GNU Emacs and XEmacs

Check the Web for Updates

To check for updates or corrections relevant to this book visit our updates page on the Web at http://www.prima-tech.com/support.

Send Us Your Comments

To comment on this book or any other PRIMA TECH title, visit our reader response page on the Web at http://www.prima-tech.com/books/book/comment.

How to Order

For information on quantity discounts, contact the publisher: Prima Publishing, P.O. Box 1260BK, Rocklin, CA 95677-1260; (916) 787-7000. On your letterhead, include information concerning the intended use of the books and the number of books you want to purchase.

GNU Emacs and XEmacs

Larry Ayers

A Division of Prima Publishing

A Division of Prima Publishing

Prima Publishing and colophon are registered trademarks of Prima Communications, Inc. PRIMA TECH is a trademark of Prima Communications, Inc., Roseville, California 95661.

Important: Prima Publishing cannot provide software support.

Prima Publishing and the author have attempted throughout this book to distinguish proprietary trademarks from descriptive terms by following the capitalization style used by the manufacturer.

Information contained in this book has been obtained by Prima Publishing from sources believed to be reliable. However, because of the possibility of human or mechanical error by our sources, Prima Publishing, or others, the Publisher does not guarantee the accuracy, adequacy, or completeness of any information and is not responsible for any errors or omissions or the results obtained from use of such information. Readers should be particularly aware of the fact that the Internet is an ever-changing entity. Some facts may have changed since this book went to press.

ISBN: 0-7615-2446-0

Library of Congress Catalog Card Number: 2001-086792

Printed in the United States of America

00 01 02 03 04 II 10 9 8 7 6 5 4 3 2 1

Publisher:
Stacy L. Hiquet

Associate Marketing Manager:
Heather Buzzingham

Managing Editor:
Sandy Doell

Acquisitions Editor:
Melody Layne

Project Editor:
Brian Thomasson

Technical Editor:
Eric Marsden

Copy Editor:
Gayle Johnson

Interior Layout:
Danielle Foster

Cover Design:
Prima Design Team

Indexer:
Johnna VanHoose Dinse

To my wife Betsy, and to Tyler and Adrian, my son and daughter.
They graciously put up with my abstraction and
much keyboard clatter during the months I was writing this book.

Acknowledgments

Many thanks go to the GNU Emacs and XEmacs development teams for creating and maintaining such versatile tools, as well as to the legions of Lisp hackers who have contributed so many useful extensions to the Emacs community.

Thanks also should go to Linus Torvalds and his many collaborators for creating such a stable and powerful platform on which to run Emacs.

Finally, I am very grateful for the encouragement and support of Melody Layne and Brian Thomasson, the two Prima Tech editors of this book, and for Eric Marsden's helpful and tactful technical review of the manuscript.

Larry **Ayers** is a free-lance writer and Open Source advocate. He lives on a small farm in northeast Missouri with his family. When not writing, he does computer consulting in his community, builds musical instruments, and operates a small portable sawmill. Larry has written for the *Linux Gazette* and *Linux Journal.*

Contents at a Glance

Contents

Chapter 3:
Overview of Basic Emacs Skills 31

Chapter 4:
Using the Built-in Customization Tools 61

Chapter 5:
Emacs-Lisp As an Entry Point to Configuration 77

Chapter 6:
Learning the Vocabulary of Emacs-Lisp 83

Chapter 10:
Changing Default Behavior 145

Chapter 11:
Modes, Major and Minor 167

Part III:
Exploring Emacs Packages 181

Chapter 12:
Introduction to Packages 183

Chapter 15:
External Convenience Packages 257

Chapter 16:
Packages That Make Programming Easier 283

Chapter 18:
Gnus Configuration and Usage 343

Chapter 19:
Editing Files on a Remote Machine 379

Part IV:
Dealing with Problems 427

Chapter 22:
Coping with Emacs Problems 429

Chapter 23:
Help Resources 445

Part V:
Appendixes 465

Appendix A:
Key Command Reference 467

E macs is one of the few software packages in use today with a history dating back to the early mainframe days. When the early versions of Emacs were being developed (about 16 years ago), they could be used only on expensive proprietary mainframe computers. Today, Emacs is used on just about any machine and operating system you can think of. A worldwide community of thousands of users and developers are continually extending and improving the editor's capabilities.

This is a brief account of how Emacs (and XEmacs) evolved.

Richard Stallman and the GNU Movement

In the early 1970s, in the days when the only computers were large and inefficient mainframes, the people who used them were an elite group. Confined largely to universities and government research labs, these early computing pioneers shared their work freely. Commercial interests had yet to enter the world of software. Copyrights and patents would arrive eventually, but in those days, most software was written for a specific machine and task.

A certain intellectual camaraderie prevailed at computing hotbeds such as Berkeley and MIT. Richard Stallman was a young MIT programmer excited by the potential of this new world of machine computation.

In those days, text editors were clumsy and difficult to use. There was no real-time display of the file being edited. The user had to type in arcane editing commands, subsequently viewing the pertinent line in the file to see whether the change was achieved. Stallman was using such an editor to write programs under the ITS (*Incompatible Time Sharing*) operating system on Digital PDP-10 machines. This editor, called TECO (*Tape Editor and Corrector*), was powerful for its time; it actually was as much a programming language as an editor. Stallman created a set of macros for TECO that made the editor much easier to use. (A macro in this context is a key sequence that executes a desired routine.) As was the common practice at the time, Stallman shared his enhancement with other programmers at MIT. From there, it began spreading to other computer-science labs.

A TECO Command

Here's an example of a TECO command:

```
[1 J^P$L$$
J <.-Z; .,(S,$ -D.)FX1 @F^B $K :L I $ G1 L>$$
```

As you can see, editing a file back then was not a task to be taken lightly!

TEMACS Evolves into Emacs

Several other people came up with their own packages of TEMACS macros. Stallman incorporated features from several of them into a new editing environment he named Emacs, which stood for "editing macros."

By 1976, Stallman realized that Emacs really didn't depend on or even have much to do with TEMACS. The concept of a "real-time, extensible, self-documenting editor" (as he described it) could be implemented any number of ways.

In 1978, computer scientist Bernard S. Greenberg worked for Honeywell, just across the street from the MIT computer lab. He was working with another early operating system called Multics. After seeing Stallman's work with Emacs (as a TEMACS enhancement), he decided to develop a Multics version. The difference was his choice of macro language. Greenberg was a proponent of the Lisp language, so he used it as the basis of his Multics version of Emacs.

What's Lisp?

Lisp stands for "list processing language". It is a computer programming language developed in the late '50s at MIT for research in artificial intelligence. An offshoot called Scheme is used as a teaching language in many university computer-science courses.

Guy Steele, also at MIT, synthesized the efforts of those who had created TECO macro sets and came up with the first version of Emacs. Stallman began to work with it and ended up becoming the primary developer.

Emacs history in the late '70s and early '80s isn't well-documented. During this period, the editor became popular with many users around the world, and other developers began helping with the project.

Also during this period, Stallman developed a smaller version of Lisp that was optimized for processing text. The first Emacs-Lisp version of Emacs was released in 1984.

The GNU Movement Is Born

In the late '70s, the computer industry began to build up a head of steam. Stallman and others began to notice an inevitable trend toward the commercialization of software. At that time, there wasn't a software industry; most software originated with computer hardware companies, who distributed the code to customers along with the machines they had purchased. At first, these programs were distributed in the form of source code, but the manufacturers noticed that their customers often made the code available to friends and coworkers. Customers (most of whom were programmers) were also making changes to the code. In order to reestablish control over what the manufacturers regarded as their intellectual property, the obvious solution was to distribute compiled binaries rather than readable code. But what if one of those binary files didn't work as advertised?

This was the situation Stallman faced sometime in the early '80s. He was trying to install a printing device in the Artificial Intelligence lab at MIT, but the driver that the printer manufacturer had supplied was faulty. Stallman knew that if he just had the source code for the driver, he could probably fix it. Contacting the manufacturer didn't help; they were adamant about their binary-only policy.

I can imagine how Stallman felt at that point. A few years before this incident, source code was shared freely, and a community spirit prevailed. Now commercial forces were robbing him of a freedom he had taken for granted.

This incident proved germinal. Stallman wrote a paper outlining his ideas about software and people's rights and posted it to some Usenet newsgroups. Here is the first paragraph:

```
From: RMS%MIT-OZ@mit-eddie
Newsgroups: net.unix-wizards,net.usoft
Subject: new UNIX implementation
Date: Tue, 27-Sep-83 12:35:59 EST
Organization: MIT AI Lab, Cambridge, MA
Free Unix!
Starting this Thanksgiving I am going to write a complete Unix-compatible software
system called GNU (for Gnu's Not Unix), and give it away free to everyone who can
use it. Contributions of time, money, programs and equipment are greatly needed.
```

The term GNU was one of the very first "recursive acronyms" that have become so common in the free software world. A recursive acronym is an acronym that, when expanded, contains the acronym itself.

After the first GNU version of Emacs was released in 1984, the movement grew steadily. Stallman quit his job at MIT and created the Free Software Foundation, an umbrella organization for software accepted by the GNU project. Much of the early GNU software consisted of replacements for utility software included with proprietary UNIX computer systems. GNU's reputation was enhanced when people began to discover that the GNU versions of these utilities had more features, were continually improved, and in general just worked better than their proprietary counterparts.

One of the long-term goals of the GNU project has been to create a free operating-system kernel to take the place of commercial UNIX kernels. This project, known as the GNU Hurd, is still underway, but the necessity for the Hurd lessened greatly in 1991.

A young Finnish computer-science student named Linus Torvalds was chafing under the limitations of Minix, a simple UNIX clone that was used mainly in computer-science classes. Torvalds thought he might be able to write a UNIX-like kernel that had more flexibility than Minix. He'd made some progress (he had a kernel that would boot), but he began to wonder if anyone else might be interested in helping. He announced his nascent project on the comp.os.minix Usenet group, and since then, the growth of Linux has been phenomenal. Many thousands of people are now involved in one way or another, and many commercial hardware and software firms now support Linux.

Linus Torvalds' project would have been very difficult or even impossible without the free GNU tools such as the gcc compiler.

Corporations Become Involved

GNU Emacs was at version 18 by 1991. The next version was supposed to include all sorts of features desired by Emacs users, but people were becoming impatient. Already a code fork called Epoch had begun at the University of Illinois.

Code Fork?

The term *code-fork* refers to a new branch of a software project, usually a branch that is incompatible with the parent project.

Sun Microsystems was using Emacs as a part of their SPARCWorks development environment and had invested programmer time in changes they needed for their product.

Another company called Lucid had been using GNU Emacs extensively as well. Lucid sold C and C++ development environments, and Emacs was a core component of their Energize product.

In effect, by the early '90s there were three forked versions of Emacs, all stemming from the official GNU version.

Programmers from both firms were eagerly awaiting promised new features of GNU Emacs 19, such as mouse support, multiple windows, and more than one font in a buffer. Emacs 19 was delayed, so Lucid became interested in the University of Illinois Epoch Emacs variant, which was beginning to support these features.

Even Epoch development seemed slow to these impatient young Lucid programmers, so they made many changes to Emacs and released it as part of their Energize development environment in 1992.

Eventually, the three variants merged as the University of Illinois (with their Epoch project), Sun, and Lucid joined forces on what was initially called Lucid Emacs.

The Rift and the XEmacs Fork

Richard Stallman for various reasons wouldn't fold Lucid's or Sun's changes to Emacs into the main source tree (there was resistance on Lucid's side to assigning copyright to the FSF); this is the point at which the code actually (and seemingly irrevocably) forked. The dispute began in 1992, and by 1994 Sun and Lucid agreed to the new name XEmacs, a neutral name that referred to neither firm.

Personality clashes had a lot to do with this fork. One of the young programmers at Lucid was Jamie Zawinski, who later went on to work for Netscape before eventually quitting in disgust when Netscape was bought by AOL. Zawinski and Stallman had their differences, partly due to age. Zawinski belonged to a new generation of programmers who had grown up in the volatile Internet environment; Stallman was of the old guard—one of the early programmers who had made the Internet and free software possible.

XEmacs development has continued ever since then, although Lucid is no more and Sun is no longer directly involved. Currently, about 20 programmers remain active in XEmacs development. An effort is made to remain as compatible as possible with the current GNU Emacs version. Many of the major external package maintainers try to ensure that their packages are compatible with both strains of Emacs, although some packages work with only one or the other.

Implications for Users

From an Emacs user's perspective, it would be nice if the maintainers of GNU Emacs and XEmacs could reconcile their efforts and merge to form one editor. This seems unlikely due to the lingering effects of past animosities. Each camp keeps a close eye on the other, and a case could be made that the resulting competition has kept both programming teams on their toes and thus has encouraged further development of both strains of Emacs.

It's possible that each flavor of Emacs appeals to a different personality type. These types are most likely reflections on the collective or group personality of each development team. If this is true, the users of both Emacs variants benefit as they gravitate toward the editor that suits them.

This book endeavors to provide information about the usage of both strains of Emacs. References to Emacs throughout this book should be understood to refer to both editors. When there are differences, the full names GNU Emacs and XEmacs are used.

Who This Book Is For

This book is for Emacs and XEmacs users who are using one or both of these editors but haven't yet tried to configure them. The default settings are usable, but there are probably certain aspects of Emacs that make you think, "One of these days, I'll figure out how to make this editor work the way I want it to!"

I've included the basics of Emacs in case you're just starting out, but one of my goals in writing this book was to provide a fairly painless introduction to Emacs Lisp. You just can't avoid this dialect of Lisp when you begin to progress past the basics. The up side is that it doesn't take long to learn enough about Emacs Lisp to actually use it to tweak Emacs to your satisfaction.

The advent of the Customize interface has reduced the amount of Lisp writing that Emacs users need to undertake. Using Per Abrahamsen's wonderful invention can greatly speed up your progress to that dimly-glimpsed goal of a perfectly configured Emacs setup, but many users are either unaware of Customize or are intimidated by it. Throughout this book, examples of Customize usage will help make you comfortable using it yourself.

If there is an underlying philosophy or message this book is meant to convey, perhaps it is to try things out! Take risks with Emacs; after all, it's just software—code on your hard disk. Nobody is looking over your shoulder. Back up your files often, and with that safety net in place, experiment with combinations of modes and settings. You will be surprised at what you can come up with if you take the time.

PART I

How Emacs Evolves to Suit Your Needs

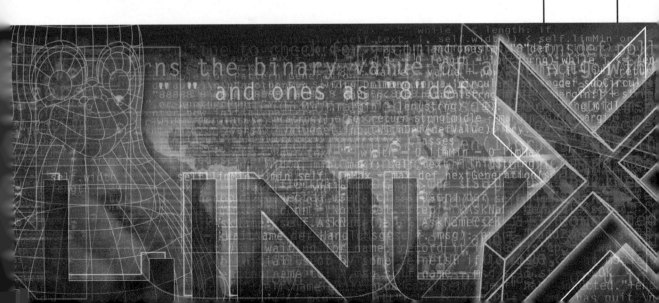

Chapter 1: How Emacs Differs from Other Software

What sets Emacs apart from other editors is the extent to which the "guts" of the program are exposed to the user. You don't have to know much Emacs-Lisp to take advantage of this trait. Throughout this book, techniques to help you delve into the inner workings of Emacs will be illustrated at whatever level you are comfortable with.

Your work with Emacs, whether motivated by curiosity or by the need to change the editor to suit your needs, can be quite a bit of fun. It tends to be an episodic activity, with bursts of customization (perhaps sparked by a Usenet posting or the release of a new package) followed by periods of just using the editor. Slowly but surely, as time passes, a new, personalized Emacs emerges. This book should speed up the process.

Software and the User

Emacs is a perfect example of the principles underlying the GNU project. The editor, including the source code, is free—with a few important qualifications. Emacs is released under the GNU General Public License. This license allows you to freely share the software but specifically forbids changing the software and rereleasing it as a proprietary application. This ensures that development will remain open and that the application remains free. In effect, the license prevents anyone from making money by selling a closed-source binary version.

Free Beer and Free Speech

The word "free" has several shades of meaning; this often leads to some confusion as to what the word really means when applied to software licensed under the GPL. Though this software can be obtained free of charge, another sense of the word "free" is more significant. The eighteenth century philosopher Thomas Locke defined this sense well:

"Exempt from subjection to the will of others; not under restraint, control, or compulsion; able to follow one's own impulses, desires, or inclinations; determining one's own course of action; not dependent; at liberty."

A comparison often encountered in GNU documentation contrasts free beer and free speech. Free beer doesn't come with the recipe!

Commercial Versus Open-Source

Although there is a thriving market for commercial software, there is also a down-side for the users. Most people have had the experience of investing money in a proprietary software application and spending time learning to use it effectively, only to see the company that developed and marketed the application either dis-continue further development or go bankrupt. Once this happens, the software is *orphaned,* and as hardware and operating systems evolve, chances are good that the application will quit functioning at some point.

Another problem from the user's point of view is proprietary binary file formats. A file saved in such a format typically can be read only by the application that gener-ated it. If the application is orphaned and quits working, the user risks losing valuable personal files.

> If a commercial software firm decides that there is no more money to be made selling one of its products, the company might quit updating it (fixing bugs and so on) and let it languish. The normal tendency is to keep the underlying source code private to prevent competitors from benefiting from their work. This soft-ware has been *orphaned.*

NOTE

When you buy a piece of commercial software, chances are that in a year or two you will be encouraged to upgrade to a new version. On the face of it, this seems to be a good thing: the company is working hard to improve its software, and you as the user/customer will benefit from bug fixes and new features. This is often the case, but on the negative side, companies sometimes change their saved-file format in such a way that a user of the old version is unable to exchange files with other users who have upgraded. What if the old version works fine for you and you have no need of the new features in the new version? Not every software firm is guilty of this "forced upgrade" practice, but it does happen.

Open-source software developers tend toward "universal" file formats—those that are written in ASCII text and can be read by other applications. Of course, many types of software that people need simply aren't available in a freely licensed version. Members of the open-source community have two different approaches to this situ-ation. The purist approach is to wean yourself from needing proprietary software, making every possible effort to find ways to accomplish your work using only open-source tools. The more moderate approach is to use free software when it suits your needs and to use commercial software when there is no open-source equivalent.

Naturally, open-source software projects sometimes lose momentum and go through static periods. Perhaps another, more useful software project has drawn away users or developers, or the maintainers have lost interest. What really matters is that the source is still available. If the software still serves anyone's needs, eventually a developer will happen across it and either take it on as a personal project or use parts of the code in a new piece of software. The work that the original developers released to the world is never completely lost; rather than reinvent the wheel, it is likely that the old code will be adapted or reused.

Writing software can be pure drudgery when done for purely monetary reasons, as any work can be. It can also be enjoyable and challenging when the results are useful to the developer and to other people using the software. There has been much speculation as to the motives which cause developers to write free software. The consensus seems to be that a personal mix of the following motives are largely responsible:

- The urge to "scratch an itch," or to solve a particular problem.
- The pleasure that accompanies any creative activity.
- Peer approval of the resulting software.
- Altruism; sometimes a little work will help many people.

Companies can also benefit from having the source to some software available. Outside developers may add features that they need and contribute them back to the company. Knowledgeable users may contribute bug reports as well.

Methods of Customization

Nobody likes software that confines the user in a straitjacket of unchangeable default settings. Most applications cater to people's natural desire for customization by allowing settings to be changed and saved in some sort of configuration file that is read whenever the application starts up. The most common approach is to have a configuration dialog box, a window that can be summoned from the menu bar and that contains a series of options. These dialog boxes can be quite extensive, but the problem with them is that each configuration option has to be compiled into the application. Expensive development time must be devoted to first figuring out what a user might want to change and then writing the code to allow that option to appear in the configuration dialog box. There is a fair chance that a default setting that you would really like to change wasn't included.

Scripting-Language Configuration

A more open-ended approach is to make available a simple scripting language with which the user can write new commands or routines. This works well if the language is simple enough to learn easily but still provides the necessary "hooks" into the application's internals. This is the route that Emacs developers have followed, but Emacs' use of Emacs-Lisp goes beyond the usual relationship of an application and its scripting language. Although the core of Emacs is written in C (for speed and window-system display purposes), the actual editing functions are written in Lisp. Since the scripting language is also Lisp, changing Emacs behavior is both convenient and powerful. While it's running, Emacs stores in your machine's memory a plethora of functions and variables. All of these are accessible and therefore modifiable using simple Lisp statements. Even the documentation for the functions and variables is instantly available, because it is stored within the Lisp files. (See Chapter 3.)

Emacs Vocabulary and Conventions

To help you learn about Emacs, I will define a few peculiar terms. Many of them are ordinary English words that have a different meaning when used in Emacs documentation. Some of these words are a legacy of the early days of computing, when Emacs and Lisp were first being developed.

Buffers and the Point

The word *buffer* refers to a text file loaded into memory (the text may be displayed or hidden) by Emacs. The word was originally a computer programmer's term for an area of machine memory set aside for a specific purpose. This term is used rather than *file* to emphasize the difference between the copy of the file being edited and the actual file on disk. When the edited buffer is saved, it is written back to the hard disk, overwriting the original file. Emacs can edit multiple files at once, so at any given time there might be many buffers.

Emacs also has internal buffers that don't correspond to any file. One of these is visible when Emacs is started up without a file name as an argument. It is called the *Scratch buffer*. It automatically appears in a special editing mode used for writing Emacs-Lisp code. A new Lisp-Interaction item appears on the menu bar whenever the Scratch buffer is visible.

Another file-less buffer is called *Messages*. This one is just a list of all the warnings and messages Emacs has generated since it was started up. This buffer can be useful when problems arise.

Point and Mark

Every buffer has a single location in it called the *point*. This is just the current location of the cursor in the buffer. Emacs remembers this spot even when the buffer is hidden.

Why Call It the "Point"?

This is another legacy term. Remember Emacs' predecessor, TECO, mentioned in the Introduction? The period (.) was the TECO command indicating the cursor position. Point, a typographical term, was probably used to refer to this command due to the lesser number of syllables in the word "point" as compared to "period."

Another name for a particular type of location in a buffer is the *mark*. Placing or setting a mark is how a specific area of text in a buffer is defined. The mark can be at the same place as the point, in which case no area is defined. The farther away from the point the mark moves, the larger the defined area of text becomes. This might sound confusing. The next section will clarify matters, because you will learn just why you might want to define areas of text.

Regions

This section will be easier to understand if you start up Emacs and load a text file so that you can try a few things. Clicking the mouse button or using the arrow keys on the keyboard, moves point to the beginning of a paragraph.

There are two ways to define an area of text, which in Emacs terminology is called a *region*. One way uses the keyboard, and the other way uses the mouse. On the keyboard, press Ctrl-spacebar, and then use the left or right arrow key to move point. Unlike most editors, GNU Emacs doesn't by default highlight the selected region. See Chapter 10 if you would like to change this. Pressing M-w (Meta-w; see the later section "Alt, Meta, and Esc") copies the region, and Ctrl-w cuts the region and stores it in memory. Ctrl-y pastes the last cut or copied region to wherever point is.

The mouse can be used to "sweep" (highlight) regions; just press the mouse button as you move the mark over the lines of text.

In effect, both pressing Ctrl-spacebar and clicking the mouse button while moving the mouse redefine the actions of pressing the arrow keys and clicking the mouse button. Normally these actions move the point, but in these cases, while point is moved a region is being defined in the process.

The Kill Ring

No, it's not the name of a murderous gang; *killing* in Emacs terms means either cutting or copying a block of text. Each time you copy or cut selected text (text that was in a region, remember?), it is stored in Emacs' memory in an area called the *kill ring*. It's a ring because you can paste from it by pressing Ctrl-y, which retrieves the most recent selection. Subsequent M-y keypresses step backwards through the selection history, retrieving the next-oldest selections. If you keep pressing M-y, you will eventually paste the most recent selection into your buffer again. You see, it loops back to the beginning, which is why it's called a ring. This feature is similar to, but more powerful than, the clipboard features of other editors.

Emacs Modes

Modes are particular combinations of Lisp functions and definitions used on particular types of files being edited. For example, Text mode is used to edit plain text files, and Emacs-Lisp mode is used to edit Lisp files. Emacs can normally determine which mode to use on a certain file by matching the file name extension with a corresponding mode. These modes typically set up the indentation, word-wrap style, syntax highlighting, and other variables.

> *Syntax highlighting*, also known as *font locking*, is the coloring of different elements of a file according to the role they play. For example, in an HTML file, tags enclosed in angled brackets are a different color than the body text. See Chapter 4 for more details.

NOTE

Key Conventions

Emacs has its own terminology for naming particular keystrokes. Some of these terms will be unfamiliar to you because many of them originated during the pre-PC era. There are a few that you need to be familiar with.

Keybindings

Keybinding is a term used throughout this book to refer to a specific combination of keystrokes associated with an Emacs command. You could think of a command being "bound" to a sequence of keystrokes. Emacs comes with many default keybindings, any of which can be changed to suit your preferences.

Alt, Meta, and Esc

Most computer users are familiar with the two Alt keys, the two Ctrl (control) keys, and the Esc (escape) key on a standard PC keyboard. Most, I imagine, have never heard of or seen a Meta key. The *Meta key* is another legacy issue from the early days of Emacs. Back when most Emacs users were typing at workstation terminals, a variety of keyboard layouts were in use. Some had a Meta key but no Alt, and some had no Delete key, but the Ctrl and Esc keys were usually found. Pity the Emacs developers who had to figure out how multi-key commands could be typed on differing keyboards! The solution they came up with was to use the Esc key as a fallback for users who lacked the Alt and Meta keys. On a PC keyboard, pressing Alt-x lets you type a command in the minibuffer. To this day, you can still substitute Esc-x to enter commands. Esc-x is two separate keystrokes, whereas when you press Alt-x (and other multi-key Emacs commands), the keys can be pressed simultaneously.

PC users just need to remember that for all practical purposes, Meta is just another name for the Alt key. This also explains the convention in Emacs circles of notating a keystroke combination such as Alt-x as M-x (which stands for Meta-x). This book follows this convention because the official Emacs documentation uses that terminology.

Many modern keyboards have 104 rather than 101 keys. Two of the additional keys are known as "Windows" keys, identifiable by a Microsoft logo on the keycaps. These keys are also useful for those not using Windows. If you are using a version of XFree86 in the 3.xx series, the right Windows key will be defined by default as the Multi key and can be used as an Emacs key-prefix (see Chapter 10 for keybinding instructions). On the other hand, if your XFree86 version is one of the recent 4.xx series you should take a look at your XF86Config file; it should contain lines similar to the following if you have one of these keyboards:

```
Section "InputDevice"
        Identifier     "Generic Keyboard"
        Driver         "keyboard"
```

```
        Option          "CoreKeyboard"
        Option          "XkbRules"      "xfree86"
        Option          "XkbModel"      "pc104"
        Option          "XkbLayout"     "us"
EndSection
```

Key Names in Lisp Files

Due to the many past versions of GNU Emacs and XEmacs, many of which are still being used, deciding just what to call a keystroke in a Lisp file can be confusing. There are many methods that work in most cases but that might not work with certain Emacs version/platform combinations. For the purposes of this book, it is assumed that you are using one of the current versions provided on the CD-ROM.

A syntax that works well with all current versions uses both square brackets and parentheses to enclose a keystroke name, as shown here:

`[(home)]`	The Home key
`[(f4)]`	The F4 key
`[(control x) p)]`	The combination Ctrl-x p
`[(meta d)]`	The combination M-d

Notice that in the three-key Ctrl-x p combination, the first two keys are enclosed in parentheses. This indicates that these two keys are pressed together as a prefix and are executed before the last keystroke, p.

Emacs and Emacs-Lisp

Ever since Emacs began using Lisp as its extension language, users and programmers have been coming up with new extension packages. Emacs was designed to be easily modified and extended, and over the past 15 years, many hundreds of these extensions have been made available. This has kept the editor from becoming outmoded, so to speak.

For example, in 1984 the idea that people would be distributing compressed music files across the Internet by the millions, as is the case today with MP3 files, would have been considered far-fetched. Recently an Emacs user wrote and made available an Emacs MP3 player mode. Another user wrote a mode that downloads and displays current headlines on Slashdot, a popular Linux-oriented Web site. Neither of these modes is terribly complicated, because each one builds on extensions that others have written.

How Emacs Evolves to Suit Your Needs

Most software is written to be fairly intuitive and powerful "out of the box," which necessarily involves some compromises. You can't please everyone, because tastes and needs can differ greatly.

The developers of Emacs have gone to some lengths to make Emacs easy for first-time users to learn and use. Nonetheless, many are somewhat taken aback by their first Emacs experiences. (See Chapter 11, which explains how to quickly change some of the puzzling default settings.)

The principal reason for this reaction on the part of many modern-day computer users is the change in computing culture in the last decade. The early Emacs developers (many of whom still work on Emacs) came from the early mainframe UNIX and pre-UNIX environments. The keyboards were different (which explains the backspace/delete issue, which still is a hurdle for many when learning Emacs), most users were programmers, and there were no graphical operating systems.

The reason Emacs has not only survived but thrived all these years is its inherent configurability. There is little that can't be changed, and a couple of hours of work setting up a personal .emacs configuration file (see Chapter 9) will make a world of difference in the editor's "feel." You won't get everything right the first time, because Emacs configuration is an incremental process. The longer you use Emacs, the more you demand of it; the editor will eventually fit like an old glove.

One reason people have adapted Emacs for unlikely tasks (for an editor, at least) such as browsing the Internet or file management is that Emacs in many ways doubles as a work environment. Why start up another application when the editor you're using can accomplish the same tasks?

Conclusion

If you haven't installed Emacs yet, the next chapter will guide you through that process. If you already have a version of Emacs installed (perhaps as a part of a Linux distribution) you might consider skipping ahead to Chapter 3, which covers basic Emacs skills.

macs is not hard to find. Source and binary packages for both GNU Emacs and XEmacs are available from many Internet sites around the world. Every Linux distribution has prepackaged versions available for installation, either from a CD-ROM or directly from the Internet. If you have a slow dial-up connection to the Internet, you will save time by installing Emacs from the CD-ROM bundled with this book.

Included are both source and binary packages of the latest GNU Emacs and XEmacs versions, as well as Bill Perry's GTK-XEmacs, an XEmacs variant that uses the GTK toolkit for a more modern look and feel. Users of the GNOME Linux desktop environment will appreciate Bill's work.

Perhaps you already have a version of Emacs installed. If so, you might want to try one of the other versions and possibly use it as a test bed for trying out some of the techniques in this book.

Though this book focuses on Emacs running under Linux, you should be aware that Emacs can be compiled on various Windows, commercial Unix, and Macintosh platforms as well. Many Emacs users dual-boot between two operating systems and use Emacs on both.

Source or Precompiled?

There are two ways to install Emacs—or, for that matter, any open-source software package. One way is to obtain the source and compile your own (which presupposes that you have the necessary development tools installed). A faster method is to use a Linux distribution packaged version, such as an *.rpm or *.deb file. It really depends on how much you trust the people who compile and package programs for your particular flavor of Linux, because they are responsible for providing a package that can use the various shared libraries on your system.

Here's another factor to keep in mind: Have you been upgrading shared libraries outside the auspices of your distribution's packaging system? It's easy to get caught that way. Your distribution's packaging system has no way of keeping track of what you've done to your Linux installation. If you install too many vital libraries on your own, you will end up having to compile everything yourself.

Whichever way you go, the objective is to end up with a smoothly-running Emacs installation. This section analyzes advantages and drawbacks of the different approaches.

Rolling Your Own

My preference is to compile and install my own Emacs. Naturally, you have to have various development packages installed, including the following:

- The gcc compiler and header files
- For XEmacs, image libraries and development packages
- The make utility
- The X Window development package
- The ncurses libraries and development package

All of these packages are easy to install from a distribution CD-ROM.

Location of Emacs

By default, most distribution packages install in the /usr hierarchy, with the executable Emacs in /usr/bin. If for lack of space or other reasons you'd like the Emacs installation to be installed elsewhere, you can build an Emacs that will install in whatever location pleases you.

You can't just move an installation to a new location and expect it to work. Emacs expects to find many subsidiary files (among them, the Emacs-Lisp files that give the editor its functionality) in a particular directory. If it doesn't find them, the editor just won't work. See the later section "Configure Switches," which explains changing the default.

Leaving out Unneeded Features

When running the Emacs configure script in preparation for compiling Emacs, several switches can be added to the command line to affect the outcome. A *switch* in this context is one of several options that affect just what gets into the makefile. The makefile is in a sense a set of instructions for the compiler, telling it what to include in the finished executable.

Here's an example from my own experience. There are several reasons I sometimes prefer to run XEmacs, but the icon toolbar isn't one of them. It's a nice feature when you're learning, but I noticed after a certain point that I rarely used it, and I began to begrudge it the window real estate it occupied.

After some investigation, I discovered that if the configure script was given the switch `--with-toolbars=no`, the result would be an XEmacs without the overhead of displaying icons beneath the menu bar. This isn't the only way to remove the toolbar.

You can also turn it off by clicking on the "Visible" check box in the Options, Toolbar Appearance sub-menu. The advantage to compiling without toolbar support is that you end up with an XEmacs executable that is smaller and uses less memory.

Another example is the built-in support for contacting a POP mail server. If you never use Emacs as a mail client, this option may as well not be included in the executable.

All versions of Emacs come with a file named INSTALL, which details the possible configuration switches.

Predumping Lisp Files

This is something not many Emacs users bother to do, but in some cases it could be advantageous. In a normal Emacs compilation, a group of essential Lisp files are "dumped" into the executable. This means that these Lisp files, which run somewhat slower when interpreted by the built-in Lisp interpreter, are preinterpreted and bundled into the executable. This is done so that these crucial files, which enable Emacs' basic editing functions, will run faster.

If you happen to know of some Lisp code that you are certain will be used constantly in your installation, you could include the code in the file /[Emacs source directory]/lisp/site-init.el, and it would also be dumped during the building process. If you also want the documentation within your Lisp code to be folded into the /lib-src/DOC file (in which case that documentation would be available using the help keys), put your Lisp code in the file /[Emacs source directory]/lisp/site-load.el.

site-init.el and site-load.el don't come with the source package. You need to create them from scratch.

Binary Distributions of Emacs for Linux

You might not find the advantages of compiling your own Emacs compelling enough to take the time to do it. Most Emacs users probably use a distribution-provided binary. It's possible that your Linux system has a functional Emacs installation of which you are unaware. During the process of installing a Linux distribution, some decisions are made for you. Often the developers of a distribution have specified a default group of software packages that are installed automatically. This helps ensure that a novice won't end up booting a new Linux installation only to find that an editor isn't available to change a file that is keeping his system from working properly.

If you are unsure, try typing `emacs` or `xemacs` in an xterm window, and see if anything happens! If an Emacs window appears, press M-x and then type this command in the minibuffer:

```
emacs-version
```

The version of Emacs you are running is displayed. Compare the version number with the version numbers of the packages on the CD-ROM. If yours is older, consider removing your installed version and replacing it with the appropriate package from the CD-ROM.

The Emacs Maintainer's Role

Part of the job of putting together a Linux distribution is picking the right people to maintain the various packages. In free-software lingo, to *maintain* a package is to be responsible for keeping up with changes in the *upstream source*, which is the source code from the developer(s) of the software the package is based on. The maintainer also forwards bug reports to the upstream developers and possibly even fixes bugs and contributes enhancements.

For many Linux users, Emacs is an important application. A well-run distribution carefully chooses its official Emacs maintainer, ideally a skilled Emacs user who keeps up with changes in Emacs.

Here are some of the tasks an Emacs package maintainer is expected to do:

- Alter the Emacs makefile so that the editor is installed in the correct directory for the particular distribution.
- Keep up with user bug reports and other mail.
- Incorporate distribution documentation and other files into the package.
- Coordinate efforts with the main distribution release team.
- Forward bug reports and fixes to the upstream Emacs maintainers.
- Apply needed patches to the current Emacs source release that might have surfaced since the last official Emacs release. These may come from users or developer mailing lists.

Red Hat Emacs

The Red Hat packages on the CD-ROM correspond with Red Hat 7.1, the most current release when this book was published. Both GNU Emacs and XEmacs packages can be found in the directory /binary/dists/redhat.

Debian Emacs

The Debian packages on the CD-ROM are a part of Debian 2.2, code-named "potato." You will find them in the directory /binary/dists/debian/potato. Readers running the unstable "woody" branch of Debian can find packages in /binary/dists/debian/woody.

SuSE

Although SuSE packages such as Redhat's are distributed in the RPM format, there are some differences. It's generally not a good idea to interchange SuSE's and Redhat's RPMs, so look for SuSE packages in the directory /binary/dists/suse.

Slackware and Others

Slackware doesn't use a dependency-checking package manager (such as RPM or Debian's dpkg) as most other distributions do. A Slackware package is in gzipped tar format. Packages that correspond to Slackware 7.1 can be found in the directory /binary/dists/slackware.

Most distributions other than the ones I've discussed can probably make use of a package from one of the mentioned directories. For example, Corel Linux uses the Debian package system; try a *.deb file from the /binary/dists/debian/potato directory on the CD-ROM.

Installation from the CD-ROM

I'm assuming that you know how to access your CD-ROM drive. If not, the command

```
mount -t iso9660 -ro /dev/[device name of your drive] /cdrom
```

should at least be close to the one you need.

Alias Your CD-ROM

If typing the command to mount your CD-ROM drive gets old, alias the command to something short like cdm. A line like this in your ~/.bashrc should do the trick:

```
alias 'mount -t iso9660 -ro /dev/[drive] /cdrom
```

This will work if you have an empty directory named /cdrom. If not, the command

```
mkdir /cdrom
```

will create one for you.

Some Linux distributions come with an /etc/fstab file that lets you mount your CD-ROM drive by merely typing

```
mount /cdrom
```

If your fstab file has a line that looks something like this:

```
/dev/cdrom /cdrom iso9660 defaults,ro,user,noauto  0  0
```

you don't need to bother with aliases.

Now that the CD-ROM is mounted, you're ready to install Emacs packages.

The CD-ROM Binaries

The binary Emacs packages were created by either volunteers for or employees of the various Linux distributions. In general, the binaries won't differ very much from those you could compile yourself. The main difference is the tweaking that the package has received to make it fit better in the distribution. In some packages, extra documentation might have been added.

Installation with Package Tools

Most Linux distributions include specialized software to ease the task of installing packages. Depending on the distribution, the package tool might check for the presence of other needed packages and set up the package as well as unpacking and installing files. Typically the same tool is used to un-install packages cleanly.

Red Hat and SuSE

Change to the Red Hat or SuSE directory (now that the CD-ROM is mounted, it will be /cdrom/binary/dists/[redhat or suse]) and then execute this command:

```
rpm -i [packagename]
```

If you happen to be missing any of the other RPM packages that Emacs depends on, RPM will let you know. You will have to find the missing packages either on the Internet or on a Redhat or SuSE CD-ROM and install them before again attempting to install the Emacs package.

Debian, Corel, and Storm

A similar procedure is used to install one of the Debian packages. The command is different, though. In this case, it is

```
dpkg -i [packagename]
```

If you have a fast Internet connection and you want to have dependencies handled automatically, you might want to use apt-get to pull down the latest Emacs *.deb files along with any needed dependencies. The package name you need will be either emacs20, xemacs21, or xemacs21-gtk, depending on your preference. A command such as this should suffice:

```
apt-get install emacs20
```

apt-get not only fetches the packages but installs them too.

Before you use apt-get to install files from the Internet, one file needs to be edited. In the directory /etc/apt is a file named sources.list. Figure 2.1 shows this file set up so that apt-get will look for files at a Debian mirror site in the United States.

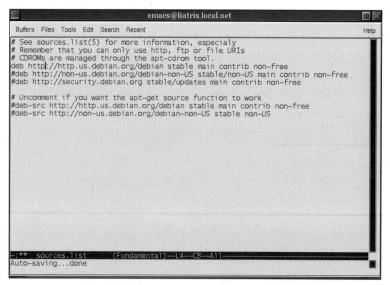

Figure 2.1   *apt-get's sources.list*

Slackware and Others

The procedure is a little different for the Slackware tar files. You have to change to the /cdrom/binary/dists/slackware directory and then copy the *.tgz file you need to a directory on your hard disk.

installpkg is a Slackware utility used to install this type of package. This command should give you a working Emacs installation:

```
installpkg /[directory to which you copied the file]/[filename.tgz]
```

If your distribution isn't covered in this section, a variant of one of the previously listed commands should get you up and running.

Binary Problems

Linux distributions change rapidly, which means that there is a chance that the binary you installed from the CD-ROM won't run. That's always dispiriting, but there is a way to see if Emacs is looking for a shared library you don't have or to find out whether your installed library is the wrong version. Run this command on the malfunctioning binary:

```
ldd emacs
```

You should see output that looks something like this:

```
libXext.so.6 => /usr/X11R6/lib/libXext.so.6 (0x401c9000)
libtiff.so.3 => /usr/lib/libtiff.so.3 (0x401e3000)
libjpeg.so.62 => /usr/lib/libjpeg.so.62 (0x40225000)
libpng.so.2 => /usr/lib/libpng.so.2 (0x40245000)
libz.so.1 => /usr/lib/libz.so.1 (0x4026d000)
libm.so.6 => /lib/i686/libm.so.6 (0x4027c000)
libungif.so.4 => /usr/lib/libungif.so.4 (0x4029b000)
libX11.so.6 => /usr/X11R6/lib/libX11.so.6 (0x402a3000)
libncurses.so.5 => /lib/libncurses.so.5 (0x4036e000)
libc.so.6 => /lib/i686/libc.so.6 (0x403ac000)
/lib/ld-linux.so.2 => /lib/ld-linux.so.2 (0x40000000)
```

This sample output shows that the Emacs binary on which I ran the ldd command is finding every library it needs.

On the other hand, if one or more of the lines of output display the statement not found after the => symbols, the reason for the broken Emacs is evident. You either have to find the proper version of the missing library or give up on that particular binary.

There is another command you can try that shows you what shared libraries are available to programs running on your system. Type this into an xterm window:

```
ldconfig -v | less
```

This command pipes the output of the ldconfig command into a pager, which lets you easily see all of the output. Using ldconfig in conjunction with the ldd command can often help resolve tricky shared-library issues.

Sometimes a library problem can be as simple as a missing symbolic link. A program looking for a library named libsomething.so might fail because that exact name wasn't found. Looking at the output of ldconfig, you might see that there is a library named libsomething.so.0 in the /usr/lib directory. Making a symbolic link between libsomething.so.0 and libsomething.so might clear up the difficulty. Do this by changing to the /usr/lib directory and running a command something like this:

```
ln -s libsomething.so.0 libsomething.so
```

This creates a symbolic link, or *symlink*, between the existing library file and the symlink itself, which functions as a pointer to a file.

Source from the CD-ROM

If you have never compiled any Linux source, Emacs is a great package to start out with. This isn't because Emacs is a simple, quickly-compiled application; it's anything but that. I'm recommending it because Emacs tends to configure and compile flawlessly. I've never seen it fail.

Years ago, when I installed my first Linux distribution, the pool of available Linux software was much smaller. There were nowhere near as many distribution software packages available. It seemed like I was constantly trying to get balky source packages to build, with mixed success. I was pleasantly surprised when I first compiled GNU Emacs and later XEmacs. Like a well-oiled machine, the build process would chug right along without a hitch, producing a shiny new executable at the end.

I later learned that not all source code is created equal. Some packages, such as Emacs, XEmacs, Apache, the Linux kernel, and quite a few others, are intensively maintained and tend to compile easily. A host of others compile easily on machines similar to the developer's, or only on certain Linux distributions, or only with certain shared libraries.

In order to compile Emacs, you need the proper development packages installed. This isn't hard to do; they are included with any Linux distribution, they don't take up a lot of space, and you're sure to need them again. You certainly need the packages containing gcc (the GNU compiler), make, and the header files that are associated with your version of glibc. Depending on which Emacs version you install, you might need the development packages for various image-rendering libraries. The development package for your version of XFree86 is also necessary.

Unpacking the Source Archive

Mount your CD-ROM drive and change to the /cdrom/source directory. There you will find source tar.gz files for two versions of GNU Emacs, 20.7 and 21.0. Two versions of XEmacs are also included, 21.1.14 and version 21.4.3, which can be compiled with GTK support. Copy the version you select to a directory on a partition with at least 150 MB of hard-disk space free. Now change to that directory and execute this command:

```
tar xvzf [filename]
```

This expands the archive file into a new directory containing the source code for the version of Emacs you've selected.

Alternatively, you can expand the file using any of the file managers that can handle tar archives, such as Midnight Commander or FileRunner.

Configuration

Configure scripts have become the standard way to set up source packages for compilation in the free-software world. These scripts are generated by Autoconf, a developer's package that emerged in the early '90s to answer a long-standing question faced by programmers: how to make a package of source code that will cleanly compile on any of the UNIX variants.

A configure script in effect asks your computer a host of questions, such as the type of processor, the operating system and version, what versions of libraries are available, and many others. If it finds a workable combination of these things, it generates a makefile. If it fails, a helpful error message is displayed that lets you know what your system is missing.

Configure Switches

Configure isn't interactive. It doesn't stop and ask you questions, but there is a way to affect its behavior when you start it. A quick way to find out which options a particular configure script will accept is to type this command:

```
./configure --help
```

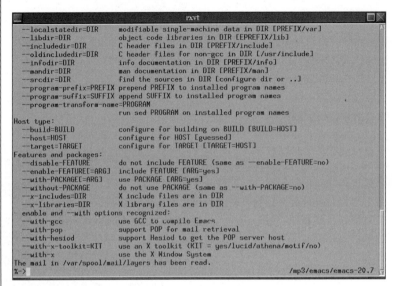

```
                              rxvt                              ☐✕
  --localstatedir=DIR     modifiable single-machine data in DIR [PREFIX/var]
  --libdir=DIR            object code libraries in DIR [EPREFIX/lib]
  --includedir=DIR        C header files in DIR [PREFIX/include]
  --oldincludedir=DIR     C header files for non-gcc in DIR [/usr/include]
  --infodir=DIR           info documentation in DIR [PREFIX/info]
  --mandir=DIR            man documentation in DIR [PREFIX/man]
  --srcdir=DIR            find the sources in DIR [configure dir or ..]
  --program-prefix=PREFIX prepend PREFIX to installed program names
  --program-suffix=SUFFIX append SUFFIX to installed program names
  --program-transform-name=PROGRAM
                          run sed PROGRAM on installed program names
Host type:
  --build=BUILD           configure for building on BUILD [BUILD=HOST]
  --host=HOST             configure for HOST [guessed]
  --target=TARGET         configure for TARGET [TARGET=HOST]
Features and packages:
  --disable-FEATURE       do not include FEATURE (same as --enable-FEATURE=no)
  --enable-FEATURE[=ARG]  include FEATURE [ARG=yes]
  --with-PACKAGE[=ARG]    use PACKAGE [ARG=yes]
  --without-PACKAGE       do not use PACKAGE (same as --with-PACKAGE=no)
  --x-includes=DIR        X include files are in DIR
  --x-libraries=DIR       X library files are in DIR
 enable and --with options recognized:
  --with-gcc              use GCC to compile Emacs
  --with-pop              support POP for mail retrieval
  --with-hesiod           support Hesiod to get the POP server host
  --with-x-toolkit=KIT    use an X toolkit (KIT = yes/lucid/athena/motif/no)
  --with-x                use the X Window System
The mail in /var/spool/mail/layers has been read.
%->                                                    /mp3/emacs/emacs-20.7
```

Figure 2.2   *Configure Script Help*

Switches will be displayed on your screen that allow you to change the installation directory and enable or disable certain features, among other things (see Figure 2.2).

An example of a switch is `--prefix=[directory]`. Let's say you wanted Emacs installed in the directory /opt instead of the default, which is /usr/local. The command to type would look like this:

```
./configure --prefix=/opt
```

This switch would cause the Emacs executable to end up in /opt/bin (after the build and install process was completed), and the other Emacs files would be installed in /opt/share/emacs.

Unless you are really short on disk space in /usr/local, you probably can just run the configure script without any switches. Change to the directory that was created when you unpacked the source archive, and then type

```
./configure
```

The `./` typed before `configure` is a Linux convention. It tells your shell to run a script or executable named `configure` in the current directory, rather than searching your path and running the first file named `configure` that it finds. See Figure 2.3.

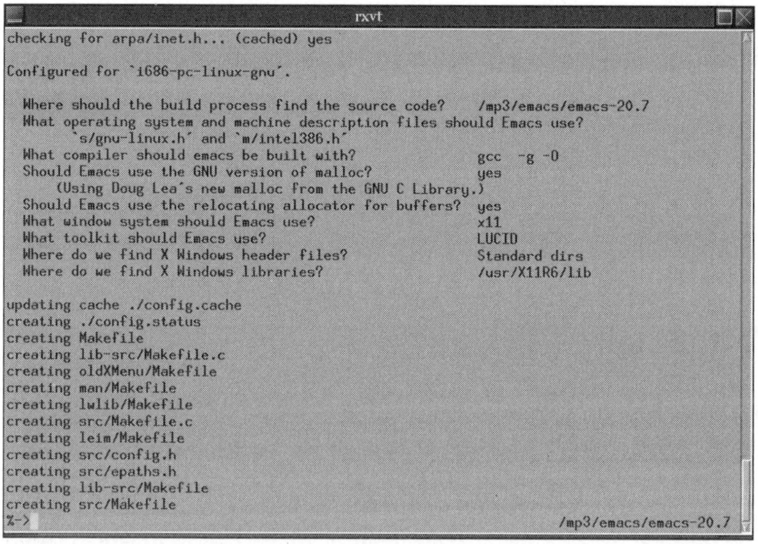

Figure 2.3 *Running the Configure Script*

An Important Switch

If you are planning to compile XEmacs, there is one important configure switch you might want to use, especially if you plan to install packages not included in the XEmacs package system. This is the command you should type:

```
./configure --with-site-lisp
```

Without this switch, XEmacs won't look for files in the site-lisp directory. You can use more than one switch on the command line. This is how you would configure XEmacs to install in /opt and recognize the site-lisp directory:

```
./configure --with-site-lisp --with-prefix=/opt
```

Compilation and Installation

The configure script takes a while to run. Messages will scroll down your screen, indicating the various tests that the script is doing. The last step is creating the various makefiles in each of the subdirectories of the Emacs source directory.

Now you can type

```
make
```

and go have a cup of coffee while Emacs is being built. Depending on the speed of your processor, it can take anywhere between a few minutes and a couple of hours.

When the build is complete, just type

```
make install
```

and the Emacs files will be copied to their new home. Once you have verified that your new Emacs binary works, you can delete the entire source directory.

Compiling XEmacs with GTK

The XEmacs 21.4 source package can also be compiled with GTK as its widget set rather than the default Athena set, the standard for X11 programs.

William Perry, developer of the Emacs Web browser W3 (see Chapter 20 for more about W3), was recently paid to rewrite the screen display portion of XEmacs so that it would make use of the GTK toolkit (see Figure 2.4).

GTK is a cross-platform development platform that has become very popular in recent years, especially in the Linux community. It was originally developed to fulfill the needs of the GIMP image-editing project, but it has since taken on a life of its own. GTK is used for many popular Linux applications, including the Mozilla project, the GNOME desktop environment, and many others.

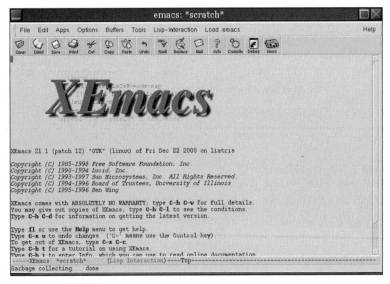

Figure 2.4   *GTK-XEmacs*

The only extra requirements for building GTK-XEmacs from source are the development packages that correspond with the versions of GTK and Glib (a library package associated with GTK) you have installed. Most Linux distributions install GTK and Glib automatically, but you might need to install the development packages manually. GTK-XEmacs also requires the GNOME development packages, but you don't have to be running GNOME to use this version of Emacs.

To enable the experimental GTK support you need to give the configure script one argument, as in this example:

```
./configure --with-gtk
```

If you are a user of the GNOME desktop environment you can add this additional switch, though it isn't absolutely necessary:

```
./configure --with-gtk --with-gnome
```

Now you can proceed with the compilation and installation as outlined above.

XEmacs Packages

Rather than bundle the most commonly used extension packages in the main source distribution, the XEmacs developers have chosen to split off nearly all packages, categorize them, and offer them individually. Without at least a few of these packages, XEmacs won't be as functional as you would like. If you know what you want, the individual packages are on the CD-ROM in the directory /cdrom/packages/ xemacs/packages/single.

If you have the disk space available, the easiest way to end up with the packages you need is to install the Sumo package, which consists of all the single packages bundled together in one tar file. You will likely end up with some packages you don't need or want, but you can delete them after you determine which packages are actually useful to you. The Sumo file is in the directory /cdrom/packages/xemacs/packages.

An XEmacs compiled from source expects to find its packages in /usr/local/lib/ xemacs/packages (unless it was configured otherwise). If you copy the desired package tar files to that directory and then expand them there, the necessary subdirectories will be created and populated with files.

XEmacs installed from binary distribution package files (*.debs or RPMs) will end up in /usr rather than /usr/local, so adjust your procedure accordingly.

You can read more about the XEmacs package system in Chapter 12.

Additional Packages on the CD-ROM

Part three of this book describes many external add-on packages for Emacs. These packages aren't included in the official distributions of Emacs or XEmacs, but some of them will doubtless be added in the future. The Emacs developers periodically evaluate new packages that, if thought to be sufficiently useful, are slated for inclusion in the next Emacs release.

You don't have to wait until a useful package is included. Simply copy packages (some are just a single Lisp file, and others are made up of several) into your /usr/local/share/emacs/site-lisp directory (the XEmacs directory to use is /usr/local/lib/xemacs/site-lisp). The next section helps you get them up and running. You can find a selection of these packages in the directory /packages/external on the book's CD-ROM.

Trying out a Package

I'm going to use a small single-file package named clipper.el as an example. Figure 2.5 shows this file loaded into an Emacs session. The beginning of the file, like most Lisp files, is commented out with semicolons. This is where the installation instructions are normally found.

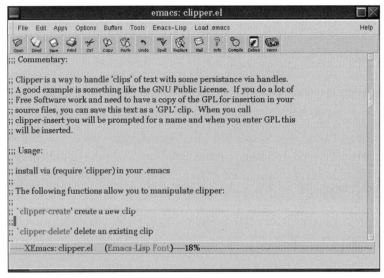

Figure 2.5 *clipper.el*

These lines are the pertinent ones:

```
;;; Usage:
;;
;; install via (require 'clipper) in your .emacs
;;
;; The following functions allow you to manipulate clipper:
;;
;; 'clipper-create' create a new clip
;;
;; 'clipper-delete' delete an existing clip
;;
;; 'clipper-insert' insert a clip into the current buffer
```

You can easily activate this file by evaluating the self-contained Lisp statement (require 'clipper). Lisp and evaluation are discussed in Chapter 7. For now, all you need to know is that placing the cursor after a parenthesized Lisp expression and then pressing Ctrl-x Ctrl-e evaluates the preceding expression. After you do this, you can use commands such as clipper-create (see the preceding excerpt) by pressing M-x and then typing

```
clipper-create
```

Chapter 15 describes what clipper.el is and what it can do; this is just an illustration of temporarily installing a package. If you were to shut down Emacs after following this example and then start it back up again, Emacs would not load clipper.el, and the commands would be unavailable.

Activating a Package Permanently

After trying out a package and finding that it suits your needs, you likely will want to install it permanently so that every time you use Emacs, the package's features will be available. You do this by copying the single Lisp statement (require 'clipper) from the clipper.el file into your .emacs file.

At this point, you might not yet have a .emacs file, an initialization file containing commands and settings that Emacs reads when it starts up. Chapter 9 goes into detail concerning this file; suffice it to say for now that a single statement copied from an extension file like clipper.el (such as the statement (require 'clipper)) can be pasted into an empty .emacs file, and it will be valid and accepted by Emacs.

Other extension packages require copying several lines into your .emacs file. It has become a custom in the Emacs community to provide instructions at or near the beginning of a Lisp file, so remember to look there first. Some multi-file packages are distributed in tar archives, which often contain README or INSTALL files.

Conclusion

You should now have a functioning Emacs installation to try out. Take some time to experiment on your own. You might try going through the Emacs tutorial by pressing Ctrl-h t.

The next chapter helps you learn the basic Emacs keyboard commands.

Chapter 3: Overview of Basic Emacs Skills

ven if you have been regularly using Emacs you will benefit from reviewing this chapter. In the remainder of the book I will assume that the basic text-manipulation commands covered here are familiar to you. You will learn to use these commands quickly if you keep an Emacs session handy while you read. Try the techniques as they are described and it won't be long before they become second nature.

You might find certain keystrokes in this chapter to be awkward to type. In Chapter 10 you will find instructions for changing keybindings, but it is worthwhile to acquire a passing familiarity with the default keybindings. You may at some point need to use Emacs on another machine and a familiarity with the defaults will prove to be helpful.

Two Basic Key Combinations

There always seems to be more than one way of doing things in Emacs. A command might have a keybinding assigned to it, but it can still be typed manually in the minibuffer. (See the section "The Modeline and Minibuffer" later in the chapter for more about the minibuffer.) Some commands involve interaction with Emacs, so the minibuffer is the best way to run them, because prompts and queries from Emacs will be visible so that you can respond to them.

Most major modes provide a subset of the available commands on the menu bar. The equivalent keystrokes are listed next to the commands on these menus. Even if you don't use the menus they can serve as a quick reference when you forget a keybinding.

The other basic command in this section is used when Emacs is involved in a process you don't need; it offers a quick way of aborting just about any Emacs process.

The M-x Command Prefix

Most Emacs commands have a corresponding keybinding. There are only so many keys and combinations on the keyboard, so commands that are used less often are typed in the minibuffer.

The prefix M-x is a signal that tells Emacs that you want to execute a command. Pressing M-x causes those characters to appear in the minibuffer, followed by a blinking cursor. Issuing this command followed by pressing the Enter key causes Emacs to execute the command. Another factor that makes the minibuffer-style command essential is that some commands, such as search-and-replace, need user input. Emacs can prompt for the needed information in the minibuffer, and you can then type it in.

The choices made by the Emacs developers when they decided which commands to bind to key combinations were necessarily arbitrary. Any command you use often can be given a keybinding. See Chapter 10, "Changing Default Behavior," for more detailed information.

Aborting Operations

Perhaps you mistyped a command, or Emacs is doing something you don't understand. Sometimes an Emacs process seems to take too long. The solution to all these problems is one key combination: Ctrl-g.

This command aborts any Emacs operation and allows you to either start over or go on to something else.

The Modeline and Minibuffer

The Emacs screen is made up of several components. Some of these are familiar, such as the menu bar, the scroll bar, and the XEmacs icon bar. Two elements of the screen are unique to Emacs and greatly enhance its usability and power: the modeline and the minibuffer. The *modeline* is a thin divider between the main editing screen and the minibuffer at the bottom, as shown in Figure 3.1. This narrow bar acts as

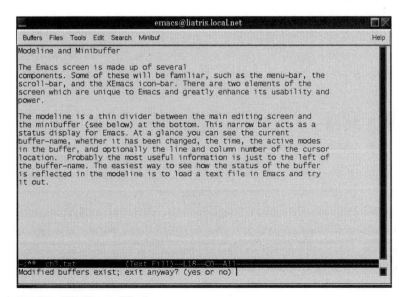

Figure 3.1　*The Emacs Window*

a status display for Emacs. At a glance, you can see the current buffer name, whether it has been changed, the time, the active modes in the buffer, and optionally the line and column number of the cursor location.

Probably the most useful information is just to the left of the buffer name. The easiest way to see how the buffer's status is reflected in the modeline is to load a text file in Emacs and try it out.

With a file loaded (press Ctrl-x Ctrl-f, or choose the File, Open File menu option), press the spacebar to insert one space in the file. Notice how two asterisks immediately appear at the far-left edge of the modeline. Now press Ctrl-x u (Undo) and watch them disappear. You could close Emacs now, because the file you loaded is in the same state as before you edited it.

The *minibuffer* is an essential part of Emacs. It is a short, full-width strip of the Emacs screen just beneath the modeline. This is the place to type commands that haven't been bound to keys. Emacs also uses this area to prompt the user for information such as file names, buffer names, search strings, the type of help requested, and any other information Emacs needs to do its work. Error messages are also displayed in the minibuffer.

There are situations in which you might be asked for confirmation in the minibuffer. Most such queries can be answered with either "y" or "n" (yes or no), but whenever your data might be at risk, Emacs insists that you answer with a full "yes" or "no". Here is one such prompt:

```
Modified buffers exist; exit anyway? (yes or no)
```

Emacs is trying to warn you that if you quit without saving the changed buffers, you might lose your unsaved changes.

Using the Help Keys

In his original description of the first Emacs, Richard Stallman referred to it as a *self-documenting* editor. This was quite an innovative feature for software at that time, and even now it is rare to encounter software written in such a way. Self-documenting means that documentation is built into the editor rather than written after the fact. The Lisp files that enable Emacs' editing functionality have documentation built into them; the result of this is that every Emacs function and variable have accessible help documentation. A set of keystrokes, all beginning with Ctrl-h, summon this help whenever it's needed:

Ctrl-h   Opens a window describing the help options available with that prefix, including all the following variations.

Ctrl-h m   Opens a window containing a description of all the currently active modes, including keybindings.

Ctrl-h k   A prompting help key. After pressing this combination, you are asked (in the minibuffer) to press the key or key sequence for which you need help. A window opens, describing just what the key does.

Ctrl-h a   Another prompting key, this one is known as apropos help. When prompted, type a word, function name, or variable name. A window displays all the Emacs commands containing the word or name. This is a good way to find commands when you don't know the exact name.

Ctrl-h f   Prompts you for a Lisp function name and then shows the documentation in a window. Since Lisp commands are functions, you can also type a command name.

Ctrl-h t   Starts the Emacs tutorial, a short introduction to Emacs for the first-time user.

Ctrl-h v   Shows you a variable's value. This is a quick way to see what default settings are in use.

Ctrl-h I   Brings up the Info help file browser, which is covered in Chapter 15, "External Convenience Packages."

Loading and Saving Files

You will use the following commands constantly, which makes them perfect candidates for rebinding to a single keystroke, such as one of the function keys (see Chapter 10 for keybinding instructions). Except for the buffer-saving command, these commands prompt you for a file name in the minibuffer. Here are the default keybindings:

Ctrl-x Ctrl-f   Loads a new file. Think of the "f" as standing for "find a file."

Ctrl-x k   Kills a buffer; if you have unsaved changes you will be asked if you want to save the buffer.

Ctrl-x Ctrl-v   Replaces a file you just loaded with another one. This can be thought of as a combination of the above two commands.

Ctrl-x I   Prompts you in the minibuffer for a file name. The contents of the file specified are then inserted at the point position.

Ctrl-x Ctrl-s   Saves the current state of the buffer to disk, overwriting the original file.

Tab Completion

Tab completion is an immensely helpful Emacs feature that ought to be one of the first time-saving techniques you learn. Any time you have to type something in the minibuffer, whether it is a file name, the name of a function or variable, or a Lisp library you'd like to load, tab completion will finish typing it for you.

If you have spent much time at a Linux shell prompt this will be a familiar concept. The common shells such as Bash use the tab key in a similar way to complete file and command names.

File Name Completion

This type of completion is especially handy when you're running an operating system (such as Linux) that supports long file names. Here's how it works: If you type Ctrl-x Ctrl-f in order to load a new file and then type (in the minibuffer) the first few characters of the file name of a file you would like to load, pressing the Tab key notifies Emacs that you want it to finish typing the name.

Emacs checks the path. If it finds only one file name in the directory you specified that starts with the same letters, the name is completed in the minibuffer; pressing Enter loads the file. Otherwise, a message appears, telling you that the initial letters you typed aren't unique to one file. Pressing Tab a second time opens a Completions window that shows all the file names in the directory that begin with the characters you typed. Clicking the second mouse button on the file name you're looking for closes the Completions window and loads the file. If you move the cursor to the Completions window, you can also select the desired file name by moving point to the entry and pressing Enter.

Help Key Completion

Help key completion works the same as the Ctrl-h help keys discussed previously. If you want help with a function whose name begins with "buffer", you press Ctrl-h f. The minibuffer becomes active and asks you to `"Describe function:"`. Type `buff` and press the Tab key. (There is no reason to type more letters than the first few. In this case, it is reasonable to assume that most functions beginning with "buff" probably refer to buffers.) The first time you press the Tab key, "buff" is completed, and "buffer" is displayed in the minibuffer. Press the Tab key again, and the Completions window opens with a list of all Emacs functions beginning with the word "buffer." Again, clicking the second mouse button summons the documentation for any of the functions listed.

Sometimes it can be quicker to type the remainder of a name rather than press the Tab key a second time if you know the exact name you're looking for.

Command Completion

Whenever you type an M-x command in the minibuffer, Tab completion saves you time. It's also a quick way to determine whether a command is available. If Emacs complains that there is "no match," either you mistyped the command, or there just aren't any available commands beginning with the letters you typed before pressing the Tab key.

Moving around in a Buffer

Editing is no fun if moving from one area of a buffer to another is slow or awkward. Emacs has a variety of built-in commands for moving around the buffer, and with a little practice, they will become second nature to you.

By Characters, Words, and Lines

Like any other editor, Emacs lets you move the cursor around with the arrow keys. Because some keyboards lack the four arrow keys, these alternative keybindings are provided:

Ctrl-f	Moves forward one character
Ctrl-b	Moves backward one character
Ctrl-right arrow	Moves forward one word
Ctrl-left arrow	Moves backward one word
Ctrl-p	Moves to the previous line
Ctrl-n	Moves to the next line
Ctrl-v	Moves to the next page (equivalent to Page Down)
M-v	Moves to the previous page (equivalent to Page Up)

These keybindings are fine for moving the cursor short distances, but they can be tedious if you have a ways to go. The next section's keybindings address this.

By Sentences, Paragraphs, and Pages

Before using the following keybindings, you should be aware that Emacs has its own idea of just what sentences, paragraphs, and pages are. The definitions are somewhat arbitrary, but some standard had to be defined in order to have consistent editing behavior. Naturally, any or all of the definitions can be changed.

To Emacs, a sentence is a series of words terminated with a period and two spaces, unless it's at the end of a paragraph, when a period alone suffices.

A paragraph is defined as a block of text separated from other text with a blank line.

Unprintable Characters

Emacs' idea of a page is different from that of a word processor. A word processor's page depends on the size of font being used and a document's formatting settings. Emacs is not a formatter; text in an Emacs file is like a continuous scroll with one portion visible in the editing window. The only reason you would need to define pages in a plain-text file would be if you were trying to accommodate a particular printer's page size.

Imagine you are using a printer that prints pages upon which 80 lines will fit, leaving room for header and footer blank areas. In typing a document to be printed on that printer, you can insert a control code every 80 lines in your file. This code is understood by most printers as a directive meaning "advance to the next page now."

The only problem is that the control code isn't on your keyboard. Emacs provides a way to insert this sort of character by prefixing it with Ctrl-q. Press Ctrl-q Ctrl-L in an Emacs text file, and what looks like ^L will appear on the screen. It's not really ^L, because ^L is two characters, ^ and L, whereas the result of pressing Ctrl-q Ctrl-L is one character, as you can see by moving the cursor over it with the arrow keys. The cursor will jump over ^L as if it were a single character, which it really is.

To sum up, Emacs considers the special control character ^L a page-break symbol. If you were to print a copy of a file that has ^L page breaks, they wouldn't show up in the printout, but new pages would begin whenever the character was encountered.

The following commands move point to a new location in the buffer:

M-e	Moves to the next sentence
M-a	Moves backward one sentence
M-}	Moves forward a paragraph
M-{	Moves back to the previous paragraph
Ctrl-x]	Moves to the next page
Ctrl-x [	Moves to the previous page

The Beginning and the End

How many times have you been typing near the end of a line and noticed a typo near the beginning? Being able to jump from the beginning to the very end of a file is handy as well.

Ctrl-a	Takes you to the beginning of the line
Ctrl-e	Puts the cursor at the end of the line
M-<	Moves point to the beginning of the file
M->	Moves point to the end of the file

I've always felt the latter two keybindings were awkward. In Chapter 10, you will learn how to assign new keybindings to common actions.

Scrolling

Scrolling a window full of text sounds like something that shouldn't need adjusting. Unfortunately, Emacs has an odd way of scrolling that can be disconcerting to new users. The text tends to scroll smoothly for a short time and then abruptly jump several lines. Here is a situation in which the editor's configurability shines, allowing you to alter the default behavior in several different ways.

Scrolling Variables

Several variables can be tweaked in order to adjust the scrolling to your satisfaction.

If you prefer to scroll while preserving the relative point position on the screen, the variable `scroll-preserve-screen-position` can be set to a non-nil value. By default, the variable's value is nil; set it to 1 to activate this behavior.

`scroll-conservatively` is a variable that by default is set to 0. Try values such as 1, 2, or 3 to prevent point from jumping to the middle of the screen while you're scrolling.

Two variables, `scroll-up-aggressively` and `scroll-down-aggressively`, offer further control of where on the screen point ends up when you're scrolling. The default value is 0.5, which tries to center point on the screen. Fractional values between 0 and 1 are valid.

The easiest way to try various values of these variables is via the Customize configuration facility, which is introduced in the next chapter. If you would like to try changing values now, you can evaluate the variable values in the Scratch buffer by typing parenthesized statements that look something like this:

```
(setq scroll-conservatively 2)
```

After you type this expression, place point just after the last parenthesis and press Ctrl-x Ctrl-e. This immediately changes the value so that you can see how you like the new behavior.

Buffers and the Buffer List

Since Emacs can handle multiple buffers in a session, it needs a way to keep track of them. Not only are the contents of each buffer stored in memory, but also the file name and buffer name associated with each buffer. The position of point in each buffer is stored, as well as its status, such as whether the buffer is read-only and whether changes have been saved.

The Buffer menu is the easiest way to switch buffers. It simply displays the current list of buffers. The list can also be accessed in a separate window that allows you to select buffers and perform operations on the selections.

The Buffer List

These two keybindings are used to bring up the buffer window:

Ctrl-x Ctrl-b   Summons the buffer list window.

Ctrl-u Ctrl-x Ctrl-b   Summons the window but shows only buffers associated with a file. Buffers such as Scratch and Messages aren't shown.

The buffer list window takes up the lower half of the screen; Figure 3.2 is a typical example.

The characters to the left of each buffer name indicate its status. An asterisk before the name indicates that the buffer has been changed but not saved. A % symbol indicates a read-only buffer, such as a Dired directory listing or the Info help browser.

There are quite a few single-letter keybindings for working with the buffers shown in the buffer list window. The most important of these bindings are included in the following list. The others can be viewed by moving point to the window and pressing Ctrl-h m (help for current mode). A window opens, showing the complete list of keybindings. Here are the most useful keys:

f   Selects the buffer at point and displays it instead of the buffer list

o   Selects the buffer and displays it in another window

s   Marks the buffer to be saved

k   Marks the buffer to be killed

x   Operates on the marked buffers (save or kill)

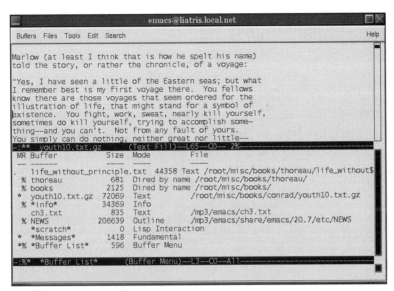

Figure 3.2   *The Buffer List Window*

Changing Buffers with the Keyboard and Menus

Ctrl-x b is the standard keybinding for switching buffers. By default, the last buffer you visited is suggested in the minibuffer; pressing Enter displays that buffer. If that isn't the buffer you want, type a few letters of the desired buffer's name and then press Tab to complete the name. As mentioned earlier, the Buffers menu is an alternative means of switching buffers; you can also pull down the menu and click on the name of the buffer to edit.

Regions, the Mark, and Point

Selecting a region of text and either copying it or cutting (killing) it is one of the most basic and useful editing operations. There are several ways to perform these actions in Emacs, using either the mouse or the keyboard.

Keyboard Selection

One end of a region is always the point position, indicated by the cursor. Pressing Ctrl-space begins the marking process; any movement commands after that extend the region. The arrow keys can be used, as well as commands such as M->.

Pressing Ctrl-space is called "setting the mark." At this time (before any motion commands are given), the point and the mark are in the same place in the file.

Subsequent motion commands leave the mark where it was set, while point moves farther from it, widening the region. Pressing M-> moves point to the end of the file, marking everything between the mark position and point's new location. M-} selects the text between the mark and the beginning of the next paragraph. In effect, Ctrl-space temporarily redefines the motion commands so that they mark rather than move. Many Emacs commands are defined in such a way that they are used in a variety of contexts. Once you know that M-f means "move to the next word," you can figure out that Ctrl-space M-f extends the marked region from point to the beginning of the next word.

While you are learning these keyboard marking commands, it's good to know that the mouse can also mark, copy, cut, and paste regions. Sometimes the mouse is more convenient, especially when you're marking smaller areas.

Mouse Selection

Mouse selection follows the usual software convention: clicking the mouse button moves point, and then dragging with the button down marks a region. Another way to do this (which is particularly useful when you're marking larger areas) is to click mouse button three at the other end of the region you want marked. The entire block of text between the cursor and the spot you clicked becomes a new marked region.

The Mark Ring

You would think that once a new mark is made, the old one would be gone forever. However, Emacs remembers up to 16 old marks. You can recover them by pressing Ctrl-u Ctrl-space. This command restores the most recent mark before the current one. Pressing this command repeatedly moves the mark to progressively older positions until finally the current mark is restored. It's called the *mark ring* because the marks loop back to the beginning.

Knowing this lets you use marks as bookmarks in a buffer.

Each buffer has its own mark ring. These rings are persistent during a single Emacs session but aren't saved between sessions. There is also a global mark ring, which records marks set in previous buffers. Pressing Ctrl-x Ctrl-space takes you to the last mark you set in another buffer. You could think of this as an alternative to the standard buffer-changing command Ctrl-x b. Ctrl-x b moves to the point position in the last-edited buffer, whereas Ctrl-x Ctrl-space displays the last mark set in that buffer.

Narrowing to a Region

Narrowing in Emacs is reducing the apparent size of the buffer to a defined area. This area can be the current page, a particular Lisp function, or the current marked region.

You might be wondering why anyone would bother to do this. One reason is to limit the scope of a global action, such as search-and-replace. Another could be to help focus attention on a particular section of a file.

When you are editing in a narrowed buffer, the remainder of the buffer is still there, but it's invisible and inaccessible until you "widen" the buffer to its original state.

Narrowing is by default disabled. The first time you try one of the narrowing commands, you are asked to confirm that you really want to do this. After you enable narrowing for the first time, it will be always available in the future. The Emacs developers set up narrowing this way so that new users wouldn't panic as they watched the bulk of their buffer seem to disappear. Here are the narrowing commands:

Ctrl-x n n   Narrows down to the selected region, the area between point and mark

Ctrl-x n p   Narrows down to the current page

Ctrl-x n f   Narrows to the Lisp function at point

Ctrl-x n w   Widens the narrowed buffer back to the original state

Cutting, Copying, and Pasting

This section could have been called "Killing and Yanking," but the familiar terms seemed more appropriate. The traditional Emacs terms, although they carry violent connotations, are expressive in their own way.

After you have defined or selected a region, several operations can be performed on the text. If you defined a region with the mouse, the contents were automatically copied to the internal Emacs clipboard (as well as the X clipboard; see the section "The Emacs Kill Ring and the X Clipboard" for information on the relationship between the two). If the region was defined with Ctrl-space followed by motion commands, further action is necessary to copy or cut the text. These commands operate on the region:

Ctrl-w   The "kill" or cut command. The selected text is cut from the buffer but remains available for yanking (which is Emacs lingo for pasting).

M-w   The copy command. The region remains in the buffer but is available for yanking from the clipboard.

Ctrl-y   Used to paste the most recent kill (which can be either a cut or copied region) into the buffer at point.

M-y   An interesting and useful variation of Ctrl-y. Instead of yanking the most recent killed text, this command yanks the next-to-last kill, replacing the region yanked into the buffer using the Ctrl-y command. If you repeat this command, it replaces the next-to-last-kill with the kill before that. When this command is repeated, it steps back through the kill ring, successively replacing yanked text with previous yanked regions. Eventually, the beginning of the kill ring is reached, and the most recent kill is again yanked into the buffer. M-y works only after either Ctrl-y or M-y. Spend some time becoming familiar with this command; it's a real time-saver.

Using the Mouse

Basic mouse usage under Emacs is intuitive; the mouse behaves as in other X applications. Clicking the mouse button moves point, dragging the mouse with the button down defines a region, and clicking the second mouse button pastes the most recent kill.

These actions are the most used, but Emacs has a variety of other mouse commands available.

There is a handy alternative to setting the mark with Ctrl-space and then moving point to define a region. Click the mouse button to set point, and then click the third mouse button at any other location in the buffer. The area between the two is copied to the kill ring. You can Page Up or Page Down between clicks; even if you can't see it, the location of the first click (the point) is still valid.

Double-clicking the mouse button on a word selects the word as a region, and triple-clicking selects an entire line.

The Emacs Kill Ring and the X Clipboard

Emacs cooperates well with other X Window programs. If you cut or copy text from another application, the selection becomes the most recent item in the Emacs kill ring. It works in the opposite direction as well: The current killed region in Emacs is also the top item in the global X clipboard. Remember that a keyboard-defined region (Ctrl-space plus motion commands) doesn't get copied to the kill ring, and thus the X clipboard, unless it has been killed with either the M-w or Ctrl-w command. The mouse-defined regions are automatically put at the top of the kill ring.

Searching

Searching for a word or phrase is an essential part of any full-featured editor. Emacs offers several ways to search, but the most useful method is a technique found in few other editors: searching incrementally. In an incremental search, the search process begins as soon as you type the first character of the search string. The cursor jumps to the first word after point that begins with that character. As successive characters are typed, the cursor jumps forward as it homes in on matching text.

This type of search can be overkill in some situations, so Emacs also supports the more traditional nonincremental and word searches.

You can cancel a search using the all-purpose abort command, Ctrl-g. The cursor returns to the previous match. Pressing Ctrl-g a second time takes you back to the original location, and editing can proceed as before.

Incremental Search

Incremental search was developed to save time. A normal search doesn't begin until the entire search word or phrase has been typed, but in many cases, just a few letters of the search term are all that is necessary to find a match.

An example will help clarify how this type of searching works. Imagine that you want to find the word "camelopard" in a buffer. Pressing Ctrl-s places the cursor in the minibuffer, waiting for search characters. As soon as you type c in the minibuffer, the buffer cursor jumps ahead to the next occurrence of c in the buffer, which would most likely be in a short word such as "can." Typing the letter a produces no result, because "can" contains "ca." Typing m might take you to the word "came." Entering the letter l might take you all the way to the first occurrence of "camelo-pard," unless the word "camel" is found first. Entering the letter o will almost certainly advance point to "camelopard," because very few words contain "camelo."

After the first occurrence of "camelopard" is found, pressing Ctrl-s again jumps the point position to the next instance. Repeat the command to jump to further matches. At any time, you can press Enter, and point will remain at the current search match. Remember that Ctrl-g backs up to the previous match, and a second Ctrl-g stops the search altogether and returns point to your original location in the file.

Describing this process takes longer than actually doing it and makes it seem more awkward than it is in practice. Try it out in one of your own buffers by searching for a word or phrase near the end of the buffer. You'll be surprised at how quick this type of search can be once you get the hang of it.

If you make a mistake while entering a search term in the minibuffer, just press Delete as many times as it takes to back up to a correct entry.

While Emacs is in search mode, the standard yank and kill commands work in a special way. After you press Ctrl-s:

Ctrl-w	Starts a search, using the word at point as the input.
M-y	Uses the most recent kill (from the kill ring) as input.
Ctrl-y	The text from point to the end of the line becomes the search string.

Standard Search

Sometimes it's easier and quicker to forgo incremental searching. A standard search (with the entire search string specified at the beginning) is a special type of incremental search.

You initiate a standard search by pressing Ctrl-s Enter. Then type [search-string] and press Enter.

The blinking cursor appears in the minibuffer, just as it does in an incremental search, but pressing Enter after pressing Ctrl-s tells Emacs to wait for a complete search string before starting the search. After you enter the search string, pressing Enter begins the search.

Exit this type of search as you would an incremental search, by pressing either Enter or Ctrl-g.

Word Search

Word search is used to search for a sequence of words. These words can be separated by either spaces, multiple spaces, new lines, or punctuation. This allows searches for word patterns that may extend over more than one line.

At first glance, this doesn't seem to be very useful. The following example shows how word search can find strings that would stymie a standard search.

Assume that you wanted to find this string in a file: "The camelopard is also known as the giraffe." You are reasonably certain that the string is somewhere in the file, but a standard search failed. The search failed because the end of the string, "as the giraffe," is on a different line in the buffer. The string you typed as a search request had a space between "known" and "as," but in the buffer the two words are separated by a line feed.

Word search doesn't care what is between the individual words in a search string. It merely looks for a sequence of words separated by non-alphabetic characters.

You initiate a word search by pressing Ctrl-s Enter Ctrl-w.

A Word-search: prompt appears in the minibuffer. Just type your string and press Enter again.

Replacing Your Search Results

Nothing is more tedious than manually replacing one word or phrase with another, especially in a large file where there might be dozens of replacements to make. Using Emacs' searching features makes this process a little faster, but combining search and replace in one operation makes the job quick and easy.

There is one drawback to doing a global replacement of a search term. What if you wanted to replace every occurrence of the word "grip" with the word "hold?" You could do this, but the words "gripe" and "Agrippa" would be replaced by the non-sense words "holde" and "Aholdpa."

In general, it's safer to use query replacement (see the next section). It takes a little longer, but the results are predictable. Global replacement is fine to use in a short file. By default, there is no keybinding for unconditional global replacement. (I suspect Emacs is set up that way to encourage the use of query replacement.) The command has to be typed into the minibuffer as an M-x command. Press M-x, type [replace-string], and press Enter.

You are prompted with the statement Replace string:. Type the string you want replaced, and then press Enter. Type the replacement string, and press Enter. The replacement will then be done from point to the end of the file. If you want the entire file processed, be sure to start the operation from the very beginning of the buffer.

Query-Replace

Query-replace is a means of making sure that only what you want replaced is actually replaced. Emacs moves from one search string to the next, each time asking whether you want the replacement done or not. Press M-% to start a query-replace. See Figure 3.3.

The prompt Query replace: appears in the minibuffer. After you type your search string and press Enter, point moves to the first search result. Now you need to respond to a new prompt, Query replacing [search-string] with:.

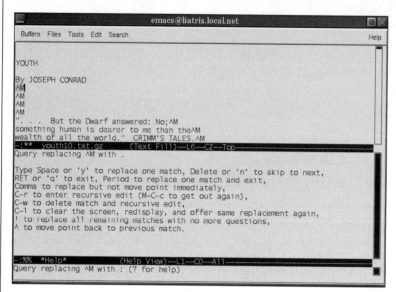

Figure 3.3   *Query Replacement*

Type in your replacement string, and press Enter. At this point, you have a range of options.

Pressing the spacebar or the y key replaces the first occurrence of the search string and then moves to the next one. You can step your way through the entire buffer this way, examining each of the search results and deciding whether you want the replacement done. If there are some instances that don't need replacement, press Delete or n.

There might come a time during a long query-replace session when you realize that the remainder of the replacements don't need individual attention. Press ! and the rest of the replacements will be processed automatically, as in a standard global replacement. This can be used at the very beginning if you are very sure of your judgment.

To exit query-replace and return to normal editing, press Enter or q.

Recursive Editing

Imagine this editing scenario: You are in the midst of a long and complex query-replace session. About halfway through the file, you notice an error on an adjacent line. Your first impulse is to try to remember where the error is and go back later.

But what if you find a second or third error? You shouldn't have to keep notes during a query-replace! Your second impulse might be to correct the error, but you would have to quit the query-replace, fix the error, and then start a new query-replace. What a pain!

The solution to this dilemma is to temporarily suspend the query-replace process, jump over to the error, and then resume the query-replace where you left off. You do this by pressing Ctrl-r. After you've given that command, you can edit to your heart's delight; just don't forget that the query-replace process is waiting for you to resume! Pressing M-Ctrl-c ends your temporary recursive-editing session and allows you to finish the query-replace.

Another way to start a recursive edit is to press Ctrl-w rather than Ctrl-r. This command deletes the current search string and allows you to replace it with something other than the replacement string. M-Ctrl-c exits this type of recursive edit as well and returns to the main search.

Searching Backwards

Any of the search commands just mentioned can be used to search backwards in a file as well as forwards. The standard incremental search command is Ctrl-s. If you substitute Ctrl-r, the search works backwards toward the beginning of the buffer. This command can be used in the middle of a forward search. While searching forward from the middle of a buffer, you might realize that you need to search the beginning of the buffer as well.

Repeating a Previous Search

Remember the kill ring and the mark ring? Emacs keeps in memory a ring of search strings as well. After you press Ctrl-s or Ctrl-r to start a search, you normally type your search string in the minibuffer. If instead you press Ctrl-s or Ctrl-r again, the last search string you entered is pasted into the minibuffer. Want the search string before that one? Press Ctrl-s or Ctrl-r yet again, and the second-previous search string replaces the previous one in the minibuffer. This can save tedious retyping of search strings you used earlier.

Uppercase and Lowercase

A standard search in Emacs is not case-sensitive. For example, searching for "wombat" will also find "Wombat." The reasoning behind this feature is to ensure that a search finds capitalized words at the beginnings of sentences. There are times when you need to search for only the capitalized form of a word, or a particular mixed-case word. An example might be a search for "Joy" in a buffer that contains the word "joy" and the proper name "Joy."

Emacs handles this issue automatically. A search string with one or more capital letters typed in the minibuffer turns on the search's case sensitivity. If you type in an all-lowercase search string directly afterwards, case sensitivity is turned back off.

Regular Expressions in Searches

A *regular expression* (also called a regexp) is a typographical symbol used in a coding system to match patterns. The basic idea is to assign seldom-used characters to match one or more common characters, such as letters and numerals. Regular expressions can be very useful in search strings, helping you find a string by specifying only a small part of it and to find strings that share only a few characters. They also let you specify the location in a line of a search string, such as searching for all instances of a certain word that occur at the beginning or end of a line.

Most Linux (and DOS) users are familiar with some of the regexps used by command shells such as Bash and DOS's command.com. Type `ls *.txt` at the bash prompt to see a listing of all files that have the .txt suffix. In this case, the asterisk matches any character or sequence of characters.

The most basic regexp is a character; any letter or number is its own regexp. In other words, "a" matches "a" in a regexp. This is seemingly trivial and not very useful. The power gained from using regular expressions comes from using ordinary characters in conjunction with specially-assigned regexp symbols.

Special Symbols

The Emacs version of regular expressions is similar to the regexp systems used by command shells and Linux utilities such as grep and sed, but there are differences. As an example, the asterisk in the bash shell is a universal wildcard, matching anything, while as an Emacs regexp the asterisk is still a wildcard of a sort, but it affects the smallest possible regexp directly before it.

The following table lists the most important symbols recognized by Emacs' built-in regular expression interpreter.

Emacs Regular Expression Symbols

`*`	Matches any number of characters, including none at all. It affects the regexp just before it. For example, `toa*s*t*[de]*` matches both "toast" and tossed," among others. (See the description of `[]` later in this table.)
`^`	Matches the beginning of a line. For example, `^algol` matches the string "algol" only if it is the first string on a line.
`$`	Matches the end of a line. For example, `p+$` matches a string composed of at least one p at the end of a line.
`.`	Matches any single character.
`[]`	Matches the range of characters within the brackets. For example, `[l-q]` matches l, m, n, o, p, or q. This can also be used to match any one of a group of characters within the brackets. For example, `[srm]` matches either s, r, or m, but not two or three of them.
`[^]`	Matches any character or range of characters not listed after the caret. For example, `[^pqz]` matches any character except p, q, or z.
`\<`	Matches the beginning of a word. For example, `\<num` matches any word beginning with "num," such as "number."
`\>`	Matches the end of a word. For example, `*ber\>` matches "number" and "encumber."
`+`	Used after a regexp to match the preceding regexp at least once.
`\`	Used to escape any of the special characters in this table. For example, `\*` would be used within a regexp to match the actual asterisk symbol.

The most commonly used regexp symbols are described in this table. There are others, but these are more than enough to get you started. If you would like to delve further into the subject, the Info help files supplied with Emacs provide more details.

Syntax of Regular Expressions

In general, regular expressions are strung together to form a complete expression. For example, `Ho[ur]s.` would match both "house" and "horse." Sometimes a subset of a regexp must be evaluated before the remainder. Expressions can be grouped in this way:

`\(...\)`

The three dots represent a regexp. This grouping ensures that the contents of the isolated group are evaluated first, with the result plugged back into the main expression.

Searching with Regular Expressions

There are four commands for regular expression searching. These are variations of the standard forward and backward search commands discussed above. Press M-Ctrl s to search forward incrementally as you type a regular expression in the minibuffer. During a standard incremental forward search each successive match is closer to the end of the buffer. When using regular expressions a match may be found before the current match as you add to the expression. As an example, say you started the regexp with `troop`. The cursor jumps to the first occurrence of the word, but now you add to the expression: `troop|squadron`. This broadens the search to include an entirely different word which happens to occur prior to the first match.

Another way to use this command is to press Enter rather than beginning to type a regular expression: M-Ctrl-s Enter.

This disables incremental searching; the search won't begin until you type a regular expression and again press Enter.

The following two commands are identical to the two above but search backwards through the buffer. Press M-Ctrl r to begin a reverse incremental regular expression search, while pressing M-Ctrl r Enter begins a non-incremental reverse regular expression search.

Query-Replace with Regular Expressions

An obscure but useful function named query-replace-regexp extends the standard query-replace command discussed previously. This command lets you use regular expression symbols in your search-string, including parenthesized groups. You can also make a back-reference in your replace-string to one of the parenthesized units of the search-string. This example shows how the command can be used.

Suppose you need to replace some of the occurrences of the words "flitter" and "flutter" with the word "fly". Start by typing the command:

```
M-x query-replace-regexp
```

Press Enter, then type this regular expression in the minibuffer:

```
fl[ui]tter
```

You will be prompted for a replacement string; type `fly` and press Enter. One at a time you will be presented with matches. The commands listed in the Query-Replace section can be used to deal with each match.

A related command is replace-regexp, which globally replaces all matches unconditionally. This can be a risky command to use unless you are uncommonly skillful at constructing regular expressions which work correctly the first time.

Formatting Commands

When you are writing text such as an e-mail, an article, a chapter of a book, or anything intended to be read by you or other people, you don't want to have to wrap lines manually. By default, Emacs doesn't automatically wrap lines, but it does a sort of pseudo-wrapping so that lines don't extend beyond the screen. This is indicated by a backslash (in GNU Emacs) or an arrow (in XEmacs). Lines are broken in the middle of a word if necessary. Most Emacs users configure the editor to automatically fill paragraphs (wrap long lines to a specific width) when in text mode or when in any modes derived from text mode (such as message mode, used when you write e-mail).

Auto-Fill Mode

Customization of Emacs is fully dealt with in Chapter 4, which shows you how to use Customize to write entries in your .emacs file automatically, and Chapter 9, which teaches you how to write your own .emacs file. But this word-wrap issue is important enough (for usability reasons) to justify jumping ahead a bit.

Emacs comes with a text-filling minor mode (a mode that coexists with and supplements a major mode) called auto-fill mode. You can easily set an option that sets that mode to be the default when no other mode is specified. This means that whenever a new file is opened, it is in auto-fill mode, and your text will wrap. Here are step-by-step instructions:

1. Start Emacs and create a new, empty .emacs file by pressing Ctrl-x Ctrl-f.
2. You are prompted in the minibuffer for a file name. Type `~/.emacs`. The screen will be empty unless you already have an .emacs file. Type in these two Lisp expressions:

```
(setq default-major-mode 'text-mode)
(add-hook 'text-mode-hook 'turn-on-auto-fill)
```

   Make sure you include all the parentheses, and don't forget the single quote just before the words `turn` and `text`.

3. Check to make sure that you typed these lines correctly by moving the cursor to the end of the first line and pressing Ctrl-x Ctrl-e. This command tells Emacs to evaluate the Lisp expression. If it's invalid, an error message appears.

4. Move the cursor to the end of the second line and press Ctrl-x Ctrl-e again. If there are no errors, text mode with auto-fill turned on will be active for the remainder of the Emacs session.

5. Save the file by pressing Ctrl-x Ctrl-s. The new setting will be in effect for future Emacs sessions.

The Fill-Column Variable

Emacs comes with the text width for auto-fill mode set at 70 columns, a reasonable default for average computer screens and Emacs window sizes. If 70 columns is too wide or too narrow for your screen, the fill-column variable can be changed. Press Ctrl-u, type [number], and press Ctrl-x f.

Substitute any desired number of columns for [number] in the command. See Chapter 9 for ways to make changes such as this one permanent.

Capitalization and Lowercase

Changing capitalized words to uncapitalized and vice versa is a common editing task. It's easy to forget to capitalize a proper name or the first word of a sentence. A tedious way to correct such typos is to move the cursor back to the offending character, delete it, and then type the proper character. That's quite a few steps for a trivial but commonplace operation.

Emacs has several built-in commands for dealing with such situations. These commands are quick to type and will quickly become second nature to you:

M-c   Capitalizes a word.

M-l   Converts a word to all-lowercase.

M-u   Converts a word to all-uppercase.

These commands don't require you to carefully place the cursor on the first character; anywhere in the word is fine.

Transposition

Another common error is transposed words or characters. You can quickly fix these annoying errors using these commands:

Ctrl-t	Transposes two letters.
M-t	Transposes two words.
Ctrl-x Ctrl-t	Transposes two lines.

Windows, Frames, and Buffers

The terms *window* and *frame* have meanings in an Emacs context that differ from their conventional meanings. Usually a window in a GUI like X Windows is defined as a rectangular, movable, and resizable bordered box within which an application runs. In Emacs lingo, this is a frame, and a window is a subdivision of a frame that displays a single buffer.

Multiple Windows

Normally, when you switch from one buffer to another, each one fills the entire frame (or the entire screen when Emacs is running on a non-X console). Sometimes it's helpful to be able to see two or more buffers at once, or two or more sections of a single buffer at once, as shown in Figure 3.4.

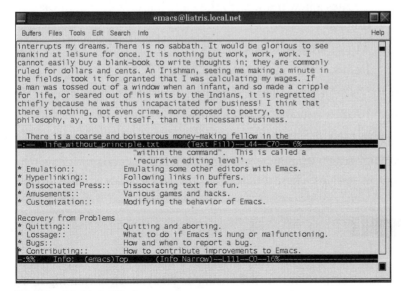

Figure 3.4   *Multiple Windows*

There are several keyboard commands for creating, destroying, and moving between windows:

Ctrl-x 2	Splits the current full-size window into two shorter windows, one above the other.
Ctrl-x 3	Splits the current window into two narrower side-by-side windows.
Ctrl-x o	Moves point to the next window or, if there are more than two, to the next window in a clockwise direction.
Ctrl-x 1	Makes the current window full-size, deleting the other one (but not deleting the other window's buffer).
Ctrl-x 0	Removes the current window, allowing the other window to expand to full size.
Ctrl-x ^	Enlarges the current window while making the other window smaller.

Frames

An Emacs frame is Emacs running in an X window, but Emacs can run in more than one frame without starting another Emacs session. These frames can be dealt with as with any X window: They can be resized, and any window manager command such as the keyboard commands for next window and previous window can be used normally. The Emacs commands for manipulating frames are analogous to the window commands in the preceding section:

Ctrl-x 5 2	Creates a new frame with the same buffer visible as in the original.
Ctrl-x 5 o	Moves focus to another frame.
Ctrl-x 5 0	Removes the currently-active frame.
Ctrl-x 5 b	Makes a new frame and displays the previous buffer in it.
Ctrl-x 5 f	Loads a new file in a new frame.

Although the concept of frames doesn't translate well to the Linux virtual console, with its individual full-screen window, recent versions of XEmacs do provide switchable frames in console sessions. These could be thought of as separate window groups.

Shell Commands

Emacs provides several ways to run external shell commands. It even allows you to devote a window to a complete interactive shell, just like your shell running in an xterm or in a virtual console.

Noninteractive Commands

M-! is a quick and simple key command that runs an external shell command and directs its output to an Emacs window called Shell Command Output. Figure 3.5 shows the output of the df command in its own new window. There are several advantages to running a command from within Emacs. You can treat the output just as you would any other text in a buffer. You can cut or copy it to another buffer, save it to file, or refer to it later in the session.

Another interesting feature is a variant of the M-! command. Use one of the standard Emacs methods of marking a region, and then press M-|.

Emacs will prompt you for a shell command in the minibuffer.

As an example, Figure 3.6 shows the result of piping a selected region of text through the GNU pr text utility (used with the -d option, which doublespaces the output).

Inserting Command Output into a Buffer

Rather than copying text from the Shell Command Output buffer, you can run an external command and have the output appear at point in your current buffer. All you have to do is precede the basic shell command with Ctrl-u by pressing Ctrl-u M-!.

This variation can also be used with the shell command on-region. The original region disappears and is replaced by the output of the shell command. Press Ctrl-u M-|.

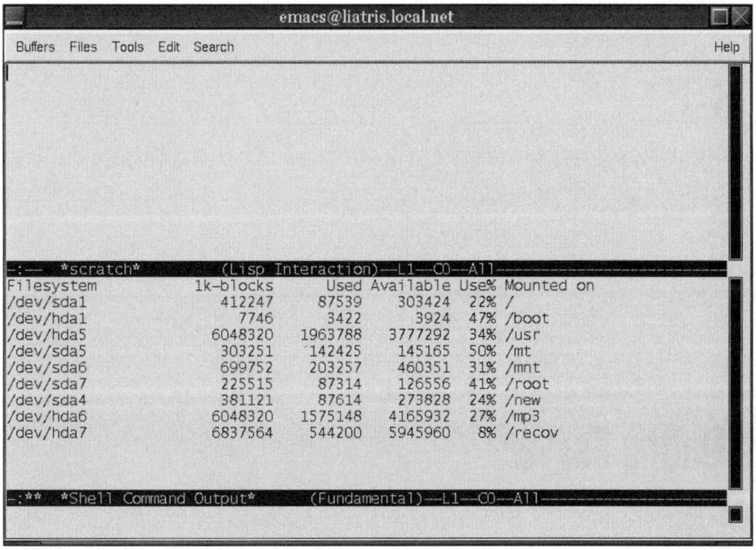

Figure 3.5   *Shell Command Output*

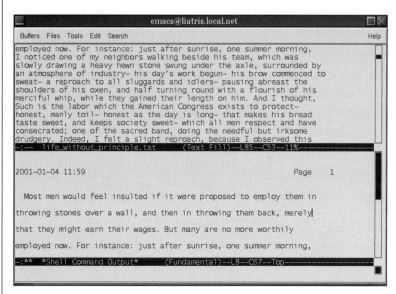

Figure 3.6 *Command on a Region*

The Shell Buffer

In the minibuffer, press M-x and type shell.

A new Shell window will open, running your normal command shell (bash, csh, and so on). From this window, you can run any command you would run in an xterm—although if you try to run ncurses-based programs (such as lynx, vim, or cftp), you will have problems. The Shell window is meant for command-line programs that output text, such as any of the basic GNU/Linux utilities such as ls, cat, and du, among many others.

As handy as the Shell window can be, I have to admit that most users don't have too many compelling reasons to use it. Since you already have the ability to cut and paste between xterm or rxvt windows and Emacs using the mouse, you might as well do that instead.

The Emacs Shell buffer gives you another option which does have some advantages. You can do incremental searches in the command output, and some feel that the Emacs command history implementation offers features lacking in the standard shells.

Emacs As an Editing Server

Once you become accustomed to the many editing conveniences Emacs provides, it can be a letdown to use the limited editors that are built in to e-mail or other programs. Luckily, most such programs have an option that lets you specify an external editor. GNU Emacs and XEmacs each have different subsidiary programs that act as editing servers so that external programs don't have to start a new instance of Emacs each time a file (such as an e-mail message) needs to be edited. Instead, a currently-running Emacs process edits the file and remains running afterwards.

emacsclient

GNU Emacs comes with a small daemon-like program called emacsclient. It can be used in two ways. The first way is to set the environment variable EDITOR to be emacsclient. This is usually set in a configuration file for your login shell. If you are a bash user, check your ~/.bash_profile file. (If you don't have one, copy /etc/profile or /etc/.profile to ~/.bash_profile and make your changes there.) Look for a line something like EDITOR=[editor-name]. Change this to EDITOR=emacsclient. Then you put the line (server-start) in your ~/.emacs file (see Chapter 9).

First you'll have to exit your shell (kill your X session, then type exit at the console prompt, log in again and restart X). Once X is running again, start up Emacs, and it'll be ready to go. Any programs that make use of the EDITOR environment variable to determine which editor to use will call emacsclient. emacsclient signals the main Emacs process, which then acts as the editor for the external program.

Many X programs these days don't bother with using the EDITOR environment variable. They typically have a configuration dialog with which you can specify an external editor. Enter emacsclient in that dialog and save the settings. The program (using emacsclient as an intermediary) will use your Emacs session as its editor.

The second way to use emacsclient is to call it directly from a shell prompt. You can type emacsclient file-name and a new frame will appear. Emacs needs to be running for emacsclient to work. The new frame is part of your main Emacs session and shares the buffer-list and kill ring just as any new frame would.

XEmacs and gnuserv

XEmacs does this a little differently. Its editing server is called gnuserv. The Lisp command (gnuserv-start), evaluated either in the Scratch buffer (see Chapter 6) or as a line in your ~/.emacs file, starts the server. Thereafter, a program that wants to use the currently-running XEmacs as its editor needs to call the editing client, which is called gnuclient. As with Emacs' emacsclient, the EDITOR environment variable can be set as gnuclient. This will cause programs that use that variable to direct editing tasks to XEmacs without starting a new process.

Conclusion

You should be becoming more comfortable using Emacs after reviewing the material in this chapter. It takes a while for Emacs' keyboard commands to become second nature, but the efforts you make will be amply repaid.

The next chapter introduces the Configure interface to Emacs customization.

Chapter 4: Using the Built-in Customization Tools

This chapter introduces two enormously useful means of customizing Emacs. The first is a point-and-click interface to nearly all Emacs settings called Customize. The second is the Emacs macro facility, which allows you to automate Emacs command and keystroke sequences and record them for reuse. Using these two tools, you can configure nearly every type of Emacs behavior without an extensive knowledge of Lisp.

Introduction to Customize

After Emacs had been under development for several years, it had become quite a complex piece of software. Although it was still completely configurable with Lisp, a sizable number of users lacked the time or ability to do so. Per Abrahamsen's introduction of the Custom library in 1996 began a new era for Emacs users. Authors of Emacs add-on packages could easily add their package variables and settings to the Customize interface with a few simple Lisp statements. Eventually, Customize was incorporated into both Emacs and XEmacs; this brought the myriad native Emacs settings into the Customize interface. Extensive Emacs customization was made possible for the many Emacs users who had been struggling with the default settings.

I've talked with several Emacs users who were unaware of Customize; they had noticed the Customize item on the menu bar but had never investigated. This is one of the drawbacks of open-source software. There is no marketing and promotion department for a "product" that is not sold by a commercial firm. Emacs doesn't have advertisements in computing magazines touting the latest new features.

Reasons to Use Customize

Even experienced Lisp programmers often use Customize, just to save time. Why do everything the hard way?

Using the Customize interface allows you to set up Emacs variables in a short time; 30 minutes spent on a first session will dramatically enhance Emacs' usability, especially for a new user. Manually making the equivalent changes in an .emacs file would probably take hours.

I probably spent a total of an hour the first time I used Customize, in two separate sessions. Since then I've used it occasionally to change one or two settings at a time. Another occasion for firing up the interface is right after you install a new Lisp package. Unless the package is small and simple, the necessary Custom hooks are usually built into the new package, causing a new group or subgroup to appear in the Customize buffers.

Any serious Emacs user will eventually absorb more than a little of the Lisp language. Using Customize lets you become productive with Emacs quickly, without the necessity of learning any Lisp until you feel ready.

How Customize Works

Any Emacs package contains a number of variables that can be changed via Lisp statements in an ~/.emacs initialization file. If the developer "wraps" those variables in a defined way, Customize can find and incorporate them when Emacs starts up, as long as the package is in Emacs' load-path.

> Emacs finds Lisp files only if they are in a directory contained in a list called the load path. The default load-path includes the native Emacs Lisp directories (part of the Emacs installation). One of these installed directories, the site-lisp directory, is empty when Emacs is first installed. This is the directory in which extra Lisp files and packages should be installed. Chapter 12 describes how to add directories to the load-path.

When Emacs is started various optional packages are loaded via statements in the ~/.emacs file. If the packages have been written with Customize support variables are created as the package is loaded. These variables add package-specific settings which the Custom library reads and translates into a Customize interface for the package whenever a Customize buffer is created. This means that every new Custom-enabled Emacs package you install will become part of the Customize interface, which is available on the menu bar and through direct M-x minibuffer commands.

The Customize interface organizes the many changeable options in a hierarchical tree-like arrangement that can be expanded and collapsed. Options are contained within groups and subgroups; this makes particular options reasonably easy to find.

Figure 4.1 shows a typical Custom session to help make this clear.

The + signs to the left of the group names can be toggled with the second or third mouse button. This action expands the group to display either expandable subgroups or individual options.

Figure 4.2 shows a single option, the default face.

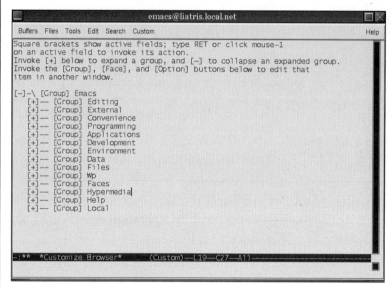

Figure 4.1 *A Top-Level Custom Screen*

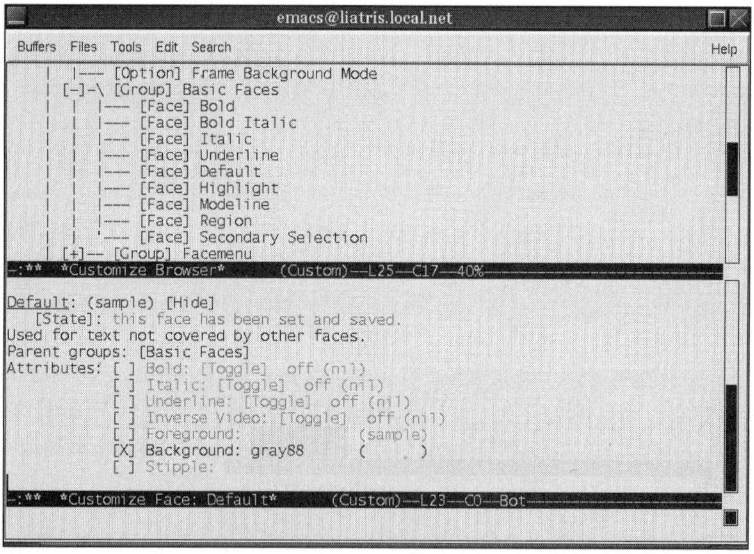

Figure 4.2 *A Custom Face Option*

The interface is not completely intuitive to a beginner, but considering the amount of information that Customize organizes, spending the few minutes it takes to find your way around is well worth your while.

Using Customize

Using the menu bar is the easiest way to bring up a Customize buffer. The Customize item is found under different headings in the various Emacs versions. In GNU Emacs versions prior to 21, Customize can be found on the Help menu, and in GNU Emacs 21 and XEmacs, you can find it on the Options menu.

The top or parent Customize group from which all the others stem is the Emacs group. If you've never used Customize, this is the place to start. The menus also offer choices that take you directly to a more specialized group, but an overview of the various groups will help you understand how Customize is organized.

In GNU Emacs, select the option Browse Customization Groups. This brings up a Customize Browser buffer. Each main Customize group is listed in a column, with a + sign to the left of each entry. Pressing the middle or left mouse button on the + sign or moving the cursor to it and pressing Enter expands a particular tree hierarchy.

XEmacs menus are slightly different. The Options, Customize item expands as you move the mouse over each Customize group, allowing you to move to any individual Customize-enabled setting. For now, choose the first item, the Emacs group. A buffer similar to the Customize Browser appears, as shown in Figure 4.3. In addition to the + sign, each group has a folder button to its left. Clicking the

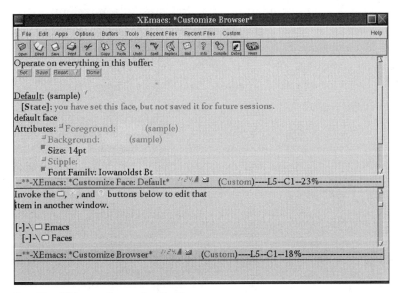

Figure 4.3 *XEmacs Customize Buffer*

middle mouse button or pressing the Enter key when the cursor is just to the right of a button opens a new buffer devoted to the button's group, which may contain subgroups. This expandable tree is implemented differently in the GNU Emacs version but the end result is the same.

Navigating the Interface

As you open successive levels of Customize buffers by clicking either the + sign or a graphic button, you will be presented with new buffers containing either subgroups or actual options. Each option has a label indicating whether it has been changed or is still set at its default value.

There are two types of options. Some have a yes-or-no value that can be toggled (these have a "toggle" button or a highlighted word), and others have a string value, such as a color or font name. String value options often have a drop-down menu (the Value menu) that has selectable choices. If there are too many choices for a menu, you have to type the string value in the entry field after deleting the default string.

Many options available in a Customize session have sensible default values that most users will not want to change. The trick to using Customize successfully is to scan each group quickly, looking for likely candidates for change, and then moving on.

Each time you choose a group or subgroup, the previous Customize buffer disappears but remains available on the Buffers menu. This can be useful if you want to back up to a previous buffer. If you are finished with a branch of the Customize tree and you don't want to change anything, click the second or third mouse button on Done or Finish. Otherwise, you will end up with many unneeded Customize buffers open.

The first time you use Customize, it might be wise not to change anything. Spend some time gaining an overview of the various groups and what they contain.

Making Temporary Changes

You might want to temporarily try out a change for a while before making it permanent. There are two places to click in a Customize buffer to make your changes active. One is at the top of the buffer—the statement Set for Current Session, directly under Operate on everything in this buffer. Clicking the second or third mouse button here activates all changes in the buffer's options until you shut Emacs down. The second spot is a mouse menu called State next to each individual option. When you click State, a drop-down menu appears. One of the items on this menu is Set for Current Session. When you click this, only the one option will be activated.

Setting Options Permanently

The same procedure is used to set an option or options permanently. At one of the just-mentioned two places in the buffer, select Save for Future Sessions. Lisp statements are added to your ~/.emacs file, which will set these options each time you start Emacs. If you don't have an .emacs file, one will be created for you.

The Lisp code inserted by Customize is in a rigid format; this helps the Custom library read it successfully. Even if you have learned some Lisp, meddling with Custom-generated code is perilous. The outcome is unpredictable and you might end up being forced to start over by deleting the entire Custom section of your ~/.emacs file and repeating your Customize sessions.

The safe course is to resist the temptation and make all Customize changes within a bona-fide Customize buffer.

Figure 4.4 shows a sample screen. The figure shows the State menu, but the menu partially obscures the State button.

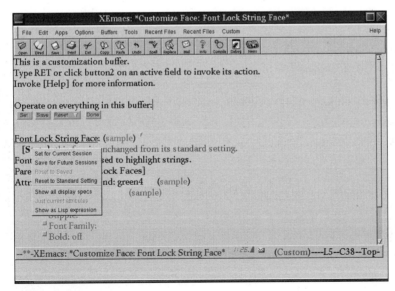

Figure 4.4 *Setting Options*

Customizing Faces

Face is an Emacs term that describes the sum total of the appearance attributes of a region of text, a cursor, a menu, or any other component of the Emacs screen. These attributes include the font (if applicable), the font's size, the foreground and background colors, the background pixmaps, and the texture.

Faces are often the first options you change when using Customize, because preferences for particular screen and text colors and fonts are very individual. Some people like light text on a dark background, and others swear by the reverse. This is one area in which the defaults, whatever they may be, won't please the majority of users.

Faces are tricky and time-consuming to set by hand. You have to write your own customization entries in an .emacs file.

How Different Modes Can Use the Same Faces

Several faces are used by most major modes, such as the various font-locking (or syntax-highlighting) faces. Among these are the String face, used to highlight quoted strings, and the Keyword, Function, and Variable faces, which are most often used in Source-code buffers. Many of these are used in other sorts of buffers, such as HTML and Mail Message buffers.

This feature allows you to change the foreground and background colors of the basic font-lock faces. After that, the changes will work without further intervention on a wide variety of files. In a sense, the modes inherit the global face settings, so you don't have to set up the face colors and fonts for every mode individually.

Dark and Light Backgrounds

Emacs maintains two complete sets of default face settings—one for dark screen backgrounds and one for light. The default set is for light backgrounds. If you change to a dark background, many of the font-lock faces will be unreadable. A quick interim solution is to use Customize to change the Frame Background Mode (which is under Faces in the Customize browser) from the default "light" to "dark." This will enable the alternative font-lock colors and make your screen more viewable. When you have time to fine-tune, you can set each of the font-lock faces individually.

Colorizing Emacs

You might be wondering where Emacs gets the specific color names it uses for foreground and background colors. They are contained in a file called rgb.txt, which is most often found in the directory /usr/X11R6/lib/X11. If it isn't there on your machine, try this command:

```
locate rgb.txt
```

This file is an ordinary text file that maps color values to names. The entries look like this:

```
255 248 220    cornsilk
```

GNU Emacs has the standard contents of rgb.txt built in, so it doesn't have to directly consult the file. XEmacs reads the color values from the rgb.txt file which is part of your X installation.

If you have a favorite shade that isn't included in the file, use a graphics program such as the Gimp to determine the red-green-blue value of the color, and insert an entry similar to the sample into the file. Any X program will be able to use the new color.

In order to add a color shade for GNU Emacs an additional step is necessary. The file [emacs-source-directory]/lisp/term/x-win.el contains a list of the rgb.txt color-names. Your new color's name needs to be added to this list as well as the rgb.txt file. Save x-win.el after adding the name, re-byte-compile it, and you will be able to use the color.

X Window and Console Faces

Many Emacs users still use Emacs in a traditional console, or virtual terminal. Console programs can use at most 16 colors, although eight colors is more common. This is in contrast to the graphics capabilities of modern video cards in X Window, which can display millions of different shades.

After you spend time setting up a pleasing combination of font-lock colors, it can be a letdown to run Emacs in a console.

GNU Emacs prior to version 21 didn't support colors in a console session, but Emacs 21 and XEmacs both do.

NOTE

If you have used Customize to set up font-lock colors, it's likely that few or none of them will be the basic eight colors supported by a console, such as red, green, and yellow. There are so many more pleasing colors available in X Windows that it would be a shame to be forced to use the eight console colors in X just so font-lock would work in an Emacs console.

Looking at a Customize buffer for font-lock faces, you would think that there is no provision for two sets of colors—one for the console and one for X. Actually, there is a way to set up colors this way, but for some reason it is hidden.

To locate this setting, first bring up a Customize buffer for one of the faces. A good first one to work with is the Default face, which controls the attributes of all text not belonging to one of the font-lock faces.

Click the middle mouse button on the State drop-down menu; this is where you saved settings earlier. Farther down the menu, notice the item "Show all display specs." Select this, and you will see a new menu called Display. Activate this menu and select "checklist." A series of labeled check boxes appears. Select the items Type and X, and make sure that TTY remains unchecked.

Now, any changes you make to the foreground and background colors will be applied only to Emacs under X Window. Repeat this procedure for all the font-lock faces. The result will be that default color choices will be used in a console Emacs session, and the more-complex colors you have chosen will be used for Emacs under X. This procedure works identically with XEmacs.

Customize from the Minibuffer

If you know the name of a particular Customize group, variable, or face, you don't necessarily need to start up the Customize browser at all. Pressing M-x and then typing

```
customize-face
```

or

```
customize-group
```

or

```
customize-variable
```

lets you access the particular Customize buffer you need. This is particularly useful when you know at least part of the Customize item's name (Tab completion helps here) but don't know in which group it can be found.

Emacs and X Resource Files

A couple of years ago, Custom was more limited in what it could control. Many Emacs users learned to make many of the changes just discussed in either their ~/.Xresources or ~/.Xdefaults file. Linux distributions use one or the other of these files to store settings for many X programs. Emacs still pays attention to these settings, but it is a good idea to phase out the use of this file for Emacs settings. It's easier to get the Emacs behavior you want if Emacs reads all its settings from your ~/.emacs file rather than trying to read from that file and the X resource file. There is less chance of conflict between the two if you comment out (with exclamation points) all Emacs settings in the X resource file and try to set up everything in Emacs using both Customize and any hand-coded Lisp you might have written.

Limitations of Customize

As the Custom library has evolved over the past few years, more and more of the many Emacs options have been made customizable. It was a massive job, both for the core Emacs developers and the external package authors, and Emacs users are grateful. There are still some little-used options that aren't included and a few packages (mostly small ones) that haven't been adapted to use Customize. The great bulk of the work has been done, though, and it's not much to ask of Emacs users that they occasionally make a manual addition to an .emacs file to enable a new package.

Introducing Emacs Macros

A *macro* is simply a recorded sequence of keystrokes that can be played back at will. Whenever you find yourself repeating a procedure in Emacs, you might want to consider creating a macro.

Macros can be temporary, lasting only until you either quit Emacs or create a new macro. You can use more than one macro in a session if you give the macros names. Once you name a macro, you can save it to a file for reuse. You can even assign a keybinding to a macro so that it can be executed quickly.

This might seem a bit abstract, so before the macro techniques are introduced, a real-world example should help you see how macros can be used to save time.

A Macro Example

Some time ago, I was writing a series of text files, each of which needed a header with the date the file was written. I didn't want to have to type the date each time; it seemed that there had to be a way to automate the process.

My first thought was to use the "insert-shell-command-output" key command. The Linux date utility returns the time and date when executed, so I tried pressing Ctrl-u M-!, typing date, and pressing Enter.

The output that was inserted into my buffer looked like this:

```
Fri Dec 29 09:36:45 CST 2000
```

That wasn't quite what I was looking for; I didn't want the time inserted, and I didn't like the order of the date's units. I read the date manual page, and next I tried pressing Ctrl-u M-!, typing date '+%A, %-d %b %Y', and pressing Enter.

This time, the output was acceptable:

```
Friday, 29 Dec 2000
```

But this command had two problems: It took longer to type the command than to type the date itself, and the cursor ended up at the beginning of the inserted date, which forced me to move the cursor to the end of the date and then press Enter for a new line.

This was a perfect situation for a macro. It was a tedious and repetitious typing task that I knew I would be doing often. I created a macro that recorded the keystrokes, including the cursor movement and newline so that after the macro executed I'd be ready to resume typing. I named the macro "mytime" and then gave it its own keybinding, Ctrl-c m. I saved it in my ~/.emacs file so that the new command would always be available. Read on to learn how to do this.

Recording and Playing Back Macros

The key command Ctrl-x (starts a keyboard macro.

Everything you type, including other keyboard commands and minibuffer M-x commands, is recorded in the macro until you end it by pressing Ctrl-x).

To execute the macro you just created, press Ctrl-x e.

Macros that are intended for temporary use in a single file can be given arguments that make the macro repeat a certain number of times. There are two ways to do this. For example, if you know that after recording a macro you will want it to repeat three times, end the macro by pressing Ctrl-u, typing 3, and pressing Ctrl-x).

If you want the last-recorded macro to repeat an indefinite number of times (such as throughout an entire file), press Ctrl-u, type 0, and press Ctrl-x e.

Here is an example of that command. Imagine that you want to add three spaces of indentation to the beginning of each paragraph. First, you record a macro that would do this once (start this with point at the beginning of a paragraph):

1. Press Ctrl-x (to start recording the macro.
2. Press the spacebar three times.
3. Press M-q to reformat the paragraph.
4. Press M-} to move forward one paragraph.
5. Press Ctrl-x) to end the macro recording.

Now that the macro is recorded, make sure that point is at the beginning of the paragraph and then press Ctrl-u, type 0, and press Ctrl-x e.

The macro will work on each paragraph in succession.

Substituting a number for the 0 in the command will execute the macro that many times rather than all the way to the end of the file.

> This macro will work in XEmacs only if adaptive-fill mode is turned off. It's turned on by default in XEmacs, and in GNU Emacs this mode is disabled.

Naming and Saving Macros

Creating macros takes time. Sometimes you have to make two or three attempts before a macro does exactly what you want. Naming a macro is the first step toward saving a macro permanently, and doing this also lets you create more than one macro in a single Emacs session.

Naming a macro requires that you execute the following rather lengthy minibuffer command: Press M-x and type `name-last-kbd-macro`

> Tab completion works well with this particular command, because there don't seem to be other Emacs commands that begin with `name`. Press M-x, type `name`, and press Tab. The remainder of the command will be completed for you. If you find yourself naming many macros, you might consider binding this command to a key.

You will be prompted for a name. This should be a name unused by any Emacs variable, command, or function. There is a custom in the Emacs community of prefixing personal macros, functions, and variables with your initials. This ensures that the names won't conflict with other Emacs names and gives an added benefit; you can view the names of all personal macros, etc. by using the Apropos help key along with your initials and using Tab completion to bring up the list.

Now that your macro has a name, you can execute it as you would any other minibuffer command. Press M-x and type `[macro name]`.

Now that you have a named macro, you can save it to a file. If you plan on using the macro infrequently, the file could be a Lisp file that would need to be explicitly loaded when needed. Perhaps the macro will be used only in a particular directory. In this case, the file containing a macro or macros can be loaded automatically through a notation in the files in that directory. Lines such as these at the end of a file inform Emacs that you would like the macro file loaded whenever the file is loaded:

```
Local Variables:
eval: (load-file "my-macros.el")
End:
```

Any macros that you anticipate using often can be inserted directly into your ~/.emacs file.

Writing the macro to a file is not difficult or involved. If you want a named macro written to a file, first load the file. Position the cursor at the desired location in the file, press M-x, and type `insert-kbd-macro`

You will be prompted for the macro's name. Type it in the minibuffer and press Enter. Lisp code representing your macro will appear in the file.

Remember the "mytime" macro I described earlier? Here is what it looks like written by the preceding command into a file:

```
(defalias 'mytime (read-kbd-macro
"C-u M-! date SPC '+%1:%M SPC %p' RET 9*<right> SPC RET"))
```

This is Lisp code. Even if you don't know Lisp, you can get the general idea of what this code is doing.

Defining new keybindings for commands is discussed in detail in Chapter 10. For now, I'll just show how the preceding macro could be given its own keybinding in an .emacs file:

```
(global-set-key [(control c) m)]  'mytime)
```

This command makes the keybinding Ctrl-c m work in all modes. Chapter 10 will show you how to make a keybinding active in just a single mode.

Macros That Query

Two types of macros stop and ask for input at specified times, similar to the query-replacement commands discussed in Chapter 3. The first incorporates the recursive-editing facility that is also used within a query-replace operation.

Recursive editing in a macro is useful when you're creating fill-in-the-blank forms. Stepping through a simple example is probably the easiest way to show you how this is done.

1. Start the macro by pressing Ctrl-x (.

2. The first item in the form is a person's name, immediately followed by the command that begins a recursive edit. Type Name: and press Ctrl-u Ctrl-x q.

3. Square brackets appear on the mode line when you are in the midst of a recursive edit. When the macro is being executed (after it is recorded), this is when you type in a name. Press M-Ctrl-c to exit the recursive edit.

4. This takes you back to macro recording. Now you type in the next field of the form, followed again by the recursive-edit command. Type Address: and press Ctrl-u Ctrl-x q.

5. Again, you leave recursive editing to type in a third field. Press M-Ctrl-c, type Date of Birth:, and press Ctrl-u Ctrl-x q. Then re-enter recursive editing by pressing M-Ctrl-c.

6. End the macro now (even though you can define any number of fields) by pressing Ctrl-x). You've just created an interactive template for writing a form. When you execute this type of macro, you have to execute the exit-recursive-edit command (M-Ctrl-c) after filling out each of the form's fields.

The second type of query macro doesn't use recursive editing. It instead stops at predefined points during the macro's execution to ask you what you want to do next.

Here is an example showing how this variant works. The purpose of this macro is to search a file for lines beginning with "Note:" and then copy the first sentence and paste it into a new file called notes.txt. The reason for the query is to let you decide if you want each sentence copied or not.

1. Press Ctrl-x (to start recording the macro.

2. Do a regexp search for Note:, but only at the beginning of a line. Press M-Ctrl-s and type ^Note:. (Remember that the caret (^) signifies that the match must be at the beginning of a line.)

3. Pressing Enter stops the search. This is where the query takes place, letting you decide whether to accept the first match.

4. Press Ctrl-x q. At this point, the macro is paused, waiting for a response. Pressing the spacebar or y signals Emacs that you want the macro to continue. Pressing Delete or n means you want to ignore this match and continue to the next one. Pressing Enter or Q means you want to quit the macro altogether.

5. Assuming that you pressed y or n (allowing the macro to continue), press Ctrl-space to set the mark.

6. Press Ctrl-e to move point to the end of the line.

7. Press M-w to copy the line to the kill ring.

8. Press Ctrl-x Ctrl-f and type `notes.txt` to create a new file called notes.txt in the current directory.

9. Press Ctrl-y to paste the copied line.

10. Press Enter to start a new line.

11. Press Ctrl-x b to go back to the original file.

12. Press Ctrl-x) to end the macro.

Conclusion

Many Emacs users find that the configurability provided by Customize and keyboard macros is all they need.

As useful as these tools are, you might eventually need to accomplish something in Emacs that is outside their scope. The next chapter introduces you to the Emacs-Lisp language, which makes this possible.

Chapter 5: Emacs-Lisp As an Entry Point to Configuration

L isp is not among the most commonly-used programming languages today, but it has several compelling advantages as an interface between a text editor and its users. It doesn't require extensive study to be useful due to its simple syntax. This chapter includes a bit of background about the language and its incorporation into Emacs.

The Origin of Lisp

If the mid-1970s, when Emacs was first being developed, was a distant period in computing history, the mid-1950s were prehistory. Computers were few, expensive, and vacuum tube-powered. The very idea of a high-level programming language was new; during this period, programming meant writing in machine language. This was (and is) a difficult skill to acquire. Computer scientists realized that a language somewhere between a spoken language and machine language would help make programming more accessible.

Early research in artificial intelligence at Dartmouth and MIT by John McCarthy and other researchers led to the formation of the Artificial Intelligence Project at MIT. The earliest forms of Lisp began to be developed and used both for AI (*artificial intelligence*) research and for mathematical programming. IBM's Fortran was an influence. Like the Internet a decade later, much of the funding for early Lisp development came from the United States military.

Through the 1960s, Lisp became more popular, and several dialects or variants evolved. One of these was MacLisp, which eventually inspired Emacs-Lisp.

Lisp As a Research Language

Lisp began as a research tool. It was intended to make the inner workings of the primitive computers of the time easier to grasp and manipulate by using human-language symbols for mathematical functions. During the first two decades of Lisp's evolution, programmers found that the language had applications beyond its theoretical use in AI research. Lisp found favor as a general-purpose programming language, especially at its birthplace, MIT.

Lisp As a Teaching Language

The 1960s and 1970s were the formative decades for computer research and teaching. There was a great need (as there still is today) for a computer language powerful enough to enable the creation of working programs but simple enough in syntax to be easily taught to computer-science students. Lisp fulfilled this need in many universities. A dialect of Lisp called Scheme is used more often today. Both Scheme and Lisp make use of parenthesized units of expression, in contrast to other languages, which tend toward a bewildering array of brackets, braces, and other punctuation. Lisp has very few hard-and-fast rules; the basics of constructing a valid Lisp expression can be taught in an afternoon.

Lisp and Java

Modern university computer science curricula often use Java, Sun Microsystems' "write once, run anywhere" language, in introductory courses. Java has many features in common with Lisp. Both can be interpreted rather than compiled languages, and both handle memory-management internally rather than forcing the programmer to deal with memory allocation issues.

Though there are similarities between the languages, Emacs-Lisp allows the user to make changes to a running system (such as Emacs), one key to the high degree of configurability and extensibility Emacs users enjoy.

One of the primary developers of Java is James Gosling. Gosling used Lisp extensively earlier in his career and even wrote a non-GNU version of Emacs.

How Emacs-Lisp Differs

It's not surprising that Richard Stallman turned to Lisp when he was thinking of possible macro languages for a new version of Emacs. Lisp was a part of the computing culture of MIT in the '70s.

Stallman realized that the current Lisp variants such as MacLisp were overkill for what he needed. A text editor is mainly concerned with manipulation of text strings rather than the algebraic formulae that Lisp handles so well.

With MacLisp as a starting point, Richard Stallman set out to create a lighter-weight Lisp that was more suitable for editing tasks. Remember that the PDP-10 computers Stallman was working with had, by today's standards, very little memory. Disk drives were slow as well, so optimized programs with little unnecessary fat were needed. Otherwise, a program would be slow to start up and sluggish to use.

A Specialized Lisp for Editing

The Lisp that Richard Stallman developed was devoid of the advanced algebraic capabilities of the parent Lisp variants. A Lisp interpreter for text must be able to do basic mathematics, such as working with integers, random numbers, and logical operators. The greater emphasis was on strings of characters: matching, searching, pasting, and all the other text-manipulation operations. Portability was another issue. Some of the older Lisp variants were optimized for particular platforms and would be difficult to port. Stallman wrote his Lisp in C, a language that can be compiled on nearly any platform.

Though some Lisp implementations have compilers, Stallman chose to make Emacs-Lisp an interpreted language. This allows on-the-fly changes of variable values and function definitions, significant assets for a programmable editor.

Lisp was designed to be an extensible language. Due to the fact that Lisp code is interpreted at runtime (rather than being compiled into a binary executable), changes in Lisp source-code files can be made and tested quickly without a time-consuming compilation. This trait fits in perfectly with Richard Stallman's idea of a user-configurable editor, an application that any user with a little knowledge of Lisp could extend for unanticipated purposes.

A Mixture of C and Lisp

Lisp has a drawback common to all interpreted languages: lack of execution speed. Programs written in compiled languages such as C run quickly. In a sense, the interpretation of the language is done beforehand, when the source code is compiled and linked into a binary executable. The downside is that in order to modify a program's behavior, the source code must be changed and the program recompiled—something an end-user shouldn't be required to do.

Using Lisp, an Emacs user can change variables and functions "on-the-fly," and they will take effect immediately. This is a direct result of using Lisp as the editing engine on top of a low-level layer of compiled C code.

Why Emacs Is Written in Two Languages

Emacs was designed to benefit from the best characteristics of both Lisp and C. Aspects of the editor that users would rarely if ever change are written in C. These components are the substructure of the editor—the parts that interact with the host operating system and windowing system. These low-level parts could be thought of as the bones of Emacs, while the Lisp components make up the flesh.

The bulk of the actual editing functions in Emacs are written in Lisp. In the background of an Emacs session, a Lisp interpreter waits for input from the user. Press a key, and the interpreter calls a function that inserts the character at the point position in the current buffer. This sounds like a slow process. In years past, Emacs has been derided for its sluggish response. This was true to a certain extent when Emacs was being used on the slow machines of the past. Modern computers are so fast in comparison that Lisp interpretation is near-instantaneous. In today's computing environment, Emacs is comparable in response to any editor written entirely in C.

Emacs and Its Built-in Lisp Functions

The Lisp files that Emacs uses can be divided into two categories. Core Lisp files that are unlikely to be changed are "dumped" into the executable when Emacs is compiled. An example is the file containing the character-insertion routine just mentioned. It's difficult to imagine why someone would want to change that behavior: when you press a character key, you want that character to appear on the screen!

The remainder of the Lisp files are available at any time, but any single user will most likely use only a small subset of them. This behavior prevents unneeded editing functions from being loaded into memory.

Why Not Perl or Java?

Over the years, a controversy has periodically erupted in the Emacs community. Someone will suggest ditching Lisp and substituting a more popular language as the native Emacs scripting and configuration language. Perl, Python, Scheme, Java, and Guile have all been suggested.

The problem with this idea (aside from the fact that nobody has volunteered to do the work) is the existence of a great number of useful Emacs add-on packages. People rely on these packages for their daily work; if Emacs suddenly began using Java rather than Lisp, they would be rendered useless. It would be a tremendous amount of work to rewrite these packages in another language.

Although Java has some similarities to Emacs-Lisp, the lack of runtime configurability is a drawback.

The recurrent controversy always dies down when this factor is pointed out. Lisp isn't a perfect language, but it has embedded itself in the Emacs community and is unlikely to be replaced in the foreseeable future.

Conclusion

This chapter has dealt with the benefits of a built-in Lisp interpreter and how Lisp and C intertwine to form Emacs. The next chapter introduces you to the building blocks of Lisp.

Chapter 6: Learning the Vocabulary of Emacs-Lisp

isp is short for *list processing*; these two words describe the action of a Lisp interpreter in a nutshell. A Lisp file has a surprisingly small number of basic building blocks, all of them lists made up of indivisible units called *atoms*. Another term for a Lisp list is *symbolic expression*, sometimes abbreviated as *s-expression* or just *expression*.

This chapter describes these basic elements. You will learn how to read a Lisp expression and then build your own. You will learn this material faster if you have an Emacs Scratch buffer handy; try out the expressions as you read. Emacs gives you immediate feedback if you evaluate an invalid expression in the Scratch buffer.

Evaluation

To evaluate a Lisp expression is to feed it to the Lisp interpreter. This is much like running a compiled program. You can evaluate any of the following examples by typing them into the Scratch buffer, leaving the cursor to the right of the last parenthesis, and then pressing Ctrl-x Ctrl-e.

The Lisp interpreter's output appears in the minibuffer.

Evaluating a very simple Lisp expression returns nothing but the expression itself.

The result of evaluation can be a value, a side effect such as copying a region or moving point, or an error message. Oddly enough, the side effect might be the actual result that the expression was written for. That might be the user's point of view, but to the Lisp interpreter, the returned value is the goal.

Lists within Lists

When the interpreter begins the evaluation, it first looks for lists contained within the main list. These are evaluated first, and the returned value is substituted for the inner list when the outer list is processed. Here is a numerical example that illustrates this:

```
(* 3 (- 20 4))
```

The contained list (- 20 4) is evaluated first, returning a value of 16. The main expression now looks like this to the Lisp interpreter:

```
(* 3 16)
```

This is evaluated and returns a value of 48.

Basic Emacs-Lisp Expressions

An expression can be as simple as a word or number enclosed in parentheses and preceded by a single quote, such as `'(125)`. The single quote tells the interpreter to accept the expression as is; without the single quote, Emacs assumes that the first member of the list is a function.

Atoms

A Lisp expression is defined as a sequence of units that can't be broken into smaller units. These units are called *atoms*. Atoms are separated by any amount of white space, usually just a single space. An atom can be either a number, a symbol, or a quoted string such as "this is a string." A symbol can be a word or an arithmetic operator, such as +, -, *, or /—the symbols for addition, subtraction, multiplication, and division.

The List

The sequence of units just described is called a *list*. Lists can be made up of just one atom, many atoms, or a combination of lists and atoms. A list can be empty; it looks like this: (). Technically, an empty list is both an atom and a list.

Emacs expects the first element of a list to be a function. It could be an arithmetic function or any other predefined Lisp function. Functions in Lisp are simply predefined Lisp commands. The above-mentioned single quote before a list forces Emacs to accept the first or left atom as nothing but a number or symbol. In other words, Emacs won't try to match the first atom with a function.

When an expression is evaluated the first element (assumed to be a function) is given the following elements to work on. If any of those elements are lists (indicated by parentheses) those elements are processed before the remainder. This is known as *recursive* evaluation.

An expression such as this:

```
(* 3 (+ 5 5))
```

when evaluated returns 30 as its value. This demonstrates again a basic principle of evaluation: A list contained in an outer list is evaluated first. Once the inner list's value is known, it is used as input for the outer part of the list. (+ 5 5) in English is "five plus five." Substituting the value 10 for (+ 5 5) in the expression would look like this:

```
(* 3 10)
```

This, in English, is "three times ten," and it yields a final value of 30.

If the expression looks like this instead:

```
'(* 3 (+ 5 5))
```

the evaluation would return this:

```
(* 3 (+ 5 5))
```

rather than 30 because the single quote forces the interpreter to accept the * and + as meaningless characters rather than arithmetic symbols.

Every list and list-within-a-list is enclosed in parentheses. This is a Lisp convention that helps the interpreter find the boundaries of any list. A list can be pages long and can contain many other lists. The Emacs-Lisp interpreter burrows down to the innermost list and evaluates its way out. Once the inner lists have been evaluated, the interpreter works its way from left to right through the list, substituting the values stored in memory earlier for each contained list.

Numbers and Strings

Emacs-Lisp recognizes both integers and floating-point numbers, distinguishing between the two by the presence or absence of a decimal point. For example, 3 and 236 are treated as integers, while 37.66 and 21.0 are seen as floating-point numbers.

Strings are most often used when a message needs to be displayed to the user. The Emacs minibuffer messages are good examples. When you see the prompt I-search: in the minibuffer, you are seeing a string variable from a Lisp file named isearch.el, one of the core Emacs-Lisp files.

Strings are also used when a Lisp program needs a changeable chunk of text. An example might be a Lisp-based add-on for Emacs that adds e-mail capabilities to the editor. Such a Lisp program would need to be able to use the user's e-mail address. The Lisp program doesn't need to know the address; this data is saved to be pasted into the From: header of an e-mail message. When text is enclosed in double quotes (making the text a string to the Lisp interpreter), the text is handled as a unit. Remember that a string is also an atom, an indivisible block.

Symbols

A symbol is a unique name in a Lisp expression. It is nothing more than a word or character that most often refers to a Lisp function or variable, though symbols can refer to anything. One symbol can refer to both a function or variable in the same statement. Remember that the Lisp interpreter assumes that the first symbol in a statement refers to a function.

Symbol names are arbitrary, but Lisp programmers attempt to give them some sort of mnemonic value, just for code clarity. A symbol can't have any white space, because Emacs would try to interpret it as two symbols.

Using the same symbol to refer to more than one function or variable will cause unpredictable results. Another possible source of problems is redefining an existing Lisp function; you're better off defining an entirely new function.

True and False Values

Many Lisp expressions can have a value of either true or false—t or nil in Lisp terminology. Here's an example:

```
(setq initial-scratch-message nil)
```

This statement sets the value of the variable initial-scratch-message to nil. Setting this value to nil (in your .emacs file) causes Emacs to start up without displaying basic usage information in the Scratch buffer, which is the default buffer you see if Emacs is started without specifying a file name on the command line.

Notice that rather than calling the variable initial scratch message, hyphens are used between the words. This is standard usage in Emacs-Lisp, ensuring that Emacs sees the variable as a unit. White space between words is always a signal telling Emacs that each word is a separate symbol.

Functions

A *function* is a self-contained Lisp procedure. You could describe a function as a program that can be called by the Lisp interpreter to accomplish a specific task. Functions can contain other functions. You can think of a function as a module that can be plugged in to other functions. In a sense, functions are like abbreviations. It is theoretically possible to write a complex Lisp program without using any functions, but the labor of defining every routine would be immense.

Emacs makes use of several *primitive* functions, which are low-level procedures written in C. They are used just as Lisp functions are. From a user's point of view, the only difference is that primitive functions can't be changed. An example of a primitive function is +, the addition function discussed earlier.

A function might need data to work with. This data can come from another function or from the user. This data is called the function's *arguments*. A function that needs no arguments has an empty list (()) in the place where arguments are listed in the function definition.

Defining a Function

Before a function can be used, it must be defined. A built-in function called defun (short for "define function") is used for this. Here is a simple function definition:

```
(defun dos-unix ()
"Strip DOS carriage return characters from a buffer."
  (interactive)
  (goto-char (point-min))
  (while (search-forward "\r" nil t) (replace-match ""))
  (message "Operation complete"))
```

The first line of this function tells Emacs that a new function named dos-unix is being defined. The empty list (()) would contain arguments (and thus would not be empty) if any were needed. This particular function needs no arguments.

The second line is optional. Notice that the line is double-quoted, the signal that tells Emacs that the line is a string. The position of this string (directly after the defun line) lets Emacs know that the string is intended to be a *docstring*, an abbreviation for documentation string. Remember Richard Stallman's original description of Emacs as a self-documenting editor? This is where the self-documentation starts—right inside the definition of a function.

Reading the Documentation of a Function

Just for fun, type the dos-unix function into the Emacs Scratch buffer.

Once you have the function displayed in an Emacs buffer, place the cursor just after the last parenthesis and press Ctrl-x Ctrl-e.

Selecting Evaluate Last S-expression from the Emacs-Lisp menu works just as well.

Now that Emacs knows about the new function, press Ctrl-h f.

When prompted in the minibuffer for the name of the function, type

dos-unix

A new window opens, and the documentation contained in the function definition is displayed. Figure 6.1 shows the results.

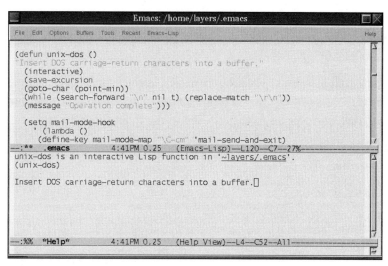

```
(defun unix-dos ()
"Insert DOS carriage-return characters into a buffer."
  (interactive)
  (save-excursion
  (goto-char (point-min))
  (while (search-forward "\n" nil t) (replace-match "\r\n"))
  (message "Operation complete")))

  (setq mail-mode-hook
    ' (lambda ()
      (define-key mail-mode-map "\C-cm" 'mail-send-and-exit)
```

```
unix-dos is an interactive Lisp function in '~layers/.emacs'.
(unix-dos)

Insert DOS carriage-return characters into a buffer.
```

Figure 6.1   *Function Documentation*

Line three determines how the function can be used. Without the `interactive` statement, the function can be loaded only if it is evaluated manually. `interactive` is a built-in function that makes it possible to run a function by typing the function name in the minibuffer.

The Function Body

The last three lines are the "body" of the function, the part in which the actual work is done. One after the other, six functions are invoked to perform the task at hand: stripping carriage-return symbols (^M) from a buffer that originated on a DOS- or Windows-based machine.

First, the function `goto-char`, a simple built-in function that moves the point position, calls another built-in function, `point-min`. `goto-char` uses `point-min` to find the position in the buffer closest to the very beginning and then moves point there. This ensures that the entire buffer will be processed by `dos-unix`.

Next, a built-in looping function called `while` enters the scene. `while` in this case runs the built-in function `search-forward`, which is given the argument `\r`. This argument is a string. The slash is a special escape character used in Lisp to represent invisible characters such as carriage returns (`\r`), tabs (`\t`), and newlines (`\n`).

Each time `search-forward` finds a carriage return, it passes the result to the next function, `replace-match`. `replace-match` is a built-in function that replaces one string with another. The argument given to `replace-match` is the empty string, `""`.

One after another, carriage returns (which look like ^M on a Linux system) are found and then passed to `replace-match`, which substitutes nothing in their place.

Remember that the `while` function is in charge of this operation. After `search-forward` has found the last carriage-return symbol and passed it to `replace-match`, `while` stops and returns the `nil` value to the Lisp interpreter. The interpreter sees that `while` has finished, and it moves on to the last line in the main function.

If the fourth and fifth lines were translated into an English command, they might look something like this:

```
Starting at the beginning of the buffer, look for carriage returns, and delete
them. When you can't find any more, stop.
```

The last line of `dos-unix` is optional. The `message` built-in function is used to display a string of text to the user. In `dos-unix`, `message` is called with a string, `"Operation complete"`, as an argument. When `dos-unix` has finished its work, that string is shown in the minibuffer.

dos-unix As a Template

The `dos-unix` function can be easily changed by simply substituting other strings for `"\r"` and `""` in the arguments given to `search-forward` and `replace-match`. Try opening a text file in one window and the `dos-unix` function in another. Change the strings in `dos-unix`, reevaluate the function, and then run it on the text file. Such experimentation is a good way to become familiar with how functions work.

Remember that all the built-in functions used in `dos-unix` have their own internal documentation. Use the Ctrl-h f help key to learn more about them.

Variables

A Lisp variable is like a variable in other programming languages. A variable is just a name used to refer to some sort of value, which may be a number or a Lisp expression. Variables can be defined using the built-in function `defvar` (an abbreviation of "define variable"). A variable can be global, affecting all Lisp procedures used by Emacs, or it may be local, in which case it is effective only in the function in which the variable was defined or set.

Internal Emacs Variables

Emacs stores in memory a great number of variables, all of which have default values. Many of these variables can be thought of as user preferences, and their values can be changed with a simple Lisp statement in your .emacs file.

The most commonly changed Emacs variables can be changed using the Customize interface, which was discussed in Chapter 4.

Defining Variables

You don't need to define a variable before using it. Emacs accepts variables as they are created, but you might want to provide some documentation and set an initial default value.

Another built-in function called `defvar` is used to provide these extra services. The syntax is

```
(defvar variable-name initial-value docstring)
```

Here's an example taken from one of the Emacs core Lisp files:

```
(defvar mark-ring nil
  "The list of former marks of the current buffer, most recent first.")
```

In this example, a variable named `mark-ring` is created with an initial value of `nil` (because a buffer starts out without any marks having been set); the quoted docstring completes the definition. Try pressing Ctrl-h v.

When prompted in the minibuffer, type

```
mark-ring.
```

You will see the `mark-ring` variable's docstring displayed in the minibuffer.

Changing a Variable's Value

`setq` is a useful built-in function that is used to change the value of a variable.

`setq` is often used in an ~/.emacs file to change default variable values. Think of these values as analogous to settings in other software. The syntax of a `setq` command syntax is simple:

```
(setq fill-column 72)
```

This is a Lisp statement that changes the variable `fill-column` (the column number at which lines are wrapped in auto-fill-mode) to a new value, 72.

Another built-in function called `let` is designed to be used within a function. Its role is threefold:

- Define a list of variables.
- Set the variables to initial values, similar to using `setq`.
- Perform an operation, usually using other built-in functions, that makes use of the newly-set variable values.

A `let` expression within a function looks something like this:

```
(let ((first-variable first-value) (second-variable second-value))
function operations on the variables)
```

The variable values (there can be more than just two of them) set within a `let` statement are valid only within the statement, and they last only as long as the statement is being evaluated. You can give a variable that is used elsewhere a new value within a `let` code block without affecting any other Emacs routines that might make use of that particular variable.

Here is a sample function that uses `let`:

```
(let ((airplane 'flies) (balloon 'floats))
   (message "An airplane %s, while a balloon %s" airplane balloon))
```

Notice that the two variable values are preceded by a single quote. Without these quotes, Emacs would try to interpret the words "flies" and "floats" as meaningful symbols, and an error message would be displayed.

In the last line of the function, the `message` built-in function is used as it was in the `dos-unix` function discussed earlier. The difference in this function's usage of `message` is that a string format placeholder, `%s`, is used. The two placeholders are replaced by the two variable values listed directly after the `message` string. The actual output to the minibuffer is

```
"An airplane flies, while a balloon floats"
```

List Operations

There are several useful built-in functions for manipulating lists. Before these are introduced, two new terms need to be defined:

- `car` is the first member of a list.

- cdr is the remainder of a list, or all elements but the first. Two built-in func-tions can extract these two portions of a list. They are `car` and `cdr`, both named for the list element they are designed to retrieve.

Here is how they are used:

```
(car '(this that other))
```

Evaluating this expression yields the car of the list (`this that other`), which is "`this`."

```
(cdr '(this that other))
```

As you would expect, the output from this expression is "`that other`."

Adding to the Front of a List

If you need to add a new item to the beginning of a list, in effect making the old car of the list a new part of the cdr, the built-in function `cons` is what you need. The syntax is not complicated:

```
(cons list-1 list-2)
```

Here is an example that inserts 25 into a list composed of the numbers 50, 75, and 100:

```
(cons 25 '(50 75 100))
```

The result is

```
(25 50 75 100)
```

You can even start a list from scratch by using `cons` to add to the empty list:

```
(cons 88 ())
```

This generates a new list with a single element:

```
(88)
```

If you `cons` a variable onto a list, the value of the variable is added to the front of the list:

```
(cons fill-column '(12 13 14))
```

This yields output something like this:

```
(70 12 13 14)
```

The numeral 70 will vary, depending on what your fill-column is set to.

As an exercise, try using `cons` to place the value of other variables at the front of a list, such as a kill ring.

...or to the End of a List

An analogous function is used to insert a list at the end of a list. This one is called append, and its usage is similar to that of cons. Here is an example:

```
(append '(oak ash) '(birch pine))
```

The output is

```
(oak ash birch pine)
```

As you can see, the second list is attached to the end of the first.

An example will show how cons can be used to add to one of Emacs' variables. The value of the variable load-path is an associated list of directories in which Emacs will look for Lisp files to load. This setq statement uses cons to add a new directory to the front of the list:

```
(setq load-path (cons [new directory] load-path))
```

Evaluation of this statement forces Emacs to look in the new directory for a Lisp file before checking the original directories in the list.

Saving an Excursion

When you write a text-manipulation function, the position of point often moves away from the starting point, leaving point at a new place in the buffer. You might prefer that, after you run a function, the point position return to the starting point—which, after all, is where you were editing.

The save-excursion built-in function is the answer to this common problem. This function acts as a wrapper around the main body of a function, allowing the point and mark positions to go wherever they need to go, but returning them to their original positions when the function operation is complete.

To illustrate this, here is a modification of the dos-unix function from earlier in the chapter:

```
(defun dos-unix ()
"Strip DOS carriage return characters from a buffer."
    (interactive)
    (save-excursion
    (goto-char (point-min))
    (while (search-forward "\r" nil t) (replace-match ""))
    (message "Operation complete")))
```

The only difference between the old version is the addition of this line:

```
(save-excursion
```

and an additional parenthesis at the end, which is needed to close the new one at the beginning of the new `save-excursion` line. The two new parentheses effectively enclose the body of the function; now the entire operation of `dos-unix` is subsidiary to the `save-excursion` function.

To help make it easier to experiment with the `dos-unix` function (you might not have any DOS-format files handy to test with), here is an opposite function called `unix-dos`:

```
(defun unix-dos ()
"Insert DOS carriage-return characters into a buffer."
   (interactive)
   (save-excursion
   (goto-char (point-min))
   (while (search-forward "\n" nil t) (replace-match "\r\n"))
   (message "Operation complete")))
```

In this function, `search-forward` is looking for newline characters rather than carriage returns. `"\n"` is the slash-escaped symbol for the invisible newline character, just as `"\r"` is the symbol for the carriage-return character (which is invisible on a DOS-based system but is visible when viewed under Linux). When you run `unix-dos`, every newline character is replaced with both a newline and a carriage return.

Try both the old version of `dos-unix` and the new, and you will see the difference that `save-excursion` makes.

How Parentheses Are Used

By now you probably have noticed how parentheses are used in a Lisp statement. Emacs looks for parentheses in a function or another Lisp statement and relies on them to separate one list from another.

Notice how in the sample function `unix-dos` each separate function operation is enclosed in parentheses. The entire `dos-unix` function is itself surrounded by parentheses.

Here's a simple rule of thumb: Each time a new function is introduced, contain it within its own parenthesized expression.

Emacs provides several convenient features that help you keep track of parentheses. In the simple function examples in this chapter, it isn't hard to see what each parenthesis is enclosing, but as a Lisp statement becomes longer and more complex, parentheses have a tendency to accumulate into difficult-to-parse heaps.

By default, Emacs blinks the matching initial parenthesis as soon as you insert a closing parenthesis. This is handy, because for a moment you can easily see the beginning of the statement you are closing. However, this doesn't help when you are looking at already-written code and are wondering which parenthesis matches a particular closing parenthesis.

show-paren-mode is tailor-made to address this need. Just press M-x and type `show-paren-mode` to enable the mode. Now, whenever point is at a parenthesis, its matching parenthesis is persistently highlighted. Figure 6.2 shows a more complex Lisp function with this mode enabled.

This mode is well worth enabling if you are writing Lisp code. The mode can be toggled on using Customize. Press M-x and type

```
customize group
```

When prompted in the minibuffer for the name of a group, type

```
paren showing
```

A Customize window will open, offering you the option of toggling the mode, along with several other parenthesis-related options.

Figure 6.2   *show-paren-mode at Work*

The Scratch Buffer

The Scratch buffer was designed to facilitate trying out Lisp code. The buffer's default mode is Emacs-Lisp, a mode that offers several useful keybindings such as the following:

M-Tab	Completes partially-typed symbols.
Delete	Deletes characters backwards, turning tabs into spaces.
Ctrl-j	Evaluates the last expression. Works just like Ctrl-x Ctrl-e, except that the output appears on a new line below.

Whatever you type in the Scratch buffer isn't saved when you exit an Emacs session. If you want to save Lisp code you have written, just save the buffer as a new file. If you give your new Lisp file the .el suffix (with a name like mycode.el), Emacs automatically switches to Emacs-Lisp mode when you later open the file.

Common Errors

The most common errors beginners cope with stem from losing track of parentheses. Use plenty of white space in your code, because this makes it easier to visually separate the various components.

Remember that documentation for the Emacs built-in functions is always available by using the help key Ctrl-h f.

Conclusion

This book can't provide you with everything you need to know to become a Lisp expert without being twice as large. After reading these chapters and experimenting on your own, you should be beginning to feel comfortable reading Lisp code with some degree of comprehension.

One of the most valuable learning aids is the vast amount of Emacs-Lisp code, a good selection of which is included on this book's CD-ROM. Try to follow the logic of a simple Lisp file to get started.

A good file to explore is simple.el, which is in the /lisp subdirectory of all Emacs installations. This file is a collection of miscellaneous functions, many of them small and easy to comprehend. Whenever you come to an unfamiliar term, use the Emacs help facilities to find out what it is.

The first source of help to consult is the function help key (Ctrl-h f), because many unfamilar terms are names of built-in functions. If that doesn't yield information, try Ctrl-h a or M-x apropos. The apropos help-facility returns a list of any symbols or keybindings related to your request.

Working your way through unfamiliar functions, puzzling out terms and syntax along the way, will eventually give you a basic grounding in the way Lisp is structured.

The next chapter goes into more detail on writing Lisp expressions and functions.

Chapter 7: A Sample Emacs-Lisp File

New Lisp Features in Clipper

The Clipper.el File

f you worked your way through the material in the last chapter, hopefully you have developed a general feel for how Lisp programs and functions are put together. This chapter could continue in the same vein, describing more built-in functions and variables and how to use them. Since this isn't intended to be a Lisp textbook, I've opted for a different approach—one that I suspect will be more interesting.

This chapter focuses on a fairly short and simple add-on mode for Emacs called clipper-mode.

A mode is simply a package of configuration settings that makes editing a particular type of file easier. There are major modes, only one of which can be active in a buffer, and minor modes, which can coexist with major and other minor modes.

Chapter 11 delves further into the subject of modes. The first sections of this chapter emphasize unfamiliar Lisp features that are used in clipper-mode.

After you have been introduced to these Lisp tools, I'll step you through the utility line by line, following and describing the path taken by the Lisp interpreter when it evaluates the file.

As in the previous chapter, understanding and absorbing this material will be much easier if you have an Emacs session running. The functions described here and clipper.el itself can be found on this book's CD-ROM in the directory /examples/ch7.

New Lisp Features in Clipper

Clipper-mode uses many of the Lisp functions and other expressions discussed in Chapter 6. Several Lisp features in the mode haven't been introduced yet, so the following sections briefly explain several. Try them out in the Scratch buffer. You might access the online help for the functions, if only to get another perspective on usage.

Association Lists

Clipper makes frequent use of another sort of Lisp list than the basic variety discussed in Chapter 6. An association list, which is more often called an *alist*, is a list of cons cells. A cons cell is an ordered pair, like a list with the usual car (first element) and with the cdr (remainder) consisting of only a single element. The car of each of the cons cells is a key, and the cdr of the cell is a value to which the key refers. In a sense, an alist is a simple database. There can be any number of cons cells in an associated list. The following example has only two:

```
(setq tools-alist
'((wrench . nut) (hammer . nail)))
```

This Lisp expression creates a new variable named `tools-alist`. This variable refers to the association list on the second line. The periods and extra spaces separating the respective keys (`wrench` and `hammer`) and their associated values (`nut` and `nail`) indicate that the association list is written in dotted-pair notation, an alternative method of representing a list that is often used in association lists. The period explicitly separates a cons cell's car and cdr. The preceding list written in standard notation looks like this:

```
'((wrench nut) (hammer nail))
```

`assoc` is the most commonly used of a group of functions that look for matches in an alist. Here is this function being used to find a match in the preceding alist:

```
(assoc 'hammer tools-alist)
```

Evaluation returns this value:

```
(hammer . nail)
```

An English translation of this `assoc` expression might read something like this:

```
In the associated list named tools-alist, which value does the key hammer match?
```

The progn Function

`progn` is a wrapper function in the same way that the `save-excursion` function in `dos-unix` is (see Chapter 6). Each function or other expression following `progn` is evaluated one by one, but the values returned are discarded, with the exception of the very last one. Typically, the changes made by the earlier-than-last functions are (from the interpreter's point of view) just side effects, but they are needed by the overall program or function that contains the `progn` function block. The side effects might be such things as minibuffer messages, moved point position, or deletions of some portion of the buffer.

The end result is that the value returned from the last Lisp statement in the `progn`-wrapped block of code is passed to the next phase following it.

The syntax is as follows:

```
(progn (expression1) (expression2) (expression3))
```

progn is one of a group of functions referred to in this book as *wrapper functions*. A wrapper function encloses a group of one or more other functions and imposes some sort of condition on the operations of these subsidiary functions. The save-excursion and while functions discussed in Chapter 6 are also wrapper functions.

if-then Statements

Remember the while looping function used in dos-unix? A similar conditional function is simply called if. It's used like this:

```
(if (this conditional statement returns a non-nil value )
(evaluate this expression)
(otherwise, evaluate this expression [and any that follow it]))
```

Rather than looping repeatedly until a condition is met, as while does, if is a one-time switch: Either the first expression following the conditional block is run, or the following ones are run.

The if and while functions are both examples of the wrapper functions introduced in the preceding section.

Buffer Functions

Clipper uses several buffer-handling functions, such as end-of-buffer and set-buffer. These functions are well-described by their names. Short descriptions will be given when they are encountered in the clipper.el file.

Sparse Keymaps

Keymap is an Emacs-Lisp term for an alist of keystrokes and the commands they run. The global keymap is used by all buffers, while individual modes usually have their own keymaps.

A small mode such as clipper doesn't need to redefine every key; it just needs to set a few new keybindings while leaving the other keymaps as they were. A function named make-sparse-keymap was designed for this situation. It lets you construct a new keymap with just a few new keybindings.

What make-sparse-keymap does involves creating a new empty association list. This function is typically used in an expression which defines the new keystrokes and their associated commands. These keystroke/command pairs are inserted into the empty alist as cons cells. This forms a new keymap for the mode.

prin1 and Friends

`prin1` is yet another built-in function; it simply outputs to the screen whatever Lisp object it is fed as an argument. There are two related functions, called `print` and `princ`. These three functions differ in how the output is formatted. Here's an example using `princ`:

```
(with-output-to-string
(princ "This is ") (princ (emacs-version)))
```

I used `princ` rather than `prin1` in this example because its output is more readable in the minibuffer. The first line of this example uses a Lisp macro named `with-output-to-string`. Lisp macros are outside the scope of this book; suffice it to say that they are used in the same way as functions in a Lisp expression. This macro takes the output of arguments given to it, formats that output as a string, and then displays that string in the minibuffer.

The statement in the second line, `emacs-version`, refers to an internal Emacs function defined at the time a particular Emacs executable was compiled. Pressing M-x and then typing

```
emacs-version
```

will result in output to the minibuffer identical to the `princ` expression just shown, but lacking the initial words `"This is "`.

Error Messages

The last of the new functions used in clipper-mode is `error`, which is used when the user needs to be informed of an error. It is very similar to the printing functions just discussed in that it sends its output to the minibuffer.

The `error` function is used as a form of communication between a running Lisp program and the user. In effect, it informs the user that something has gone wrong and that the user should either repeat a command with valid arguments or restart the program.

Further Preparation

The next sections dissect clipper-mode in an attempt to trace the path that the Emacs-Lisp interpreter takes when evaluating the mode. Loading the file clipper.el into Emacs wouldn't be a bad idea at this point. Make sure that font locking is turned on by pressing M-x and then typing

```
font-lock-mode
```

The differently-colored strings, keywords, and so on that font locking provides are a big help when you are trying to puzzle out the structure of a Lisp file.

If you come across a function or variable that still seems unclear, remember to check the help documentation with the help keys Ctrl-h a or Ctrl-h v for different perspectives.

The Clipper.el File

An abbreviated outline of clipper-mode could be presented like this:

- Introductory comments
- Setting variables
- Defining functions

Each of these logical subdivisions is dealt with in the following sections. By the time you have read through this material, you should be well on your way to being able to make sense of other Lisp files.

Introductory Comments

There is a convention when writing Emacs-Lisp files in which a block of lines at the top of a file is commented out with semicolons, causing the Lisp interpreter to ignore the lines (see Figure 7.1). After a couple of lines that list the file name and copyright notice, the comment section begins with a five-line summary listing the author, maintainer, location (often a Web site), keywords, and version. The author and maintainer are often the same person; the categories are kept separate because some Lisp authors have either lost interest in the file they wrote or are no longer accessible via e-mail. In these cases, someone else with an interest in the file might step in as maintainer—a person who will accept bug reports or fixes and try to improve the file and release enhanced versions.

A block of GNU- and Emacs-related "boilerplate" information usually comes next, detailing the file's licensing and distribution terms. Incidentally, one of Kevin Burton's motivations for writing clipper.el was to make it easier to insert unchanging blocks of text into files.

The next section of comments is the most useful. Its title is often "Commentary" (see Figure 7.2). This is where you find usage information and instructions for installing the mode or utility. Often the author includes lines of Lisp code that can be cut and pasted into your .emacs initialization file (see Chapter 9 for more on the .emacs file).

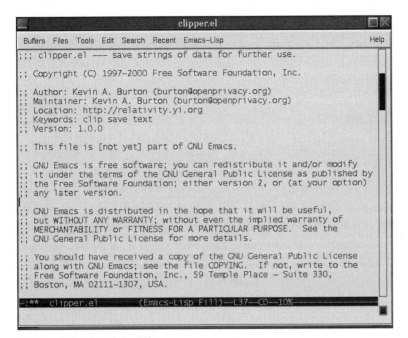

Figure 7.1   *The Top of the File*

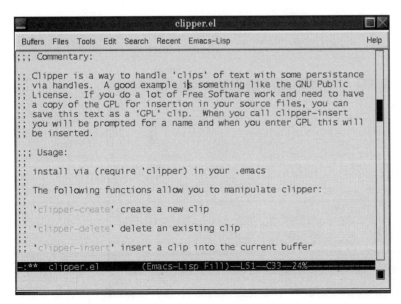

Figure 7.2   *The Commentary Section*

These lines either automatically load the file when Emacs starts up or cause it to be loaded when a file name with a particular extension is opened. For example, a utility used only when editing HTML files might be loaded only when a file with an .html or .htm suffix is opened.

Setting New Variables

When you write a Lisp utility such as clipper-mode, there are certain advantages to first creating new global variables to be used elsewhere in the code. Putting the variable definitions at the beginning of the Lisp code allows the following function definitions to make use of them by name. This has the side effect of making the code easier to read and comprehend. The alternative would be to create the variables as they are needed within the functions. However, this would tend to obscure a function's meaning—at least for humans reading the code. The Lisp interpreter wouldn't care.

The clipper.el Lisp code begins with several variable definitions, as shown in Figure 7.3.

A variable can have any name (as long as it doesn't contain white space), but a custom has evolved of choosing names that at least partially reflect the variable's purpose.

The first variable defined is an empty association list called `clipper-alist`. Here is the definition:

```
(defvar clipper-alist '() "Associated list for holding clips.")
```

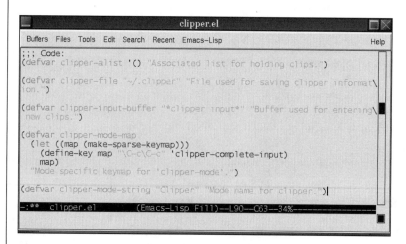

Figure 7.3   *Creation of Variables*

See the empty list ()? It's empty because no "clips" have yet been made. The alist exists because it has been defined, but it won't have any content until someone creates a clip. This won't happen until clipper-mode is in use, but when it's needed, the alist will be ready to receive the first clip.

The next variable gives a name to the clipper file, a file that stores saved clips between Emacs sessions:

```
(defvar clipper-file "~/.clipper"
"File used for saving clipper information.")
```

The file name is arbitrary and could easily be changed, but it is necessary to have a name assigned to the file so that when clipper-mode tries to save a clipped piece of text, it will know where to put it.

```
(defvar clipper-input-buffer "*clipper input*"
"Buffer used for entering new clips.")
```

This variable gives a name to a dedicated buffer for writing a new clip. The buffer name is surrounded by asterisks to indicate that the buffer isn't associated with an actual file, similar to the Scratch buffer.

The next variable creates a single keybinding for clipper-mode:

```
(defvar clipper-mode-map
(let ((map (make-sparse-keymap)))
(define-key map "\C-c\C-c" 'clipper-complete-input) map)
"Mode specific keymap for 'clipper-mode'.")
```

This definition is a bit more complex than the previous ones. It starts out by using the `let` function (see Chapter 6 for examples). `let` defines a temporary variable `map` using the function `make-sparse-keymap`. The result is an empty keymap named `map`. The `define-key` function in this case adds the keybinding Ctrl-c Ctrl-c to the empty `map` keymap and associates that keybinding with something called `clipper-complete-input`. Remember that a variable, `clipper-mode-map`, is in the process of being defined. The output returned by the `let` statement is a keymap containing a single keybinding. This becomes the sole value in `clipper-mode-map`.

In the third line of the code-block `clipper-complete-input` appears, but up to this point no function with that name has been defined in clipper.el. It might seem odd to bind a key to a command that doesn't yet exist, but it really doesn't matter. By the time a user has a chance to press Ctrl-c Ctrl-c, clipper.el will have been evaluated in its entirety, and farther down in the file, a function with that name will be defined.

The last part of this variable declaration is the optional docstring. If you evaluate the whole variable definition and press Ctrl-h v, and then enter `clipper-mode-map` when prompted, that documentation will appear.

The last variable simply gives a name for the mode that will be visible in the modeline when clipper-mode is active:

```
(defvar clipper-mode-string "Clipper" "Mode name for clipper.")
```

Clipper Functions

The remainder of clipper.el is a series of function definitions, each of which defines and enables a particular facet of the mode's behavior. You will see all of the variables just discussed crop up in several places in these definitions.

The first function is a series of instructions that the mode follows when saving a file:

```
1  (defun clipper-save()
2   "Save the clipper information to file."
3   (find-file clipper-file)
4   ;;whatever is in this buffer is now obsolete
5   (erase-buffer)
6   (insert "(setq clipper-alist '")
7   (prin1 clipper-alist (current-buffer))
8   (insert ")")
9   (save-buffer)
10  (kill-buffer (current-buffer))
11  (message "Wrote %s" clipper-file))
```

It starts out, as usual, by giving the name of the function and its docstring (lines 1 and 2).

The first real work done by this function is in line 3. A simple built-in function called `find-file` looks for and loads `clipper-file`, which is one of the variables defined earlier. This line with the variable's value substituted would look like this:

```
(find-file "~/.clipper")
```

Notice the comment in the fourth line, reassuring anyone who might be reading through the file that there is a reason for the destructive operation in line 5. Another simple built-in function, `erase-buffer`, is called. It deletes the entire contents of the ~/.clipper buffer.

At first, this doesn't make a lot of sense. Isn't the whole purpose of clipper-mode to allow persistent clippings of text to be saved between Emacs sessions? Now all the patiently saved "clips" have been deleted!

Those clippings might be gone from the file, but they still exist as an association list in Emacs' memory. The function `clipper-save` (which wants to delete the contents of ~/.clipper) isn't a usable function unless clipper.el has been loaded. If clipper.el has been loaded, the contents of ~/.clipper have been incorporated into Emacs' current state of memory as a variable linked to the value `clipper-alist`. You can see this for yourself by evaluating clipper.el, pressing the variable help key Ctrl-h v, and responding to the minibuffer prompt by typing `clipper-alist`. The alist will be empty unless you have already created some clips.

The sixth line calls another simple built-in function named `insert`. All `insert` does here is copy a string into the now-empty ~/.clipper file. The string inserted, `"(setq clipper-alist '"`, is the first part of a Lisp statement, complete with left parenthesis.

The seventh line calls the function `prin1`, which was described earlier in this chapter. `prin1` prints or copies the current value of the `clipper-alist` variable into the clipper file, ~/.clipper. The previous action of `insert` left point at the end of the string that it copied into the same file. `prin1` takes up where `insert` left off, and the value of `clipper-alist` ends up just after the insert string. This is what the clipper file looks like at this point:

```
(setq clipper-alist '((name-of-first-clip . first-clip)
(name-of-second-clip . second-clip))
```

This isn't quite a valid Lisp expression, because the parentheses don't balance. One more is needed at the end to match the one just before `setq`, so the `insert` function is called again to insert a single parenthesis in line 8.

Three built-in functions are called in sequence to complete the work this function accomplishes. First, `save-buffer` saves the buffer (which means that the ~/.clipper file with its new contents is written to disk), followed by the `kill-buffer` function, which closes the buffer (Emacs discards it from memory). `kill-buffer` knew which buffer to kill because the argument to `kill-buffer` was the value returned by yet another function, `current-buffer`.

The last line invokes the `message` function, whose role here is to display a line of confirmation text in the minibuffer. The string format placeholder `%s` is replaced by the value of the variable defined at the beginning of clipper.el, `clipper-file`, so this string is output to the minibuffer:

```
Wrote ~/.clipper
```

The usage of the `message` function isn't really needed here, as the `save-buffer` function outputs the same message to the minibuffer, but this redundancy really doesn't hurt anything.

The reason the variable was used in the message string rather than the file name itself is to give clipper-mode a degree of user configurability. If a clipper-mode user decided that ~/.Repository is a better name for the file ~/.clipper, he would only need to edit the value of the variable `clipper-file` in clipper.el. The variable definition would then be

```
(defvar clipper-file "~/.Repository"
"File used for saving clipper information.")
```

and the minibuffer output generated by `message` would be

```
Wrote ~/.Repository
```

The order of the functions in a Lisp utility such as clipper-mode isn't important, even when the functions refer to other functions later in the file. The definitions of the functions are stored in Emacs' memory when clipper.el is evaluated, but none of them are run until they are called while actually using clipper-mode.

In the interests of clarity, the next function to be teased apart will be the third rather than the second: `clipper-create`:

```
1   (defun clipper-create()
2   "Create a new 'clip' for use within Emacs"
3   (interactive)
4   (set-buffer (get-buffer-create clipper-input-buffer))
5   (erase-buffer) ;; just in case
6   (clipper-mode)
7   (setq clipper-clip-name (read-string "Name of new clip: "))
8   ;;make sure the clip that the user just specified doesn't already   exist.
9   (if (null (assoc (intern clipper-clip-name) clipper-alist))
10  (progn
11  (insert "CLIPPER:---------------------------------------------
12  ----------------------------\n")
13  (insert "CLIPPER: Lines beginning with 'CLIPPER:' are removed
14  automatically.\n")
15  (insert "CLIPPER: Enter new clip.  Type C-c C-c when complete.\n")
16  (insert "CLIPPER: \n")
17  (pop-to-buffer clipper-input-buffer)
18  (end-of-buffer)
```

```
19 (message "Enter new clip. Type C-c C-c when complete."))
20 (error "The specified clip already exists")))
```

After the obligatory name creation and brief docstring, an `interactive` statement signals that this function can be run by the user. Other functions in clipper-mode, such as `clipper-save`, are part of the mode's internal workings and aren't meant to be run separately. This means that after you install clipper-mode, pressing M-x and typing `clipper-create` will run this function.

Three buffer-related built-in functions follow in quick succession. The first, `set-buffer`, makes sure that the current buffer is set to be the output of the second function, `get-buffer-create`. This function does one of two things: If the argument to the function is the name of a buffer in the buffer list (buffers that Emacs has open), that buffer's name will be passed to `set-buffer`. Otherwise, a new buffer will be created using the argument as a name. This is what happens in this function.

The name ultimately passed to `set-buffer` ends up being `clipper-input-buffer`. When the Lisp interpreter happens upon a name, it checks to see if the name matches any variables that have been defined. At the beginning of clipper.el, `clipper-input-buffer` was given the value `*clipper-input*`. In this case, `get-buffer-create` creates a new buffer (rather than "getting" an existing one), since no other open buffers have the name `*clipper-input*`, and gives it that name. Remember that the asterisks surrounding the name indicate that the buffer is temporary and isn't associated with a file, similar to the Scratch buffer.

Another small, single-purpose function (`erase-buffer`) is called next to erase the contents of the new buffer. There shouldn't be any contents in this brand-new buffer, but, as the comment states, "just in case" there is some content in the buffer, it is erased.

At this point, a new buffer called `*clipper-input*` is displayed on the screen. The next statement, `(clipper-mode)`, sets the mode of this file. (`clipper-mode` is a function that is simple enough to be left as an example at the end of this chapter.)

The variable-setting function `setq` appears in line 7. Its job is to set the value of the variable `"clipper-clip-name"`. It's now time for some user interaction, as the different clips are named by the user. The function needs some way of prompting the user for a name for the new clip.

Another built-in function called `read-string` was designed for this sort of situation. This function takes a string for its argument—in this case, `"Name of new clip: "`. The string appears in the minibuffer. Whatever the user types after the string becomes the output of the `read-string` function. Imagine that `clip3` was typed as a response to the prompt. Substituting that for the `read-string` statement would yield this for line 7:

```
(setq clipper-clip-name "clip3")
```

The next block of code is moderately complex. A `progn` function is wrapped in an `if` function. The outer `if` function's job is to make sure that the user isn't trying to use a clip name that already exists.

Remember that any existing clips are being held in memory (while clipper-mode is active) in the form of an association list. Somehow, that list needs to be checked to make sure that the new clip name that the user just entered isn't already in that alist.

Here is a more schematic view of this portion of the function:

```
(if (null (assoc (intern clipper-clip-name) clipper-alist))
[progn function snipped]
(error "The specified clip already exists"))
```

The first new function here is a simple one: `null` returns a value of `t` (or yes) if the value of the following list is `nil` (or no).

The `null` function looks at the value of an `assoc` function statement. What `assoc` does here is check to see if its first argument (`intern clipper-clip-name`) can be found in `clipper-alist`. Another little function, `intern`, looks for a symbol associated with its argument, `clipper-clip-name`, and returns whatever it finds. Previously in the function, the user was prompted for a name for a new clip. The `setq` function gave the variable `clipper-clip-name` the name as its value.

Since this chunk of code can be hard to unravel, an English translation should make it clear:

If the new clip's name can be found in the existing list of clip names, give the user an error message so that he will choose a unique name. On the other hand, if the new name really is new, run the `progn` section of the function.

This `if-then` wrapper around the `progn` function could have been left out, but the `clipper-create` function would probably hang or stall if the user mistakenly chose an already-used name. Think of this as an error-catching feature in the function.

Now onward to the `progn` code block. At this point, a new buffer called `*clipper-input*` has been created and given a unique identity, which distinguishes it from other clips created earlier. The buffer isn't visible yet, because a little more work needs to be done before it is ready for user input.

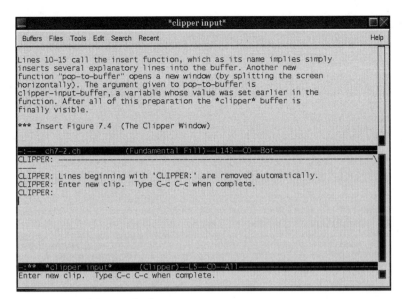

Figure 7.4   *The Clipper Window*

Lines 11 through 16 call the `insert` function, which, as its name implies, simply inserts several explanatory lines into the buffer. Another new function, `pop-to-buffer`, opens a new window (by splitting the screen horizontally), as shown in Figure 7.4. The argument given to `pop-to-buffer` is `clipper-input-buffer`, a variable whose value was set earlier in the function. After all this preparation, the `*clipper-input*` buffer is finally visible.

After you type the new clip, saving it with Ctrl-c Ctrl-c overwrites the ~/.clipper file with the contents of the clipper alist, which now includes the new clip. This action isn't done by the `clipper-create` function; the Ctrl-c Ctrl-c keybinding calls a new function called `clipper-complete-input` (see the value of the variable `clipper-mode-map` near the beginning of clipper.el).

Here is the new function:

```
1   (defun clipper-complete-input ()
2   "Called when the user is done entering text. "
3   (interactive)
4   (set-buffer (get-buffer-create clipper-input-buffer))
5   ;;make sure font-lock is off in this buffer
6   (font-lock-mode -1)
```

```
 7  ;;clean up the input buffer by removing commentlines.
 8  (save-excursion
 9  (beginning-of-buffer)
10  (while (re-search-forward "^CLIPPER: .*$" nil t)
11  (message "removing region")
12  (delete-region (match-beginning 0) (match-end 0))
13  (kill-line 1)))
14  ;;now get the value of the buffer.
15  (let (clipper-input begin end)
16  (save-excursion
17  (beginning-of-buffer)
18  (setq begin (point))
19  (end-of-buffer)
20  (setq end (point)))
21  (setq clipper-input (buffer-string))
22  (add-to-list 'clipper-alist (cons (intern clipper-clip-name) clipper-input)))
23  ;;now clean up...
24  (kill-buffer clipper-input-buffer)
25  (delete-window)
26  (clipper-save))
```

The first six lines of the function are straightforward, similar to other function operations already discussed. Line 7 is the beginning of an interesting section contained within a `save-excursion` wrapper, which ensures that point will be returned to its original position.

This code block begins by invoking the `beginning-of-buffer` function, which does what you would expect: moves point to the first character in the buffer. The remainder of the block is a `while` loop that makes use of a variation of the `search-forward` function called `re-search-forward`. This function adds regular expression capability to the search.

Chapter 3 introduced the concept of regular expressions. In order to make sense of the `re-search-forward` function, you might review the regular expression special characters, because several of them are used in this part of `clipper-complete-input`.

This `while` loop has a condition: as long as `re-search-forward` keeps finding lines that match the criteria given the function, the `delete-region` and `kill-line` functions will do their work.

So what criteria is `re-search-forward` looking for? The regular expression `"^CLIP-PER: .*$"` matches lines that start with the word "CLIPPER:" followed by a single space. . * matches any sequence of zero or more characters, and the $ character signifies the end of a line. Another way to describe a matching line is any whole line that begins with "CLIPPER: ", no matter what the remainder of the line might be.

Each time a matching line is found, the function `delete-region` is turned loose. This killing function takes two arguments: the beginning of the region (or selected area) and the end. Two small functions are used to indicate the region's boundaries. `match-beginning` finds the beginning of the matched line, the result of the latest `re-search-forward`. `match-end` finds the end of the matched line. Therefore, the region given to `delete-region` is the entire matched line.

One by one, the searched-for lines are deleted; when they have all been processed, the `while` loop's condition has been satisfied.

Just to make sure that the buffer is thoroughly purged of the temporary lines, the function `kill-line` is called. This kills the top line in the file. The only lines left should be the new lines of clipped material that the user has entered.

The next step is to do something with the text entered as a new clip. Somehow, this function needs to save the new clip and its unique name in such a way that it will be available in the future.

The code block that does this is made up of a `let` function wrapped around a `save-excursion` function and two additional function calls.

The `let` function gives names to three variables (`clipper-input`, `begin`, and `end`) that are valid only within the `let` wrapper.

Within the `save-excursion` wrapper function, point is moved to the beginning of the buffer (with the `beginning-of-buffer` function), and the `let` variable `begin` is set (with `setq`) to that point position. Point is moved to the end of the buffer (with the `end-of-buffer` function), and the second `let` variable, `end`, is set to the new point position. `save-excursion` now does its job and moves point back to the beginning of the buffer.

In line 21, `clipper-input`, the last of the `let` variables, is given a value with `setq`. The value is the output of a simple function called `buffer-string`, which turns the content of the current buffer into a string.

The next function called is `add-to-list`, which takes as arguments the name of a list (a variable) followed by an element to add to that list. The list specified is the association list `clipper-alist`. An alist needs cons cells consisting of two members—a key and a value associated with that key. The basic function `cons` is called to construct a new cons cell from the values of two variables. The first is generated by a simple function called `intern`, which returns the symbol associated with its argument, `clipper-clip-name`. This is the user-defined name of the recently-typed clip. The second member of the list is the value of the variable set in line 21, which is the contents of the clip buffer.

The cons cell that `add-to-list` is preparing to add to `clipper-alist` would look like this:

```
(name-of-the-clip . contents-of-the-clip)
```

As the comment in line 23 indicates, all that is left to do is a little clean-up. The last lines kill the buffer and get rid of the window. Finally, one last function is called, `clipper-save`, which was the first new Clipper function discussed earlier.

So far, the functions for creating and saving clips have been described. The whole purpose of the mode is to let the user insert named clips of text into a buffer, so functions are needed to choose and insert a clip. The next two functions set up a framework that lets a user ask for a clip by name.

The second of these two functions, `clipper-insert`, is a user command that can be used as an M-x minibuffer command or can be bound to a key. `clipper-insert` needs to somehow prompt you for the name of a clip and retrieve from the `clipper-alist` a clip that matches the name. To do this, `clipper-insert` calls the first function, `clipper-get-clip`. This function attempts to build a completion list in order to make choosing a clip easier.

Here is the function:

```
1    (defun clipper-get-clip()
2    "Use completion to ask the user for a clip"
3    ;;build a list for completion
4    (let(clip i completion-list)
5    (setq i 0)
6    ;;(setq
7    (while (< i (safe-length clipper-alist))
8    (setq clip (symbol-name (car (nth i clipper-alist)))))
9    (message clip)
10   (add-to-list 'completion-list
11   (list clip 1))
12   (setq i (1+ i)))
13   (completing-read "Clip name: " completion-list nil t)))
```

This function is the first one in this chapter that uses a counting mechanism, an incrementing `while` loop that adds 1 to the previous number and then runs a sequence of functions on the new value. It keeps doing this until it runs out of elements—in this case, the members of `clipper-alist`.

As with the preceding function, a `let` wrapper sets up three new variables that are defined further along in the function.

Before the `while` loop begins its repetitious action, one of the new `let` variables is given a value with `setq` in line 5. This is the beginning of the counter. After each run through the `while` loop, line 12 adds 1 to the value of the variable `i`. What's to keep this `while` loop from spinning off into an endless series of repetitions?

The condition clause in line 7 sets a boundary for the `while` loop's cycles. Line 7 in English could look like this:

```
As long as the number of elements (or cons cells) in clipper-alist is greater than
the current value of i, while has permission to cycle through its actions once more.
```

The `safe-length` function in line 7 is a counting function with a safety feature: If a list being counted is circular, `safe-length` restricts itself to counting only unique items.

`safe-length` returns the number of elements in `clipper-alist`. Now the function needs some way of putting together a list of clip names.

The `setq` statement in line 8 does much of the work. It sets the value of the `let` variable `clip` to a different value during each cycle of the `while` loop, depending on what the current value of `i` is. The `nth` function uses the value of `i` to retrieve the corresponding member of `clipper-alist`. This function takes two arguments: the first is a number, and the second is a list. If `i`, which is the number in the function, is 3, the function returns the third member of the list.

A problem arises, however: The members of `clipper-alist` are cons cells, composed of a clip's name and its content. The function is trying to build a completion list from clip names; the contents of a clip are superfluous here. This where the list operator car comes in handy.

The `nth` function has extracted a particular cons cell from `clipper-alist`. Taking the car of that cons cell results in the clip name alone. The `setq` function in line 7 takes that result and sets the value of `clip`.

In line 9, the `message` function displays the clip name in the minibuffer.

The current value of the `clip` variable, which is different each time through the `while` loop, is added to a temporary completion list by the function `add-to-list`.

When the `while` loop has finally processed each member of `clipper-alist`, the result is a completion list containing every clip name in the alist.

This serves the function in line 13, `completing-read`. This function takes two arguments. The first is a prompting string to display in the minibuffer, and the second is a completion list to search for matches. When the user types a letter in the minibuffer in response to the prompt, `completing-read` searches the completion list for matching items. The Emacs native completion mechanism is called into play, allowing Tab completion on clip names.

The bulk of the work has now been done by `clipper-get-clip`. `clipper-insert` is much shorter and easier to grasp, because much of the details have already been taken care of by `clipper-get-clip`.

Here is `clipper-insert`:

```
1   (defun clipper-insert()
2   "Insert a new 'clip' into the current buffer"
3   (interactive)
4   (let (value)
5     (setq value (assoc (intern (clipper-get-clip)) clipper-alist))
6     (insert (cdr value))))
```

Unlike the preceding function, this is an interactive function, directly called by the user. Line 3 brings in the `interactive` function, followed by the `let` wrapper, which encloses the remainder of the function. Just a single local variable, `value`, is named by `let`. Line 5 uses `setq` to give `value` a value.

Compare the `assoc` statement in line 5 with line 9 of the `clipper-create` function discussed earlier. As in that function, `assoc` is used to extract a member of an association list by referring to the key value. The key value here is returned by the `intern` function, which finds the current value of `clipper-get-clip`. At this point, the value of the `value` variable is a two-element list retrieved from `clipper-alist`. In `clipper-get-clip`, the needed member of the list was the first, which was the key value or clip name. In `clipper-insert`, the contents of the clip are what is needed.

In line 6, the cdr list operator is called by the `insert` function. The remainder (everything but the first element) of the `value` list is extracted by cdr, and `insert` pastes it into the buffer.

So far, functions have been defined to create and insert clips, but not to get rid of old and unneeded clips. The next function addresses this need:

```
1   (defun clipper-delete()
2   "Delete an existing 'clip'"
3   (interactive)
4   (let (clip)
5   ;; get the clipper to delete
6   (setq clip (clipper-get-clip))
7   (if (yes-or-no-p
```

```
8      (format "Are you sure you want to delete clip: %s? " clip))
9      (progn
10     ;;remove it...
11     (setq clipper-alist
12     (delq (assoc (intern clip) clipper-alist) clipper-alist))
13     ;;save the alist to disk
14     (clipper-save)))))
```

This is another interactive function beginning with a `let` function wrapper. A single temporary `let` variable called `clip` is given a name in line 4.

As in `clipper-insert`, the `clipper-get-clip` function is called within the `setq` statement in line 6. `setq` sets the value of the variable `clip` as the output of the `clipper-get-clip` function. This output will be the clip name for which the user was prompted.

Line 7 begins an `if` statement. A function called `yes-or-no-p` displays a question in the minibuffer. This function has two possible outputs, depending on how the user answers the question. If the user types `no`, `yes-or-no-p` returns `nil` to the `if` function, which responds by aborting the function altogether. Alternatively, a `yes` response executes the remainder of the `if` code block.

This section of the function is controlled by the `progn` function, which runs one line after another, discarding all output except that of the last command, which is the function `clipper-save`. Lines 11 and 12 are where the actual work gets done. `setq` sets the value of the variable `clipper-alist` by giving it the returned value of a `delq` function.

The `delq` function hasn't been discussed yet. Its role here is to delete a particular member of `clipper-alist`. The `assoc` function is used to extract the proper member of the list; the previously-defined variable `clip` is what `assoc` is told to extract. The new `clipper-alist` is just the old one with one item deleted. The function ends with a call to the `clipper-save` function, which writes the modified `clipper-alist` back to disk.

Conclusion

There are a few more functions left in clipper.el, but for the most part they make use of functions that have already been discussed. While these concepts are still fresh in your mind, try stepping through the remaining functions in clipper.el, using the function help key (Ctrl-h f) as you go.

Now that you have seen how this small mode works, try reading through some other Emacs-Lisp files. In Chapter 6, a function found in the Emacs core file simple.el was analyzed. That same file contains many small text-related functions that aren't too difficult to understand. Look for simple.el in either /usr/share/emacs/lisp or /usr/local/share/emacs/lisp, depending on how you installed Emacs.

The next chapter introduces you to the Emacs byte-compiler, a utility that optimizes Lisp files so that they run faster.

Chapter 8: Byte-Compiling for Efficiency

E macs-Lisp is a human-readable language. It might not be as easy to read as English, but words and phrases are identifiable, and the characters are all ASCII text. This readability is a plus for people, but it is a stumbling block for programs that need to read Lisp files, such as the Emacs-Lisp interpreter.

A computer program doesn't read a file the way we read text. Like people tend to do, a program starts at the beginning of a file and makes its way to the end. A big difference between a machine's and a person's reading technique is that people don't scrutinize every character and every chunk of white space (such as tabs and spaces), searching for meaning. A computer program doesn't have ideas concerning the relative importance of spaces, indentation, and characters.

The very traits that make it possible for the programmer to quickly scan a Lisp file, noting the various function and variable declarations and the file's general logical flow, are nothing but a time-consuming hindrance for a program. A Lisp interpreter spends time laboriously plowing through the very white space that makes a program human-readable in order to get at the "meat" of a file.

This was more of a problem in the early days of Emacs, when machines were slow and every means was taken to squeeze more efficiency from computer programs.

The Byte-Compiler

The solution the Emacs developers came up with is a Lisp program called the byte-compiler. This program is made up of several related Lisp files that join forces to transform a normal Lisp file into a more compact form.

The byte-compiler can be thought of as a virtual machine, an emulated Lisp computer running within the actual hardware machine. Compiled-code executables, such as Emacs or any other C or C++ program, directly access the computer's hardware (though the operating system acts as an intermediary layer). The byte-compiler evaluates Lisp code and passes the results to Emacs. This additional evaluation is responsible for the relative slowness of byte-compiled as compared with compiled code, but there are advantages to this approach. Byte-compiled code is machine- and platform-independent. A byte-compiled Lisp file from a Linux machine will run equally well on a Windows or Sparc machine as long as the Emacs versions are the same.

The idea of a virtual machine is also used in the Java language. A *.java source file is compiled into a *.class file; this is analogous to an Emacs Lisp *.elc byte-compiled file. A *.class file is also portable between platforms because it is run within a Java virtual machine.

Byte-Compiler Files

If you are interested in the inner workings of the byte-compiler, you might want to read through the actual Lisp files that do the work.

They can be found in /usr/share/emacs/[version-number]/lisp/emacs-lisp. If you are running XEmacs, the files are in /usr/lib/xemacs-[version-number]/lisp.

The main file to look at is called byte-comp.el; the other files used are referred to within this one.

This file is very well-commented. The comments will help you understand what's happening when a Lisp file is byte-compiled.

The new file is not human-readable, but it can be loaded by the Lisp interpreter many times faster, and will use less memory.

Figures 8.1 and 8.2 are before-and-after screen shots of a small Lisp file.

The Lisp code produced by the byte-compiler is known as byte code. Due to the compression that takes place during byte-compilation, the resulting file is about half the size of the original.

The byte-compiler works mainly on function definitions, which make up the bulk of most Lisp files. Functions in the original Lisp file are replaced by their byte-code equivalents. The documentation strings within the definitions are left alone and can still be read in the byte-compiled file. These strings are left intact so that the built-in function help will still be available to users. The comments that often

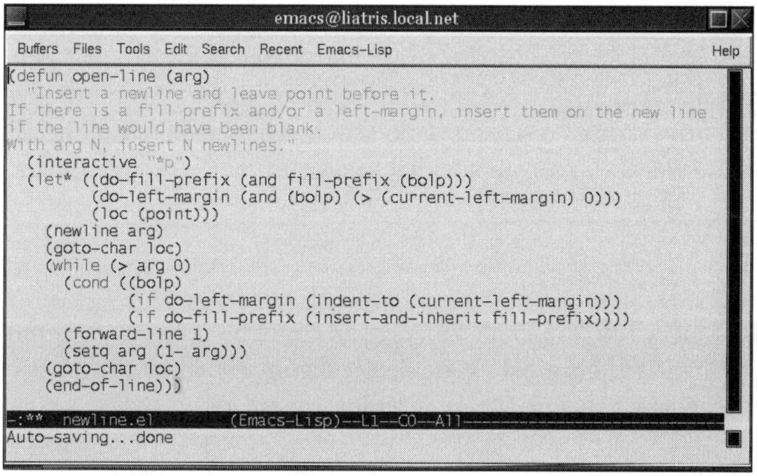

Figure 8.1 *Before Byte-Compilation*

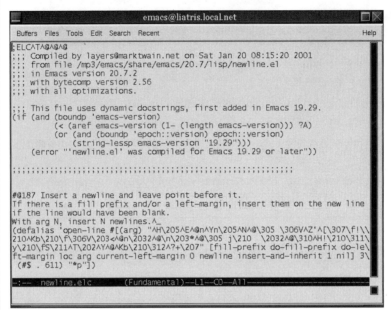

Figure 8.2 *The Byte-Compiled File*

make up a significant portion of a Lisp file are discarded by the byte-compiler; after all, they mean nothing to the program.

The Lisp files that are a part of an Emacs installation have already been byte-compiled, and in some Linux distributions, the byte-compiled versions are the only Lisp files supplied. When this is the case, the uncompiled Lisp files are available as a separate package.

The byte-compiler is useful for newly-written Lisp files as well as for files that were byte-compiled for a different version of Emacs or XEmacs. Sometimes transferring byte-compiled Lisp from version to version works fine, but it's a good rule of thumb to byte-compile these files with the compiler that belongs to your version of Emacs.

How to Run It

The byte-compiler can be run on a single function, an entire file, or a directory full of Lisp files. A file that has been byte-compiled is distinguished by the letter c appended to the file name: filename.el becomes filename.elc.

Keyboard Commands

The most commonly used command is

```
M-x byte-compile-file
```

You are prompted for the file name; the suggested default is the file name of the current buffer. Just press Enter to accept the default, or type in a different file name to choose some other file.

The following command byte-compiles all Lisp files in a particular directory:

```
M-x byte-compile-directory
```

Non-Lisp files are ignored. If you don't anticipate changing the parent *.el files for a while, you can save some disk space by gzipping them with the following command in a shell window:

```
gzip *.el
```

This command is a Linux rather than an Emacs command, so you should run it from a terminal window or an Emacs shell buffer.

You can also gzip groups of marked files in a Dired directory listing, using either the menu or the Dired keyboard commands.

Emacs needs to be run noninteractively for the next command, because the Emacs process is killed at the end. This command is called `batch-byte-compile`. Like the last command, this one is run from a Linux terminal or console:

```
emacs -batch -f batch-byte-compile *.el
```

Running this starts up Emacs without creating the usual editor window. This command is used by Lars Magne Ingebrigtsen as part of the Gnus mail/news-reader installation. He does this so that he can distribute *.el files for all versions of Emacs. The user installing Gnus uses the local flavor of Emacs to byte-compile the files, ensuring that the *.elc files will work well.

The last keyboard command is mainly used by Lisp developers. It allows you to run the byte-compiler on a single function rather than the entire file:

```
M-x eval-defun
```

This command also has a keybinding in Emacs-Lisp mode:

```
M-Ctrl-x
```

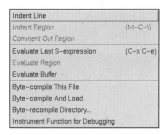

Figure 8.3 *The Emacs-Lisp Menu*

Using the Menu

The first two of the keyboard commands just discussed are also available from the Emacs-Lisp menu, which appears automatically whenever Lisp files with the *.el prefix are loaded.

There is another useful byte-compiling command: Byte-compile And Load (see Figure 8.3). Here is a scenario that shows how this command can be used.

Imagine that you have discovered a new and intriguing Emacs utility posted on the Usenet newsgroup gnu.emacs.sources. You save it to a file and move the file into your site-lisp directory, just to try it out. The first thing you do is load the file into Emacs so that you can read the comments and decide whether it might be useful. You could try it out by evaluating the entire buffer, selecting Evaluate Buffer from the Emacs-Lisp menu.

An alternative approach is to select Byte-compile And Load from the menu. This will give you a better idea of how quick and responsive the utility is, because Emacs will load the faster byte-compiled version.

Interpreting Error Messages

While the byte-compiler is working its way through a Lisp file, a stream of messages might flash by in the minibuffer. These might be error messages. If an error is severe, the compilation will stop. If there were no errors, a message similar to this appears in the minibuffer:

```
Compiling file /usr/local/lib/xemacs/site-lisp/square-braces-as-parens.el at Thu
Jan 18 09:38:08 2001
```

A log of all messages is available in an impermanent buffer named *Compile-Log*. This log is useful when you're trying to track down the source of an error.

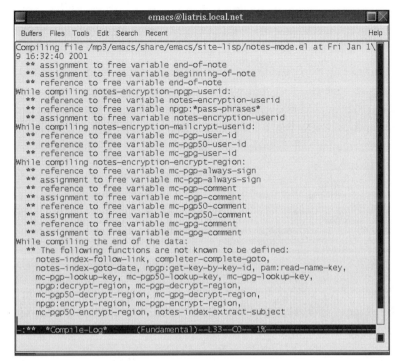

Figure 8.4 *Harmless Errors*

Many Lisp files cause the byte-compiler to spew out a stream of errors that don't prevent the successful generation of a usable *.elc file. Figure 8.4 shows a typical example of a *Compile-Log* buffer.

If any of the errors are fatal (meaning that the Lisp file just won't work), an error message appears in the minibuffer when you attempt to load the compiled file.

Error Types

There are two error messages that almost always are symptoms of a parenthesis problem:

```
Invalid read syntax: ")"
End of file during parsing
```

These are the easiest errors to fix. Use one of the Emacs parenthesis-matching modes to find unbalanced pairs.

You can also step your way through the buffer by repeatedly pressing Ctrl-M-f. This key-command moves point to the next valid function definition and will signal an error if parentheses don't match.

An error message such as this:

```
Warning: the function font-lock-add-keywords is not known to be defined.
```

means that an external function called from within the Lisp file couldn't be found. This is most often because the Lisp file was written with a particular version of Emacs in mind, and that version knows about the missing function, but your Emacs doesn't. Lisp files and packages can be written so that any recent Emacs version can use them. The developer will include some if/then clauses that could be translated into English like this:

```
If the version of Emacs running this byte-compiler is GNU Emacs version 20.0 or
later, call function x. If the Emacs version is XEmacs later than 21.0, call
function y instead. If the Emacs version is neither of these, abort and send this
message to the user: "You need to upgrade your Emacs to a newer version in order to
use this package."
```

Another possible reason for a function error is that the new package requires another package to be loaded first. This should be documented in the commented-out installation instructions in the new file.

Another, usually less-serious error message complains of an uninitialized variable. Figure 8.4 shows several examples.

This sort of error rarely results in problems with using the file. You usually encounter errors like this when byte-compiling a single file of a multifile package. An uninitialized variable or seemingly missing function might be in one of the other files in the package—files that aren't currently loaded. When the package is actually used, the main file refers to the others when they are needed.

Problems with Different Emacs Versions

When migrating Lisp add-ons from one Emacs version to another, re-byte-compiling every file is a good rule of thumb. There is a chance that the new Emacs will accept the *.elc files generated by another Emacs, but why risk it? Byte-compiling doesn't take long and removes any uncertainty.

If you spend much time at all experimenting with Emacs add-on packages, you will certainly find some that just won't run with your chosen version of Emacs. It takes quite a bit of extra effort on the part of the Lisp programmer to make a program version-neutral.

The proverbial motivation behind the creation of open-source software is to "scratch an itch." After the personal itch has been taken care of (that is, when the program fulfills its creator's needs), not every programmer is immediately compelled to make the program useful to any and all Emacs users. That might come later, after e-mail messages begin to arrive from users of the new package. One of the new users might even contribute a patch.

If you are determined to force a balky package to work, you might consider posting a question on the gnu.emacs.help Usenet newsgroup. Many knowledgeable veteran Emacs users frequent this group, and a polite query might yield useful replies.

If all else fails, consider e-mailing the author of the Lisp add-on. Most free-software authors enjoy hearing from users, but there is a certain etiquette to keep in mind. An ill-mannered and demanding message will likely be deleted without a reply. Remember, the author doesn't owe you anything. Try to emphasize what you liked about the add-on, if only the concept itself.

Edits That Seem to Have No Effect

When Emacs is instructed to load a Lisp file (perhaps from your ~/.emacs initialization file), the suffix of the file is omitted. Suppose you want Emacs to load the file utility.el; the statement in the ~/.emacs file might look like this:

```
(load 'utility)
```

When Emacs encounters such a line, the first action it takes is to look for a file named utility.elc. The byte-compiled file will run faster than a plain Lisp file, so Emacs by default uses the *.elc file if it exists. If it can't find utility.elc, Emacs next looks for utility.el and loads it.

This behavior can lead to problems. Imagine that you (or someone on the Net) have come up with an improvement to utility.el. You start up Emacs to try out the new version, only to find that nothing has changed. What could have gone wrong?

What has happened is that Emacs found the utility.elc file, which had been generated from the old utility.el, effectively ignoring the new version. The solution to this situation is to get in the habit of re-byte-compiling Lisp files whenever a change is made.

Emacs notices when an *.el file is newer than the corresponding byte-compiled version. Look in the Message buffer (shown in Figure 8.5), and you might see entries like this:

```
Source file '/usr/share/emacs/site-lisp/notes.el' newer than byte-compiled file
```

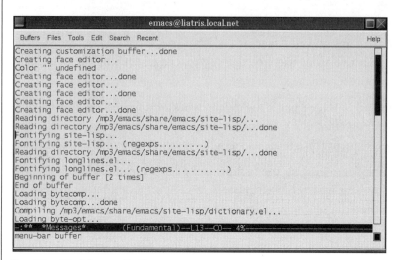

```
                        emacs@liatris.local.net                      ☐ ✕
  Buffers  Files  Tools  Edit  Search  Recent                         Help
 Creating customization buffer...done
 Creating face editor...
 Color "" undefined
 Creating face editor...done
 Creating face editor...
 Creating face editor...done
 Creating face editor...
 Creating face editor...done
 Reading directory /mp3/emacs/share/emacs/site-lisp/...
 Reading directory /mp3/emacs/share/emacs/site-lisp/...done
 Fontifying site-lisp...
 Fontifying site-lisp... (regexps..........)
 Reading directory /mp3/emacs/share/emacs/site-lisp/...done
 Fontifying longlines.el...
 Fontifying longlines.el... (regexps...........)
 Beginning of buffer [2 times]
 End of buffer
 Loading bytecomp...
 Loading bytecomp...done
 Compiling /mp3/emacs/share/emacs/site-lisp/dictionary.el...
 Loading byte-opt...
 -:**  *Messages*       (Fundamental)--L13--C0--- 4%
 menu-bar buffer
```

Figure 8.5   *The Message Buffer*

The Message buffer is a record of every message or warning that Emacs generates during a session. It isn't saved when you quit Emacs; it's the same sort of nonpersistent buffer as the Scratch buffer. It isn't a bad idea to take a look at it every now and then, just to check for Lisp files that might need to be re-byte-compiled.

You can find the Message buffer on the GNU Emacs Buffers menu. Under XEmacs, select the Show Message Log entry from the Edit menu.

Conclusion

A good way to familiarize yourself with the byte-compiler is to spend some time fooling around with it. Try deleting some *.elc files in your /usr/share/emacs/[version-number]/lisp directory, first making certain that the matching *.el files are installed. Load the *.el files into Emacs, and try the byte-compilation commands discussed in this chapter. The Lisp files that are a part of your Emacs installation will byte-compile with no problems. This should give you confidence before you try byte-compiling third-party Lisp files.

The next chapter's goal is to help you become comfortable with a crucial Lisp file—the ~/.emacs initialization file. This will open the door to a multitude of possible Emacs customizations.

PARt II
Learning to Configure
Emacs with Lisp

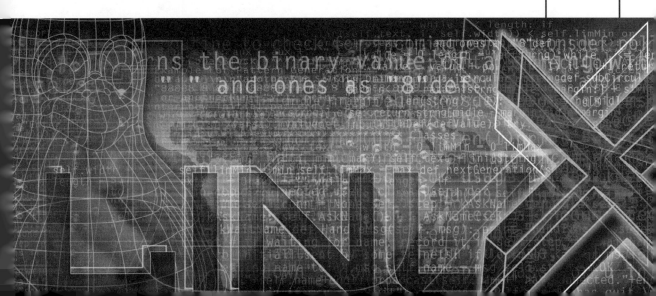

Chapter 9: First Steps in Customization: Your .emacs File

This File Makes Your Editor Unique

If you work with Emacs for a while, you will eventually be confronted with the prospect of editing your .emacs file. Perhaps you've tried this and inadvertently ended up with a plain-vanilla Emacs that refused to even load your configuration file! This chapter shows you how this important file is put together and how to bend it to your will.

Building Blocks of the File

Customizations of Emacs' default behavior are contained in a single Emacs-Lisp file named .emacs, which lives in your home (~/) directory. This file doesn't exist in a new user's Emacs installation. It can be created from scratch by the user or indirectly via the Customize utility, when options you've changed are saved for future sessions.

> I don't recommend making numerous changes to an .emacs file in one editing session. Doing this makes it difficult to track down the source of any problems that might arise.

Functions

An .emacs file consists of a series of self-contained functions called expressions, each one made up of a function name followed by arguments. For example:

```
(global-set-key (kbd "<f4>") 'end-of-buffer)
```

is a complete Lisp statement. It calls the built-in function `global-set-key` with arguments telling the function to make the F4 key move point to the end of the buffer. The arguments call two other built-in functions, `kbd` and `end-of-buffer`. See Chapter 6 for more about Lisp functions.

Definitions

Much of Emacs' behavior is determined by the values stored in Emacs Lisp variables. These variables are available to the user and can be changed at any time; the most common method of changing these values is with statements in your ~/.emacs file.

A built-in function used for this purpose is `setq`, as in this example:

```
(setq initial-scratch-message nil)
```

setq explicitly sets a variable to a value. The default value of the variable initial-scratch-message is t, or true. When the value is true, a "splash screen" appears in the Scratch buffer every time Emacs starts up. This screen contains basic information about the editor and directions for finding help. The preceding line in your .emacs file suppresses the initial message screen.

The Lisp terms t, meaning true, and nil, meaning false, are frequently found in Lisp expressions (see Chapter 6).

Troubleshooting the File

When Emacs is starting up, it reads your .emacs file, starting at the first line and proceeding to the end. If any error is encountered, the built-in Emacs-Lisp interpreter immediately rejects the file and instead loads the default settings. A message beginning with the phrase "error in init file" appears in the minibuffer, with a reference to the line number where the first problem occurred.

Handling Parentheses

Any Emacs user who has experimented with settings in an .emacs file has probably inadvertently broken the file at one time or another. Lisp needs the parentheses in a Lisp file or statement to balance; that is, for every opening parenthesis, there must be a matching closing one. A Lisp function often contains several nested parenthesized statements. One missing parenthesis is not necessarily noticeable to the human eye, but it can make the Lisp function make no sense at all to the Emacs interpreter. Emacs just gives up on the malformed .emacs file and reverts to its compiled-in defaults.

Parenthesis Modes

The developers of Emacs long ago tired of manually counting stacks of parentheses. A mode called blink-matching-paren is by default turned on in a new GNU Emacs installation. This mode causes the parenthesis at one end of a parenthesized expression to blink whenever point is on the other end. An X Windows-specific variant called show-paren-mode can be turned on or off with the minibuffer command M-x show-paren-mode. This mode highlights the corresponding opposite parenthesis to the one the cursor is on. XEmacs has three parenthesis-matching modes that you can activate by selecting Options, Paren Highlighting. Any of these modes will help you spot unbalanced parentheses.

You can also use the key-commands Ctrl-M-f and Ctrl-M-b to move forward and backwards from one correctly parenthesized expression to another.

Other Sources of Errors

Another potential cause of error can be a missing or superfluous single quote (ˈ). Remember that a single quote before a list tells the interpreter that the list is not a function to be evaluated (see Chapters 6 and 7). A missing quote causes Emacs' Lisp interpreter to unsuccessfully try to link the list with a function definition, and an error occurs. Conversely, a single quote accidentally placed before a legitimate function causes Emacs to ignore and thus fail to execute the function.

There are several techniques for finding and dealing with Lisp errors. If you suspect a certain routine of problems, select the entire function or statement to focus Emacs' attention on that region only. Do this either by pressing M-x and typing

```
eval-region
```

or by selecting Evaluate Region from the Emacs Lisp menu. Another method of confining the evaluation is to place the cursor directly after a single Lisp expression and pressing Ctrl-x Ctrl-e. You might remember this from Chapter 6 as the keystroke for Evaluate Last S-expression, a function also available on the Emacs Lisp menu.

Another technique for tracking down .emacs file errors is to start Emacs in such a way that the Lisp debugger is invoked if an error occurs. Do this by using this switch when starting Emacs:

```
emacs -debug-init
```

See Chapter 22 for information about the Lisp debugger.

Comments

Most programming languages are designed to allow the programmer to include text intended for human readers within their source code. These sections or lines are known as *comments;* they are used to help the programmer (and whoever else might later see the code) understand what the code is intended to do.

Comments are ignored by the compilation or interpretation software that transforms the code into a form that a computer can execute. A special character is used to inform the software that a particular line or block of code should be ignored. Surrounding or prefixing an area with this character is known as *commenting out* the area. Here is an example:

```
;; Make F8 be "start macro", F9 be "end macro",
;; F10 be "execute macro"
(global-set-key [(f8)] 'start-kbd-macro)
```

```
(global-set-key [(f9)] 'end-kbd-macro)
(global-set-key [(f10)] 'call-last-kbd-macro)
```

The first two lines are comments explaining the purpose of the following three lines.

As you can see in the example, Emacs-Lisp uses the semicolon as its commenting character. Emacs ignores any text following a semicolon when the file is evaluated or byte-compiled. A good habit to cultivate is to comment your Lisp files liberally. Code that is crystal clear just after being written has a remarkable tendency to become difficult to understand as time passes. The Lisp files that are a part of Emacs tend to be very well-commented.

Backing up Your .emacs File

Once you have Emacs configured and adapted to your working style, you might understandably be reluctant to tinker with your .emacs file in an attempt to gain further ease and efficiency. It takes time to backtrack to a usable state after an .emacs file has been rendered unusable. It's always a good idea to save a copy of your .emacs before you start making extensive changes. Put the copy somewhere other than your home directory, and it will serve as insurance: At any time, you can replace a botched and unusable .emacs file with the known-to-be-good copy. Another approach is to create a new user on your Linux system; most distributions of Linux use a command called adduser. Copy your working .emacs file from your home directory to the new user's home, and then log in as that new user. This user account can be used as a developmental sandbox. Whatever changes you make to the new user's Emacs setup, good or bad, you still have your unaltered original Emacs to use from your main account. If changes you make to the new user's .emacs are beneficial, you can eventually migrate them into your "real" .emacs.

Another way to access earlier versions of a file such as .emacs is to use a version control system such as CVS or RCS. These systems were designed for maintaining program source code; they give you the ability to revert to any earlier version of any file which you edit. It is likely that your Linux distribution provides packages for both of these systems. Install one of them and read the included documentation in order to learn how to maintain different versions of files which are subject to frequent changes.

Byte-Compiling .emacs

Chapter 8 introduced byte-compilation of Emacs-Lisp files. When your .emacs file and the subsidiary files it loads have accumulated a sizable number of functions and statements, it is a good idea to byte-compile them. Emacs will start up faster (although, with the speed of modern computers, this isn't as significant as it was a few years ago). Just remember that any further changes you make to the original Lisp files won't have any effect until the file is again byte-compiled. The .elc file is then overwritten by an up-to-date version that reflects the changes made to the .el file. As a review, to byte-compile the file currently being edited, press M-x and type

```
byte-compile-file
```

GNU Emacs displays the file's directory path in the minibuffer and prompts you for the file name. Just type enough characters of the file name to allow Tab completion to finish the name. XEmacs assumes that you want the file you are editing to be byte-compiled and prompts you with its file name. With either editor, pressing Enter causes the operation to begin. Don't even bother to byte-compile until you are sure that there are no typos or Lisp errors.

Learn by Example

Other Emacs users' personal .emacs files are a valuable resource. Many long-time users have publicly posted their .emacs files on the World Wide Web. (See Chapter 23 for a list of URLs.) Over the years, an .emacs file gradually accumulates more and more useful and time-saving additions, while others that haven't worked out are commented out or deleted. Since the files are small and portable, they can accompany a user from job to job and from machine to machine.

Splitting Your .emacs File

Your .emacs file inevitably grows larger as you tailor the editor to your needs. These files tend to become unwieldy and filled with commented-out sections. The additions made by the Customize utility are not meant to be easily read by humans and can occupy quite a bit of space. Splitting your .emacs file into several single-topic files can help make the whole initialization scheme easier to deal with. To do this, first create a subdirectory, perhaps in your home directory. In this example, I'll call it /home/user/emacs. Load your .emacs file into Emacs, cut out chunks of the file dealing with keybindings, and paste them into a new file called /home/user/emacs/ keys.el. Do the same with sections of .emacs that set options for various major modes; they can be pasted into a new file called modes.el. Macros that you have generated are good candidates for a new file as well. What is left after this dissection of the file is likely to be miscellaneous Emacs settings, along with options that

Configure has saved. The miscellaneous options could be pasted into a misc.el file, leaving nothing but the Configure-generated lines in the .emacs file.

Loading the New Files

The next step is to find a way to let Emacs find and load these split-off Lisp files. In Chapter 4 the basic built-in function `cons` was introduced. As a reminder, it is used to insert an atom (or single element) at the front of a list. This function is just what you need now. `load-path` is a variable that Emacs uses to find the files it needs to run. This variable is simply a list of directories that contain Lisp files, such as /usr/share/emacs. `cons` can be used to insert the new Lisp directory /home/user/emacs (a single element) at the front of this list. The code looks like this:

```
(setq load-path (cons "/home/user/emacs" load-path))
```

This brief line of code creates a new value for the `load-path` variable, with the new path the first element of a list of directories. The remainder of the list is the former value of `load-path`. An interesting aspect of this procedure is that you don't need to know what the value of the variable is to `cons` a new element onto the beginning or append a new element to the end.

Insert the preceding line of Lisp at the end of your .emacs file, and then evaluate it to make sure it's proper Emacs Lisp. Now Emacs is aware of the new directory, but it hasn't been instructed to do anything with the files there. Emacs automatically loads the ~/.emacs file when it starts up, but it has to be explicitly told to load any other files. `load` is a built-in Emacs function that is invoked to load Lisp files. In this case, the following statements do the job:

```
(load "keys")
(load "modes")
(load "macros")
(load "misc")
```

These lines should immediately follow the preceding `load-path` line in the .emacs file.

Did you notice that the .el suffix is missing from the `load` commands? Emacs doesn't need this suffix. One reason is that some Lisp .el files are byte-compiled for faster execution and have an .elc suffix, whereas the human-readable uncompiled Lisp files have the .el suffix. Emacs looks for files with either suffix, loading by preference the .elc files (if they exist) over their .el counterparts.

Now that your initialization file is split into separate special-purpose files, you will find that making changes is easier. If you want to change or add a keybinding, the keys.el file presents you with a simple list of your keybindings. No longer will you need to page through a large .emacs file, looking for a particular keybinding.

Edit and Then Re-Byte-Compile

If you have byte-compiled .emacs, don't forget to repeat the process if you make any changes to the original .el file. Emacs always loads the speedier byte-compiled .elc files rather than the human-readable .el files, so any changes you make will not take effect until byte-compilation is repeated.

A Little Reassurance

If this account of broken .emacs files and malformed Lisp statements sounds daunting, take heart! The usual method of customizing Emacs with Lisp is slowly incremental, and dealing with a single problem at a time isn't really much work. As time permits, you will eventually develop an initialization file that smoothes your work.

A custom in the Emacs community is very helpful to the newcomer. The vast majority of Emacs add-on packages include a section of commented-out installation instructions at the beginning of the primary Lisp file. These instructions nearly always include several lines of Lisp code that can be copied and pasted into an .emacs file. These lines are necessary for the proper usage of the package. The programmers who write these packages primarily write them for their own use, but when other people begin using them, the impulse to fix bugs and develop the package further seems to increase. One way to encourage this is to make the package accessible to new users. Sometimes a package ends up serving an entire community of users, many of whom contribute patches and bug reports, thus enhancing the package for everyone. The Gnus news-and-mail reader, maintained by Lars Magne Ingebrigtsen, is a perfect example. Over the past several years, this very complex and featureful extension to Emacs has gained enough adherents to merit a Usenet newsgroup of its own, nntp://gnu.emacs.gnus.

Trying out the Sample Files

On the CD-ROM that accompanies this book are several sample .emacs files located in the directory /lisp/samples. These files are meant for experimentation and would need to be adapted to your system in order to actually be useful. Look at them as a source of Lisp snippets that can be copied and pasted into your personal file.

Don't Forget to Make a Backup

If you are already using an .emacs file, be sure to move it somewhere out of the way so that it won't be overwritten. Remember that Emacs automatically tries to load any file in your home directory that is named .emacs or .emacs.el. Now you're ready to copy one of the sample files into your home directory and fire up Emacs.

Copying Files from the CD-ROM

Mount the CD-ROM to a suitable mount point with a command such as

```
mount -t iso9660 -ro /dev/[cd drive] /cdrom
```

If you use data CD-ROMs often, aliasing that command to something short, like `cdmnt`, will save you from typing it out in full. Go ahead and copy all six of the samples from the directory /cdrom/lisp/samples to your home directory. In order for Emacs to use a particular sample, it should be soft-linked to .emacs with a command like this:

```
ln -s .emacs-html .emacs
```

When you're done experimenting with a sample, the command `rm .emacs` deletes the symbolic link without affecting the file it was linked to. This process can be repeated for each file that interests you.

Sample .emacs Files

The sample files on the CD-ROM are each set up for a specific task. Feel free to copy sections from one to another or to merge two files into one. For example, you could make a new file that is tailored for both HTML and LaTeX editing. Remember that these are just examples, so they need to be modified in order to be very usable. Many lines are commented out; uncomment just a few at a time so that you can evaluate the changes.

An .emacs Optimized for HTML

The file .emacs-html contains lines that automatically load html-helper-mode when Emacs loads an HTML file. Before starting Emacs, you have to copy the html-helper-mode files from the /packages/html-helper directory on the CD-ROM into your Emacs site-lisp directory (which is usually either /usr/share/emacs/site-lisp or /usr/local/share/emacs/site-lisp). This is a quick way to try out one of the most popular HTML modes for Emacs. After you've started Emacs and loaded an HTML file, you should notice the new HTML menu on the menu bar. Pull down that menu and toggle the Turn On Expert Mode item. Now the menu should display a wide choice of HTML tags that can be inserted into your document. Note that the menu also shows the equivalent keybindings for each tag. If you use this mode very much, it pays to learn the keyboard commands for the most commonly-used tags, while saving the menu for the rarely-used tags.

This file also contains a large commented-out section that, if uncommented, initializes hm—html-menus mode. This is another mode for editing HTML that some users prefer. If you uncomment these lines, you should comment out the html-helper lines. See Chapter 13 for details about these two modes.

If you would like to use either of these modes regularly, just open both the .emacs-html file and your saved .emacs file in Emacs, and then copy the lines that initialize the mode into your saved .emacs file. Use this same procedure with any of the following examples.

A Programmer's .emacs

The sample file .emacs-prog sets several variables used by C, Perl, and Python modes. Several alternative choices are included in the file but have been commented out. These alternative variable values can easily be enabled by commenting out (with semicolons) the active values, uncommenting one or more of the alternatives, and then evaluating the newly-uncommented statement. (As a review, I'll remind you that placing point after a statement, followed by pressing Ctrl-x Ctrl-e, evaluates the expression.) As in the previous example, in order for the mode to be active, the relevant Lisp files must be either part of your Emacs installation or located in your site-lisp directory.

cc-mode, which is used in this sample file, is included with GNU Emacs. python-mode and cperl-mode would have to be installed in the site-lisp directory. XEmacs bundles all three modes in the prog-modes package, and, of course, they are also included in the giant Sumo package.

A LaTeX Writer's File

You can install AUCTeX from the CD-ROM in order to try out the .emacs-tex file. An XEmacs AUCTeX package can be found in the directory /external/auctex/

xemacs. AUCTeX is most conveniently installed for usage with GNU Emacs by using the source package, which can be found in the directory /external/auctex/emacs. See Chapter 12 for installation instructions. AUCTeX is useless without a complete TeX-LaTeX installation. If you lack the necessary TeX setup, and you have no interest in this sort of text processing, you might as well skip ahead to the next section.

New Keybindings

The file .emacs-keys is filled with a variety of alternative keybindings, most of which are commented out. Just uncomment bindings that interest you, evaluate them, and try them out. Copy and paste the bindings you prefer to your .emacs file. The F-key bindings are particularly useful, because Emacs doesn't assign bindings to these keys by default. Multikey bindings that are awkward to type can be reassigned to F keys. This can speed up your work considerably.

An .emacs with Macros

I've written several sample macros in the file .emacs-mcr. These examples show the sort of Lisp that is written out by the `save-kbd-macro` function. Read the comments, because one of the examples works only with XEmacs.

A Gnus User's .emacs

The file .emacs-gnus contains several of the many variables that can be set or changed by a Gnus user. These Lisp statements can be placed either in your .emacs file or in a file named .gnus, which, like .emacs, should be placed in your home directory.

XEmacs, GNU Emacs, and Their .emacs Files

It is theoretically possible to run both XEmacs and GNU Emacs, with both editors using the same .emacs file. There have been times in the past when that has worked for me, but inevitably the acquisition of one add-on package or another causes one of the editors to complain and malfunction. Some packages are specifically designed for GNU Emacs, and others for XEmacs. The best course to follow is to make sure that each program uses its own initialization file.

The easiest way I've found to do this is to run one of the two (preferably the least-used) with another user's .emacs file. I use XEmacs most of the time, so I let it use the .emacs file in my home directory. I created another user just so I could keep a

GNU Emacs .emacs file in that user's home directory. When I run GNU Emacs, I start it with a shell alias. In my ~/.zshrc file is this line:

```
alias emacs emacs -u [username]
```

> A line similar to this will also work with the more-popular Bash shell.

This line allows me to type `emacs` in a terminal window and have the command `emacs -u [username]` executed. I use the zsh shell, but other shells such as Bash support the same syntax in their init files (such as .bashrc). A similar result can be obtained by editing the mouse menu configuration file of your favorite window manager.

Conclusion

Trying new things and not being afraid to experiment are keys to becoming comfortable working with your .emacs file. As long as you have a backup of a working .emacs as a safety net, it really pays to spend some time cutting and pasting blocks of Lisp code into a trial .emacs file.

Download from the WWW copies of experienced Emacs users' .emacs files, and try some of their routines and functions in your own file. There are Emacs aficionados out there who have been polishing and refining their Emacs setup for years, and you can profit from their experience.

> Start up Emacs with the `-q` switch (`emacs -q`) from time to time, just as a reminder of the default behavior you started out with. You'll be surprised at how much easier to use Emacs can be than it is "out of the box."

By now you should be well on your way toward understanding the Emacs initialization process and what it takes to mold Emacs to your preferences and working style. In the next chapter, you will learn of many more possible changes that can be made in your ~/.emacs file, as well as other methods of tailoring Emacs to your preferences.

Chapter 10: Changing Default Behavior

F irst impressions are important, even in the realm of software. Most people have had the experience of trying a new software application only to find the user interface awkward and difficult to learn. If the application is required for work, people generally bite the bullet and learn to use it; otherwise, the first impulse is to look for other software that will do the same job.

Emacs has more reasonable defaults than it did in the past, but some new users still find the editor frustratingly unintuitive. This can be attributed to the UNIX (and pre-UNIX) background of the early Emacs developers. The situation has been exacerbated by the influx of new Emacs users who come from a Windows background. Now that both GNU Emacs and XEmacs have functional ports to Windows, the number of users accustomed to CUA applications has increased.

> CUA stands for Common User Access, a set of guidelines developed by IBM for computer programs. Microsoft used these standards as a guide when developing its own standards for Windows applications. CUA is responsible for many familiar conventions. Common hot keys and menu contents and locations found in many popular applications owe much to this standard.

Two approaches are available to the frustrated new user: Get used to the default settings, unfamiliar as they might be, or bend Emacs to your will and make it conform to your tastes and preferences. This chapter emphasizes the second option. It introduces you to techniques that make Emacs a more comfortable work environment.

Puzzling Defaults

A first-time Emacs user can't be blamed for wondering about odd keybindings, occasional annoying beeps, and the drab appearance. These defaults are holdovers from an earlier era of computing, when a sizable number of potential users were running computers with very limited capabilities. Computers have developed so rapidly in recent years that some of the defaults seem antiquated. However, it's worthwhile to consider that many Emacs users are in third world countries where the computing environment is primitive compared to the standards of the wealthier countries.

Backspace and Delete

Users of mass-market consumer PCs might be surprised to learn that the 101-key keyboard so ubiquitous these days isn't the only type of keyboard in use. Mainframe computers, servers, and workstations used in business, research, and government environments have a bewildering array of keyboard types, and many are still in daily use. Emacs was originally developed on such nonstandard keyboards, and the editor still retains some traces of its history.

Odd as it might seem to users accustomed to CUA operating systems and programs, a debate about the proper roles of the Backspace and Delete keys periodically surfaces in the Emacs community. The users of Sun and other nonstandard keyboards maintain that both the Delete and Backspace keys should remove the character before point (in other words, delete backwards). This accommodates users who have keyboards that either lack a Delete key or have a Backspace key labeled "Delete". The default Emacs key for deleting forward is Ctrl-d, and many Emacs users have become accustomed to using this keybinding rather than the Delete key.

I assume that most readers of this book are using a standard 101-key keyboard, complete with a Delete key, which, in Emacs, annoyingly does the same job as the Backspace key.

In order to change the behavior of the Delete key, you first need to determine how X11 uses these keys. X11 comes with a handy utility called xev that gives real time output in a terminal window, displaying how X11 interprets every keystroke and mouse motion. Try it out by typing xev in an xterm or rxvt window; a small white Event Tester window appears. Move your mouse cursor into this window, and make sure the window has focus. Press the Backspace key and then the Delete key, and note what appears in the terminal window. It should look something like Figure 10.1.

If your output is different, you might need to modify an X11 configuration file that modifies X11's internal keymapping. The individual user's file is called ~/.Xmodmap, and the system-wide file is usually called /etc/X11/Xmodmap. If you are the only

```
                              rxvt
    root 0x3e, subw 0x0, time 833765656, (75,15), root:(907,426),
    state 0x0, keycode 22 (keysym 0xff08, BackSpace), same_screen YES,
    XLookupString gives 1 characters:  "

KeyRelease event, serial 24, synthetic NO, window 0x1c00001,
    root 0x3e, subw 0x0, time 833765768, (75,15), root:(907,426),
    state 0x0, keycode 22 (keysym 0xff08, BackSpace), same_screen YES,
    XLookupString gives 1 characters:  "

KeyPress event, serial 24, synthetic NO, window 0x1c00001,
    root 0x3e, subw 0x0, time 833766729, (75,15), root:(907,426),
    state 0x0, keycode 107 (keysym 0xffff, Delete), same_screen YES,
    XLookupString gives 1 characters:  ""
```

Figure 10.1 *xev Output*

user of your computer, you might as well modify the system file in /etc/X11. Here is a sample Xmodmap file that maps the two keys to standard values:

```
keycode 64 = Meta_L
keycode 113 = Meta_R
keycode 0x6D = Multi_key
keycode 22 = BackSpace
keycode 107 = Delete
```

You can ignore the first three lines if you are running GNU Emacs; however, they might be useful to users of recent XEmacs versions.

The file /etc/X11/Xmodmap most likely exists on your system, and it might already contain the last two lines in the preceding sample. If the lines are there, they are probably commented out with ! characters, which is the commenting character for X Window configuration files. Delete the comment characters at the beginning of the two lines, save the file, and log out of your X session. The next time you start X, the new keycodes will be active.

If the lines aren't there, just type them in as shown. Make sure that the s in BackSpace is capitalized; if it isn't, the line will have no effect.

These changes to X11 will affect all other X11 applications, resulting in uniform behavior for Delete and Backspace.

Now that X11's handling of the two keys has been reconfigured, all that remains is to convince Emacs to use these keybindings. There are several ways to change the Delete key's behavior, but the simplest is to insert this line in your ~/.emacs file:

```
(define-key global-map [delete] 'delete-char)
```

This line calls the function define-key, which takes three arguments. The first one is the particular keymap in which the newly defined key should be placed. In this case, the map is the global map, which affects all buffers. The second argument is the keyboard key to map, and the third is the action that the key should perform. The action here is a basic built-in Emacs function called delete-char, which simply deletes the character following point.

Defining a key in this way overrides any other definition of the Delete key.

XEmacs users can accomplish the same task by setting a variable's value rather than by calling a function:

```
(setq delete-key-deletes-forward t)
```

Placing this line in your ~/.emacs file toggles the value of the variable delete-key-deletes-forward from the default, which is nil, to t (true).

You might wonder why the default behavior of the Delete key is to delete backward in both GNU Emacs and XEmacs. There is still a sizable contingent of non-PC Emacs users, and many of them are active in the ongoing development of the two editors. Think of this as an Emacs tradition that some are reluctant to abandon, and be glad that Emacs is configurable enough to allow you to ignore that tradition if you so wish.

Beeping

I remember when I was first trying to learn to use Emacs. A new user inevitably makes errors, and those errors were signaled by piercing beeps. After a time, Emacs began to seem somewhat ill-tempered, complaining in shrill tones after each error, many of which seemed to be incredibly trivial. When I scrolled down in a buffer, the cursor ran into the end. Beep! Reaching the end of a file is an error?

Perhaps some people aren't bothered by this error-beeping, but I was annoyed enough to search for a way to turn it off. It turns out that there is a variable that as a side effect can be used to turn off the beeping.

This variable bears the mysterious-sounding name `visible-bell`. This name is another artifact that still survives within Emacs. The computers of the '70s and early '80s didn't have the miniature loudspeakers common to nearly all modern machines—the very speakers that emit both the Emacs beep and the beep generated when a computer boots up.

Instead of a speaker, the older mainframe computers had an actual bell inside, similar to the semispherical bells on antique rotary telephones. Computer programs of that era were said to "ring the bell" when signaling error messages.

This led to the idea of a visible bell. Some early computer users were also bothered by audible error signals, especially if many computer terminals were in a single room. A visible bell is a substitute for the audio bell that briefly blinks all or part of the screen.

In Emacs, `visible-bell` is a variable that by default is set to `nil`. Set the variable to `t` with this line in your ~/.emacs file:

```
(setq visible-bell t)
```

This setting causes the modeline and the first visible line in the current buffer to flash a contrasting color. As a side effect, it disables the beep.

This variable can also be set using Customize. Figure 10.2 shows the Visible Bell Customize buffer.

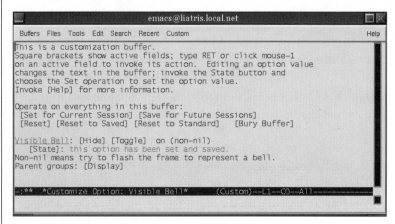

```
┌────────────────────────────────────────────────────────────────┐
│ ■                    emacs@liatris.local.net             □ ⊠     │
│ Buffers  Files  Tools  Edit  Search  Recent  Custom       Help   │
│ This is a customization buffer.                                  │
│ Square brackets show active fields; type RET or click mouse-1    │
│ on an active field to invoke its action.  Editing an option value│
│ changes the text in the buffer; invoke the State button and      │
│ choose the Set operation to set the option value.                │
│ Invoke [Help] for more information.                              │
│                                                                  │
│ Operate on everything in this buffer:                            │
│  [Set for Current Session] [Save for Future Sessions]            │
│  [Reset] [Reset to Saved] [Reset to Standard]    [Bury Buffer]   │
│                                                                  │
│ Visible Bell: [Hide] [Toggle]  on (non-nil)                      │
│    [State]: this option has been set and saved.                  │
│ Non-nil means try to flash the frame to represent a bell.        │
│ Parent groups: [Display]                                         │
│                                                                  │
│ -:** *Customize Option: Visible Bell*      (Custom)--L1--C0--All─ │
│                                                                  ■ │
└────────────────────────────────────────────────────────────────┘
```

Figure 10.2   *Customizing the Visible Bell*

You can summon the Customize buffer by pressing M-x and typing

`customize-variable`

When prompted for a variable, type

`visible-bell`

A single-option Customize buffer will appear. See Chapter 4 for more details about using Customize.

Syntax Highlighting

Syntax highlighting is a way to display text in a buffer with the different categories of text shown in different colors. The Emacs term is *font locking*. Think of it as variable and configurable foreground colors locked to the font that Emacs uses to display text.

What makes font locking particularly useful is that what it colors depends on the type of file. For instance, an HTML file's text is contained within different types of tags using different colors, making the file easier to read and edit. The angle-bracket tag indicators are colored as well, making them easier to ignore while reading the file.

Font locking is most often used by programmers. Source-code files tend to be full of words and phrases with a defined function, such as strings, variables, functions, and comments. When these elements are distinguished from each other by their colors, the logical structure of the file is easier to read.

Many other types of files can benefit from font locking. E-mail messages can be displayed with their headers, and quoted blocks can be highlighted. Even shell scripts and Linux configuration files improve in readability.

By now, you might be wondering why all your buffers are a uniform color. If you haven't yet spent much time customizing Emacs, you might not have turned font locking on. It's off by default. The reason for this setting is that there is no way for a packager of an Emacs distribution to know how many colors your monitor and video card can display. After all, some people still use monochrome monitors. The choice to leave font locking off helps ensure that no matter what your hardware might be, Emacs will start up without errors.

Setting up font locking used to be a serious undertaking that involved writing Lisp code in the ~/.emacs file for each font-lock type and color. It was fun if you like that sort of tweaking, but many users settled for the default color values. The advent of Customize simplified font-lock configuration. Customize writes the necessary Lisp code for you, and the interface is not difficult to navigate with a little practice (see Chapter 4 for an introduction).

You probably won't create an ideal font-lock configuration in one Customize session. Like other Emacs configuration tasks, it's an incremental process. You change a few things, see how you like it, and, when time permits, change some more.

Rather than start the Customize Browser and click around, looking for the font-lock group (it's a subcategory of Faces, if you go that route), you can go directly to the group by pressing M-x and typing

```
customize-group
```

When prompted, type

```
font-lock
```

in the minibuffer. Figure 10.3 shows the screen that appears.

In the figure, take a look at the fifth underlined item from the top. Global Font Lock Mode is a setting that can be toggled on or off. When you have the Customize buffer displayed in an Emacs session, click the Toggle button if it is set to off. You might want to try font-lock mode for a while before turning it on permanently; use the State button to activate font locking either way.

The default font-lock faces might or might not work well with your screen background. Try loading a file that contains several font-lock faces; I recommend a Lisp file, perhaps the clipper.el file discussed in Chapter 7.

Read through the file. Are some of the newly-colored sections hard to read? A certain amount of contrast is necessary for good readability. If the contrast between the foreground and background colors is too small, something needs to be done. Don't settle for marginally readable files when a little effort can enhance readability so profoundly!

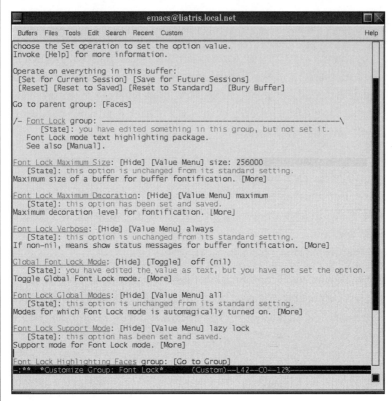

Figure 10.3   *The Font-Lock Customize Group*

Now that global font locking has been enabled, the next step is to look at the default setting for screen brightness. There are two sets of default font-lock faces; which one is used is determined by the value of the variable frame-background-mode. You can get to the Customize buffer containing this variable by clicking Faces in the Customize Group: Font-lock buffer. Go to parent group: [Faces] is the line to look for.

The first item you will see in the Customize Group: Faces buffer is the setting for frame-background-mode. The default setting is nil, which lets Emacs decide whether you have a light or dark background. I don't know just how Emacs determines this; why not directly set the variable to either light or dark? Most people have a decided preference for either light or dark screen backgrounds. After you have set this variable to your preference (and saved it either temporarily or permanently), switch back to the Lisp (or whatever you chose) font-locked buffer. Perhaps setting the background mode changed the colors for the better. If you still think the coloring could be improved, you can individually set each font-lock face.

To do this, you need to go back to the Font Lock Group Customize buffer (it should be listed on the Buffer menu). The seventh item down (this might vary, depending on which Emacs version you are running) should be Font Lock Highlighting Faces.

Select this item, and a new buffer will appear with items for many different font-lock faces. The first nine are the most important. A sample of the current setting is shown for each one, allowing you to judge whether it harmonizes with your default face's background. Click Show for any face you would like to change, and a menu of possible settings appears (see Figure 10.4 for a representative screen shot).

By default, only the Foreground setting is marked with an X. In most cases, this is the only setting you would want to change. The background should be controlled by the Default Face background (see Chapter 4).

You get immediate feedback when you change a foreground or background color as soon as the setting is activated by selecting either State, Set for Current Session or State, Save for Future Sessions. The word "sample" will be highlighted with the color name you typed into the text entry field just after Foreground:.

Emacs will accept any color available to your X11 session. The names of these colors and their RGB values are stored in a text file called rgb.txt; this file can usually be found in /usr/X11R6/lib/X11, or possibly in /etc/X11. If you can't find it, type the following at a terminal prompt:

```
locate rgb.txt
```

A periodically updated database of files on your system will be consulted, and the location of rgb.txt will appear.

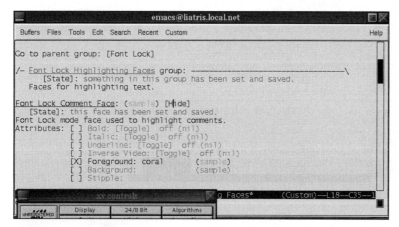

Figure 10.4 *A Font-Lock Face*

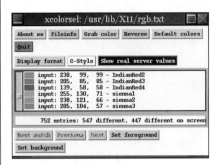

Figure 10.5   *The xcolorsel Window*

With about 750 colors available in this file, you should be able to find what you need. Looking through rgb.txt, the inevitable first reaction is "But what do they look like?". A handy little utility called xcolorsel comes to the rescue. It displays each of the colors and even allows you to "capture" a color from your desktop or an application and determine which of the available colors is closest to it. Figure 10.5 shows xcolorsel in action.

xcolorsel is available from your Linux distribution CDs and from any of the Linux software archive sites.

Start out with an xcolorsel window visible right next to an Emacs window displaying the Font Lock Highlighting Faces buffer. Work your way through the faces, and try to set each one to a color that harmonizes both with your default face background and with the other font-lock faces. You don't need to know what they all mean; each face gets used in a variety of modes that provide font locking. Unless you are a VHDL programmer, you can safely ignore the items at the bottom of the list; they are faces used exclusively by VHDL mode.

The new font-lock faces will be automatically used by any future add-on modes you might install. See Chapter 4's section "X Window and Console Faces" if you want to set up console font-lock faces separately.

GNU Emacs provides another way to evaluate the various foreground and background font-lock colors. Press Ctrl-mouse-button-2 to bring up the Text Properties menu. The last two items on the menu are Display Faces and Display Colors. Select both of them, one after the other, and you will end up with a horizontally-split screen similar to the one shown in Figure 10.6.

It takes some practice and experimentation to come up with a harmonious set of font-lock faces. Too many brilliant contrasting colors are hard on the eyes, in what has been called the "angry fruit salad" effect. Colors that are too similar defeat the purpose of font locking. A period of trial and error usually results in a setup you can live with.

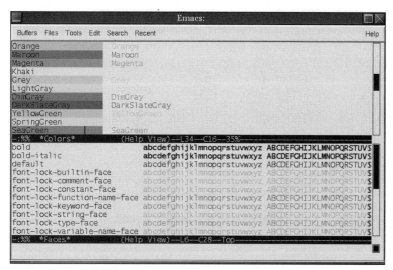

Figure 10.6   *Colors and Faces*

Word Wrapping

Years ago, before Emacs began diversifying into an all-purpose editing and work environment, most Emacs users were computer programmers. Programmers writing source code don't have a need for automatic word wrapping. This might explain why writing a text file in a default Emacs installation can be frustrating for new users.

Emacs uses a sort of pseudo-line wrapping by default. When typed text reaches the edge of the buffer window, a continuation character appears; if you type more text, it appears on the next line. In GNU Emacs, the continuation character is a backslash, whereas XEmacs uses a little curved arrow.

The continuation characters aren't part of the file and aren't saved. They are there to let you know that the lines of a file are too long to display in the buffer window. Notice in Figure 10.7 that the wrapping can happen right in the middle of a word. This makes the file difficult to read.

Not many people would choose to read or write a text file with Emacs if pseudo-wrapping were the only choice. Luckily, a line-wrapping mode can be automatically enabled for all text files.

Auto-fill-mode is a minor mode, which means that it can coexist with major modes such as text-mode. You can enable this mode by pressing M-x and typing

```
auto-fill-mode
```

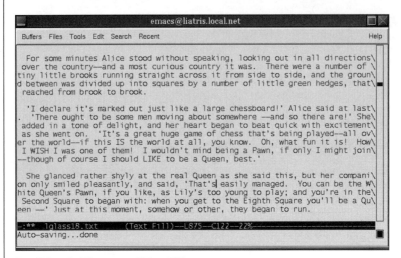

Figure 10.7 *An Unwrapped Text File*

You probably don't want to be forced to manually start this mode every time you need it. Inserting the following line into your ~/.emacs file will cause the mode to be loaded whenever it's needed:

```
(add-hook text-mode-hook (lambda () (auto-fill-mode 1)))
```

The next chapter deals with mode hooks. For now, think of this line as a way of adding a new setting to an existing mode—in this case, text-mode.

By default, only files with the *.txt suffix are automatically put in text mode. If you have files with a different suffix that should be in text-mode, a statement like this in your ~/.emacs file should do the trick:

```
(add-to-list 'auto-mode-alist (cons "\\.jrn\\'" 'text-mode))
```

Substitute any suffix for jrn in the expression.

Emacs maintains in memory an associated list called `auto-mode-alist`, which matches file suffixes with major modes. The preceding add-to-list statement effectively creates a new alist by adding a new cons cell associating the suffix *.jrn with text mode. After this line has been evaluated, any file with the *.jrn suffix will automatically be in text mode. You might want to take a look at the current value of `auto-mode-alist`. Just press the variable help key, Ctrl-h v.

You will be asked for the name of a variable. Respond with

```
auto-mode-alist
```

A window will open, containing a description of the variable and its current value. In this case you will see all of the file-type associations in the form of cons cells.

Here is one last Lisp expression you might want to add to your ~/.emacs file:

```
(setq default-major-mode 'text-mode)
```

This line is a way of letting Emacs know that if a file is loaded with an unknown extension, text-mode should be enabled. It uses the `setq` variable-setting function to change the value of the `default-major-mode` variable. By default, the variable's value is `fundamental-mode`, a fairly useless mode.

Fonts

The fonts you see in an Emacs session are provided by the X server, not by Emacs. Unlike a word processor, a text editor such as Emacs doesn't save font information along with a document's text. Printing a text file depends more on the capabilities of the printer than the editor that produced the text.

In order to produce formatted text with Emacs, you need to use a markup language such as LaTeX or groff. Many Emacs modes provide convenient features for writers using these languages. See Chapter 13 for more about these modes.

The main reason for choosing a different display font for Emacs is to enhance screen readability. The right font can vary widely, depending on the size and resolution of your monitor and the condition of your eyesight.

GNU Emacs and XEmacs differ on how fonts are handled. XEmacs lets you set the default font and its size from the Options menu as well as in the Customize Default Face buffer.

You can try a font for one session to see how you like it. Start Emacs with this command:

```
emacs -fn "font-name" &
```

For a permanent change, GNU Emacs requires the font to be set externally, in either the ~/.Xresources or ~/.Xdefaults file. (You might not have such a file; create a new one, and your X server will use it.) This font must be a fixed-width rather than proportional font. It also must use the standard X syntax for font names. Here is a sample line from an ~/.Xresources file that sets the base Emacs font:

```
Emacs*font: *-b&h-lucidatypewriter-medium-r-normal-sans-17-120-100-100-m-100-iso8859-1
```

Some of the fixed-width fonts supplied with your X installation have short names, such as 9x15; these are aliases for the longer forms, such as the preceding ~/.Xresources line.

Two utilities, xlsfonts and xfd, should be available on your Linux system. The first one lists the X11 fonts , and the second displays a font and its properties in a window.

Here is how to use xlsfonts to generate a list of fixed-width fonts. Run these two commands, one after the other, and the lists will be saved to the file fonts.txt:

```
xlsfonts -fn '*-*-*-*-*-*-*-*-*-*-*-m*' > fonts.txt
xlsfonts -fn '*-*-*-*-*-*-*-*-*-*-*-c*' >> fonts.txt
```

With the new fonts.txt file open in an Emacs session, you can copy the line referring to your desired font to an `Emacs*font:` line in an ~/.Xresources file similar to the preceding example. You could alternatively use the standard X11 mouse cut-and-paste facility to paste a font name into an X11 terminal window after `emacs -fn`, as in the earlier example.

The xfd (X Font Display) utility can be used to preview any of the fonts that xlsfonts listed for you. Paste any of the lines from fonts.txt into this command:

```
xfd -fn [font-name]
```

xfd displays a window with all the font's characters shown actual size. Figure 10.8 shows an example.

This might seem like quite a bit of work, but you have to do it only once. You will be amply repaid by an Emacs display that is easier on the eyes.

You can set up the default font for XEmacs through Customize. Press M-x and type

```
customize-face
```

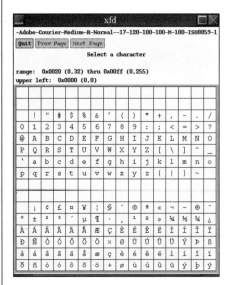

Figure 10.8 *xfd Window*

When prompted, enter

```
default
```

The Customize buffer for the default face has an entry field for Font Family, as well as for the familiar foreground color and background color entry fields discussed earlier. The entire long font name doesn't have to be typed in, just the font family name, such as Times or New Century Schoolbook. The font family and size can also be set from the Options menu; remember to select Save Options from the same menu if you want the change made permanent.

Faces and Fonts

It's easy to confuse faces and fonts. The thing to remember is that every face has a font that in most cases is the default font. Faces also include other text attributes, such as color, the font's size, and whether the font is italic, bold, or underlined.

Proportional Versus Fixed

Text editors traditionally have used only fixed-width fonts. One reason for this is that text such as program source and columnar data look neater due to the equal character widths. Proportional or variable-width fonts have long been used in publishing because of their enhanced readability and more refined character design. In general, proportional fonts give a document a more polished and formal look. The mechanical typewriters of yore had only fixed-width fonts, which is why popular fixed-width fonts such as Courier are sometimes called "typewriter fonts".

Which should you use? It's a matter of taste and preference. Currently, GNU Emacs doesn't support proportional fonts, but the upcoming version 21 will. XEmacs has supported these fonts for several years.

In my opinion, the only proportional fonts worth using in X are TrueType fonts (discussed next). The increase in sharpness and clarity in all font sizes is very noticeable. If your system isn't set up to render TrueType fonts and you don't plan to upgrade, you probably are better off sticking with the tried-and-true fixed-width fonts.

TrueType Fonts

Font display was for several years one of X11's weak points. Some fonts looked OK, but others, especially scalable fonts (another name for proportional fonts), tended to look jagged and blocky. The first time I ever saw uniformly good-looking fonts in

X Window was several years ago, when I discovered that font servers for TrueType fonts were available.

TrueType fonts were developed in the late '80s by Apple as part of an agreement with Microsoft. The motivation of the two companies was to counter the impending dominance of Adobe's font technology in the emerging personal computer market. Apple's new fonts were designed to look clear and sharp on a computer monitor. Naturally, the Microsoft-Apple alliance hoped that the new style of fonts would supplant Adobe's rival PostScript Type 1 font standard. This didn't happen. PostScript fonts are still the norm in the publishing industry, but for on-screen display, TrueType fonts are exceptional.

The 4.0x releases from the XFree86 Project are a milestone for the Linux user. The major Linux distributions are making the transition from the old 3.3x releases. Because of this, the installation and use of TrueType fonts has become easier. The new XFree86 releases come with built-in support for TrueType fonts. The xfs font server can make them available to applications, a job that previously required the services of a third-party font server.

After you have installed some good-quality TrueType fonts, they will show up in the Font section of the XEmacs Options menu.

Your Own Keybindings

Only so many keystroke combinations are available on a standard keyboard. The Emacs developers tried to assign keystrokes to the most commonly-used commands while making other commands available as M-x minibuffer commands. There's a good chance that you don't entirely agree with their decisions. Some keybindings might feel awkward, while others that you use constantly deserve to be elevated from multikeystroke to single-keystroke bindings.

This is an area where the sheer configurability of Emacs shines. After you learn to use some fairly simple Lisp functions, any or all keys can be rebound to other keystrokes.

One note of caution: If you go hog-wild with massive keybinding changes, using another Emacs configured "normally" could be a painful experience. If you work in a corporate environment and you occasionally need to use Emacs on other users' machines, it might be wise to keep at least the basic key commands on your machine close to the default. This is one reason why the supposedly more-efficient Dvorak keyboard layout isn't used more widely: A Dvorak user at a QWERTY keyboard can be reduced to the hunt-and-peck style of typing.

How Keys Can Be Represented in Lisp

Emacs-Lisp interpreters understand several valid systems of key notation. Unfortunately, some of the systems aren't portable between different versions of Emacs. The system I'll present here isn't as compact as some, but it has the advantage of being usable on any modern version of GNU Emacs or XEmacs.

This system uses basic English terms for the modifier keys: Ctrl-x is `control x`, and M-x is represented as `meta x`. Shift is `shift`; the arrow keys are simply `left`, `right`, `up`, and `down`; and the function keys are `f1`, `f2`, and so on.

Whenever two or more keys are intended to be pressed at the same time (known as a *key chord*), they should be enclosed in parentheses. The entire key sequence, including chords, is enclosed in square brackets. Here are several examples as they would appear in a Lisp expression:

```
[(control c) d]

[(shift f1)]

[(control c) (control shift f5)]

[(meta shift right)]

[(control mouse-1)] GNU Emacs

[(control button 1)] XEmacs
```

The last two examples demonstrate the only difference between GNU Emacs and XEmacs in these representations: The term for mouse-button clicks differs slightly.

Now you can write any sequence of keystrokes in such a way that Emacs can decipher it, but that's just the first step. Somehow, that keystroke representation needs to be put with all the other keybindings, along with the command it is supposed to execute.

Keymaps, Global and Local

Chapter 7 briefly introduced the idea of keymaps while clipper.el was being dissected. To recap, a keymap is a variable whose value is an associated list, a list that is made up of keystroke/command pairs.

> In XEmacs a keymap is not an associated list. It is a primitive type, but from a user's perspective there is no difference. The built-in functions such as make-sparse-keymap are used just as in GNU Emacs.

A keymap can be global, effective in all Emacs buffers and modes, or local, confined to buffers of a certain type. Each time you use a keyboard command, Emacs first looks for that key sequence in the local keymap (which may be part of a mode). If the key sequence isn't found, the global keymap is consulted; if a match is found, the associated command is executed. If Emacs draws a complete blank, the error message [keys pressed] not defined appears in the minibuffer. This sounds like a slow process, but because the keymaps are maintained in memory, access to them is near-instantaneous.

The global keymap isn't merely a jumbled heap of keybindings. It's sorted according to prefix; each prefix (such as Ctrl-x) has its own subkeymap. All key commands that begin with Ctrl-x (such as Ctrl-x k, the kill buffer command) are part of the ctl-x-map.

Adding a new keybinding to the global keymap requires a Lisp expression like this one:

```
(global-set-key [(control c) c] 'fill-region)
```

The function global-set-key is a built-in Emacs function; its first argument is the key representation, and the second is the command to run. In this example, I've defined the keybinding for the built-in function fill-region (which refills all the paragraphs in the selected region) to be Ctrl-c c. This function has no default keybinding. If there had been one, it would still be in effect and you would end up with two keybindings for the same command.

The single quote just before fill-region is necessary, because it forces the global-set-key function to treat fill-region as a symbol rather than as a variable's value.

Many Emacs commands use the Ctrl key pressed simultaneously with a letter key (known as the *modifier*), followed by either a single letter key or another Ctrl key-modifier combination. One of these combinations has been reserved for your new keybindings: the Ctrl-c prefix. This prefix is easy to type and should be your first choice when you need a keybinding for a newly-created command.

Another possibility is to change a default Emacs keybinding. This is called *rebinding* a keyboard command. There are most likely several keybindings that you never use and can't foresee using in the future. As an example, consider the Ctrl-z keybinding. Pressing it suspends Emacs and iconifies the frame. Any Linux window manager provides the same action, either with a title-bar button or as a menu item, so this might be a candidate for rebinding.

Perhaps you find the default keybinding for beginning-of-buffer (M-<) awkward to press. The following line in your ~/.emacs file assigns Ctrl-z to this command:

```
(global-set-key [(control z)] 'beginning-of-buffer)
```

After this line has been evaluated, pressing Ctrl-z moves point to the beginning of the buffer. The old Ctrl-z keybinding will be superseded, but the M-< keybinding will still be functional.

You can create a new family of usable keybindings by creating a new prefix if the Ctrl-c prefix doesn't provide enough comfortable keystroke combinations. What if you decided that Ctrl-z, because it's easy to type, would make a great prefix for new keybindings? A line like this one:

```
(global-set-key [(control z) a] 'eval-region)
```

would result in an error. Because Ctrl-z is already associated with a command, it can't be used as a prefix. You must first explicitly disassociate Ctrl-z from all keybindings with a statement like this:

```
(define-key global-map [(control z)] nil)
```

After this has been evaluated, the preceding `global-set-key` statement will be valid.

You can use the preceding expression to disable any keybinding, even if you don't plan to replace it with another. For example, every now and then, I accidentally press the Insert key without realizing it. Normally the Insert key switches from the default insert mode to overwrite mode. I never use overwrite mode when editing, so the following statement in my ~/.emacs file disables the keybinding:

```
(define-key global-map [(insert)] nil)
```

The function keys are good candidates for rebinding. F1 is by default bound as a prefix to the internal Emacs help system (as is Ctrl-h), but do you really need two keybindings for help? In GNU Emacs F2 pressed twice (or F2-2) is bound to the command that splits the screen vertically for two-column editing, a rarely-used command. F10 is handy if you run Emacs from a console, because it sets up the keyboard menu interface (no version of Emacs has console menus). Most users these days run Emacs as an X Windows application; for these users, this binding is useless. What I'm getting at is that all the function keys are fair game for rebinding.

Which Emacs commands do you use most often? I would guess that killing buffers, saving to disk, and running ispell (the Emacs spell checker) would qualify. These are the sort of commands that are suited to a single key rather than a multikey combination. You might want to try out the following `global-set-key` expressions in your ~/.emacs file. If they don't suit you, change or delete them.

```
(global-set-key [(f1)] 'kill-buffer)
(global-set-key [(f2)] 'ispell-word)
(global-set-key [(f3)] 'beginning-of-buffer)
(global-set-key [(f4)] 'end-of-buffer)
```

```
(global-set-key [(f7)] 'save-buffer)
(global-set-key [(f8)] 'start-kbd-macro)
(global-set-key [(f9)] 'end-kbd-macro)
(global-set-key [(f10)] 'call-last-kbd-macro)
```

Remember that you don't have to go to the trouble of actually putting these (or any previous) examples in your ~/.emacs file to try them out; type any of them into the Scratch buffer and evaluate the expression (with Ctrl-x Ctrl-e). The binding will remain active until you either change it or quit Emacs.

Mode-Specific Bindings

Another type of keybinding is active only within a particular mode (see Chapter 11 for more about modes). You don't have to do anything to set these up. When a mode is loaded and thus made active, a local keymap is created (if needed) that might override some of the global keybindings.

Keys and the Console

If you use Emacs in a virtual console, there is a possibility that some keys that work fine in X Window will behave differently. It all depends on how your Linux distribution is set up. The usual culprits are the Backspace and Delete keys and possibly the Alt keys.

Linux comes with a utility called loadkeys that can load a different console keymap. Check your distribution's documentation for information about the location of console keymaps; there is a good chance that you will find at least one keymap optimized for Emacs usage with a name such as emacs.kmap. Read the manual page for loadkeys, load the new keymap, and then start a console Emacs session. If the new keymap improves the keyboard situation, you can edit one of the init scripts so that the Emacs keymap is loaded automatically whenever you log in at a virtual console. Your distribution's documentation will tell you how.

The Title Bar

By default, the title bar of an X Window Emacs window displays a line that looks like this: emacs@[your machine's hostname]. You can change the title bar text so that it shows more useful information. The variable frame-title-format controls this text, and its value can be changed. Perhaps you would like the file name of the current buffer, including its directory, shown in the title bar. Try putting this Lisp expression in your ~/.emacs file:

```
(setq frame-title-format '("Emacs: " ("%f")))
```

This variable uses several built-in codes that are shared with another Emacs variable, `mode-line-format`. The `"%f"` statement is one of them; it stands for the current buffer's file name with path. Any quoted string, such as `"Emacs: "` in the example, will be inserted verbatim into the title-bar text. Here are some of the other codes you might want to experiment with:

`%b`	Prints the buffer name.
`%m`	Prints the current mode name.
`%p`	Prints the percentage of the buffer above the window, or Top.
`%P`	Prints the percentage of the buffer below the window, or Bottom.

Here's another example:

```
(setq frame-title-format '("XEmacs: " ("%b" (" %m"))))
```

This one sets the frame title to something like this:

```
XEmacs: buffername Text-mode
```

In these examples, note that spaces have been inserted within the quotes. These spaces appear on the title bar and help keep the fields separated.

You can read more about the structure of this variable by consulting the Emacs help (Ctrl-h v) for the variables `frame-title-format` and `mode-line-format`.

Conclusion

This and the previous chapter should have helped you progress beyond the scope of Emacs changes that Customize provides. Experiment with the Lisp sample expressions. Remember that when you evaluate a Lisp statement, Emacs picks up on the change in real time. This allows you to try things out temporarily without disturbing your currently working setup.

The next chapter explores Emacs modes, which have been briefly discussed in previous chapters. Modes give Emacs tremendous power and flexibility, because they allow Emacs to become a specialized editor for specific types of files.

Chapter 11: Modes, Major and Minor

B y now you most likely have an idea of what an Emacs mode is, because several have been mentioned so far. Think of a mode as a collection of configuration values, which might include font-lock colors, keybindings, new menus, and specialized functions.

This chapter introduces the different uses of major and minor modes and how they interact. Since modes are composed of one or more Lisp files, they can be edited and re-byte-compiled if you want to alter their behavior; the final sections of this chapter give examples of this.

Introducing Modes

There are two varieties of modes—major and minor. A buffer can be in only one major mode at any given time. Minor modes are less exclusive. More than one minor mode can be active at once, and they can coexist with the dominant major mode. You could think of a minor mode as a mode that supplements a major mode, adding new features or capabilities.

Modes can be loaded in two ways: explicitly, via a minibuffer command, or automatically, when a file name with a certain extension is loaded. Chapter 10 introduced the variable `auto-mode-alist`, an associated list of all mode-to-extension pairings. Why not take a look at the value of this variable? Press Ctrl-h v and when prompted, type

```
auto-mode-alist
```

A Help window opens and displays the variable's help (see Figure 11.1), which consists of a brief description and the variable's current value, which is one long, jumbled-looking list.

Look closely and you will see the individual elements that make up the overall associated list. Here's one of them:

```
("\\.[ch]\\'" . c-mode)
```

Way back in Chapter 3, in the section "Regular Expressions in Searches," the basic Emacs regular expression (regexp) syntax was introduced. This two-element dotted-pair cons cell uses two of the regexp symbols. The `ch` pair of characters is within a pair of brackets, which indicates that either c or h is valid. The backslashes are the regexp escape characters, forcing the period to be taken literally rather than interpreted as the regexp symbol it would normally be. The backslashed single quote is a special case; it signifies that the suffix must be the end of the string which makes up the file name. The result of all this is that any file with a c or h suffix matches the regular expression and will be opened in c-mode.

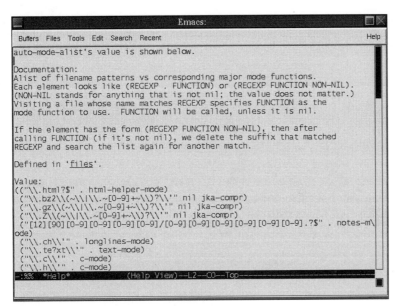

Figure 11.1   *The* `auto-mode-list` *Help Window*

Another associated list matches scripting-language files to major modes. Instead of using the file-name suffix, the interpreter-mode-alist matches strings found in the first line of such files. Here is a cons cell from that a-list:

```
("python" . Python-mode)
```

Python files often begin with a line such as this:

```
#! /bin/env python
```

When such a file is loaded into an Emacs session the interpreter-mode-alist will find a match in that first line and the file will be opened in Python mode. The reasoning behind this alist is that scripting-language files might not have a suffix which would allow auto-mode-alist to associate the file with a major mode.

What a Mode Does for You

A mode specialized for editing certain types of files transforms Emacs into an editor optimized for that particular type of file. This is all effortless and transparent to the user. You open an HTML file, and an HTML mode comes into play, a LaTeX file is opened, and AucTeX takes over. This happens only if the file's suffix is included in the auto-mode-alist variable. Many varieties of files are included in the variable, but you need to add new and obscure types yourself. Instructions for doing this are often included in the comments of a new mode. If they aren't, the example from the preceding chapter can serve as a template:

```
(add-to-list 'auto-mode-alist (cons "\\.jrn\\'" 'text-mode))
```

Substitute the suffix of a file type for `jrn` and the name of a mode for `text-mode`. This will cause any file with that suffix to be opened in the specified mode. The expression can be included in your ~/.emacs file if you want it to be permanent.

The regular expression in `auto-mode-alist` doesn't necessarily need to match a file's suffix. Let's say that you have decided to use Emacs as the external editor for the Mutt e-mail program. You would like Emacs to automatically switch to text-mode when you write e-mail messages originating from Mutt.

Mutt's name for its temporary message files is in this format:

```
mutt-[user-name]-xxxxx-x
```

with the x characters replaced by digits that are different for every message. The only unchanging part of these file names is at the beginning, so the regexp should search for and match any file whose name begins with `mutt-`. Here is the `setq` statement that does this:

```
(setq auto-mode-alist (cons '("^mutt-" . text-mode) auto-mode-alist))
```

The ^ just before `mutt-` in the regexp section indicates that only files with `mutt-` at the beginning of the file's name should match.

Syntax Highlighting

The syntax highlighting (or font-locking) system that Emacs uses was designed to be applicable mainly for programming languages, but it has been adapted to work well in a variety of other types of files. The nine main font-lock faces bear names reflecting their original usage in programming modes, such as the Variable, Constant, and Keyword faces. This doesn't mean that these faces can't be used in nonprogramming modes. These faces are largely differentiated by their foreground colors. Rather than create new faces, many modes elect to use existing font-lock faces even though their names might have little to do with the type of text being highlighted.

This makes life easier for the user who is installing a new mode. Once you have gone to the trouble of configuring font-lock faces to your liking, a new mode that uses the already-configured faces will be ready to use.

Keybindings

Modes generally don't need an entirely new set of keybindings. Many of them use the `make-sparse-keymap` function to construct a local keymap, which is a set of bindings limited to the current buffer.

The Ctrl-c prefix is reserved for use by modes as well as for user-defined keybindings. Several characters that can follow Ctrl-c are reserved for use by major modes:

- Ctrl-c Ctrl-[character]
- Ctrl-c [digit]
- Ctrl-c [{,},<,>,;, or :]

You can be certain that if you use Ctrl-c followed by a letter character for your own keybindings that there will be no conflict with a major mode's keybindings.

Certain special-purpose modes aren't used for actual editing. Inserting text is not what they are intended for; thus, they can take over the keyboard completely. The Dired file-management mode is a good example. Dired uses many of the letter keys to perform various file operations, such as marking and deleting.

Another such mode is dictionary mode, an add-on that acts as an Emacs interface to a dictd dictionary server. Dictionary mode is used with keybindings that allow you to look up the definition of the word at point. The definition is displayed in a new dedicated dictionary window. When this happens, the following code kicks in:

```
(setq dictionary-mode-map (make-sparse-keymap))
(suppress-keymap dictionary-mode-map)


(define-key dictionary-mode-map "q" 'dictionary-close)

(define-key dictionary-mode-map "h" 'dictionary-help)

(define-key dictionary-mode-map "s" 'dictionary-search)

(define-key dictionary-mode-map "D" 'dictionary-select-dictionary)

(define-key dictionary-mode-map "M" 'dictionary-select-strategy)

(define-key dictionary-mode-map "m" 'dictionary-match-words)

(define-key dictionary-mode-map "d" 'dictionary-search-word-at-point)

(define-key dictionary-mode-map "l" 'dictionary-previous)
```

This Lisp code starts out by creating a new variable, `dictionary-mode-map`, which starts out with the value returned by `make-sparse-keymap`. In the next line, the normal keymap is replaced using a built-in function called `suppress-keymap`. This function replaces the current keymap with the value of the argument to the function, which in this case is `dictionary-mode-map`. At this point, `dictionary-mode-map` is empty, but the following lines add keybindings to the keymap—bindings that previously were normal character-insertion commands.

In each of the lines, the last element is the name of a function defined elsewhere in dictionary.el.

Later in dictionary.el, the following line makes the new keymap active in the dictionary window but nowhere else:

```
(use-local-map dictionary-mode-map)
```

Indentation

Programming modes such a c-mode, python-mode, and lisp-mode redefine indentation behavior. For example, some programmers like to be able to indent functions as a unit. The Emacs C/C++ mode (cc-mode) provides keyboard commands for this as well as the indentation of entire parenthesized or bracketed statements. Other language modes provide these features to a greater or lesser degree.

Word Wrapping

Text-mode isn't the only mode that can make use of auto-fill-mode. The various mail message composition packages, such as Gnus and rmail, by default load either auto-fill-mode or a related mode called adaptive-fill-mode.

The above-mentioned cc-mode uses word wrapping only within comment blocks, the areas of a source code file in which wrapping is appropriate or needed.

Later in this chapter, the concept of mode derivation will be introduced. It's a means by which one mode can "inherit" traits from another. Several modes use this device to add features to a new mode without having to rewrite function code.

Minor Modes

Every buffer is always in some major mode, even if it's only fundamental mode. Usage of minor modes is optional. When one of these smaller modes is enabled, it adds something to the behavior of the dominant major mode without interfering with the major mode's features.

An example of this is auto-fill-mode, a minor mode, in conjunction with text-mode. All text-mode does by itself is set up a few keybindings (such as M-Tab, which calls on ispell to complete a partially-typed word) and define a blank line as a paragraph separator. The auto-fill minor mode adds word wrapping to the basic text-mode behavior.

Any number of minor modes can be active in a buffer, but more than two or three is uncommon.

A minor mode may install a new keymap that can redefine some of the keys in the major mode's keymap. The documentation summoned by the mode help key Ctrl-h m lists the keybindings of all active modes, including minor modes.

The Advantages of Multiple Modes

You might use a major mode for a particular type of file but find that one small feature is missing. The prospect of trying to edit the major mode's Lisp files in order to add that feature can be daunting. The mode works fine now, and you hate to risk making it unusable somehow. Chances are there is a minor mode available that will add that missing capability, but if you can't find one, you can try writing your own without risking damage to the major mode files.

Mode Hooks

The idea of providing hooks for modes is an inspired one. Imagine that a mode is some sort of material object. Imagine further that this object has hooks mounted on it on which can be hung smaller objects that change the object's behavior. That is the idea behind mode hooks: Build into a mode a facility for modifying the mode with a simple Lisp expression. This is similar to the idea of the minor mode, but the Lisp expression that hooks on to a mode hook need not be as complex as a full-blown minor mode. This is what you use if you just need to add, say, a single new keybinding to a mode.

Here is an example of a line that enables hooks for text-mode (this line was extracted from the text-mode.el file):

```
(run-hooks 'text-mode-hook))
```

Now here's a line that could be in ~/.emacs that adds a hook to text-mode:

```
(add-hook 'text-mode-hook 'turn-on-auto-fill)
```

The hook in this example is a simple instruction: execute `turn-on-auto-fill`, a built-in function that unconditionally turns on auto-fill-mode.

Mode hooks make it easy to add one or more features to a mode. Keybindings, new faces, and running an existing function can all be done with an `add-hook` statement.

Here's another example:

```
(add-hook mail-mode-hook
    (lambda ()
    (define-key mail-mode-map [(control c) (x)] 'mail-send-and-exit)
    (define-key mail-mode-map [(control c)(c)] 'mail-cc)
    (setq fill-column 65)))
```

This one adds two new keybindings to mail-mode and changes the `fill-column` setting. It does this using the `lambda` function, which is an anonymous function, unnamed because it has no use outside this particular `setq` variable definition.

Notice the difference between these two examples. The first one adds a hook, so if other text-mode hooks have been defined, this one will be added to the list rather than replacing the earlier hooks. The second example is a `setq` variable definition, which replaces any value that `mail-mode-hook` might have had. Use this form when you are certain that no other hooks have been attached to the mode. Because these hooks are normally defined in the ~/.emacs file, it's no great chore to check the file for previous hook entries pertaining to the mode in question.

How to Associate Modes

Some modes aren't useful unless they're used along with one or more other Lisp libraries. The `require` function is used near the beginning of a Lisp mode file to force the loading of features from another file before the body of the mode is evaluated (see the following section for more about `require`). This is often how multifile packages are constructed. The advantage to the user is that only one statement in your ~/.emacs file is needed to load the entire package. Notes-mode is a good example. The first two lines of notes-mode.el cause two related files, notes-variables.el and notes-aux.el, to be loaded before the main body of notes-mode.el is evaluated:

```
(require 'notes-variables)
(require 'notes-aux)
```

Splitting a large mode into several files makes life easier for the developer. Related functions and variables can be segregated into a separate file. This also separates possible errors, making it easier to track them down.

Different Ways to Load a Mode

Three ways of writing Lisp expressions in your ~/.emacs file activate a mode. They each have their advantages and limitations, and an add-on mode might be written in such a way that only one will work. I have encountered mode packages that wouldn't work with a certain method, even though the documentation claimed otherwise. Sometimes experimenting with another of the three loading methods can help get a mode working for you.

Load

The most basic way to load a Lisp file is with the built-in function `load`. A `load` statement looks like this:

```
(load '[file-name])
```

`load` first looks for file-name.elc; if it can't find that, it looks for file-name.el, and if that doesn't exist file-name will be used.

The disadvantage to this function is that the file is loaded immediately, even if it isn't needed until later. Using `load` would be appropriate for a heavily-used Lisp file which needs to be available quickly. The next two methods are more commonly used due to their greater flexibility.

Autoloading

There are probably some modes that you seldom use but that you would still like to have available when needed. Autoloading such modes is the ideal technique, because the mode isn't loaded until you call it, with either a keystroke or a minibuffer command. `autoload` is a built-in function. An `autoload` command looks like this:

```
(autoload 'follow-mode "follow")
```

This is a simple example; the complete syntax of the `autoload` command looks like this:

```
(autoload function-name Lisp-file docstring interactive type [last three are optional])
```

The `follow-mode` example just shown uses just the first two of the syntax example elements. It leaves out the three optional switches, as they are unnecessary when you are using autoload on a Lisp file which is in a directory on your load-path. Autoload uses the load function to actually load the file when you request it, so as described above an *.elc file is used if present.

Translated into English the above autoload statement might read like this:

```
"Find an Emacs Lisp file on the load-path  named follow.elc, follow.el, or follow,
preferably the first. Find a function named follow-mode within the file and be
prepared to load that function if the user requests it".
```

If only the first two required arguments are present `autoload` considers the values of the missing arguments to be nil. In other words, there is no docstring, the function isn't interactive, and the single argument refers to a function (the default).

Here are two examples from an ~/.emacs file that loads two functions from dictionary-mode rather than the entire file:

```
(autoload 'dictionary-search "dictionary"
 "Ask for a word and search it in all dictionaries" t)


(autoload 'dictionary-search-word-at-point "dictionary"
 "Search the word at point in all dictionaries" t)
```

These two expressions load functions from `"dictionary"`, which is expanded by the `autoload` function to `"dictionary.elc"`. If the function can't find a file by that name on the load-path, it looks for dictionary.el instead. The `t` at the end of the expressions is meant to make the `dictionary` function interactive—t meaning yes or true. This means that pressing M-x and typing

```
dictionary-search
```

would cause the `dictionary-search` function to be loaded from dictionary.elc, which would result in the minibuffer prompt `Search word:`.

Require

Some packages are necessary for your daily work; you want them to be loaded when Emacs starts and to be quickly available thereafter. The `require` function is tailor-made for this need. A `require` expression can be as simple as this:

```
(require 'clipper)
```

This function doesn't explicitly load a function or a Lisp file. It loads a *feature*, an Emacs term meaning a collection of functions and/or variables.

The full syntax is

```
(require '[feature-symbol] '[file-name])
```

The second argument is optional; if it is absent the function will look for a file name with the same name as the feature.

In order to use `require` a statement such as this one must be present in the Lisp file:

```
(provide 'clipper)
```

The function `provide` adds the feature-symbol given as its argument to an Emacs variable named `features`, which is a list of all available features available in the current Emacs session.

An advantage of `require` is that the function first checks to see if a file has already been loaded; if it has, `require` does nothing. This prevents a file from being loaded more than once in a session.

`require` is often used in a Lisp file to make available features existing in another file.

The difference between the `require` and `autoload` functions is that `autoload` loads just the name of the file and its docstring into memory, deferring actual loading until an explicit request is made.

The choice of which of the three functions to use is normally up to the package author. The commented-out documentation in the source file usually provides sample lines that can be inserted in your ~/.emacs file. If you have trouble convincing a package to load or autoload, it is worthwhile to try one of the other functions.

Deriving One Mode from Another

Mode derivation is a time-saving technique. Here's a common situation: You need a mode that makes editing a certain type of file easier. A mode designed for another sort of file is almost what you need, and it seems a shame to start from scratch. You can derive one mode from another, retaining the core functionality of the old mode but changing certain features so that the new mode works the way you need it to. It helps prevent that "Am I reinventing the wheel?" feeling.

What makes this possible is a Lisp package called `define-derived-mode`. It has a simple syntax:

```
(define-derived-mode new-mode's-name old-mode's-name mode-line-string
docstring
expression-1
expression-2
etc.)
```

Here's an example from gametree.el, a file bundled with the Emacs game modes:

```
(define-derived-mode gametree-mode outline-mode "GameTree"
  "Major mode for managing game analysis trees.
Useful to postal and email chess (and, it is hoped, also checkers, go,
shogi, etc.) players, it is a slightly modified version of Outline mode.

\\{gametree-mode-map}"
(auto-fill-mode 0)
(make-variable-buffer-local 'write-contents-hooks)
```

```
(add-hook 'write-contents-hooks 'gametree-save-and-hack-layout))


;;;; Key bindings


(define-key gametree-mode-map "\C-c\C-j" 'gametree-break-line-here)
[etc]
```

The first line sets the scene: `define-derived-mode` is being called to make a new mode, `gametree-mode`, using `outline-mode` as a foundation. `mode-line-string` is a short, descriptive piece of text that is displayed in the mode-line—in this case, `"GameTree"`.

The next three lines are the docstring, the optional built-in documentation found in most well-written modes. Notice that the first line breaks prematurely (right after `trees`). It's an Emacs custom to start a docstring with a single-sentence summary on a line by itself. The apropos help facility looks for that summary line and displays it if you press Ctrl-h a after `gametree-mode` has been loaded. The docstring ends with an odd-looking expression beginning with two backslashes. This is a code understood by the Emacs internal help system; it means "Evaluate the expression between the curly braces, and substitute the result for this line." If you had a buffer in gametree-mode and you summoned help for the mode by pressing Ctrl-h m, the Help buffer would look like Figure 11.2.

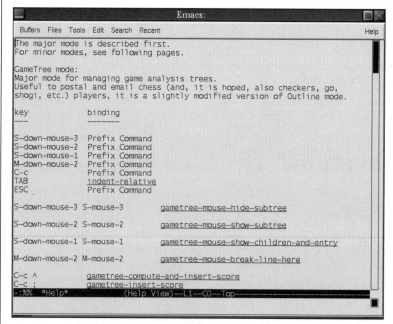

Figure 11.2   *Gametree Help*

Notice how the docstring has been altered: The backslash-prefixed line is gone, and the list of keybindings (`gametree-mode-map`) has been substituted in its place.

Following the docstring is the actual body of the expression, which is made up of a sequence of function definitions and/or variable declarations. The `define-key` function in this example uses an alternative way of showing a keybinding. Backslash escape characters are used as a substitute for the bracket-parenthesis system illustrated in the preceding chapter. This keybinding is equivalent to `"[(control c) (control j)]"`.

Modifying a Mode

Sooner or later, every Emacs user finds the thought "I wish there were a mode to make this sort of editing easier!" passing through his or her mind. Perhaps you are editing a new type of file and wish there were font locking for the file type or a new key command that would speed up a repetitious task.

I would be willing to bet that many accomplished Lisp hackers who create new modes from scratch got their feet wet by changing an existing mode. The Lisp source is freely available for nearly every mode; all you need to do is find one that comes close to what you need.

One Lisp skill that is essential if you want to get very far in adapting a mode is facility with regular expressions. They are used in one way or another in just about every mode, especially in the font-locking routines.

You need to be able to tell the font-locking engine how to recognize a particular chunk of text, and regular expressions are the only practical means to do so. Take a look at this font-locking code snipped from rmail.el:

```
(defvar rmail-font-lock-keywords
  (eval-when-compile
    (let* ((cite-chars "[>|}]")
      (cite-prefix "A-Za-z")
      (cite-suffix (concat cite-prefix "0-9_.@-`'\"")))
      (list '("^\\(From\\|Sender\\):" . font-lock-function-name-face)
      '("^Reply-To:.*$" . font-lock-function-name-face)
      '("^Subject:" . font-lock-comment-face)
      '("^\\(To\\|Apparently-To\\|Cc\\|Newsgroups\\):"
        . font-lock-keyword-face)
          [remainder of defvar statement cut]))))
```

This is how the rmail Emacs mail client determines which lines to highlight. Note the numerous regular expression symbols used throughout, such as the caret (^) to indicate that the regular expression that follows it is a match only at the beginning of a line. The second-to-last line illustrates a regular expression convention that is often seen in font-locking expressions: the double-backslash escape characters, which allow characters such as parentheses and the pipe symbol (|) to be passed to the Emacs regular expression interpreter rather than the Lisp interpreter.

Regular expressions can seem baffling to a beginner. A good way to learn to read them is to keep a list of the regexp special symbols handy while puzzling through some of the Lisp files that are a part of Emacs.

Conclusion

The chapters in this part of the book should have left you with a good grounding in basic Lisp and Emacs configuration. If you want to learn more about Emacs Lisp, I highly recommend two packages of Info format documentation. "Emacs Lisp Reference" and "Programming in Emacs Lisp: An Introduction" are both included on this book's CD-ROM (in the directory /cdrom/docs).

The next part of the book explores the variety of Emacs packages that are available—both those that are included in the standard GNU Emacs and XEmacs distributions and the packages written by other members of the Emacs community.

PART III

Exploring Emacs Packages

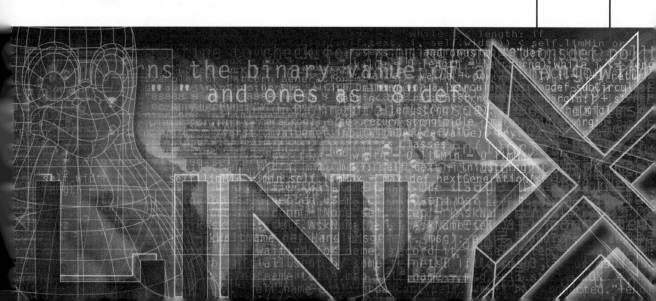

The Rationale behind Packaging

GNU Emacs Packages

The XEmacs Packaging System

Installation Methods

In the early days of Emacs, it was taken for granted that most users had a certain amount of Lisp experience. The sheer volume of available packages was much smaller, and the packages themselves were simpler, many of them single-file Lisp utilities. In the years that followed, several major multifile packages were developed, some (such as the Gnus news/mail reader) almost baroque in their intricacy.

Emacs users began to become more diverse. As the word spread about this free editor with so many clever and time-saving features, Emacs began to be used by nonprogrammers, first mainly by users of various flavors of UNIX, and more recently by more mainstream users of Microsoft operating systems.

The developers in the Emacs and XEmacs camps realized that times had changed and that efforts to streamline the installation of add-on packages would greatly benefit the user community.

This chapter discusses the differences between the GNU Emacs and XEmacs package systems. The usage and features of each will be considered separately.

The Rationale behind Packaging

Ideally, packages would be carefully adapted to each new release of Emacs, leaving a minimum of configuration for the user. Default settings would make the package at least minimally usable. To a large degree, this goal has been attained: Both GNU Emacs and XEmacs, although their systems differ, come with a great variety of usable packages. The package developers make an effort to keep abreast of changes in the two Emacs variants, while the official Emacs maintainers try to maintain communications as well.

Naturally, this fairly informal system doesn't always work. A package can become obsolete and refuse to function with a recent Emacs version. The developer might have lost interest, or a better and more popular package with a similar purpose might have come along.

As with any other sort of open-source software, it is ultimately the state of the users that drives further development. The larger the community of users, the more bug reports and fixes that flow "upstream" to the developer. More users also means that some will be fluent in Lisp, providing a pool of possible new maintainers further down the road.

GNU Emacs Packages

Every few years, a new version of GNU Emacs is released. During the intervening years, the developers work on the source code for Emacs itself, improving it and dealing with bugs. In parallel with this work on the core of the editor, old packages are updated and new ones evaluated for inclusion in the official distribution. There is a two-way exchange between the author who submits the new package and the Emacs maintainers. The Emacs people might suggest some changes to the package that will help it work correctly with the next Emacs version. Certain legal papers must also be signed by the package author and returned to the GNU Emacs team. These documents assign rights to the Free Software Foundation, a safeguard that the FSF feels is necessary to preserve Emacs from legal challenges. An ambiguously copywrited package could conceivably taint the legal status of an entire Emacs distribution.

Not every package author agrees to sign the papers. Some don't want to take the time, and others feel that the GNU GPL license included with their package should be sufficient protection of its freedom.

The upshot of this occasional disagreement is that not every worthwhile add-on package ends up being bundled with GNU Emacs. All this means for the Emacs user is that the package must be obtained separately from the package author's Web or FTP site.

How Packages Are Activated

The current version of GNU Emacs contains a wide variety of packages, many of which you will probably never use. Most of them are in a dormant state. Actually using them requires an explicit command, either in the minibuffer, as a keyboard command, or as an entry in your ~/.emacs file. Others are ready to go, so you don't need to do anything to enable them.

There are good reasons for this variety of activation methods. Some packages are used rarely, and others are used every day. Naturally, the packages that fall into these categories are different for every user. Any package you use often can be elevated from minibuffer loading to automatic loading. See the sections in Chapter 11 on `autoload`, `require`, and `load-library`, three functions that can be used in your ~/.emacs file to load packages.

The ready-to-go packages are typically modes that are paired in the `auto-mode-alist` or `auto-interpreter-alist` variables with file name extensions or contents of the first line. Chapter 11 has more about the details of these variables.

Finding Installation Instructions

If you want to learn how to install one of the more prominent Info-documented packages (such as Gnus), just press Ctrl-h i and read the instructions in the relevant Info manual. The smaller and/or more obscure packages are internally documented.

One slight drawback of Emacs (and XEmacs) is that many interesting and useful modes and packages are installed, but the supplied documentation (the Info files) covers only the larger and most-used packages, such as Dired, Gnus, and Ediff.

The Package Finder is an effective way to browse the Commentary sections of the packages supplied with Emacs. Press Ctrl-h p to bring up a Finder window (or select Find Emacs Packages from the Help menu). A buffer listing categories of packages appears. Click the second or middle mouse button on a category to see a Finder category window, as shown in Figure 12.1.

The Lisp files listed in the second window can be clicked on to access a third window, one containing the actual Commentary section of the file. In most cases, this documentation is sufficient to get you started using the package.

Another way to learn about packages is to take a look at the actual Lisp files. They can be found in the /[prefix]/share/[version-number]/lisp directory and in various categorized subdirectories under it. Sometimes a package's Commentary section is scanty. The actual Lisp code can be a useful source of information.

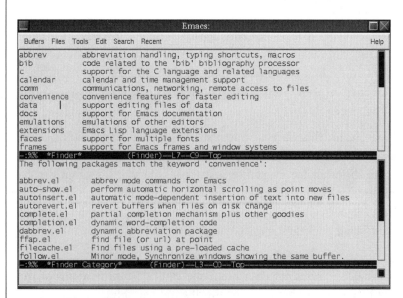

Figure 12.1   *Finder Windows*

The bracketed [prefix] in the directory path can vary, depending on how you installed Emacs. Most commonly, the prefix is /usr or /usr/local, but Emacs can be installed in a nonstandard location if it was built from source. An example of this is shown in Figure 12.2; this particular Emacs has /mp3/emacs as its prefix. The bracketed [version-number] might be 20.7, 21.0, or something else, depending on which version of Emacs you have installed.

The Emacs file manager mode Dired is ideally suited to help you browse through a directory of Lisp files. Any files that you want to investigate will be easy to read in a font-locked Lisp mode Emacs buffer. Just press Ctrl-x d, and you will be prompted for a directory name. Type the name of the /lisp directory of your Emacs installation, and you will be all set.

Browse through the *.el files you find there. Often, the name of the file gives you some idea of what it does.

You'll need to load the Lisp file (or the main file if it's a multifile package) and look for instructions in the commented-out portion near the top of the file. The section to look for is called the Commentary. You will find usage notes and examples of activation lines that can be inserted in your ~/.emacs file.

Figure 12.2 shows the Commentary section of a utility called desktop.el, which saves the state of your current Emacs session, including major mode, open buffers, and other aspects, and restores it the next time you start Emacs.

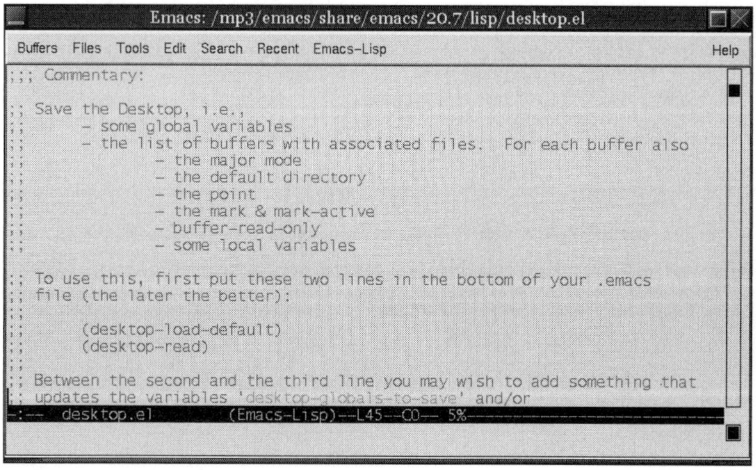

Figure 12.2 *Instructions for desktop.el*

> You don't need to restart Emacs after adding a line or two to your ~/.emacs file. Instead, select the new lines as a region (using Ctrl-spacebar and the arrow keys), and then select Evaluate Region from the Emacs-Lisp menu.

Installing a New Version

Some Emacs modes and utilities, especially the simpler ones, were written years ago and still work well. They do their job without fail, so why would anyone be tempted to change them?

Other packages are in a state of intermittent flux. If a certain package is important to your work, you might benefit from keeping up with the development process. There might be a mailing list to monitor; nearly all package releases are announced on one of the Emacs Usenet newsgroups.

Installing a new release of a package can be as simple as dropping the files into the Lisp directory, thus replacing the old files. It might be prudent to move the old files into a temporary directory (one that isn't in your load-path) just in case there is a problem with the new version.

Don't forget to byte-compile the Lisp files (see Chapter 8). It isn't absolutely necessary, but the files will load quite a bit faster.

The Site-Lisp Directory

The site-lisp directory in a new Emacs installation is empty. It exists to give you a place to install third-party packages, meaning Lisp add-ons that aren't a part of the Emacs installation. This directory is included in `load-path`, a variable whose value is a list of directories that Emacs searches for Lisp files. Figure 12.3 shows the help screen for the `load-path` variable.

If your ~/.emacs file contains these lines:

```
(autoload 'html-helper-mode "html-helper-mode" "Yay HTML" t)
(setq auto-mode-alist (cons '("\\.html?$" . html-helper-mode) auto-mode-alist))
```

and you load a file named index.html, Emacs first checks the `auto-mode-alist` variable to see if the html suffix is matched with the name of a mode. A match is found (due to the second line). Since `html-helper-mode` was autoloaded (in the first line), the mode is made active as an index.html buffer appears in an Emacs window. Emacs found `html-helper-mode` because it was located in the site-lisp directory.

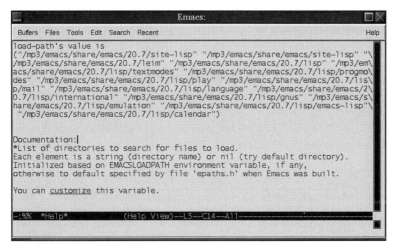

Figure 12.3 `load-path` *Help*

There are actually two site-lisp directories. The first one's path is /[prefix]/share/ emacs/[version-number]/site-lisp, and the second one is found at /[prefix]/share/ emacs/site-lisp. Both of these directories are on the load-path.

Why two of them? Some users have more than one version of Emacs installed. The second site-lisp directory makes it possible to have add-on packages that can be found by any Emacs version. The first directory is tied to a specific version of Emacs. A particular package might be picky about which version of Emacs it can work with. Installing the package in the version-specific site-lisp directory allows the package to be used by only that version.

This sort of situation is rare. The vast majority of packages happily cooperate with any recent Emacs version and thus can be installed in the second (version-neutral) site-lisp directory.

The XEmacs Packaging System

For the past couple of years, the XEmacs development team has been creating a new packaging system. XEmacs has traditionally included a great number of packages in the standard distribution. The downside of this is that the download size of a complete binary XEmacs package was becoming larger as time went on, to the point that some users were reluctant to upgrade to a new version. An idea arose: Perhaps the Lisp packages could be maintained independently from the editor. A side benefit is that users would be able to pick and choose the packages they needed rather than get them all.

A New Way to Manage Packages

This new system relies on several intertwined features. A standard directory structure for packages to inhabit lets XEmacs find the packages. Category package names were created (the single-file packages described in the next section), such as edit-utils (containing editing-related packages) and os-utils (utilities that interface with the host operating system). A file format was decided on that lists and briefly describes all available packages.

To minimize the time spent keeping a collection of packages up-to-date, several utilities were written. These package tools allow the user to choose an FTP site from which packages can be retrieved and download an updated package database (the package list just described). From within XEmacs, a connection can then be opened with the FTP site, and any number of packages can be downloaded and installed. Previously installed packages can also be updated to new versions. Once initiated, this process takes place in the background. The menu interface to these tools is described in a moment.

Types of Packages

There are two types of packages—regular and single-file.

A regular package is a group of Lisp files that are related and need each others' presence. You shouldn't delete any of the files in this type of package, because the package itself is a unit. Gnus, VM, Dired, and Viper are examples.

A single-file package is not really a package in the way the word has been used in this chapter. This sort of package is a bundle of smaller Lisp utilities or modes, each one a single file. The prog-modes package is an example. Every file in this package is a mode for a programming language, such as perl-mode, python-mode, and pascal-mode. Another is the misc-games package, a collection of text-mode amusements such as doctor.el, gomoku.el, and life.el.

Individual files can be deleted from single-file packages. As an example, if you have no interest in programming in the Pascal language, the file might as well be deleted from the prog-modes package directory.

The Directory Structure

The XEmacs directory layout is quite a bit different from the GNU Emacs system shown earlier in this chapter. There are two directory hierarchies. The first is a version-specific directory tree located at /[prefix]/lib/xemacs-xxx/, with the x characters at the end replaced with the XEmacs version number. This directory contains the

XEmacs core Lisp files, the Info documentation, and miscellaneous executables. The actual XEmacs executable (the program itself) is installed in /[prefix]/bin.

The second directory tree contains the site-lisp and package directories. This tree is version-neutral and survives XEmacs upgrades. It is located at /[prefix]/lib/xemacs, and the package directory is /[prefix]/lib/xemacs/packages.

Installation Methods

There is a bit of a chicken-and-egg problem if you have installed XEmacs but don't have any packages yet. Two packages must be installed before the package utilities will work: the efs package (which gives XEmacs the ability to make Internet FTP transfers) and the xemacs-base package. All of the package files are available on this book's CD-ROM in the directory /cdrom/xemacs/packages. If you would rather get them from the Internet (ensuring that you are getting the most recent versions), there is a list of XEmacs mirror FTP sites at http://www.xemacs.org. Pick the site that is closest to you.

Download and install the two required packages, following the directions in the later section "Installing Individual Packages Manually". After you have done this, the next section guides you through the process of automated package installation.

Installing Individual Packages Manually

If you are accustomed to retrieving files with an FTP client such as gftp, ncftp, or the original FTP program, installing one or more packages is not difficult. Packages can be found at ftp://ftp.xemacs.org/pub/xemacs/packages.

After you have downloaded the files, just move them into /[prefix]/lib/xemacs/packages. Use this shell command to expand the tar archive:

```
tar xvzf [package].tar.gz
```

You can also copy the packages from the directory /cdrom/packages/xemacs/packages/single on the book's CD-ROM.

When the packages are in place, they will be usable the next time you start XEmacs.

Using the Menu Interface

The package utilities available under the Options, Packages menu option work only while you have an open Internet connection, so open one before you start. The first step is to choose the menu option Add Download Site, as shown in Figure 12.4.

Figure 12.4   *Package Download Sites*

Select a nearby FTP site, and then select the third item from the top, List and Install. In the background, an FTP connection is opened to the site you selected. The current index database (a file named package-index-LATEST.pgp) is downloaded to a temporary directory on your machine. The information in this file is compared to the packages you already have installed. A Packages buffer appears, showing the status of all installed and installable packages (see Figure 12.5). You can quickly determine if any of your installed packages are out-of-date and decide which ones (if any) you want to update to the current version. You can also select new packages to install.

The new Package menu, shown in Figure 12.6, can be used to install or delete tagged files, among other things.

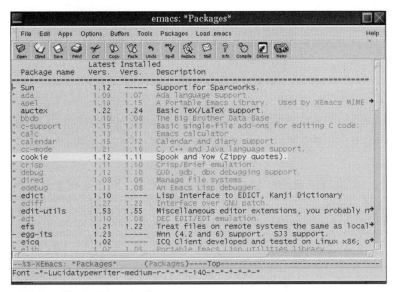

Figure 12.5 *The Packages Buffer*

Figure 12.6 *The Packages Menu*

The Package buffer has its own keybindings:

Enter	Tags or untags the current package for installation.
d	Tags or untags the current package for removal.
r	Adds any packages needed by those that were tagged.
x	Installs or deletes the tagged packages.
I	Displays more information about the package in the modeline.
g	Refreshes the package list.
v	Toggles between detailed and terse display.
q	Kills the buffer.

When you have tagged the packages that interest you, pressing x or selecting Install/Remove Selected from the Packages menu fetches the files from the download site that you specified earlier and installs them.

One menu item/keyboard command you might take note of is Add Required. This is an automatic method of pulling down any packages that your selected packages need in order to function properly. This feature is analogous to the Debian Linux `apt-get` command, which provides the same service for Debian packages.

If for some reason you have trouble with any phase of this process, you might need to use Customize to change one or more of the default package tool variables. Press M-x and type

```
customize-group
```

When prompted, type

```
package-tools
```

The resulting Customize buffer allows you to change and save the settings.

Linux Distributions and XEmacs Packages

Each Linux distribution handles XEmacs packages a little differently. Most of them bundle all the packages in the distribution package, so the one file is all you need. If you installed an RPM-based distribution's XEmacs package, you should have the necessary XEmacs packages already installed.

Debian splits the packages from the core XEmacs distribution, placing them in a separate *.deb file. The package file you need is on the book's CD-ROM in the same directory as the binary.

Installing a Sumo Tarball

Some XEmacs users prefer the old package policy. If disk space isn't at a premium and the Internet connection is fast, they reason, why not just download all the packages in one fell swoop? To accommodate these people, a large single archive file containing all the packages is made available whenever a series of packages is released.

This file is known as the Sumo Tarball, and its file name is xemacs-sumo.tar.gz. This is actually a symbolic link; the actual filename includes the release date.

The Sumo Tarball can be found in the same directory on the FTP sites as the individual packages. You can also find a copy on the book's CD-ROM in the directory /cdrom/xemacs/packages.

To install one of these files, simply move it into the /[prefix]/lib/xemacs/packages directory and execute this shell command:

```
tar xvzf xemacs-sumo.tar.gz
```

The /lisp, /etc/, /info, and several other directories will be created if they don't already exist, and the files will populate those directories and be ready to use.

Conclusion

Now that you know how to obtain and install these packages, the following chapters will introduce you to a sampling of them.

Although programming was the purpose for which Emacs was developed, it has now become just as important as a writer's tool. The next chapter is an overview of packages used to produce readable text in one form or another.

Chapter 13: Text Processing Packages

ASCII text is the Emacs native file format. ASCII (*American Standard Code for Information Interchange*) is a character encoding standard meant to be platform- and manufacturer-independent. Each character is represented by 7 bits (the smallest unit of storage for computers, equivalent to a binary digit). Here are some advantages of ASCII text:

- It is a worldwide standard that can be read by all software.
- It has minimal storage requirements.
- The files are relatively small.
- ASCII is not tied to the fate of any commercial entity.
- It's versatile.
- It's used for programmers' source code, e-mail, and input to text processors.

The simplicity of ASCII text comes at a cost. No formatting information is built into the files beyond the breaking of lines with line feeds and/or carriage returns (these are invisible non-printing characters that make line-wrapped files possible). Font information is lacking; the appearance of such files depends on the capabilities of the video display or the printer's built-in fonts. It is a bare-bones file format, but you can be sure that anything saved in plain text will be readable in the future, a guarantee that can't be made by vendors of proprietary binary file formats.

> A binary file cannot be read in a text editor. Executable or shared library files on your Linux system are binary files. Commercial applications such as word processors and spreadsheets have traditionally used binary file formats for a user's documents. These file formats can be changed at the whim of the software vendor and often aren't read accurately by other manufacturers' products.

Although formatting information isn't a part of a plain-text file, a variety of text-processing languages and systems can be used to add that formatting to an ASCII text file in the form of markup or tags, special characters that tell the text-processing system how to represent sections of text. This chapter introduces several methods of writing text with Emacs, processing the file, and ending up with a professional-looking printable file.

Text Processing and Word Processing

Word processors have become ubiquitous in recent years. They provide an easy way to produce formatted documents, but they do have a few limitations. The proprietary binary file format locks the user into using one application, and the documents' portability is compromised.

Tag-based formatting languages give you the advantage of separating the document's content from its formatting instructions, although they both are in the same file. Your content can be extracted and used with another formatting language or exported to a word processor. This approach is also more dependable when you're writing longer documents, such as research papers or books.

Another advantage to text-formatters is that they don't have to be used interactively, i.e. you don't necessarily have to be present. A formatter such as TeX can be set up to periodically generate printable documents from an input source which changes over time, such as a database or logging facility. Word-processors in general are best used interactively.

A variety of applications are available for Linux that translate files written in one text-processing language into equivalent files written in another language. As an example, a file written in LaTeX can be translated into HTML, and vice versa.

Several modes for Emacs simplify writing documents in these tag-based languages, providing hot keys, menus, and font locking.

When a Word Processor Is More Appropriate

In some situations, using a word processor is the best choice. Many companies, universities, and government agencies have made Microsoft Word their standard for document exchange. Many law firms use WordPerfect. In these environments, most users feel they have no choice.

After you have used Emacs enough to realize how well it can expedite the writing process, you might find yourself wanting to export text files to a word processor, making these documents more accessible to colleagues and coworkers. If you have ever tried this, you might have noticed that most word processors don't handle text very well that has been wrapped into paragraphs with `auto-fill-mode`.

The problem is that word processors store paragraphs internally as one long line. They tend to get confused when importing ASCII text and often reformat the paragraphs inconsistently, requiring you to do a lot of cleanup before the file is acceptable.

There are a couple of ways to remedy this situation. One way is to first change the `fill-column` setting (the column number at which auto-fill wraps a line). Change it to a large number, such as 1,000, by pressing Ctrl-u and typing `1000`. Then press Ctrl-x f.

Ctrl-u is the "universal argument" prefix, a keystroke combination that allows you to give an argument to the command that follows. Ctrl-x f runs the function `set-fill-column`. The combination of the two sets the `fill-column` to `1000`, which in effect gives you paragraphs made up of one long line. If you write paragraphs that contain more than 1,000 characters, you can use a higher number.

The next step is to press Ctrl-x h. This is the keybinding for the "mark the entire buffer" command. The entire buffer is now a selected region.

The last step is to press M-x and type

```
fill-region
```

Each paragraph will now be one line, although the pseudo-wrapping that Emacs uses keeps all the text visible. This sequence of commands doesn't take as long as you might think after reading the description. If you find yourself doing this often, you can turn the entire command sequence into a keyboard macro and give it a keybinding.

Here are some lines that could be inserted into your ~/.emacs file to define two macros and assign keybindings:

```
(defalias 'unwrap
  (read-kbd-macro "C-u 1000 C-x f C-x h M-x fill- region RET"))
  (global-set-key '[(control c) (u)] 'unwrap)


(defalias 'wrap
  (read-kbd-macro "C-u 72 C-x f C-x h M-x fill- region RET"))
  (global-set-key '[(control c) (w)] 'wrap)
```

The second macro, named `wrap`, reverses the effect of the first one. You could use it after unwrapping a file and exporting it to a word processor. It re-wraps the paragraphs to a usable `fill-column` setting for further editing.

LaTeX, HTML, and Lout As Alternatives

HTML (*HyperText Markup Language*) is the easiest way to produce formatted text if your needs are fairly simple. HTML is a tag-based markup language that supports images, tables, different fonts, and various text and header sizes. It has formatting ability roughly equivalent to that of a rudimentary word processor. The major Web browsers can export files to a printer. With Linux, successful printing depends on a working GhostScript setup (or a PostScript printer), because Netscape translates files to PostScript format before sending them to the print queue.

There is no text-processing step, because the file is interpreted and displayed by a Web browser, an application present on nearly all computers.

Using LaTeX or Lout is a bit more involved. Although effective Emacs modes exist for both of these text systems, you need to have the appropriate text-processing systems installed and configured before you can view or print your files. Setting up a TeX/LaTeX installation once was a difficult task, but a good Linux distribution should have preconfigured packages available. Lout has never been difficult to set up, but the distribution packages still help.

LaTeX (which is based on Don Knuth's TeX system) and Lout are both well-suited for producing complex and lengthy book-length documents, but they also can be used for tasks as simple as writing a business letter. Excellent support for mathematical symbols and equations has resulted in LaTeX's (and, to a lesser degree, Lout) becoming a standard in the scientific community.

The ultimate output of both the LaTeX and Lout text processors is a PostScript file. As with printing HTML with a Web browser, a working GhostScript installation along with the proper printing filters for your printer are necessary for viewing and printing your files.

Printing Filters

A printing filter is a convenient layer between you and the printing daemon (often lpr or lprng). These filters put a new entry in your /etc/printcap file that sends a file being printed to GhostScript with all the arcane command switches your printer needs in order to produce the highest-quality output. The two most popular filters are magicfilter and apsfilter. magicfilter hasn't been under active development lately, but it works fine with older models of printers. apsfilter is the one to choose if you have a newer inkjet printer. Both should be available as packages for your Linux distribution.

HTML Modes

You have two choices when you decide that you need to generate HTML files. You can use a WYSIWYG HTML editor, which hides the tagging and displays the text as it would appear in a Web browser. If you aren't familiar with HTML, this might seem like a godsend, but there are some drawbacks. Using this type of application necessarily insulates you from what is really happening behind the scenes. The developers of your application can't anticipate every user's needs, so the resulting Web page might not be quite what you had in mind. These applications often produce HTML that is practically unreadable in a text editor.

Other commercial HTML editors do show you the tags in your file as you write it. This is the approach that the Emacs HTML modes use. You end up with greater control over how your file is ultimately displayed, but you need to know a bit more about what those tags actually mean.

It's not difficult to learn the basics of HTML. There exists a popular superstition (promulgated by some writers of HTML) that HTML is a programming language; thus, people who write HTML are programmers. This isn't true. HTML is one of the simpler text markup languages, and it doesn't take much more than an afternoon to pick up the basic principles. Many Web sites (as well as books) can help you learn these basic ideas, although an hour or so fooling around with one of the Emacs HTML modes will help you learn enough to get started.

Setting up to Write HTML

Nobody should have to manually type in the tags in an HTML file. There are too many convenient means of avoiding this tiresome task—among them, the various Emacs HTML modes. Take a look at Figure 13.1. It gives you an idea of the appearance of a typical HTML file.

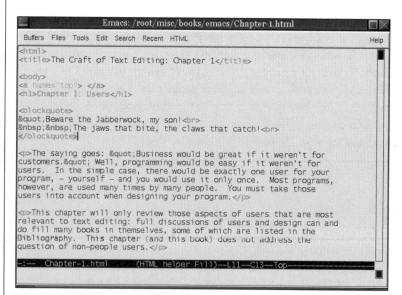

Figure 13.1 *An HTML File*

Notice how all the tags are enclosed in angle brackets (<>). These brackets are awkward to type because they are shifted characters (like uppercase letters)—Shift-, and Shift-..

Several modes ease the task of writing HTML documents. Which one should you choose? Try them all and see which one suits you. I prefer `html-helper-mode`, but the others have their faithful adherents.

GNU Emacs' Built-in Mode

The default HTML mode that comes with GNU Emacs is fine for occasional use, but it doesn't offer many features. I won't describe it here, because mode-help (Ctrl-h m) will explain it if you are interested. If you do use this mode, you will notice that HTML buffers aren't font-locked by default. You can turn on font-locking for this mode at any time by pressing M-x and typing

```
font-lock-mode
```

If you'd like automatic syntax highlighting for all HTML buffers, insert this line into your ~/.emacs file:

```
(add-hook 'html-mode-hook 'turn-on-font-lock)
```

If you write HTML often, consider learning either `html-helper-mode` or hm—html-menus, both of which offer shortcut keys and menus for the majority of HTML tags.

html-helper-mode

This mode was written over a period of several years by Nelson Minar; recently, Gian Uberto Lauri became the new maintainer. This mode isn't quite as complex and feature-rich as hh-html-menus and psgml-html, but it has enough menu items and hot keys to expedite writing all but the most involved HTML.

Two versions are available on the net (and on this book's CD-ROM). Nelson Minar's most recent version is 2.19.1.1. This one isn't being actively maintained, but it works well in both XEmacs and GNU Emacs. Gian Uberto Lauri has been releasing new versions regularly, but the most recent releases I've tried have worked for me only in GNU Emacs. The improvements he has made involve support for *.php and *.asp files (*Personal Home Page* and *Active Server Page*), as well as Java support. He also has incorporated an interface to Customize so that user variables can be set easily.

Either version is easy to install. After copying the file to your site-lisp directory, insert these lines into your ~/.emacs file, and you will be ready to edit HTML:

```
(autoload 'html-helper-mode "html-helper-mode" "Yay HTML" t)
(setq auto-mode-alist (cons '("\\.html$" . html-helper-mode) auto-mode-alist))
```

Restart Emacs and load an HTML file. It should look similar to Figure 13.1.

The menu that `html-helper-mode` generates can appear in two forms, Novice and Expert. I recommend switching to Expert mode, because many more tags are available from this menu. If you want to make this the default, load the html-helper-mode.el file into Emacs and change these lines:

```
(defvar html-helper-use-expert-menu nil
  "*If not nil, then use the full HTML menu.")
```

to this:

```
(defvar html-helper-use-expert-menu t
  "*If not nil, then use the full HTML menu.")
```

Finding these lines can be quick and easy if you use the incremental search facility. Press Ctrl-s and type

```
expert-menu
```

This should take you to the lines that need editing. Edit them, save the file, and select Byte-compile This File from the Emacs-Lisp menu. The next time you start Emacs and load an HTML file, the Expert menu will appear (see Figure 13.2). Don't be put off by the name; you don't have to be an expert to use this menu! It just gives you many more choices for tag insertion.

The menu is handy, but the keybindings (which use the Ctrl-c prefix) are quicker to use. Let's take a look at how they are organized by secondary prefix. The primary prefix is Ctrl-c, which is followed by another Ctrl prefix that has (for the most part) a mnemonic value.

For example, Ctrl-c Ctrl-l is a dual prefix for list-related tags. Those keystrokes followed by u will insert the tags for an unordered list, whereas following them with o inserts tags for an ordered list. An i results in another list item.

Rather than fill several pages with a complete list of keybindings (there are a quite a few!). I recommend that you use the menus as a learning aid. Each tag on the menu is followed by its keybinding. You should learn just a few at the beginning— the ones that are used constantly. Using the menu to insert these tags would rapidly become annoying.

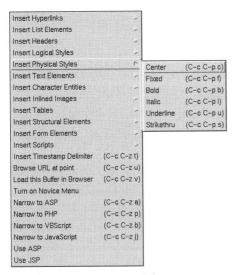

Figure 13.2   *The html-helper Menu*

These keybindings are enough to get you off to a good start. You will gradually absorb other keybindings by repeatedly seeing them on the menu.

M-Enter	Inserts the <p> paragraph tag.
M-Tab	Completes a partially-typed tag.
Ctrl-c Ctrl-t [1-6]	Inserts a header tag <h1></h1>, from 1 (the largest) to 6 (the smallest).
Ctrl-c M-h [1-6]	Gian Uberto Lauri's newer version uses this rather than Ctrl-c Ctrl-t [1-6] for headers.
Ctrl-c -	Inserts the horizontal rule tag, <hr>.
Ctrl-c Enter	Inserts a forced line break, .
Ctrl-c Ctrl-a l	Inserts an HTML link, <a href=""></a>.
Ctrl-c Spacebar	Inserts a nonbreaking space, .

Another category of tag helps you insert special characters in the HTML language. What if you wanted to use an angle bracket in an HTML file? If you just typed one in, the HTML interpreter (such as Netscape or Lynx) would think it was part of a tag and would be confused. The ampersand (&) character is also a special character (as in the nonbreaking space tag,) and can't be included directly. There are special HTML tags to handle these situations:

Ctrl-c <   Inserts a literal less-than character, <.

Ctrl-c >   Inserts a literal greater-than character, >.

Ctrl-c &   Inserts a literal ampersand, &.

You might have noticed that there are two types of tags: single tags, like <hr>, and double tags, which enclose some sort of content, like the header tag <h1></h1> . html-helper-mode is smart enough to realize that if you insert a double tag, the next thing you will do is fill in the content, such as the header title between header tags. In order to make this easier for you, the cursor is automatically placed between the tags when a double tag is inserted.

If you are an HTML beginner, you might insert a double tag and not realize that content needs go between the tags. You can tell the mode that you would like to be prompted in the minibuffer whenever such a tag is inserted. This variable can be changed with Customize. Press M-x and type

```
customize-variable
```

When prompted, type

```
tempo-interactive
```

The default value is `nil`, which results in no prompting. Toggle the value to `t` in the Customize buffer to turn on prompting.

With the value set to `t`, try inserting a header tag in an HTML buffer using the appropriate keybinding from the list shown earlier. The left tag is inserted, and a minibuffer prompt appears:

```
Header:
```

Type a header name and press Enter. The tag is filled in with your content, followed by the closing tag.

This prompting will occur with all two-element tags. After you've gained some facility with HTML, you will probably want to change the variable back to `nil`, because it is quicker to have the cursor waiting between tags rather than use the minibuffer.

Timestamps in HTML files are a useful convention. A timestamp is a piece of text inserted into a file stating the author's name and the date and time of the file's last modification. Many HTML files are intended for use on the World Wide Web, a dynamic medium compared to hard-copy printouts. These files are regularly updated (at least on maintained sites), and both the HTML writer and the reader like to be able to determine when a Web page was last updated.

`html-helper-mode` has an automatic timestamp feature. When this is turned on, the timestamp is updated whenever the buffer is saved. You turn on this feature by pasting this line into your ~/.emacs file, right after the other `html-helper-mode` lines:

```
(setq html-helper-do-write-file-hooks t)
```

If you want your name and e-mail address to appear along with the time and date, insert these lines too:

```
(setq html-helper-address-string
    "<a href=\"mailto: user@your.net\">Your Name&lt;user@your.net&gt;</a>")
```

Built into the mode is a template for new HTML files. If this feature is turned on, the necessary elements that an HTML file needs are inserted into every new HTML file. Figure 13.3 shows such a newly-created file.

This feature is also activated with an entry in your ~/.emacs file:

```
(setq html-helper-build-new-buffer t)
```

Like the native GNU Emacs mode, html-helper-mode can invoke the browse-url package, which loads the current buffer into your preferred Web browser. This can be anything from the text-mode Lynx browser to Netscape. Use Customize to choose the browser and any command-line switches by pressing M-x and typing

```
customize-group
```

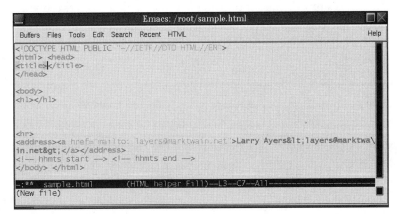

Figure 13.3 *An HTML Template*

When prompted, enter

```
browse-url
```

This speeds up HTML composition when you can view your file in a browser easily, reloading the file periodically as you make changes.

Many HTML files were originally plain-text files to which tags were applied later. Some HTML authors even prefer to work this way, writing the content first and then converting the file to HTML. This often results in a common situation: You are reading back over the file, and you see a phrase that should have been tagged as bold. If you press Ctrl-c Ctrl-p b (the bold font key sequence), you end up with `<b></b>`. But you need that phrase to be surrounded by the opening and closing tags.

The solution? First, select the area to be tagged as a region, and then press Ctrl-u before you press the key sequence. The tags will neatly surround the selected text. This works with all paired tags. html-helper-mode has co-opted the Ctrl-u "universal argument" key sequence so that its effect is "tag the selected region".

hm——html-menus

If you prefer to use the mouse rather than the keyboard to insert HTML tags, this package might be just the thing. Heiko Münkel wrote hm—html-menus as a package that could be used by the HTML novice but that had enough features to attract HTML veterans. The most recent version (5.9) is a couple of years old, but it works well with both GNU Emacs and XEmacs. The XEmacs package maintainers have modified it somewhat so that the mode integrates well into the new packaging scheme. Install the XEmacs package following the instructions in Chapter 12.

Installing GNU Emacs is simply a matter of copying the Lisp files from this book's CD-ROM. You can find the necessary files in the directory /cdrom/packages/ hm—html-menus. Install the files in your site-lisp directory and the Info documentation file in /usr/local/info. You can also obtain the package from ftp:// ftp.tnt.uni-hannover.de/pub/editors/xemacs/contrib.

Activating this package and making it the default mode for HTML files requires adding a rather large chunk of Lisp to your ~/.emacs file. I imagine that you would rather not retype the necessary code, so I've put it in a file named config.el, which you can find in the /cdrom/packages/hm—html-menus directory on the CD-ROM. You can copy and paste from that file or from the hm—html-menus Info file, which is included with the package. If you have installed `html-helper-mode`, you need to comment out with semicolons the activation lines for that mode.

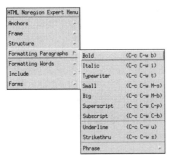

Figure 13.4   *The hm—html
Mouse Menu*

This package differs from html-helper in that most of the functionality is in mouse-button-menus rather than menu-bar menus. Figure 13.4 shows the main mouse menu and one of the submenus.

This package has more tag keybindings than html-helper-mode, but many of them are lengthy enough to be difficult to remember and use. For example, the binding for the table tag is Ctrl-c Ctrl-s Ctrl-t t. This is why I earlier suggested this package for users who prefer mouse to keyboard commands. It is quicker to select from a menu than to type such finger-twisting commands.

For some reason, the XEmacs package maintainers changed many of the keybindings when they made hm—html-menus into an official XEmacs package. This could be annoying and confusing if you use both GNU Emacs and XEmacs.

hm—html-menus has a clever way of dealing with the recurring need to surround selected regions of text with tags. Notice in Figure 13.4 that the menu title is HTML Noregion Expert Menu. If you select some text, the title changes to HTML Region Expert Menu; any tag selected from the menu will now enclose the selected region.

A template minor mode is included with hm—html-menus; it's called tmpl-minor-mode.el, and it can be used for template expansion with any major mode. This minor mode comes into play when you create a new HTML file. You are prompted in the minibuffer for the location of your template files. Type in the directory where you installed hm—html-menus, and it will be remembered for future sessions. A sample template is included with the package, but you need to edit it or use it as a model when writing your own.

psgml and HTML

psgml is a large and complex package developed by Lennart Stafflin to help writers working with SGML documents. Since HTML is a subset of SGML, it is also possible to use psgml to write HTML documents, although XEmacs has better support for this.

This package as distributed isn't set up to work specifically with HTML documents, but hm—html-menus used as a minor mode in conjunction with psgml is a quite effective, if complex, HTML editing environment. psgml has file-parsing abilities. In other words, it can read through a file, checking for syntax errors. It can also be used in conjunction with the sgmls external parser.

Installing psgml for XEmacs is just a matter of retrieving the preconfigured package, as detailed in Chapter 12. The XEmacs package version of psgml is quite different from the release version. Large portions of `html-helper-mode` have been folded in; in general, the mode is much more suited for HTML editing.

In order to use hm—html-menus as a minor mode (assuming you have already installed the hm—html-menus package), insert this line into your ~/.emacs file:

```
(add-hook 'html-mode-hook 'hm--html-minor-mode)
```

Try psgml both with and without hm—html-menus as a minor mode; the two together might be more than you need. Figure 13.5 shows the menu layout with both modes enabled.

This is a complex array of menus and submenus with three sections. The new items toward the left are psgml menus: Modify, Move, Markup, and DTD. You can ignore most of the items under these menus while writing HTML, because they pertain to SGML rather than specifically to HTML. The DTD menu is applicable to HTML files.

A DTD (*Document Type Definition*) is a text file that corresponds to a particular type of SGML document. A DTD defines the valid elements that can be used in a markup language like HTML. The SGML parser (like the one included with psgml) parses (reads and absorbs) the HTML DTD and uses this information when validating an HTML file. Think of validation as error-checking that helps you write proper HTML.

HTML has evolved into a rather sloppily-enforced language. A Web browser can process and display malformed or incomplete HTML. In order to take advantage

Modify Move Markup DTD HM-HTML HTML Insert

Figure 13.5   *XEmacs psgml Menus*

of psgml's validation features, an HTML file should have a first line that states the DTD, because there are several versions of HTML and thus several possible DTDs. That first line should look something like this:

```
<!DOCTYPE HTML PUBLIC "-//W3C//DTD HTML 4.01 Transitional//EN">
```

All the HTML modes discussed in this book include such a line in their default templates for new files.

Among the files that make up the XEmacs psgml package are a collection of DTDs for different versions of HTML, Docbook (an SGML package used for technical documentation), and XML. One of these files will be consulted when you use psgml to check your HTML files.

Moving toward the right along the menu bar, you will find the hm—html minor mode menu, which is similar to the menu displayed when hm—html-menus is the major mode. The most useful items on this menu are the toggle item for setting the skill level (Novice or Expert) of the mouse menu and the item that loads the current buffer into a Web browser. The mouse menu when hm—html-menus is a minor mode under psgml is the same as the hm—html-menus major mode mouse menu (see Figure 13.4).

The last two new menus belong to psgml's HTML mode. The HTML menu, shown in Figure 13.6, contains several useful functions, some of which duplicate items on the hm—html-menus menu, such as the file-previewing items. The Validate item on this menu checks your file against the appropriate DTD and points out any syntax errors. This is psgml's strong point.

The Insert menu, shown in Figure 13.7, is a series of nested menus full of tag-insertion commands. These are the commands incorporated from html-helper-mode but with different keybindings. A significant difference between this menu and the original html-helper menu is that the keybindings aren't displayed next to each menu item. This is unfortunate, because their presence in both html-helper-mode

Figure 13.6   *The HTML Menu*

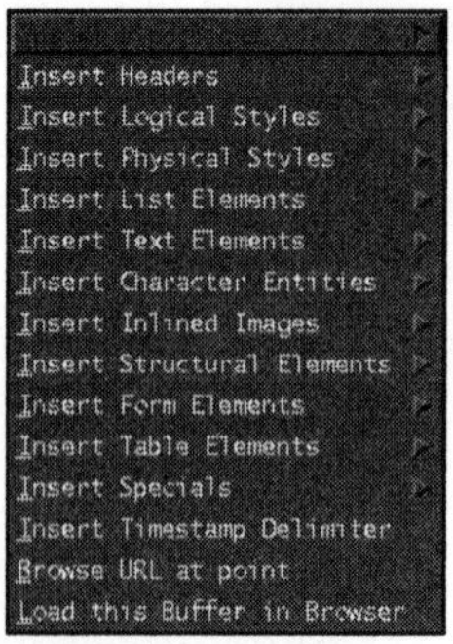

Figure 13.7   *The Insert Menu*

and hm—html-menus serves as a convenient learning aid. You can view a list of psgml's keybindings by pressing Ctrl-h b, the mode keybinding help key.

Unlike the first two HTML modes described, the XEmacs psgml-based HTML mode doesn't come with any specific documentation. psgml itself has a comprehensive set of Info files, but the emphasis is on SGML in general, with no mention of HTML editing. You can learn this mode by trial and error. Select various menu items and see if what they do is useful to you. Eventually, you will develop a toolkit of helpful commands while learning to ignore others.

The main advantage of this HTML mode lies in its validation and error-checking abilities. The tag-insertion menus are more difficult to use than in the other HTML modes, and for keyboard-oriented users, the keybindings are overly long. One possible approach to using this mode is to do the bulk of your editing in one of the other HTML modes and then use psgml-html to check your file.

psgml for GNU Emacs is another matter. Evidently, some people have learned to be productive writing HTML with psgml alone, but it isn't easy. If I had a spare chapter or two, I could outline the procedure, but I have a feeling that the audience would be small. If hm—html-menus as a minor mode could automatically be linked to psgml, it might be more usable, but unfortunately that works only with the XEmacs version of psgml.

Any of the three HTML modes discussed here can be useful. Try them all, and you'll most likely settle on one that fits your working style.

LaTeX or Lout?

Either of these text-processing systems can produce high-quality documents. Each has pros and cons.

Here are the LaTeX pros:

- A large user community, which results in a wider variety of add-on packages.
- Accepted by more scientific publications (mandatory in some cases).
- It's been around longer; the code is more mature and bug-free.
- Commercially printed documentation is available.

Here are the LaTeX cons:

- It's more difficult to adapt to your needs; changing the defaults can be difficult.
- A much larger installation.
- It's more difficult to add new fonts.

Here are the Lout pros:

- Including graphics is easier.
- Making new document styles requires less expertise.
- Uses standard PostScript fonts.
- The Lout distribution fits on a single floppy disk.
- Ships with copious documentation.

Here are the Lout cons:

- Smaller user community.
- The Emacs modes available are less refined than AUCTeX.
- Lout uses more of your computer's memory.

There is no reason you can't use both systems, although each has a learning curve that might make this impractical. Try them out, and see which one fits your needs.

LaTeX

Typing a document marked up with LaTeX tagging can be a tedious and time-consuming job. The Emacs TeX/LaTeX modes, especially AUCTeX, can make writing this sort of markup nearly as easy as writing an ordinary text file. Figure 13.8 is a typical LaTeX document.

As you can see, the tagging characters are highlighted, which helps you keep them mentally separate from the actual content of the file. The backslash indicates a LaTeX command, and curly brackets, dollar signs, and percent symbols abound. This is the sort of file that an Emacs mode can handle well, full of elements you would rather not have to type repeatedly.

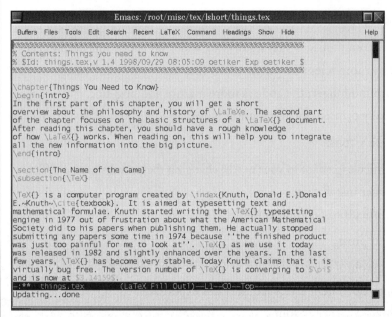

Figure 13.8   *A LaTeX Buffer*

TeX, LaTeX, and Linux

There isn't much point in generating LaTeX documents without some means of running them through the TeX processor. Even if you don't intend to print a hard copy on your local machine, you need to be able to preview a TeX-generated PostScript file, just to make sure that the document is satisfactory.

Luckily, any Linux distribution worth its salt has preconfigured TeX and LaTeX packages available. Most distributions use Thomas Esser's well-maintained teTeX package as the basis for their distribution packages. A teTeX installation is bulky, taking up to 60 MB of disk space. This isn't really all that much compared to most word-processor installations, and the output has the potential of being consistently higher in quality.

Not sure if teTeX is installed? Type

```
locate latex
```

This will result in

```
/usr/bin/latex
```

if the package is installed. If it isn't, consider installing your distribution's package or packages before finishing this chapter so that you will be able to try the examples.

TeX and LaTeX can be run from the command line, but AUCTeX, the Emacs mode recommended in this book, can run the necessary commands for you as well as take you to trouble spots in your LaTeX buffers.

A Basic TeX Mode

Both GNU Emacs and XEmacs provide a simple tex-mode for editing TeX and LaTeX files; the XEmacs version is part of the Texinfo package. Neither version is described in detail in this chapter, because these modes aren't very full-featured. If AUCTeX hasn't been installed, tex-mode is the default mode for *.tex files. Font locking and a few keybindings are provided, but there are no tag-insertion commands or menus. The Ctrl-h m mode-help key command tells you all you need to know about this mode. One advantage for the casual TeX user is that this mode doesn't take long to learn.

AUCTeX

AUCTeX is a hoary old package in the compressed chronology of computer programs, where a couple of years sees many changes. It even antedates Linux by several years. In 1986, Lars Peter Fischer wrote some macro extensions for the Emacs version 16 TeX mode. Per Abrahamsen made his first contributions the following year, and soon after, Kresten Krab Thorup released the first version of AUCTeX. Per Abrahamsen is the current maintainer. New versions are released regularly, and there is a large worldwide community of users, many of whom contribute patches and enhancements. AUCTeX lets you avoid typing environment tags due to its impressive array of menus and keybindings.

Installation

XEmacs users can install AUCTeX by installing the AUCTeX package (see Chapter 12 for instructions). One more step is necessary to activate the package. Insert this line into your ~/.emacs file:

```
(require 'tex-site)
```

and you will be ready to edit TeX and LaTeX files.

GNU Emacs users can find the AUCTeX archive file on this book's CD-ROM in the directory /cdrom/packages/auctex. Expand the archive in a temporary directory, and load the makefile into an Emacs session.

This makefile will byte-compile and install the necessary files for you, but a little editing is in order before you run the `make` command. You can also create a subdirectory of the site-lisp directory named auctex and install the files there. This isn't absolutely necessary, but it is helpful to keep the many files AUCTeX installs in one place rather than mix them up with other site-lisp files.

The section of the makefile that needs to be changed is near the beginning and looks like this:

```
##-------------------------------------------------------------------
##   YOU MUST EDIT THE FOLLOWING LINES
##-------------------------------------------------------------------


# Where local software is found
prefix=/usr/local


# Where info files go.
infodir = $(prefix)/info


# Where local lisp files go.
lispdir = $(prefix)/share/emacs/site-lisp


# Where the AUC TeX emacs lisp files go.
aucdir=$(lispdir)/auctex


# Name of your emacs binary
EMACS=emacs
```

Edit these lines so that they reflect your Emacs installation, and then (from a terminal window) run the `make` command after switching to the directory that contains the unarchived AUCTeX files. Just type

```
make
```

The makefile invokes Emacs in noninteractive mode. The result is that the AUCTeX Lisp files will be byte-compiled by your version of Emacs. When this process is finished, type

```
make install
```

The files will be copied to the directory you specified in the makefile.

One last step, and you will be ready to use the package. Insert this line into your ~/ .emacs file:

```
(require 'tex-site)
```

The next time you start Emacs, load a *.tex file. The AUCTeX menus should appear.

Syncing with Your TeX Installation

The default settings should work on most Linux systems. If AUCTeX balks when you try to process files with TeX, your TeX installation might be different than usual. Take a look at the tex-site.el file installed in your site-lisp directory; it has default paths and settings that might need to be changed. Luckily, AUCTeX also has extensive Customize support. Press M-x and type

```
customize-group
```

When prompted, type

```
AUC-TeX
```

A multilevel AUCTeX Customize buffer appears. Most settings can probably be left as is, but you might find one that makes all the difference.

Menus and Keybindings

This aspect of AUCTeX saves you time and makes writing LaTeX files tolerable. Why not create a new, empty buffer so that you can try these features? Give the buffer a name like xxx.tex so that AUCTeX will be loaded automatically. Notice the two new menus on the menu bar, Command and LaTeX. Setting aside the Command menu for the moment, take a look at the LaTeX menu, shown in Figure 13.9.

The Insert Environment item on this menu is one of the most frequently-used commands, and it is the first one to run on a new LaTeX file. If you use the keybinding Ctrl-c Ctrl-e instead of the menu item, you are prompted for an environment name. AUCTeX has reasonable defaults for this command. If your file is empty, the default environment (shown in parentheses in the minibuffer) is `documentclass article`. Pressing Enter inserts the correct tags and places the cursor between them.

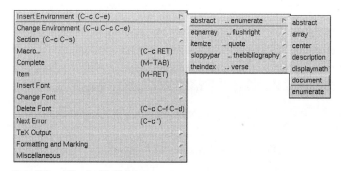

Figure 13.9 *The LaTeX Menu*

> In LaTeX jargon, an *environment* is the category of text between two defining tags. This includes lists, quotations, various mathematical forms, tables, and many others. Environments can be nested. For example, the outermost environment is the document class, which sets parameters for the entire document, such as what subsections are valid. This book's document class uses chapters for subsections, whereas an article uses sections. Many LaTeX environments are analogous to the various HTML tags, although LaTeX has many more possibilities.

LaTeX files need a few basic tags in order to be valid. The first is the document class tag, which lets TeX know whether the file is intended to be a book, an article, or a report. Immediately following a backslashed tag can be a statement in curly brackets. This can be a section or chapter name or any variable value that might apply to a tag. Think of them as the arguments to a formatting command.

The actual content of your chapter or section is typed like any other text. You don't need to worry about formatting, because TeX does this for you when you process the file. There are things you need to keep in mind while writing this type of file. Eight characters have a special meaning to the TeX program, and they can't be inserted literally unless you precede them with a backslash:

$	}
&	-
%	\
{	^

For example, if you needed a numerical dollar amount in a file, you would write `\$32.00`. The backslash is an exception to this rule, because `\\` is defined as the "force a new line" command. To insert a backslash in a file, you need to write it like this:

```
$\backslash$
```

Another possible source of errors to keep in mind is that all "begin" tags must be balanced by an "end" tag, and all curly brackets must be in matched pairs. AUCTeX helps you keep track of these, because it always inserts both beginning and ending tags when you use the menu or keybindings to insert environment tags.

Here is something else to try in your new file. Select List from the Insert Environment submenu. A pair of tags defining a list appears in your buffer, along with the first "item" tag, and your cursor will be where it needs to be so that you can easily write the list item. Write something there, and then press M-Enter. A new list

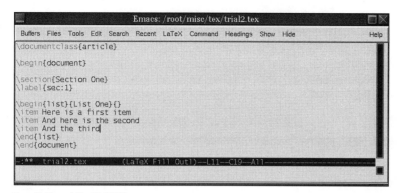

Figure 13.10 *A LaTeX List*

item appears, and again the cursor is repositioned. The result should look something like Figure 13.10.

AUCTeX can also complete partially-typed tags for you. If you do much writing of LaTeX files, you will eventually use tags that aren't on the menu or bound to keys, and this feature lets you type just the first few characters of a tag. AUCTeX scans the LaTeX files you are editing and builds an internal list of the tags you have been using. It uses this list as a source of completions.

The limitations of this chapter prevent me from going into more detail about LaTeX usage. This book's CD-ROM has an excellent LaTeX introduction and tutorial by Tobias Oetiker called "The Not So Short Introduction to LaTeX2e". It is in the form of unprocessed LaTeX files. I recommend that you copy this file, lshort.tar.gz, to your hard disk and unarchive it. You can find this file in the CD-ROM directory /cdrom/doc. You can use these files as practice material in the next section. As a side benefit, you will end up with a printable PostScript file of this book.

Running TeX

The Command menu is where you find AUCTeX's interface to the actual TeX processing commands. These commands can be run from any terminal window; the advantage of using AUCTeX is that it keeps track of errors in your files and takes you right to the trouble spots so that you can deal with them.

Try this out by loading the master LaTeX file from the lshort.tar.gz archive. The file you need is lshort.tex.

Once you have this file in an Emacs buffer, select LaTeX Interactive from the Command menu. This hands the file over to your TeX system. A new window opens, displaying the messages that TeX emits as it goes about its task. If the process is successful, a message is displayed in the minibuffer, as shown in Figure 13.11.

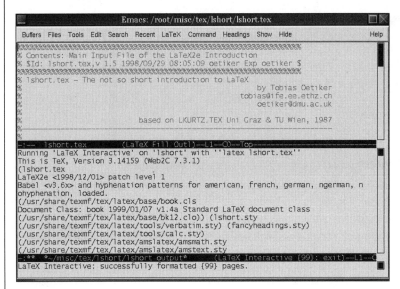

Figure 13.11   *A LaTeX Interactive Session*

Viewing and Printing Your File

If you want to view the resultant DVI file, select View from the Command menu. A command line invoking xdvi (which should be part of your TeX installation) appears in the minibuffer so that you can edit it if necessary. If you want to generate a printable PostScript file, select ps from the Print submenu. The dvips command line appears in the minibuffer. You need a PostScript viewer such as gv or GhostScript to view the file. See the sidebar titled "Printing Filters" earlier in this chapter for information about printing PostScript files.

Many more commands and features in AUCTeX are beyond the scope of this brief introduction. The Info files that come with AUCTeX are well-written and complete and should be your next source of learning material.

Lout

The Lout text-processing system is the brainchild of Jeffrey H. Kingston at the University of Sydney in Australia. (Lout is a contraction of "layout.") It has most of the capabilities of TeX/LaTeX, with a fraction of its size and complexity. Lout has been under development for 16 years. It began as a university research project and evolved into a package of GNU-licensed free software. As users began to contribute features and suggestions, over the years Lout became quite versatile and powerful, yet with less of a learning curve than LaTeX. See the earlier section "LaTeX or Lout?" for a comparison of the two.

From a user's point of view, the two formatting systems have much in common. Tags are indicated by certain reserved characters. These tags control not only structural formatting, such as sections and chapters, but character-level characteristics such as font selection.

Eric Marsden has written a Lout major mode for Emacs called lout-mode.el. It isn't as large and complex as AUCTeX, but it does have keybindings and menu items for the majority of tags. Font locking is supported, allowing the tags to be displayed in a subdued color. You can run the Lout processor from within the mode and step through errors just as in AUCTeX.

Installing Lout

You can find both RPM and *.deb packages on this book's CD-ROM in the directory /cdrom/packages/lout. A source archive is also included in case you prefer to compile your own. Use your distribution's package tools to install the prebuilt packages. The source package isn't much more difficult to install. You have to edit the makefile, but the instructions at the top of the file are clear. After you have done this, type

```
make ; make install
```

and you should have a new Lout installation ready to use.

The documentation for Lout is in a separate distribution RPM or *.deb. It's also included in the source archive in the form of unprocessed Lout files.

Using lout-mode

You can find lout-mode.el in the CD-ROM directory /cdrom/packages. Copy this file to your site-lisp directory and insert these lines into your ~/.emacs file:

```
(autoload 'lout-mode "lout-mode" "Major mode for editing Lout text" t)
(setq auto-mode-alist
      (append '(("\\.lout\\'" . lout-mode)) auto-mode-alist))
```

The latter two lines cause any file with the *.lout suffix to be edited in lout-mode. If you want to use a different suffix for your Lout files, edit the last line, changing \\.lout\\' to whatever you like. Don't forget to byte-compile the file: Load lout-mode.el and select Byte-compile File from the Emacs-Lisp menu.

If you are unfamiliar with Lout, you are probably wondering just what Lout markup looks like. Even if you installed the prebuilt Lout and documentation distribution packages, you might want to unpack the source archive from the CD-ROM into a temporary directory. Delete everything but the /doc directory, and then use Dired to visit that directory. The files there lack an identifying suffix. They are Lout files that, if processed, would become the Lout documentation PostScript files. You don't need to process them, because presumably you already installed the Lout documentation. They are good examples of Lout files that give you an idea of how these files are marked up.

Click the middle mouse button on one of the files in the Dired buffer to load it. It appears in Fundamental mode rather than in Lout mode, because the files don't have a suffix. Press M-x and type

```
lout-mode
```

Then press M-x and type

```
font-lock-mode
```

You should see something like Figure 13.12. (The `font-lock` command might or might not be necessary, depending on your Emacs configuration.)

Rather than the backslash, which LaTeX uses, Lout uses the @ symbol as a tag indicator. Unlike LaTeX, which interprets a blank line as a paragraph separator, Lout uses @PP to indicate the end of a paragraph.

The lout-mode menu lets you select from among the most commonly-used tags, most of which have keybindings assigned.

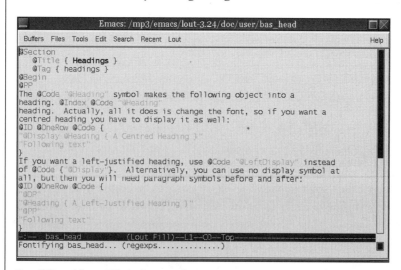

Figure 13.12   *A Lout File in lout-mode*

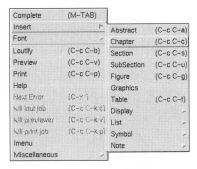

Figure 13.13   *The lout-mode Menu*

Figure 13.13 shows the lout-mode menu, which combines the functions of the two AUCTeX menus into one.

A few variables in lout-mode.el might need to be edited to match your system. You can find them at the beginning of the Lisp file:

```
(defvar lout-view-command "gv -safer"
  "*The name of the Postscript previewer on your system.
This program is called from \\[lout-view]. You can include command-line
arguments such as \"-dSAFER\" to protect against dangerous Postscript
commands.")


(defvar lout-print-command "lpx -Fps"
  "*How to print Postscript files on your system.
If this is a string it will be sent to a subshell, after having the
name of the Postscript file appended to it. If it is a function it
will be called with the name of the Postscript file as a parameter,
and should return a string which when passed to a shell, will print the
file.")
```

In the first line, you might need to change gv to ghostview if you don't have gv installed. You might consider installing gv, because it is a more featureful and convenient PostScript viewer than ghostview.

The print command varies, depending on your Linux distribution, print spooler, and filter setup. On many systems, a simple lpr is all you need.

Processing and Printing

Selecting Loutify from the Lout menu (or pressing Ctrl-c Ctrl-b) sends your file to the Lout text processor. A new window opens, displaying messages as the file is compiled into PostScript format. If errors occur, you can select Next Error from the menu (or press Ctrl-c '), and point will move to the spot in your source file that needs attention. The menu items and keybindings for Preview and Print let you view the completed PostScript file with your PostScript viewer and then send it off to be printed.

The file user.ps is a comprehensive and well-written guide for the Lout user. This file can be found in the Lout documentation package. If you installed Lout from the source archive, you need to run Lout on the file named "all" in the /doc/user subdirectory of the Lout source directory. You need to run Lout several times on the "all" file, because in a complex indexed document such as this, multiple compilations are necessary to resolve the cross-references.

Conclusion

Although HTML and LaTeX are the most popular formatting languages, Emacs also has modes for some of the lesser-used languages.

troff (and its GNU descendant, groff) was used extensively on early UNIX systems for document formatting and is still the standard for the production of UNIX, BSD, and Linux manual pages. nroff-mode offers font locking and keybindings for creating such documents.

psgml, aside from its use as a basis for the XEmacs HTML mode, is also a full-featured aid for those writing SGML and XML files.

As new methods of formatting documents are developed, undoubtedly Emacs support will follow shortly thereafter.

The next chapter introduces many time-saving Emacs modes and utilities.

Chapter 14: Built-in Convenience Packages

Abbreviation and Expansion

Bookmarks

Dired, the Emacs File Manager

Differences between Files

Spell Checking with ispell

Running a Shell in Emacs

Outline Mode

The Calendar and the Diary

ach time a new version of GNU Emacs is released, new modes and utilities are included. They are submitted by the authors or recommended by Emacs users. One benefit of using an extensible editor with such a long history is that the editor extensions have proliferated over the years.

It's not uncommon while using any piece of software to run into situations that make you exclaim, "This is so tedious! Why wasn't this software designed with a feature to make this easier?" The reason, of course, is that all software is written by human beings with limited time and foresight.

With Emacs, chances are good that someone else in the Emacs community has experienced the same frustration with a limitation of the editor and decided to write an extension. In this and the following chapters, many of these extensions, both simple and complex, are described, along with instructions for their use. This chapter focuses on the extension modes and utilities that are a part of the Emacs distributions.

Abbreviation and Expansion

Two abbreviation modes are supplied with Emacs. The idea is that rather than repeatedly typing long or awkward-to-type words, you type a few letters (the abbreviation), followed by a keybinding that expands the partial word to its full length. abbrev-mode uses previously-defined abbreviations, whereas dynamic abbreviation uses other words in the current buffer and thus requires no setting up. They each have their uses and can be used simultaneously. These modes are especially useful if you aren't a speedy typist. A short trial doesn't do them justice. After using one or both of them regularly for a period of time, you will be surprised at how much quicker typing can be.

abbrev-mode

This mode can be used in a variety of ways. You can load an abbreviation file in your ~/.emacs file so that it is always available. Alternatively, you can load such a file only when you need it. You might create a special abbreviation file for use on a particular project.

Here are the two main entry points:

Pressing M-x and typing

```
abbrev-mode
```

starts abbrev-mode so that you can define abbreviations.

Pressing M-x and typing

`edit-abbrevs`

opens your abbrev file so that you can edit, add, or delete abbreviations. After you enter abbrev-mode using the `abbrev-mode` command, you need to decide whether you want a global abbreviation, valid in all buffers and major modes, or an abbreviation that will be confined to a particular mode. Type in the new abbreviation (it doesn't matter where; the Scratch buffer will do). Depending on which type you choose, one of these two commands will begin the process:

Ctrl-x a i g	Adds a new global abbreviation.
Ctrl-x a i l	Adds a new abbreviation that will be active only in your current major mode.

You will be prompted for the string to which the abbreviation refers. Type it in the minibuffer. It will be added to a list called the global-abbrev-table.

Abbreviations don't have to be actual abbreviations; they can also be a means of correcting words you habitually mistype. For example, I have a habit when I'm typing quickly of typing "teh" rather than "the". I defined "teh" as an abbreviation for "the". Therefore, as long as abbrev-mode is turned on, this typo is corrected automatically.

A good time to add this sort of abbreviation is just after you've mistyped a word for the hundredth time. Correct the word and then use one of these commands:

Ctrl-x a g	This command uses the word before point as the expansion. You're prompted for the abbreviation, which in this case is the word as you habitually mistype it.
Ctrl-x a l	This does the same thing as Ctrl-x a g, but the abbreviation is confined to buffers in your current major mode.

When abbrev-mode is turned on, expansion of an abbrev-mode takes place only when a word-separator character is typed, such as a space or a period. If for some reason you don't want a particular abbreviation to be expanded, type the abbreviation, and then press Ctrl-q followed by whichever word separator is appropriate.

Saving Abbreviations

Any abbreviations you define are lost when you quit Emacs. If you want to save all abbreviations you've created in a session, press M-x and type

```
write-abbrev-file
```

This command writes the abbreviations to the default abbrev file, ~/.abbrev_defs. You are prompted for a file name, which you supply if you plan on using several abbrev files. Otherwise, just press Enter, and the default file will be used.

If you become a fan of this approach to abbreviations, you probably will want to add lines to your ~/.emacs file that load your abbreviations and turn on abbrev mode. These are the lines:

```
(setq-default abbrev-mode t)
(read-abbrev-file "~/.abbrev_defs")
```

Dynamic Abbreviation

I didn't discover dynamic abbreviation until a couple of years ago, but I'm an addict now. All you need is the easy keybinding

M-/

to start using dynamic abbreviation right away. This keybinding searches the current buffers for any word that begins with the characters you have already typed and then completes the word. Naturally, this only works well after you have typed a significant amount of material, but after you have used a word once, you never have to type the whole word again. There might be several words that begin with the letters you have typed. If the first result isn't what you need, press M-/ repeatedly until the proper completion is entered. That's all there is to it.

The default settings will satisfy most needs, but several variables can be altered with Customize. By default, dynamic abbreviation searches other open buffers for matches, ignoring buffers such as the Buffer List and the message log. As you can see in Figure 14.1, you can change the behavior so that searches occur only in the current buffer or, alternatively, in the current buffer along with a list of other defined buffers. How dynamic abbreviation searches respond to the case of a word is changeable, as well as whether searches are backward-only in a buffer or both forward and backward.

You can browse the Customize groups to find the Customize buffer shown in Figure 14.1 or go directly to the buffer by pressing M-x and typing

```
customize-group
```

Figure 14.1   *abbrev Customize Buffer*

Respond to the prompt with

```
abbrev
```

The Dynamic Abbreviation group buffer can be accessed from the parent group buffer (Abbreviations), which the `abbrev` command invokes. Before you select the Dynamic Abbreviations buffer, you might look through the Customize options in the parent group buffer, which affect `abbrev-mode`.

Bookmarks

Bookmarks aren't very useful in a short file, but in a long file, they can save you time spent looking for the place you need to return to. It isn't a complicated interface. If you are at a location in a file to which you know you will need to return, just press Ctrl-x r m Enter.

The default name of a bookmark is the parent buffer's name. It is suggested in parentheses (in the minibuffer) when you set or visit a bookmark without specifying a name.

If you will be setting more than one bookmark in a file, you need to give each one a name, using this variation on the preceding command: Press Ctrl-x r m, type [Name], and press Enter.

It's easy to forget bookmark names if you set several of them. Press Ctrl-x r l Enter to see a list of all the bookmarks you have set.

> XEmacs users need to install the edit-utils package in order to use the book-marks facility. See Chapter 12 for instructions.

You can set as many bookmarks as you like. Each buffer you edit has its own private bookmarks, although all of them are lost when you quit Emacs unless you save them to a bookmark file (see the next section).

Saving and Revisiting Bookmarks

You can go back to any bookmark you have set by pressing Ctrl-x r b and typing

```
[optional name]
```

You can use this command as an alternative way to change buffers, because it is a side effect of visiting a bookmark.

You can even use this command to load files. The file containing a particular named bookmark is automatically loaded when you give that name to the command. Give your bookmarks short names—just two or three characters is all that is necessary.

Not every bookmark needs to be available in all buffers. Perhaps you have a directory containing files associated with a project, and you want to keep those bookmarks separate from your main bookmark file in your home directory. Use the bookmark-save command: Press M-x and type

```
bookmark-write
```

You are asked for a file name. Type one in, and a new bookmark file is created.

If you want the bookmark to be saved to your global bookmark file, press M-x and type

```
bookmark-save
```

If you want to use the suggested default (~/.emacs.bmk), just press Enter. This default file is loaded whenever you start Emacs, whereas you must load any other bookmark file explicitly by pressing M-x and typing

```
bookmark-load
```

Use this for directory- or project-specific bookmark files.

The default bookmark file ~/.emacs.bmk is compatible across every version of GNU Emacs and XEmacs I've tried, including beta versions.

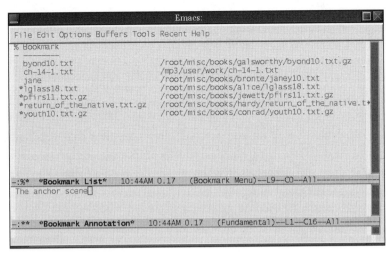

Figure 14.2   *The Bookmark List*

Another feature of Emacs' bookmarking facility is annotations. You have to enable this feature before you can use it. Go to the Customize Bookmarks buffer by pressing M-x and typing

`customize-group`

Respond to the prompt with

`bookmarks`

Toggle the Use Annotations item to on, and save the setting. You will be queried for an annotation whenever you save a bookmark. An annotation is a description or any text you want to be associated with your bookmark. This isn't really necessary in a short bookmark file, but if you have dozens of bookmarks saved, this can help you remember why you saved them. The annotations are visible in a bookmark list summoned with the Ctrl-x r l `bookmark-listing` command (see Figure 14.2). This feature can also be used as a means of keeping bookmarked notes on a file.

The Bookmark List buffer has its own set of keybindings. Here are the most important ones:

a	Shows bookmark annotations in another window (annotated bookmarks are marked with an asterisk).
1	Selects this bookmark in the current full-frame window.
j	Replaces the bookmark list with the selected bookmark.
o	Splits the window and loads the bookmark in the other window, retaining the bookmark list in its window.

k	Marks a bookmark for deletion and moves down one entry.
Ctrl-d	Marks for deletion and moves up one entry.
x	Deletes marked bookmarks.
s	Saves the list to the default bookmark file (~/.emacs.bmk).

Bookmarking works perfectly well on compressed files, assuming that you have enabled auto-compression. This feature automatically inflates a compressed file when you load it and then recompresses it when you're finished editing. You can turn this on by pressing M-x and typing

```
customize-group
```

Then type

```
jka-compr
```

when prompted. A Customize buffer appears without any apparent reference to auto-compression. Toggle the Show button next to the Compression Info List item. Your buffer should now look similar to Figure 14.3.

Most of the subitems have reasonable defaults, dealing mainly with regular expressions for recognition of compressed files. Each section has a toggle at the bottom labeled Auto Mode. Toggle this to on for each type of compression, and select Save For Future Sessions from the State menu.

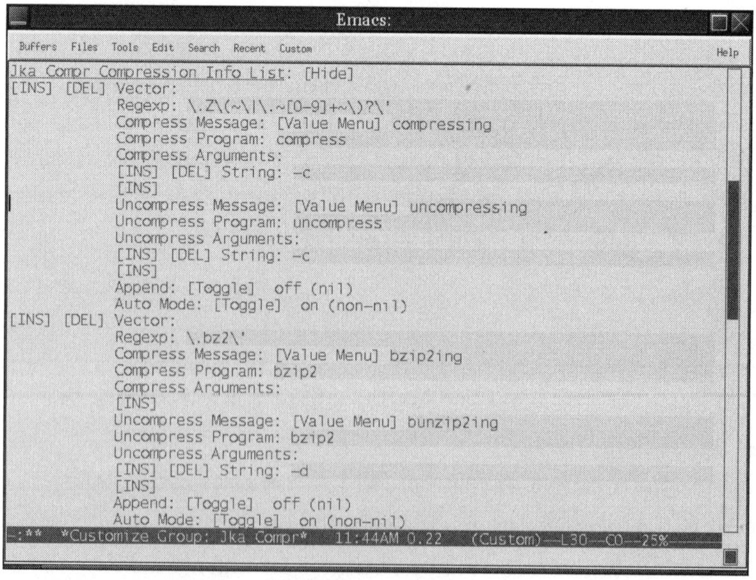

Figure 14.3   *jka-compr Customize Buffer*

Loading, saving, and bookmarking compressed files will now be nearly unnoticeable. A brief message flashing by in the minibuffer and a delay of a fraction of a second are the only signs of the behind-the-scenes activity.

Dired, the Emacs File Manager

Dired has been a part of Emacs for many years, dating from the days before file-management programs were available. Essentially, Dired is an Emacs wrapper around ls, rm, mv, and other file utilities.

Many stand-alone file managers are available for Linux these days, and most can be configured to use Emacs as the default editor for selected files. This lessens the importance of Dired for many Emacs users, but it is undeniably handy at times to be able to browse files from within Emacs. Figure 14.4 shows a typical Dired buffer.

A complex set of menus appears in Dired mode, offering a wide array of file and directory operations. One thing to keep in mind is that the file and directory listings aren't automatically updated if another program changes the contents of the directory. Typing g causes the listing (which is the output of the ls command) to be reread. Any change to the Dired buffer made with a Dired command (such as the deletion or creation of a subdirectory) is immediately reflected in the Dired listing.

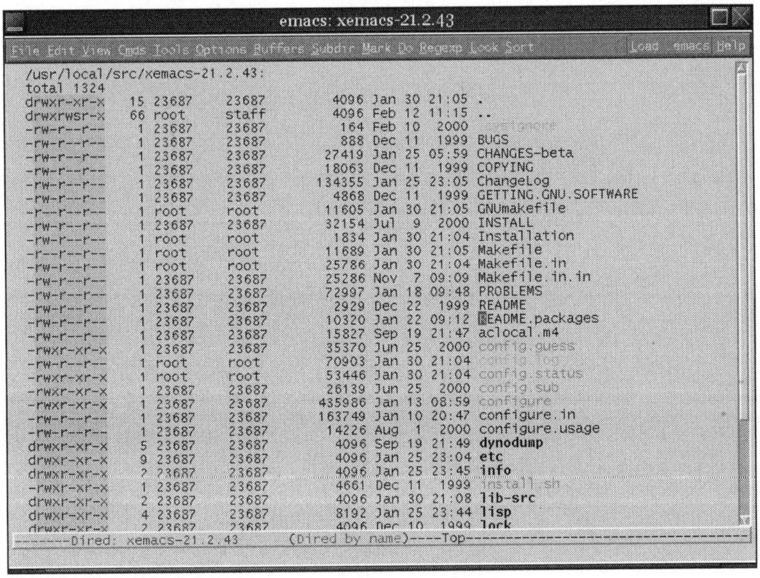

Figure 14.4   *The Dired Buffer*

Dired Keys

The key command for loading a Dired buffer is Ctrl-x d. You are prompted for a directory name. The default (shown in parentheses) is the directory of the current buffer's file. Just press Enter if you want the default; otherwise, type a directory name in the minibuffer.

When a Dired buffer appears, the default keymap is replaced with a Dired keymap. Many of the letter keys are remapped to Dired commands. These keybindings are shown in the menus next to the relevant items. Dired has many bindings, but a handful of them are all you need to get started. You will pick up others while using the menus.

Basic Dired Keys

d	Tags a file or directory for deletion.
x	Deletes tagged files, asking for confirmation first.
m	Marks or tags an item (a file or directory) for other operations.
C	Copies an item or marked files.
S	Symlinks an item (with a prompt for the name to symlink to).
R	Renames an item.
Z	Compresses an item with gzip.
v	Loads a file in View mode—read-only, with spacebar paging

The Regexp Menu

One of the more useful groups of Dired commands are those listed on the Regexp menu. These commands use regular expressions to mark or operate on files. This allows you to change quantities of files with a single command. Suppose you have a number of files that have names beginning with "QUOT", and you want them to begin with "quotes_2000". Selecting Rename from the Regexp menu would produce this prompt in the minibuffer:

```
Rename from (regexp):
```

You would type ^QUOT* in the minibuffer. Remember that the caret character (^) is the regular-expression symbol for "only at the beginning of the line".

The next prompt would be

```
Rename ^QUOT* to:
```

You would type `quotes_2000`, and all the file names would change. These regular-expression operations are confined to the left portion of file names; the file suffix is ignored.

GNU Emacs and XEmacs each provide a grep file-searching function in their respective versions of Dired, but the commands differ slightly and are found on different menus. grep is the classic GNU file utility that is used to perform regular-expression searches for text in single or multiple files. You can mark files in a Dired buffer and use a menu command to search for either a particular string of text or a regular-expression match.

The GNU Emacs grep command is Mark Containing on the Regexp menu, and the XEmacs equivalent is Grep for on the Look menu.

A new window opens, displaying the results of the search.

Customizing Dired

The Dired Customize group has several settings that can be changed. One that affects the layout of Dired buffers is the choice of switches given to the `ls` command, Dired's back end. Read the ls Info file (which should be installed on your system). ls, like many of the Linux GNU utilities, is provided with an abundance of possible switches. Unfortunately, the options acceptable to Dired need to be compatible with the `-l` long listing switch, which includes a file's owner, group, and permissions.

Several faces are used by the XEmacs version of Dired to display different sorts of file and directory names. Backup files, executables, soft and hard links, and directories all have separate faces that can be changed with Customize. Selecting Edit Faces from the Options menu opens a Customize buffer showing all the faces used by XEmacs. They are listed in alphabetical order; the Dired faces all begin with `dired-`.

Dired Tips

One thing to remember when you are traversing a directory hierarchy with Dired is that each Dired buffer hangs around indefinitely until you explicitly kill it. It's easy to drill down through nested subdirectories without realizing that you are leaving a trail of active Dired buffers in your wake. Not that they are really harmful, but they do clog your buffer list and eventually use memory for little reason. You can avoid this by being more specific when using the Ctrl-x d command and by killing Dired buffers when you are finished with them. You can also append a subdirectory listing to the current Dired buffer by pressing i and kill it by pressing k.

Dired has good mouse support. While sweeping the mouse cursor over a file name in a Dired buffer, notice how the name is highlighted. If you click the middle mouse button on the file name, the file is loaded into an Emacs buffer. The XEmacs Dired has additional mouse functions:

Ctrl-Button 2	Pops up a menu of possible file operations.
Button 3	Shows another menu with different viewing and editing options.
Shift-Button 2	Tags the file or directory for subsequent operations.

If you explore the numerous Dired menu entries, I'm certain you will come across other useful commands.

Differences between Files

Just as Dired is an Emacs front end for ls and friends, Ediff provides a convenient way to use the GNU file-comparison tools diff and diff3, as well as Larry Wall's patch utility. Michael Kifer wrote Ediff and continues to maintain the package.

Ediff makes good use of font locking. Lines that differ between two files are shown in a different font-lock face, allowing you to see at a glance the areas of difference.

When you compare two or three files, each one appears in its own window or frame. You can copy highlighted differences between two buffers. Figures 14.5 and 14.6 give you an idea of the interface.

The Compare submenu is under Tools on the menu bar. The menus are handy, because they can take the place of minibuffer commands. The first two items on this menu, Two Files and Two Buffers, are equivalent to the minibuffer commands

M-x `ediff-files`

and

M-x `ediff-buffers`.

You can see a list of the other Ediff minibuffer commands by pressing M-x, typing `ediff-`, and pressing Tab twice.

A completions window appears, listing the numerous commands, many of which would be awkward to type—all the more reason to use the menus!

When you run Ediff from the menu bar or by using minibuffer commands, the files you specified are first compared in the background. Unless the files are exceptionally long, this doesn't take long. Files in Ediff buffers are in their normal modes, and editing is done normally. When the Ediff buffer windows appear, the mouse

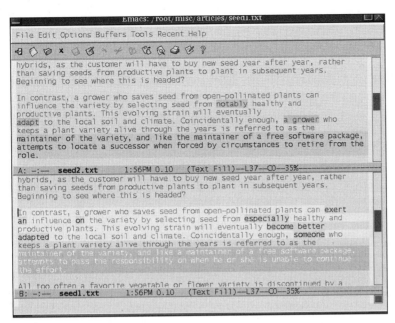

Emacs: /root/misc/articles/seed1.txt

File Edit Options Buffers Tools Recent Help

hybrids, as the customer will have to buy new seed year after year, rather
than saving seeds from productive plants to plant in subsequent years.
Beginning to see where this is headed?

In contrast, a grower who saves seed from open-pollinated plants can
influence the variety by selecting seed from notably healthy and
productive plants. This evolving strain will eventually
adapt to the local soil and climate. Coincidentally enough, a grower who
keeps a plant variety alive through the years is referred to as the
maintainer of the variety, and like the maintainer of a free software package,
attempts to locate a successor when forced by circumstances to retire from the
role.

A: -:-- seed2.txt   1:56PM 0.10   (Text Fill)—L37—C0—35%

hybrids, as the customer will have to buy new seed year after year, rather
than saving seeds from productive plants to plant in subsequent years.
Beginning to see where this is headed?

In contrast, a grower who saves seed from open-pollinated plants can exert
an influence on the variety by selecting seed from especially healthy and
productive plants. This evolving strain will eventually become better
adapted to the local soil and climate. Coincidentally enough, someone who
keeps a plant variety alive through the years is referred to as the
maintainer of the variety, and like a maintainer of a free software package,
attempts to pass the responsibility on when he or she is unable to continue
the effort.

All too often a favorite vegetable or flower variety is discontinued by a
B: -:-- seed1.txt   1:56PM 0.10   (Text Fill)—L37—C0—35%

Figure 14.5   *Two Files in Ediff Buffers*

Search Files (Grep)...	
Compile...	
Shell Command...	(M-!)
Shell Command on Region...	(M-|)
Debugger (GUD)...	
Spell Checking	⌐

Compare (Ediff)	▶	Two Files...
Merge	⌐	Two Buffers...
Apply Patch	⌐	Three Files...
Ediff Miscellanea	⌐	Three Buffers...
Version Control	⌐	Two Directories...
PCL-CVS	⌐	Three Directories...
Read Net News (Gnus)		File with Revision...
Read Mail (with RMAIL)		Directory Revisions...
Send Mail (with sendmail)	(C-x m)	Regions Word-by-word...
Directory Search	⌐	Regions Line-by-line...
Display Speedbar		Windows Word-by-word...
Display Calendar		Windows Line-by-line...
Games	⌐	This Window and Next Window

Figure 14.6   *The Ediff Menu*

cursor is immediately placed in the Ediff control window, a small window that
shows the number of difference regions along with instructions for getting help
(see Figure 14.7).

As with Dired, the keyboard is completely remapped, but only when the mouse
cursor is in the control window. Clicking ? while the control window is active
expands the window so that it is large enough to display the keybindings (see
Figure 14.8). Click ? again to reduce the window to its original state.

Figure 14.7 *The Ediff Control Window*

```
|   Move around       |    Toggle features      |       Manipulate
======================|=========================|=============================
p,DEL -previous diff  |    | -vert/horiz split   |a/b  -copy A/B's region to B/A
n,SPC -next diff      |    h -hilighting         | rx  -restore buf X's old diff
    j -jump to diff   |    @ -auto-refinement    |  *  -refine current region
   gx -goto X's point |                          |  !  -update diff regions
  C-l -recenter       |   ## -ignore whitespace  |
  v/V -scroll up/dn   | #f/#h -focus/hide regions | wx  -save buf X
  </> -scroll lt/rt   |    X -read-only in buf X | wd  -save diff output
    ~ -swap variants  |    m -wide display       |
======================|=========================|=============================
    R -show registry  |    = -compare regions    |  M    show session group
    D -diff output    |    E -browse Ediff manual|  G   -send bug report
    i -status info    |    ? -help off           | z/q  -suspend/quit
----------------------------------------------------------------------------
For help on a specific command:   Click Button 2 over it; or
                               Put the cursor over it and type RET.
-- *Ediff Control Panel*   At start of 6 diffs        Quick Help
```

Figure 14.8 *The Ediff Help Window*

If you would rather see the help in one of the Ediff buffer windows, click the middle mouse button on the "quick help" panel of the control buffer.

You don't have to work with entire files. Toward the bottom of the menu are commands that let you compare either two entire windows of text or selected regions within those windows. You can either use a coarser line-by-line comparison or have word-by-word differences shown.

Navigation within Ediff Buffers

The keys you will use the most are the v and V keys, which scroll both (or all three) buffers simultaneously; the n or spacebar key, which takes you to the next difference; and the p or Delete key, which moves to the previous difference.

Working with Directories

It's common to have more than one Ediff session at once, a session being a pair or triplet of files that have had their differences determined. Comparing two similar directories is one way to try this out and get a feel for how Ediff works with multiple sessions. Select Tools, Compare, Two Directories. You are prompted for two directory names. The ideal candidates are a directory and its backup from long enough ago that you have made changes to some of the files. Figure 14.9 shows an Ediff Session Group Panel showing the results of comparing directories of two different AucTeX releases.

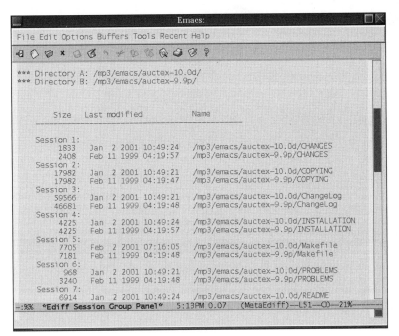

Figure 14.9 *Ediff Session Groups*

Each pair of files is listed, with their sizes and last modification time, making it easy to see which pairs differ from each other. Pressing Enter or clicking the middle mouse button on a session turns Ediff loose on the pair, and before long you will see a split-window Ediff session similar to Figure 14.5.

Working with Differences

As soon as the differences between files are accessible and highlighted, several operations are available. The a and b keys copy the highlighted regions from one buffer to the other, and ra and rb restore the buffer by undoing the action. A numerical argument restricts the copying. For example, typing 3a copies just the third difference region from buffer A to buffer B. Typing ! recalculates the differences between the two buffers.

A common scenario involves an original file that was edited by two different people. You end up with three different files, with one being the "ancestor" of the other two. Select Three Files from the Compare menu. You are prompted for the three file names. An Ediff three-way session appears, looking something like Figure 14.10.

The same commands can be used as in a two-file session, but to copy differences, you need to specify both source and destination. cb copies differences from buffer C to buffer B.

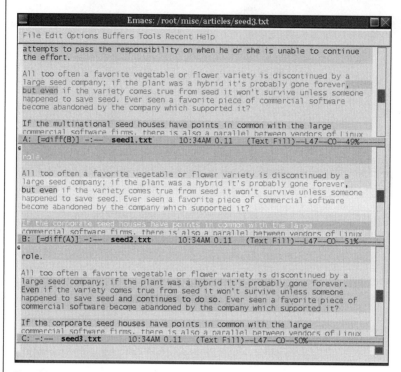

Figure 14.10   *Two Files and Their Ancestor*

Merging Files

Directly beneath the Compare menu is another Ediff menu, Merge. The various commands on this menu can work with files, buffers, and directories. The basic idea is to take the differences in two newer files and incorporate them into the original file, the ancestor. These commands are often used in conjunction with version control systems such as CVS.

Merging operations don't always do exactly what you want, but you can always undo the command. Pressing & offers you a choice of merging methods; press the Tab key to see what those choices are.

Patching Files with Ediff

Ediff offers a convenient interface to the patch program, a useful tool used in many software projects. A patch is in effect a collection of file differences generated by the diff program with a variable amount of context lines before and after the differences. This context is used by the patch program to find the right locations to insert the differences.

Just beneath the Merge submenu is the Apply Patch submenu. You can choose to patch either a single file or an entire directory. The latter option is more commonly used. Most patches include sections of differences, each of which is intended for a different file in a directory of source code.

If you are patching a directory, an Ediff session group is displayed, with each file affected by the patch becoming a session. This allows you to patch each file individually if you wish. The buffer is similar to Figure 14.9.

Learning More

Ediff comes with an informative Info manual that contains more details than this book can give. A good way to become comfortable and gain facility with Ediff is to try it out on unimportant files. It takes a while to get used to the dual-keyboard mode (commands working only while the control window has the focus), but a little practice will help.

If you use Ediff often, consider taking a look at the variables that can be changed with Customize. The Ediff Customize group is quite large and contains dozens of changeable settings, including the highlighting faces used on difference regions.

Spell Checking with ispell

Most, if not all, word processors offer some form of spell checking, a service that can be a time-saver for those who can't spell well. Typically, the dictionary database used by the application isn't used by other programs. This can lead to multiple bulky dictionaries, each used by a different piece of software. The philosophy behind UNIX and UNIX-like systems like Linux includes the idea of small but powerful tools that cooperate with each other. One dictionary available for all programs is a natural outgrowth of this view.

Emacs doesn't come with a dictionary, yet checking the spelling for entire documents, a selected region, or a single word is just a keystroke away. This is possible because Emacs makes use of the default system-wide dictionary system present on nearly all computers running Linux, ispell.

ispell has been around in one form or another since 1971, when an ancestral version was written for the WAITS operating system on DEC PDP-10 computers. The current maintainer is Geoff Kuenning. It is an international program with dictionaries available for many languages.

ispell is a stand-alone command-line program that is used like this:

```
ispell [file-name]
```

The program steps through the file and displays what it considers to be misspelled words one at a time, with a bit of context included. It offers likely replacement words and the option of accepting the word and moving on to the next one.

It wasn't too long after Emacs began to be popular that an Emacs extension was written, effectively integrating ispell into Emacs. You don't have to load ispell.el or enable it. It's ready to go whenever you feel the need.

ispell Commands

The command for checking a single word is

M-$.

This checks the spelling of the word at point. When you execute this command, a small Choices window opens at the top of the screen. As you can see in the modeline of the Emacs session shown in Figure 14.11, the two main commands are pressing the spacebar to ignore the word or pressing a numerical character to use one of the possibilities in the Choice window.

Another useful command is pressing i. This saves the word in your personal dictionary, called ~/.ispell_default unless you have specified otherwise. The first time you use this option, the file is created. You can build up a list of words such as proper names and technical terms, which will be accepted as valid words by ispell.

The command that M-$ executes is called `ispell-word`. You don't need to type an entire word of which you are unsure; type part of it, and let ispell suggest the remainder of the word.

Spell checking the entire buffer isn't bound to a key; press M-x and type

`ispell-buffer`

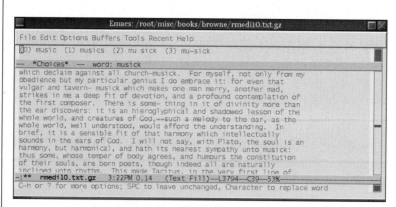

Figure 14.11   *Spell Checking a Single Word*

If you use this command, often you can bind it to a key with a statement like this one in your ~/.emacs file:

```
(global-set-key [(control c) i)] 'ispell-buffer)
```

Speaking of keybindings, the default M-$ binding for a single word is rather awkward to type; I've rebound it in my ~/.emacs file to use a function key instead:

```
(global-set-key 'f6 'ispell-word)
```

Dictionaries for ispell

Another command can be used to change the default dictionary. Press M-x and type

```
ispell-change-dictionary
```

You are prompted for the name of another dictionary (perhaps a dictionary in another language).

ispell dictionaries are in a special hashed format. The ispell distribution comes with a separate program called buildhash, which is used to process word lists into compact dictionary databases. Consult the ispell and buildhash man pages for instructions.

Checking HTML and LaTeX Files

ispell has native support for spell checking tagged LaTeX and HTML files. It will ignore the tagging and concentrate on the content of these files.

Customizing ispell

Many of ispell's settings can be changed with Customize. The default dictionary, the highlighting of misspelled words, and ispell's stance toward HTML can all be changed, as well as many other variables. To bring up this Customize buffer, press M-x and type

```
customize-group
```

When prompted, respond with

```
ispell
```

Programmers might be interested in the Customization item Ispell Check Comments. The default is "on," meaning that all text within a commented-out block will be checked. This is fine, but what if you would rather not check the program code itself? ispell will likely flag as misspelled odd function and class names, and this could become annoying after a while. There is a value menu for this variable; a choice you might want to try is "exclusive". Setting the variable to this value restricts ispell to spell checking only comments. This would be useless in ordinary text files, but it could be set that way on a per-session basis.

Flyspell

Recent Emacs releases come with an automatic on-the-fly spell checker called Flyspell, written by Manuel Serrano. XEmacs users can find it in the text-modes package.

This mode highlights every word that ispell regards as misspelled as you type. It doesn't make you stop and correct a highlighted word, but if you want to deal with one, clicking mouse button 2 displays a menu of choices. These are the same words that would have appeared in the Choices window when using the default ispell interface.

If you would like to enable this mode on an optional basis, so that the mode would be active only when manually enabled, insert these lines in your ~/.emacs file:

```
(autoload 'flyspell-mode "flyspell" "On-the-fly spelling checking" t)
(autoload 'global-flyspell-mode "flyspell" "On-the-fly spelling" t)
```

After these two lines have been evaluated (Ctrl-x Ctrl-e), or Emacs has been restarted, press M-x and type

```
flyspell-mode
```

to enable the mode. The command is a toggle. In other words, the same command will turn Flyspell off.

If you try it out and want to use it in every Emacs buffer, insert this line instead:

```
(global-flyspell-mode t)
```

Flyspell was written with extensive Customize support. You might find the default behavior distracting, but settings can be changed to make the mode less obtrusive. You can set it up so that duplicate words aren't highlighted, and you can even give it a greater time delay. More delay forces Flyspell to wait a configurable amount of time before highlighting a word, lessening the feeling that Flyspell is looking over your shoulder and urging you to correct these errors right now!

You can access this Customize buffer by pressing M-x and typing

```
customize-group
```

Respond to the prompt with

```
flyspell
```

If you spend some time tweaking the ispell and/or Flyspell settings, you should be able to come up with a level of spell-checking activity that is effective and unobtrusive.

Running a Shell in Emacs

Emacs has its own shell mode, a window that is similar to a login shell session in an xterm or at a virtual console. Your familiar shell, whether it is bash, tcsh, zsh, or any other command shell, is used with the same startup scripts as in any login session.

To open a shell buffer, just press M-x and type

```
shell
```

You can run other command-line programs from this shell buffer as long as they don't manipulate the display. ncurses-based programs won't work. Any of the GNU file and text utilities such as ls or cat are good examples of programs that output nothing but text and thus are appropriate. Programs run from a shell buffer run asynchronously, which means that they are running in a process outside of Emacs and don't affect the editor's behavior.

So why would you bother, when xterm or rxvt windows are a dime a dozen and don't have the limitations of the shell buffer? One (the only?) reason is that the output of a command in the shell buffer can be manipulated like text in any other Emacs buffer. You can copy the text and paste it into another buffer. Probably programmers are the main users of the shell buffer these days. The GNU gcc compiler is used by a great majority of free software developers, and its output (especially error messages) can be useful in an Emacs session.

Consider also that the Emacs shell buffer was developed in an era of slow, resource-hungry computers; in those archaic times, it was a truly useful and good concept. Nonetheless, even with today's powerful and memory-rich machines, the Emacs shell buffer can still be worth using.

Shell Buffer Keybindings

You might have become accustomed to the usual shell keybindings, but the Emacs Shell buffer bindings are different.

In most Linux shells, the previous commands are kept in memory, and you can bring one back in order to run it again by pressing either the up-arrow key or M-p. The Emacs shell buffer supports only the latter binding. Tab file name completion works, but some of the bindings for process manipulation are different in the Shell buffer. In a normal shell session, pressing Ctrl-c interrupts a running process. That key combination is reserved as a prefix in an Emacs session; press Ctrl-c Ctrl-c to interrupt a process. Starting a Shell buffer results in three new menus on the menu bar: Complete, In/Out, and Signals. Most users won't have much use for many of the commands on these menus aside from the basic keybindings outlined earlier.

Shell Buffer Problems

The Shell buffer generally works well, since your login shell does the real work and Emacs just displays the output. A recurrent problem users have reported is a garbled display when using the ls command. The output will be littered with ^M characters, making it difficult to read. If you see something like Figure 14.12 when using ls in the Shell buffer, read on.

This happens when the user has ls set up to display various types of files and directories in contrasting colors. Many Linux distributions have made this setting the default. ls displays colors by using terminal code that the Linux console and X terminals understand. They respond by translating the code into the appropriate colors; unfortunately, Emacs shell mode can't do this.

There are at least two solutions to this problem. The first is to set up ls so that colors aren't displayed. This can be done with a shell alias in one of your shell init files, such as ~/.bashrc. Insert these aliases:

```
alias lsn='ls --color=no'
alias lln='ls -la --color=no'
```

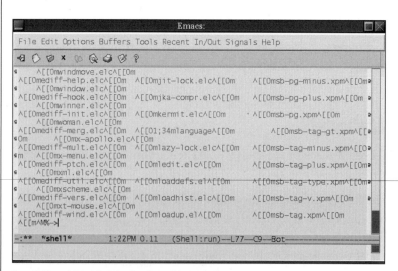

Figure 14.12 *A Bad ls Display in a Shell Buffer*

These aliases give you good results in a Shell buffer. In a normal terminal session (console or xterm), you can use the standard `ls` and `ls -l` commands, and the output will be colored as before.

When Emacs starts up your default shell in a Shell buffer it will use an Emacs-specific initialization file rather than the default ~/.bashrc if one exists. You can put the above aliases in a file named ~/.emacs_bash and they will only be effective in Emacs. This works with any shell, not just Bash; as an example Zsh users can name the file ~/.emacs_zsh.

Another alternative is to use Eshell rather than standard shell mode.

Eshell

Eshell is a new package written by John Wiegley. It is still under active development, but in its current state, it is a viable replacement for standard shell mode.

Rather than using your normal command shell, Eshell provides a new shell written completely in Emacs Lisp. Many of the standard shell commands are emulated in Lisp to such an extent that for casual use you won't be able to tell the difference. The emulated `ls` command's output is very similar to the colored `ls` output seen in an xterm.

Command completion, aliases, zsh-like globbing, and many other features of the standard Linux shells are all provided by Eshell.

Eshell comes with its own scripting language, but the documentation hasn't been written yet.

Eshell will be included with Emacs 21. It is currently available as an XEmacs package. Emacs 20-and-earlier users can install Eshell from the tar archive, available on this book's CD-ROM in the directory /cdrom/packages.

You might want to check out the following Web site, because a newer version might be available by the time you read this: http://www.gci-net.com/users/j/johnw/.

Installation for pre-21 versions of Emacs isn't too involved. Just copy the *.el files to the site-lisp directory and byte-compile the files. Then insert this line into your ~/.emacs file:

```
(load "eshell-auto")
```

After you have it installed, start an Eshell session by pressing M-x and typing

```
eshell
```

John Wiegley has ambitious plans for Eshell. It might eventually become the default Emacs shell.

Outline Mode

Outline mode is used when you're writing structured documents that have a predictable hierarchy. Any document that is divided into sections is suitable for this mode. Outline mode allows you to "collapse" a buffer so that only the section titles or headers are visible. Figure 14.13 shows the same document in both windows. The upper window is the normal expanded view, and the lower window has been collapsed with the command Hide Leaves from the Hide menu.

Outline mode uses a tree analogy when referring to the various parts of a document; the "leaves" are the actual text content under a heading or subheading. A parent-child analogy is also used, with the content under a heading (including subheadings and their content) thought of as the children of a parent heading.

Starting Outline Mode

You can turn on Outline mode by pressing M-x and typing

```
outline-mode
```

This makes Outline mode the major mode. Outline mode is designed to work in conjunction with text-mode, so your text-mode settings will still be in effect.

Outline mode doesn't have to be a major mode. You might want to use it along with another mode, such as one of the programming-language modes. Outline minor mode is really the same mode, but the keybindings are different so that it

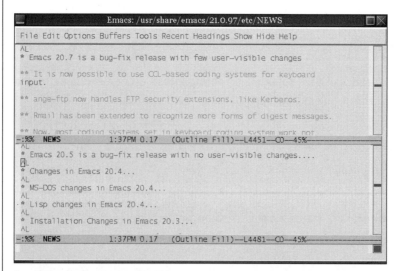

Figure 14.13   *Buffers in Outline Mode*

won't conflict with a major mode's keybindings, which often begin with the same Ctrl-c prefix that Outline mode uses. You can start minor mode by pressing M-x and typing

```
outline-minor-mode
```

Local Variables

Outline mode is different from many major modes in that it isn't associated with any particular file suffix. Because of this, you can't expect a file written using this mode to automatically be in Outline mode each time you edit the file. Emacs uses a file's suffix to determine which mode is appropriate for it.

You can force Emacs to use Outline mode for a file by including a Local Variables line at the beginning of the file. When Emacs loads a file, it looks at the first line. If it finds a line like this one:

```
-*- mode: Outline -*-
```

it makes Outline mode the file's major mode. This works for the Outline minor mode as well:

```
-*- mode: Outline-minor -*-
```

The Local Variables line can be used to set any Emacs variable. It will be set for only that file and not in other Emacs buffers. More than one variable can be set in the line. They need to be separated with semicolons.

Outline Levels

When you are in Outline mode, you must follow certain conventions if you want the mode to be able to recognize the different sectioning levels of your document. Asterisks at the very beginning of a line indicate a level heading: One asterisk indicates the top level, two the second level, and so on. Here is a simple example:

```
* Section 1
This is called the body of this top-level header; this part can be hidden and
revealed using Outline mode commands.


** Sub-section 1
More body material, but under a second-level header.


** Sub-section 2
```

```
Another second-level section, but still a part of the top-level Section 1.


*** Part 1
A third-level header, this one belonging to Sub-section 2.


* Section 2
The second top-level subdivision of the document.
```

If this example were to be collapsed, it would look like this:

```
* Section 1 ...


** Sub-section 1 ...


** Sub-section 2 ...


*** Part 1 ...


* Section 2 ...
```

It isn't absolutely necessary to use the default asterisks as section-level indicators. A variable called outline-regexp can be changed to correspond to heading levels of a particular type of document. The default value is [*^L]+, which can be translated as "one or more of either * or the control character ^L, a single character that is used to indicate page boundaries". A built-in limitation of Outline mode is that the higher the level, the shorter the level indicators must be. You can get around this by using just part of a word indicator, a part shorter than the next-lower indicator in the hierarchy. An example will clarify this. Suppose you were editing documents that used (in descending order) the levels Part, Chapter, and Scene. Part is a short word, but the word Scene is shorter than Chapter and longer than Part. Chapter is the one level indicator that doesn't follow the "lower level requires a longer name" rule, so Chapter needs to be truncated to fit the rule. A problem arises: If Chapter is shortened to Chapt to make it longer than Part, it ends up the same length as Scene. There is nothing to do here but add a character to Scene to make it longer. Using an asterisk as that character, the three strings for the new regular expression are Part, Chapt, and *Scene. Plugging these into a Lisp statement results in this:

```
"\\(Part\\)\\|\\(Chapt\\)\\|\\(\\*Scene\\)"
```

This is a complicated-looking regular expression. The numerous backslashes are necessary to "escape" the characters that otherwise would be interpreted as regular-expression special characters.

You can summon a Customize buffer to change the `outline-regexp` variable by pressing M-x and typing

```
customize-variable
```

Respond to the prompt with

```
outline-regexp
```

You can change the variable in that Customize buffer for all buffers, either permanently or for the duration of your Emacs session. You might consider setting this variable so that it applies only to the file you are editing, by including a Local Variables line at the top of files that need this variable set differently. The line would look something like this:

```
-*- mode: Outline; outline-regexp:"\\(Part\\)\\|\\(Chapt\\)\\|\\(\\*Scene\\)"-*-
```

Make sure you include the semicolon between the various settings you might include in a Local Variables line.

Expanding and Collapsing Outlines

The keybindings for the major and minor Outline modes are different; the major mode bindings are based on the Ctrl-c prefix and aren't hard to type. The minor mode bindings unfortunately have finger-twisting bindings based on the Ctrl-c @ prefix, surely one of the more awkward prefixes in existence. If you plan on using Outline minor mode on a regular basis, I advise you to change the minor-mode prefix to something more comfortable. All you need to do is insert a Lisp statement similar to this one in your ~/.emacs file:

```
(setq outline-minor-mode-prefix [(control z)])
```

Ctrl-z is a fairly useless prefix in an X Window Linux session. By itself, this key command iconizes and suspends an Emacs session. Most window managers provide this service with title-bar buttons or keybindings, so this prefix is fair game for usage in Emacs mode configuration. Another prefix you might prefer is Ctrl-v. By default, this runs the scroll-up command, but the Page Up key does the same thing.

The following are the Outline mode keybindings. Substitute Ctrl-c for [prefix] when you are in Outline major mode and Ctrl-c @ (or Ctrl-z if you have changed the variable) when you are using Outline as a minor mode.

The Headings Menu

[prefix] Ctrl-n	Moves to the next entry.
[prefix] Ctrl-p	Moves up to the parent header.
[prefix] Ctrl-f	Moves to the next entry at the same level.
[prefix] Ctrl-b	Moves to the previous entry at the same level.

The Show Menu

[prefix] Ctrl-a	Shows all. Expands the tree so that everything is visible.
[prefix] Ctrl-e	Expands the entry at point.
[prefix] Ctrl-k	Displays subcategories of the current level.
[prefix] Ctrl-i	Shows "children," or subsidiary-level headings.
[prefix] Ctrl-s	Like [prefix] Ctrl-i, but shows entries as well.

The Hide Menu

[prefix] Ctrl-l	Hides the "leaves," or the entries within the current level.
[prefix] Ctrl-t	Hides everything but the outline headings.
[prefix] Ctrl-c	Hides just the entry belonging to the current heading.
[prefix] Ctrl-d	Hides the headings and entries beneath the current level.
[prefix] Ctrl-q	Hides all but the top-level headings.
[prefix] Ctrl-o	Hides everything but the heading and entry at point.

It takes some practice on a multilevel file to get the hang of this mode. Every version of Emacs comes with a file—the NEWS file—detailing the changes made in the current and previous Emacs releases. You can load this file simply by pressing the help key Ctrl-h n. It appears in Outline major mode, so the Ctrl-c prefix will work with the keybindings just discussed.

You might be wondering just what would happen if you did an incremental search on a collapsed Outline mode buffer with the Ctrl-s command. The search will penetrate collapsed and invisible portions of the buffer, and any affected sections that were invisible will become visible and will still be visible afterwards. You can hide them again with the Ctrl-c Ctrl-c, Ctrl-c Ctrl-l, or Ctrl-c Ctrl-t commands.

Deletion and Outlines: A Warning

You need to be cautious and avoid the willy-nilly cutting of text while you are getting the hang of this mode. If you delete a heading while your document is collapsed, everything under the heading is deleted as well. Remember, those three periods at the end of the heading line stand for hidden content; when they are deleted, so is your content. Until you quit Emacs, that deleted content will still be in the kill ring and could be pasted back again, but if you shut down Emacs, that cut text is lost. You might be able to retrieve accidentally deleted text from a backup file, but the best strategy is "Think twice; delete once".

Other Outline Modes

If you find outline mode useful, you might consider trying one of the other similar modes. Folding mode (introduced in the next chapter) offers a different approach to showing and hiding levels of a document, as does the Foldout minor mode extension to Outline mode. Foldout minor mode is documented in the Emacs Info files. One of the features it adds to Outline mode is the use of narrowing—making one level of headings the only visible part of the buffer. This confines global editing actions to the part of the buffer you can see. You can try it out by including this line in your ~/.emacs file:

```
(eval-after-load "outline" '(require 'foldout))
```

This automatically makes Foldout a minor mode whenever Outline mode is enabled. Don't forget that if you don't like this minor mode, you should comment out or remove this line.

The Calendar and the Diary

You can use Emacs to keep track of appointments, anniversaries, holidays, and any other days you want to remember. The entry point to this facility is Calendar mode, a small window displaying calendars for three months, with the current month in the middle. Open a Calendar window by pressing M-x and typing

```
calendar
```

It doesn't look like much at first glance, but an array of useful commands are associated with this mode. You can easily move from month to month, both in the future direction (toward the right) and left into the past. The keybindings shown in the Calendar modeline (Ctrl-x < and Ctrl-x >) shift the display one month at a time in either direction. If you want to move faster through the months, the Page Up and Page Down keys jump three months per keystroke. The cursor keys move from day to day, and the mouse can be used to move point just as in any Emacs buffer.

Notice how a date is highlighted when the mouse moves over it. Two mouse menus are available for each date. The middle mouse button brings up a menu of commands that are associated with that date, and Ctrl-mouse button 3 displays a menu of more-general calendar functions (XEmacs doesn't need the Ctrl key for this menu).

The commands shown in Figure 14.14 are mostly concerned with the Diary, which is really more of an appointment and scheduling tool than an actual diary.

The keybindings shown in Figure 14.15 are valid when point is in the Calendar window. They apply to the date at point.

The Calendar menu or menus on the main menu bar offer many more commands. GNU Emacs has them divided between four different menus (Goto, Holidays, Diary, and Moon), and XEmacs has consolidated all the commands into one multilevel Calendar menu.

Using these menus, you can display the Mayan or Chinese date, see lists of holidays for various years and time periods, see the current phase of the moon, and a

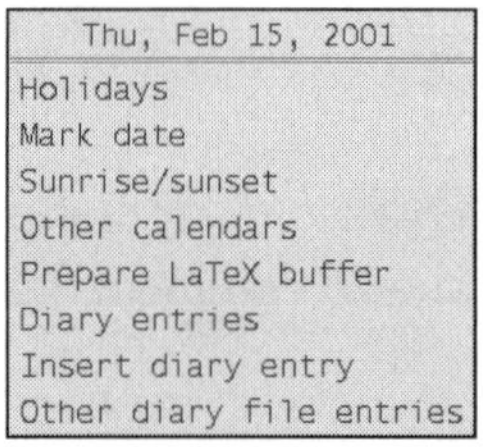

```
      Thu, Feb 15, 2001
  Holidays
  Mark date
  Sunrise/sunset
  Other calendars
  Prepare LaTeX buffer
  Diary entries
  Insert diary entry
  Other diary file entries
```

Figure 14.14 *The Diary Mouse Menu*

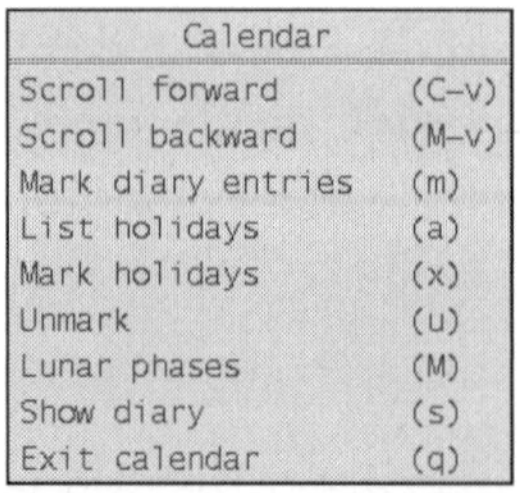

```
          Calendar
  Scroll forward         (C-v)
  Scroll backward        (M-v)
  Mark diary entries     (m)
  List holidays          (a)
  Mark holidays          (x)
  Unmark                 (u)
  Lunar phases           (M)
  Show diary             (s)
  Exit calendar          (q)
```

Figure 14.15 *The Calendar Mouse Menu*

variety of other date-related commands. Many of these you might seldom (if ever) use, but they are available.

The Diary File

The Calendar mode Diary functions are similar to those of a Personal Information Manager (PIM) program; you can keep track of one-time, weekly, or cyclical appointments, anniversaries, or reminders. Selecting Insert Diary Entry from the Diary menu or submenu opens a file named diary in your home directory. This file is created if you're just starting out with Calendar mode. The date is inserted in the file, and the rest of the line is intended for your notes. Figure 14.16 is an example of a diary file. Notice how the dates referred to in the file are highlighted in the Calendar window. You turn this on by pressing m and turn it off by pressing u.

One feature that helps makes the Diary useful is the variety of entries possible. For example, look at the fourth entry in the diary file shown in Figure 14.16. This is a cyclic entry. You don't need to know the format of an entry like this, because it is created automatically for you after you are prompted for the length of the cycle. The entry shown marks every fourth day. You create an entry like this by selecting Insert Cyclic from the Diary menu or submenu.

You can create another useful type of entry by selecting the Insert Block command. This creates an entry that includes a consecutive sequence of days. Before selecting this command, you need to set the mark (Ctrl-spacebar) on the first day of the block and then move the cursor to the last day. The last diary entry in Figure 14.16 is an example of a block entry.

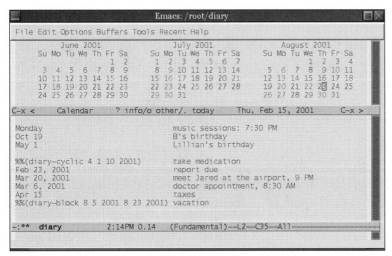

Figure 14.16   *Calendar with Diary File*

```
                Tue, Jul 3, 2001
Daily (1 page)
Weekly (1 page)
Weekly (2 pages)
Weekly (other style; 1 page)
Weekly (yet another style; 1 page)
Monthly
Monthly (landscape)
Yearly
Yearly (landscape)
Filofax styles
```

Figure 14.17   *The Prepare LaTeX Menu*

When you have a Diary and Calendar screen layout similar to Figure 14.16, the diary file isn't always shown in its entirety. If you select Diary Entries using the middle mouse button menu, only the entries pertaining to the date at point are shown. A pop-up ToolTip window also shows those entries in Emacs 21 and XEmacs. Press s to make all entries visible again.

If you want to print a calendar (and have LaTeX installed), select Prepare LaTeX buffer from the middle mouse button menu. The menu shown in Figure 14.17 appears; choose the calendar you prefer, and a LaTeX buffer is created. You can process the buffer with LaTeX and dvi2ps and end up with a printable PostScript file of your calendar. (See Chapter 13 for more about LaTeX and Emacs.)

The Calendar and Diary have many other features; to learn more, consult the Calendar section of the Emacs or XEmacs Info files.

Conclusion

This has been a tour of the more popular and useful of the "official" Emacs extensions, but you might enjoy investigating others that are included with Emacs. One way to learn the names of packages worth looking at is to spend some time browsing the comp.emacs.* and gnu.emacs.* newsgroups. If an extension is useful and well-written, chances are other Emacs users will be talking about it or asking questions.

The next chapter deals with a number of external Emacs add-ons. Although they aren't distributed with Emacs, these packages can be as high-quality as the included ones. Some will eventually be incorporated into the official Emacs and XEmacs distributions, but until that happens, they are available from various Internet sites.

The packages discussed in this chapter were developed by Emacs users who had an itch that needed scratching (in other words, they needed a task that Emacs couldn't perform). "Scratching" in this context meant writing a new extension for Emacs, a mode or utility that adds yet another costume for this quick-change artist of an editor.

These are external packages, meaning that they aren't bundled with the official distributions of Emacs (although some might be available as an XEmacs package).

Several volumes the size of this one would be required to adequately describe the myriad Emacs extensions that have been written in the past 15 years. Here are my criteria for including packages in this chapter:

- The extension must work with current versions of Emacs and/or XEmacs. Some of the older packages haven't been updated to work with the recent versions. In many cases, a newer extension with the same functionality has been written.
- It should be freely licensed, preferably under the GNU GPL.
- The add-on should be of use to a reasonably large percentage of readers. Some packages are quite specialized, such as a mode for an obscure programming language that few people use.
- The package shouldn't have too many bugs and preferably should have an active maintainer.
- It should have enough documentation included. Figuring out how to use the extension shouldn't be an exercise in interpreting Emacs-Lisp.

All the packages described in this chapter can be found on this book's CD-ROM in the directory /cdrom/packages.

Clipper: A Persistent Clipboard

You might remember clipper.el from Chapter 7. At the end of that chapter, the Lisp file was lying motionless on the marble slab, its still-quivering organs (pardon me; I meant to say functions!) scattered haphazardly. In the meantime, it has been put back together and sewn up. In this section, you will see what it can do.

Clipper is a fine example of a compact single-file Lisp package (a little over 6 KB). Small as it is, it adds a new mode and an easy-to-use interface to an Emacs session.

Kevin Burton wrote the mode because he was tired of manually copying and pasting the same blocks of text into the comment sections of Lisp files he had written. One of these blocks of text was the obligatory GPL statement found at the beginning of most Emacs-Lisp files. This is how many Emacs extensions are born: Someone faced with repetitive tasks thinks, "Wouldn't it be nice if Emacs could…".

The idea that Kevin came up with was a permanent file that would act as a repository or memory containing these chunks of text. The hard part was coming up with a way of easily retrieving the units of text by name, plus a quick method of adding new-named text blocks to the repository file. See Chapter 7 if you are interested in the gory details.

Installation

A single-file package such as Clipper is easy to install. Just copy the file from this book's CD-ROM into your site-lisp directory, and then insert this Lisp statement into your ~/.emacs file:

```
(require 'clipper)
```

If you evaluate this line (press Ctrl-x Ctrl-e), you will have several new Clipper-related commands to try out:

M-x `clipper-create`	Creates a new clip.
M-x `clipper-delete`	Deletes an existing clip.
M-x `clipper-insert`	Inserts one of your clips into the current buffer.

All three of these commands result in a prompt for a clip's name.

You might also want to set up keybindings for the two commands used most often:

```
(global-set-key [(control c) (control i)] 'clipper-insert)
(global-set-key [(control c) (control n)] 'clipper-create)
```

Although Kevin Burton designed Clipper for inserting "boilerplate" text such as the GNU license, the mode is open-ended enough to be used for any text you repeatedly need to insert, such as your name and mailing address. You could think of Clipper as another form of abbrev-mode (discussed in Chapter 14) but adapted toward larger chunks of text that aren't needed as often as an abbreviation might be.

Notes Mode

Notes mode was developed by John Heidemann several years ago as an aid for keeping academic notes organized and accessible. It will probably never be incorporated into the official Emacs distributions, because it isn't simply an Emacs extension written completely in Lisp. Much of the mode's functionality derives from several Perl scripts designed to be run periodically and noninteractively in the background. Thus, Notes mode is an unusual hybrid mode, not useful without Emacs as a host (like most modes) but also not useful without a Perl installation and a means of running processes automatically at defined intervals. Luckily, just about every Linux installation fulfills these two requirements: Perl is normally installed by default, and a daemon named cron is available to run programs or scripts periodically.

Notes mode supplies an environment for writing notes and keeping them organized and indexed by date and topic. Like many Emacs extensions, it can be used for purposes not envisioned by the author. Notes mode can be used as a personal database or even as a framework for a journal or diary.

Prerequisites

You need to have Perl installed, and the version should be at least 5.00. Any recent Emacs or XEmacs version should work. You should have at least several megabytes of disk space available, because the note files and directories inexorably grow in size over time.

Installation

Notes mode installation is a bit more involved than usual. If it's done incorrectly, the mode won't work at all. First, unarchive the distribution file to a temporary directory. Notes mode uses a configure script and makefile system to adapt some of the Lisp files to your system, byte-compile them, and finally copy both the Lisp files and a set of Perl scripts to their new homes.

Running the configure script creates a customized makefile, but the configure process might need to be run with at least one switch, because it might not find your site-lisp directory. The default installation destination for the non-Lisp components is /usr/local, but this can be changed with a switch as well. Here is a sample command:

```
./configure --with-prefix=/usr --with-lisp-dir=/usr/share/emacs/site-lisp --
infodir=/usr/info
```

Use the `--infodir` switch if you would rather have the Info documentation files somewhere other than the default /usr/local/info.

Now load the newly-created makefile into an Emacs session, and look near the top of the file for this section:

```
##########################################
#
# user configurable parameters
#
prefix=/usr
# LIB_DIR should be a private place for notes-mode stuff.
LIB_DIR=${prefix}/share/notes-mode
# EL_DIR should be where your site-specific emacs .el{,c}'s go.
EL_DIR=/usr/share/emacs/site-lisp
# INFO_DIR is for emacs info files.
INFO_DIR=${prefix}/info
INSTALL_INFO=/usr/sbin/install-info
# must be perl 5.000 or better.
PERL=/usr/bin/perl
# must be 19 or greater
EMACS=emacs
MKDIR_P=mkdir -p
#
# end of user configurable parameters
#
##########################################
```

Check to see if the parameters accurately reflect how you want the package installed. Make any necessary changes and save the file to disk.

XEmacs users need to make one extra edit; change this line:

```
EMACS=emacs
```

to this:

```
EMACS=xemacs
```

This assumes that the XEmacs executable is in your path. Otherwise, type in the path as well—something like this:

```
EMACS=/opt/bin/xemacs
```

Now that the makefile is ready, you can type

```
make install
```

The Lisp files will be byte-compiled in the background by a noninteractive Emacs or XEmacs process and then copied to your site-lisp directory. The Perl scripts are copied to /usr/local/share/notes-mode (or elsewhere if you specified a different prefix), and the Info documentation files join your other Info files. You need to add a line such as the following to the dir file in your Info directory:

```
* Notes Mode: (notes-mode).          On-line note organizer
```

There is one last step before you can begin using Notes mode. Change to the directory in which the Perl scripts were installed (the default location is /usr/local/share/notes-mode). Execute one of these scripts by typing

```
notesinit
```

This an interactive script. You will be asked various questions, such as where you want your notes directory to live, and the script uses your answers to complete the setup, creating directories if necessary. Each user on your system must run this script if they want to use the mode.

One task the notesinit script undertakes is setting up your crontab file so that the other Perl utilities are called at the proper intervals. This might or might not work, depending on how cron is configured in your Linux distribution.

Read your cron documentation to find out where the crontab configuration files are located, and check to see if an entry for the Notes mode `mkall` command has been added. If something went wrong and it's not there, you need to add a daily cron job. The following command needs to be executed during the daily cron session:

```
/usr/local/share/notes-mode/mkall
```

For example, on my Debian system, the various cron jobs are in the form of shell scripts located in the directories /etc/cron.daily, /etc/cron.weekly, and /etc/cron.monthly. Here are the contents of a shell script called notes-mkall, which runs the mkall Perl script once a day:

```
#!/bin/sh
# notes-mode cron daily
/usr/local/share/notes-mode/mkall
```

A script like this needs to be made executable by a command such as this:

```
chmod +x  /etc/cron.daily/notes-mkall
```

You really need to make sure that cron is set up to run mkall every day, although I suppose you could run the command yourself every day or two. It's nice, though, for your notes index to be kept up-to-date without needing to remember to do it yourself.

One result of running notesinit is that a sample notes file is created and inserted into your new notes directory. This file gives you an idea of the format of a notes file. Here's what the sample looks like:

```
* Today ------


to do list goes here?



* Environment/notes -----------------


Set up notes with notesinit.
```

The mkall Perl script (which is run every day as a cron job) indexes and cross-references all your existing notes files. Each notes file you create is automatically given a numerical name reflecting the day it was created. As an example, I'm writing this paragraph on the 17th of February, 2001. The notes file created for me this morning has this file name and path: /home/layers/Notes/200102/010217.

You interpret the directory-name 200102 as the second month of 2001, and the file name 010217 uses the last two digits of the year, followed by the month and the day of the month. These name aren't really for your use; they are intended to be used by the indexing Perl programs that work behind the scenes to keep your notes organized and accessible.

The Perl scripts daily generate a new index of your notes sorted by subject headers, with the individual notes files arranged chronologically. Each item in the Index buffer, which can be summoned from any Notes mode buffer, is a clickable link to one of your note files.

Entries that have a particular subject line can be copied from all existing notes into one Summary buffer with a key command. This is a handy way to view every note that has the same subject, an alternative to advancing chronologically and by subject from note to note.

Figure 15.1 shows a Summary buffer. This is a temporary buffer, but it could be saved to a file.

Another task accomplished by the scripts is updating all the links within the notes files. If you wrote a note a week ago with a subject line of "* Politics" and you wrote another note with the same subject today, a new "next" link would be inserted in the week-old file, pointing to today's file. Your old notes are continually being updated with links to newer notes.

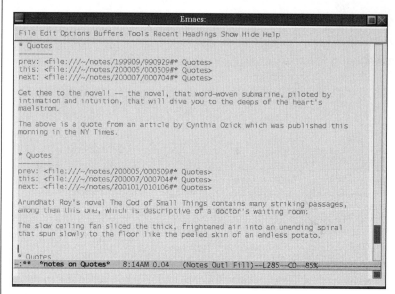

Figure 15.1   *The Notes Mode Summary Buffer*

Notes mode recognizes any line beginning with an asterisk followed by a space as a subject heading. The "* Today————" heading is a special one. This heading and any content that follows it are copied from the previous note file into the next new one. This is a place to insert "to-do" items; they appear in all subsequent notes until you delete them. If you aren't in the habit of making to-do lists, just delete the sample entry and use the "* Today" category as a means of navigating to the previous day's note.

You can create new categories at any time, as long as the line begins with an asterisk and has one space before the name. After you have used a subject line once and it has been indexed, you can use Tab completion on the name the next time you type it.

You begin a new note by pressing Enter after entering the subject prefixed with its asterisk-space identifier. The subject line will be automatically underlined, and pseudo-URLs will be created for the note. A pseudo-URL for the previous note with that subject header (if there is one) is inserted as well, so you can immediately go back to that note if you wish.

External links are pointers to other files on your machine or network. They work just like an HTML link, as a sort of pseudo-URL. They look like this:

```
file:////usr/local/articles/mencken.txt
```

The power and convenience of Notes mode really can't be appreciated until you have amassed a fair quantity of notes. Navigating from one note to another by either date, index, or subject is analogous to browsing the World Wide Web, except that it's your personal web of notes.

Keyboard and Mouse Commands

Note navigation can be either mouse- or keyboard-based. The keybindings are based on the Ctrl-c prefix:

Ctrl-c Ctrl-n	Moves to the next note that has the same subject.
Ctrl-c Ctrl-p	Moves to the previous note that has the same subject.
Ctrl-c Ctrl-i	Moves to the Index buffer, which has links to every note.
Ctrl-c Enter	Follows a pseudo-URL link.
Ctrl-c Ctrl-k	Copies the pseudo-URL of the current note to the kill ring.
Ctrl-c Ctrl-s	Collects all notes that have the current note's subject header into a single Summary buffer.
M-Ctrl-a	Jumps to the beginning of the current entry.
M-Ctrl-e	Jumps to the end of the current entry.

The Ctrl-c Ctrl-k binding is an interesting and useful one. It lets you grab the pseudo-URL of the current note as a unit. You could also do this by selecting the region and copying it, but the keystroke is quicker. Paste the pseudo-URL into another note, and you have linked the two. Sometimes it is helpful to link two notes that don't share the same subject category.

The mouse commands provide another means of navigation:

mouse button 2	Clicked on a link to a note in the Index buffer takes you there.
Shift-mouse button 2	Clicked on a pseudo-URL in a Notes buffer opens the note.

Notes mode also supports the encryption of individual notes. Outline-minor-mode can be used in conjunction with Notes mode so that a notes buffer can be collapsed, leaving only the subject header lines visible. Refer to the Info, PostScript, or HTML documentation that comes with the package to learn more about these and other features not described here.

Auto-Reverting Notes

If you are in the habit of leaving Emacs running all night, and you wrote and saved a Notes mode note the previous day, you might notice the next morning that your note has been "unsaved." Asterisks in the modeline indicate that the note has been changed but not saved.

No, you didn't neglect to save the note. The Perl script mkall did its job during the night and reindexed all your notes. Part of this cron job is inserting the pseudo-URL links between notes, including the still-loaded note from yesterday. Emacs notices if one of its buffers has been changed on disk by another process, and if you try to resave the note, you are asked if you really want to do this. Type yes, save the note, and consider using an add-on called auto-revert-mode, which does this for you automatically.

Reverting a buffer means interpreting the file on disk as the desired version and reloading that file as an Emacs buffer.

autorevert.el is included with GNU Emacs; XEmacs users can find the file on this book's CD-ROM or at this URL (this is author Anders Lindgren's page):http://www.csd.uu.se/~andersl/emacs.shtml.

You can activate this mode in such a way that only Notes mode buffers will be affected by inserting this line in your ~/.emacs file:

```
(add-hook 'notes-mode-hook 'turn-on-auto-revert-mode)
```

auto-revert mode is designed to do its job only when Emacs is idle, because it would be disconcerting and annoying if the mode tried to revert a file while you were editing it.

Folding Mode

Anders Lindgren's Folding mode has become popular in recent years as an alternative to Outline mode. The extension is another approach to the idea of selectively hiding and revealing portions of a buffer.

In Outline mode, asterisks are used to indicate section headers—one asterisk for top-level sections, two for second-level subsections, and so on. There is no "end-of-section" marker. Folding mode uses three curly braces to indicate both the beginning and end of a section, and the levels in section hierarchies all use the same triple opening and closing braces. Folding mode determines what level a section belongs to solely by how deeply nested the brace-enclosed section is. Here is a skeletal Folding mode section with an embedded subsection:

```
{{{ Section One
[upper-level content]
     {{{ Sub-section 1
     [sub-section content]
     }}}
}}}
```

The opening fold-marker should always be followed by some identifying text. Folding mode requires this in order to work properly, and it also makes a folded buffer more comprehensible.

A good way to understand how Folding mode works is to install it and then load a good-sized multilevel file written with folding in mind. It just so happens that folding.el itself serves as an excellent example of how the mode can be used.

Installation

GNU Emacs users can find folding.el on this book's CD-ROM. XEmacs users need to install the text-mode package, which includes the extension.

There are two ways of activating the mode with lines added to your ~/.emacs file. The first method automatically starts Folding mode when a file is opened that contains the fold indicator braces:

```
(if (load "folding" 'nomessage 'noerror)
            (folding-mode-add-find-file-hook))
```

You might not want Folding mode to be loaded until you explicitly start it by pressing M-x and typing

```
folding-mode
```

In that case, autoload statements in your ~/.emacs file are what you need:

```
(autoload 'folding-mode          "folding" "Folding mode" t)
(autoload 'turn-off-folding-mode "folding" "Folding mode" t)
(autoload 'turn-on-folding-mode  "folding" "Folding mode" t)
```

After these lines have been evaluated (either manually with Ctrl-x Ctrl-e or by restarting Emacs), you are ready to open the folding.el file and try out some folding and unfolding commands.

Figure 15.2 shows folding.el with just one section unfolded.

```
┌─────────────────────────────────────────────────────────────────────┐
│           Emacs: /usr/share/emacs/21.0.97/site-lisp/folding.el    □ X │
├─────────────────────────────────────────────────────────────────────┤
│ File Edit Options Buffers Tools Recent Emacs-Lisp Fld Help            │
│ ;;{{{ GPL...                                                          │
│ ;;{{{ Introduction...                                                 │
│ ;;{{{ Installation...                                                 │
│ ;;{{{ Documentation...                                                │
│                                                                       │
│ ;;{{{ Customisation...                                                │
│ ;;{{{ Examples                                                        │
│                                                                       │
│ ;;  Example: personal setup                                          │
│ ;;                                                                    │
│ ;;     To define your own keybinding instead of using the standard ones, │
│ ;;     you can do like this:                                         │
│ ;;                                                                    │
│ ;;          (defconst folding-mode-prefix-key "\C-c")                 │
│ ;;                                                                    │
│ ;;          (defconst folding-default-keys-function                   │
│ ;;             '(folding-bind-backward-compatible-keys))              │
│ ;;                                                                    │
│ ;;          (defconst folding-load-hook 'my-folding-load-hook)        │
│ ;;                                                                    │
│ ;;                                                                    │
│ ;;          (defun my-folding-load-hook ()                            │
│ ;;             "Folding setup."                                       │
│ ;;                                                                    │
│ ;;             (folding-install)  ;; just to be sure                  │
│ ;;                                                                    │
│ ;;             ;; ........................................... markers ... │
│ ;;                                                                    │
│ ;;             ;; Change text-mode fold marks. I ussually program my │
│ -:--  folding.el    12:46PM 0.16    (Emacs-Lisp Fld Isearch)--L18--C0-- 1%─ │
│ Quit                                                               ■  │
└─────────────────────────────────────────────────────────────────────┘
```

Figure 15.2   *A Partially Folded Buffer*

Keyboard and Menu Commands

The default prefix for Folding mode commands is Ctrl-c @, a prefix I refuse to use. Casting about for a superfluous Emacs keybinding to co-opt as a prefix for Folding mode, I happened across Ctrl-v. The default binding runs the `scroll-up` command, which also happens to be the command called by the Page Up key. Since I never use Ctrl-v, preferring single keystrokes when possible, Ctrl-v seemed like a good candidate. If you would like to do the same, you first need to unset the current binding with this line in your ~/.emacs file:

```
(define-key global-map [(control v)] nil)
```

This line needs to be earlier in the ~/.emacs file than your Folding mode initialization lines. Now you are free to assign a new meaning to the Ctrl-v prefix. This can be done with Customize. Bring up the Folding Group Customize buffer by pressing M-x and typing

```
customize-group
```

When prompted, type

```
folding
```

Several folding settings can be changed in the resultant Customize buffer. The default prefix key is the first setting.

But since you've been mucking around in your ~/.emacs file anyway, instead of using Customize, you can add one more line directly after the `define-key` line just shown that will change the prefix for good:

```
(defconst folding-mode-prefix-key [(control v)])
```

Even the menus will pick up this change, because they are generated from scratch each time Folding mode is started.

Figure 15.3, a screen shot of the Fld menu after this change has been made, illustrates the numerous folding-related commands that are available.

If you retained the default Folding mode prefix, each command would be prefixed with Ctrl-c @ rather than Ctrl-v.

Spend some time with folding.el after starting Folding mode, and you will develop a feel for navigating through a folded file. Creating your own file isn't difficult as long as you remember to keep the opening and closing fold-markers balanced.

Folding mode has built-in support for the particular commenting characters used by most programming languages. Notice how the fold indicators in Figure 15.2 are prefixed with semicolons (the Emacs Lisp comment character), but the mode still recognizes the folds. Braces prefixed with a double forward slash (signifying C++ comments) will be recognized as folds in a C++ source file. New comment characters can be added to the list with a statement such as this:

```
(folding-add-to-marks-list 'major-mode  "@{{{"   "@}}}" )
```

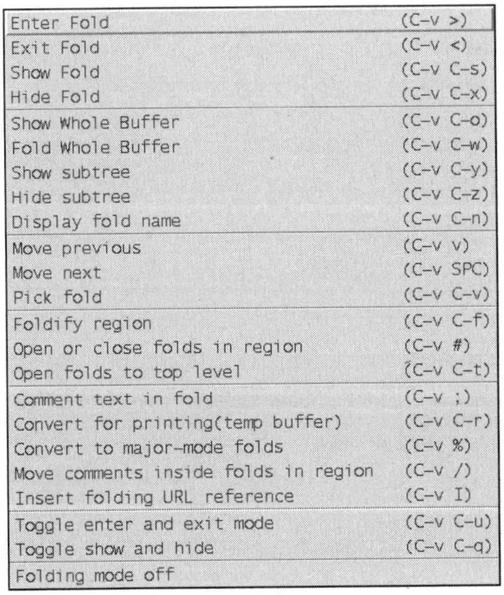

Enter Fold	(C-v >)
Exit Fold	(C-v <)
Show Fold	(C-v C-s)
Hide Fold	(C-v C-x)
Show Whole Buffer	(C-v C-o)
Fold Whole Buffer	(C-v C-w)
Show subtree	(C-v C-y)
Hide subtree	(C-v C-z)
Display fold name	(C-v C-n)
Move previous	(C-v v)
Move next	(C-v SPC)
Pick fold	(C-v C-v)
Foldify region	(C-v C-f)
Open or close folds in region	(C-v #)
Open folds to top level	(C-v C-t)
Comment text in fold	(C-v ;)
Convert for printing(temp buffer)	(C-v C-r)
Convert to major-mode folds	(C-v %)
Move comments inside folds in region	(C-v /)
Insert folding URL reference	(C-v I)
Toggle enter and exit mode	(C-v C-u)
Toggle show and hide	(C-v C-q)
Folding mode off	

Figure 15.3   *The Folding Mode Menu*

This line is for an imaginary major mode that uses the @ character as its comment indicator.

If you would like to see if a particular language is supported, press the "help-on-variables" help key, Ctrl-h v.

Respond to the prompt with

```
folding-mode-marks-alist
```

A window opens, displaying the numerous comment characters that Folding mode recognizes.

An Interface to Online Dictionaries

The Dict project (http://www.dict.org) has made available a free client/server dictionary system for computer users. It works by employing a server daemon running as a background process that handles requests from client software such as dict, which is part of the distribution.

Dict is a command-line program. You type `dict [word]`, and the word is passed to the dictd server, which looks it up in one or more dictionary files that are compressed with a specialized compression program called dictzip. The definition is in turn passed to a pager such as less, where the definition can be read. This entire process is near-instantaneous.

The compressed dictionary files from which dictd plucks definitions are all public-domain files, including an unabridged Merriam-Webster dictionary circa 1913 and the complete WordNet database. Others include a gazetteer, a Bible dictionary, and two compendiums of computer terms.

These dictionary files can be either on a remote dictd server on the Internet or local files on your own machine. Linux distribution packages are available for the client, the server, and the dictionary files.

The Dict system is worth using on its own, but it wasn't long before some Emacs users began to write modes that would allow access to these dictionaries from within Emacs. One such user was Torsten Hilbrich; he wrote a feature-filled mode called dictionary.el. Rather than act as an Emacs front end to the dict client program, this mode takes its place and contacts the dictd server directly.

Dictionary.el Installation

Installation consists of unpacking the dictionary-1.2.1.tar.gz file, copying the *.el files to your site-lisp directory, and byte-compiling the files. These lines pasted into your ~/.emacs file will activate the mode:

```
(autoload 'dictionary-search "dictionary"
  "Ask for a word and search it in all dictionaries" t)
(autoload 'dictionary-lookup-definition "dictionary"
  "Search the word at point in all dictionaries" t)
(autoload 'dictionary-match-words "dictionary"
 "Ask for a word and search all matching words in the dictionaries" t)
(autoload 'dictionary "dictionary"
 "Create a new dictionary buffer" t)


(global-set-key [(control c) (d)] 'dictionary-lookup-definition)
(global-set-key [(control c) (s)] 'dictionary-search)
(global-set-key [(control c) (m)] 'dictionary-match-words)


(setq dictionary-server "localhost")
```

The last line makes your machine the default dictionary server. If you want to use a remote server, substitute the server's IP address for `"localhost"`. The keybindings can be changed to suit your setup.

Dictionary mode offers several function commands. `dictionary-lookup-definition` looks up the word at your cursor location and then opens a Dictionary buffer and displays the definitions that were found. A variation called `dictionary-search` displays the word at point in the minibuffer, allowing you to edit it before pressing Enter. `dictionary-match-words` prompts you for a partial word and then displays lists of words containing the pattern, sorted by dictionary. Each word in the list is a clickable link that fetches the definition.

Figure 15.4 shows a typical Dictionary window.

At the top of the Dictionary window are several mouse-activated buttons that run the various Dictionary mode commands; the results appear in the window.

An empty Dictionary window appears if you press M-x and type

```
dictionary
```

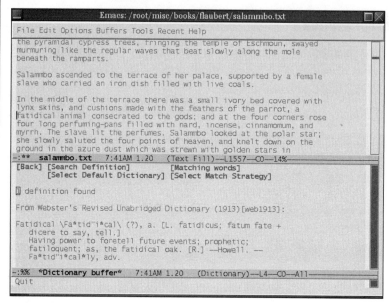

Figure 15.4   *A Dictionary Mode Window*

You can use the empty Dictionary window to access the command buttons.

One of the buttons in the Dictionary window can be used to select the default dictionary, which can be changed at any time. Figure 15.5 shows the menu of choices brought up by this button.

Dictionary mode is a great aid for the writer. Not only can you use ispell to check a word's spelling, but with this mode, you can refer to definitions quickly.

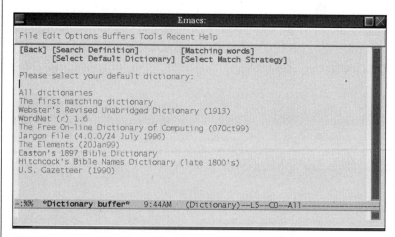

Figure 15.5   *Dictionary Selection*

The mode is also useful for those who read the Project Gutenberg public-domain texts. I've found that I'm much more likely to look up a word if I can do it quickly with a single key command.

Emacs CD and MP3 Players

Plenty of command-line music players are available for Linux. This section focuses on Emacs interfaces for the mpg123 MP3 player and the cda and cdcd music CD players. These Emacs music modes aren't as fancy as the stand-alone X11 players such as gcd and xmcd, but if you use Emacs a lot and don't mind sacrificing a portion of one of your Emacs frames, they can be quite convenient. X11 players can become buried behind stacks of windows or might be in another virtual desktop. It is distracting to shuffle through a complicated screen layout when all you need is to find the player's controls. An Emacs music player is just another buffer and can be accessed from the Buffers menu.

A CD Interface

Matthew Hodges wrote cdi.el, a versatile CD-playing mode that displays the track, artist, and disc names in a narrow window and offers the expected commands for the various playing operations. Both of the command-line players support look up CDs (if you are on the Internet) by accessing a CD database server and pulling down the title, artist, and track information for current and future use.

cdi.el is a single-file package that can be dropped into your site-lisp directory. These two lines in your ~/.emacs file enable the extension:

```
(require 'cdi)
(global-set-key '[(control c) (z)] 'cdi-start)
```

The second line is optional and could be set to any convenient and available binding.

If you don't choose to assign a keybinding, pressing M-x and typing

```
cdi-start
```

will start a new cdi session.

The Cdi interface is a short window with the disc, track, and elapsed time displayed at the top.

While the Cdi window has focus, press Ctrl-h b (the bindings help key), and a window similar to the top one in Figure 15.6 will appear. This mode assigns mnemonic keys such as p for play/pause and > for next track.

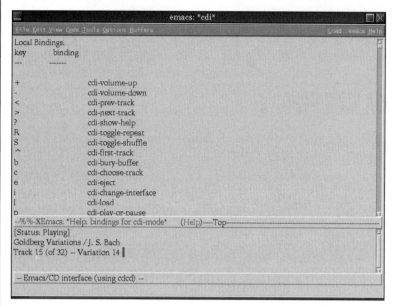

Figure 15.6 *The Cdi Window with the Help Window*

Playing Lists of MP3s

This mode for playing MP3 compressed music files was written by Hirose Yuuji. It acts as a front end to the command-line programs mpg123 and the aumix mixer, both of which should be available as packages for your Linux distribution.

It's somewhat similar to Cdi, with playlists taking the place of CDs, as you can see in Figure 15.7.

A convenient feature of mpg123.el is that in addition to specifying a single MP3 file to play, you can give the name of a playlist. The playlists have a simple format: one file name per line. You don't even need to manually type a list. You can generate a list with a simple shell command:

```
ls */*.mp3 > list
```

For a single directory list, you can omit the initial */ from the path.

You can also generate a list by loading an entire directory rather than a single file. When the individual MP3 file names are displayed, press s to save to a list. Why even bother when the mode can load a directory full of files? You can load the playlist into Emacs and sort and rearrange the file names into a pleasing playing order. If you just want the playing order shuffled randomly, the s command followed by r mixes up the list you see on-screen.

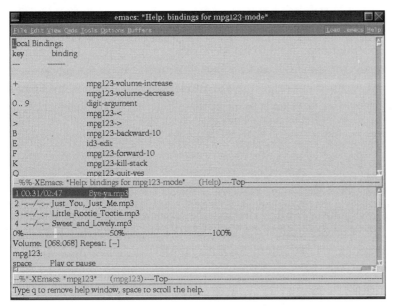

Figure 15.7 *The mpg123 MP3 Player*

An ABC Mode for Musicians

ABC is an ASCII file format that was originally developed as a compact means of transferring traditional tunes over the Internet via e-mail or the Web. In its ten years of existence, the format has been tweaked and refined to the point that even complex European art music pieces can be translated into ABC format.

What makes ABC truly useful for musicians is that programs have been developed for converting music written in this format to high-quality PostScript scores that can be printed. Music publishers might not be too excited about ABC, but for musicians, the vast amount of music in this format available on the Web is an invaluable resource.

Visit the ABC home page at http://www.gre.uc.uk/~c.walshaw/abc/ to find sources of both ABC tune files and the Linux software needed for PostScript conversion. I recommend abc2ps, which is the converter software that abc-mode is set up to use.

Michael Shulman wrote abc-mode.el as an Emacs interface to the ABC file format and the software used with it. The extension provides font locking and a variety of keyboard commands for processing and viewing the tune files. One command even transposes tunes to a different key.

Installation

To benefit from abc-mode, you need to have GhostScript installed and configured, abc2ps (and optionally the abc2midi package) installed, and a PostScript viewer such as gv. The mode is contained in a single file, abc-mode.el, which you need to copy to your site-lisp directory. The last step is to insert these lines into your ~/.emacs file:

```
(autoload 'abc-mode "abc-mode" "Major Mode for ABC files" t)
(add-to-list 'auto-mode-alist '("\\.abc\\'" . abc-mode))
```

Using abc-mode

Aside from PostScript conversion and viewing, abc-mode also allows you to search for tune names. This is very useful with some of the large ABC files available, which might contain more than 100 tunes. Here are the available commands:

M-Ctrl-b	Goes backward one measure in a tune.
M-Ctrl-f	Goes forward one measure.
Ctrl-c Tab	Inserts a standard ABC header.
Ctrl-c Ctrl-b	Converts the entire buffer to a PostScript file.
Ctrl-c Ctrl-c	Converts just the tune at point to a PostScript file.
Ctrl-c Ctrl-g	Goes to a particular tune.
Ctrl-c Ctrl-i	The same as Ctrl-c Tab: Inserts an ABC header.
Ctrl-c Ctrl-n	Converts the selected region to a PostScript file.
Ctrl-c Ctrl-p	Converts the entire buffer to a PostScript file.
Ctrl-c Ctrl-r	Transposes tunes to a different key.
Ctrl-c Ctrl-s	Searches for a tune.
Ctrl-c Ctrl-t	Jumps to the body of a tune.
Ctrl-c Ctrl-v	Runs a PostScript viewer on a PostScript file.

abc-mode is a good demonstration of how Emacs can facilitate work with external programs that use text files as input.

The Remembrance Agent

Software that has a completely new function is rare. Most applications are refinements of ideas that are ten or 15 years old—a better spreadsheet, a word processor with new features, and so on. Bradley Rhodes managed to come up with a novel job for software to undertake when he began writing the Remembrance Agent (RA). In his words:

> The Remembrance Agent is one of the projects being developed by the MIT Media Lab's software agents group. Given a collection of the user's accumulated email, Usenet news articles, papers, saved HTML files and other text notes, it attempts to find those documents which are most relevant to the user's current context. That is, it searches this collection of text for the documents which bear the highest word-for-word similarity to the text the user is currently editing, in the hope that they will also bear high conceptual similarity and thus be useful to the user's current work. These suggestions are continuously displayed in a small buffer at the bottom of the user's Emacs buffer. If a suggestion looks useful, the full text can be retrieved with a single command.

> The Remembrance Agent works in two stages. First, the user's collection of text documents is indexed into a database saved in a vector format. After the database is created, the other stage of the Remembrance Agent is run from Emacs, where it periodically takes a sample of text from the working buffer and finds those documents from the collection that are most similar. It summarizes the top documents in a small Emacs window and allows you to retrieve the entire text of any one with a keystroke.

Of the packages described in this book, the Remembrance Agent is perhaps closest to Notes mode, because this is another hybrid package that depends on external programs to function. Both packages index and organize collections of text files and make them accessible through an Emacs interface. One large difference between the two is the dynamic nature of the RA buffer, which automatically responds to the text in your active buffer as you type.

The engine behind RA is two compiled C programs, ra-index and ra-retrieve. The first one must be run manually on files and directories you want indexed for later use by RA. ra-retrieve is automatically called by the Emacs Lisp component of the system; its responsibility is to periodically search for similarities in your indexed files. ra-retrieve's input is the text surrounding point in your active buffer, and its output supplies links for the RA window.

Due to the unprecedented nature of RA, it takes some practice to get the hang of using it. The main factors controlling the relevance of the links in an RA window are the files you have chosen to index and make available. This requires some experimentation.

Users are accustomed to software that responds to your input and then patiently and passively waits for more. RA is akin to the background daemons on a Linux system that scurry and bustle about, doing their work behind the scenes, but daemons don't periodically show you what they've been up to, as RA does.

Unpacking and Installation

Unpack the remem-2.09.tar.gz archive and change to the new directory, where you will find a Configure script. If you are running GNU Emacs, there is an excellent chance that running the script will produce a usable makefile. Try this first:

```
./configure ; make ; make install
```

The make process generates the two binary executables ra-index and ra-retrieve and byte-compiles the two Lisp files in the subdirectory /other. The make install command copies the executables to /usr/local/bin and the Lisp files to your site-lisp directory.

XEmacs users need to change the middle command in the preceding line to

```
make EMACS=xemacs
```

However, due to some changes recently made to the way XEmacs loads nonpackaged extensions, some further tinkering might be necessary. Recent XEmacs versions have deprecated the old site-lisp directory and replaced it with /usr/local/lib/xemacs/ site-packages/lisp. You could go to the trouble of modifying the makefile so that the byte-compiled Lisp files get installed to the proper directory, but it is easier to do this by hand. Just make sure that remem.elc and jimminy.elc are copied to the proper directory, the one that XEmacs searches for local Lisp files. The two binaries should have ended up in /usr/local/bin even if the Lisp files weren't copied to the correct location.

The last step is to insert these activation lines in your ~/.emacs file:

```
(load "remem")
(load "remem-custom.el")
```

At this point, you might be saying, "There's no such file as remem-custom.el! How can Emacs load it!?"

Well, you're right; there is no such file. It needs to be created. This step isn't absolutely necessary (and if you don't do it, ignore that second ~/.emacs line!), but it makes it easier to customize RA without needing to re-byte-compile remem.el while you are tweaking your RA setup.

All you need to do is load the file remem.el into an Emacs session and copy the lines near the top of the file between this commented line:

```
;; CUSTOMIZATIONS
```

and this one:

```
;; END OF CUSTOMIZATIONS
```

Now load a new, nonexistent file by pressing Ctrl-x Ctrl-f and typing

```
/[your site-lisp directory]/remem-custom.el
```

Paste the copied lines into the new file and save it.

Now the second line in the preceding ~/.emacs entry will do something, but only if you edit remem-custom.el so that it includes the directories you need to create before RA will function.

Setting up Searchable Sources

You need at least one directory containing files generated by ra-index. The first step is to create the directory ~/RA-indexes. This is the default name. If you want to use a different name and location, you need to edit the remem-custom.el file and change the value of the variable `remem-database-dir`.

XEmacs Font Locking

XEmacs users might want to change a couple of lines in remem-custom.el to enable syntax highlighting (although this might have been fixed by the time you read this). These lines:

```
(cond ((and (boundp 'hilit-background-mode)
            (equal hilit-background-mode 'dark))
```

should be changed to this:

```
(cond ((and (boundp 'frame-background-mode)
            (equal frame-background-mode 'dark))
```

Choose a directory of text files and then create a subdirectory under ~/RA-indexes that mnemonically reflects the text-file directory's contents, such as "mail" or "notes". Now you need to tell RA what directory to use. Edit the remem-custom.el file again, and add at least one *scope,* a Lisp statement that sets up some lines in the RA display buffer so that they display search results from a particular directory. The variable definition to change looks like this:

```
(defvar remem-scopes-list '(("books" 2 5 500)
                            ("articles" 2 5 500)
                            ("common" 2 5 500)
                            ("notes" 2 5 500))
    "The list of scopes, where each scope is (DIRN NUM-LINES UPDATE-TIME QUERY-RANGE)")
```

A scope is a series of lines in the RA window that display the search and matching results from a particular subdirectory of ~/RA-indexes. You need only one scope, but you can use several, as in the preceding example. The word in quotes (such as "books" in the example) is the name of one of the subdirectories of your ~/RA-indexes directory. The number 5 in the sample entries is the number of seconds between updates; ra-retrieve will wait this long before searching again and updating the RA buffer. The QUERY-RANGE (500 in the example) is the number of words on either side of point (in your editing buffer) that should be taken into consideration when searching. Save the file when you are finished, and evaluate the buffer to update any changed variables.

Now you are ready to run ra-index with this command:

```
ra-index -v ~/RA-indexes/[subdirectory] [directory-to-be-indexed] -e
[subdirectories-to-ignore]
```

An example might look like this:

```
ra-index -v ~/RA-indexes/articles ~/articles -e ~/articles/economist
```

You need to run this command once for every directory for which you have included a scope in the remem-scopes-list variable.

This is quite a bit of preparation, but you need to do it only when you want to add, update, or exclude directories.

RA Commands

The RA keymap is based on the prefix Ctrl-c r. To start (or stop) the Agent, press Ctrl-c r t.

An RA window opens. There is a delay of a few seconds while the index directories are scanned. Once it's initiated, the window looks something like Figure 15.8.

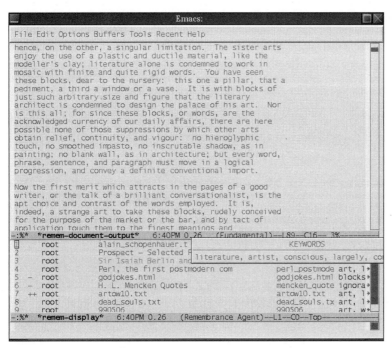

Figure 15.8 *The Remembrance Agent Window*

You can control RA activity with these key commands:

Ctrl-c r t	Toggles RA on and off.
Ctrl-c r v	Displays the results. Bypasses the built-in timer and updates the RA window.
Ctrl-c r [number]	Copies the full text of an indexed source file to a temporary buffer.
Ctrl-c r r [number]	Rates the suggestion's relevance. Ratings are saved to a log file that can be e-mailed to the author, who uses this information to evaluate and improve the software.
Ctrl-c r f	Performs a search on one of the fields in the RA display: Body, Location, Date, Subject, or Person.
Ctrl-c r q	Brings up a query buffer so that you can fill in keywords in more than one field. Pressing Ctrl-c r v (just described) initiates the search and updates the RA window with the results.
Ctrl-c r d	Database change. This is how you tell RA to begin using a subdirectory of ~/RA-indexes other than the defaults you defined in remem-custom.el.

The mouse can also be used to control the RA window.

Mouse button 1 is the equivalent of Ctrl-c r [number]. Clicking on the line number at the left edge of the window displays that indexed file.

The first mouse button can also be clicked on a particular field, such as Location or Subject. A search begins on the contents of the field, and the new results are displayed.

Mouse buttons 2 and 3 will pop up a small window with the keywords that caused that file to be deemed relevant.

Because the work done by RA is new and unfamiliar, it takes practice to get any benefit from the package. Experiment with different combinations of indexed directories, different scope sizes, and different update intervals, all of which can be changed in the remem-custom.el file. This file shouldn't be byte-compiled, because it is small and changes frequently.

The RA window can be distracting if it is constantly visible. If you maximize your main editing window (Ctrl-x 1), RA will remain running in the background. This is the way I like to run RA, checking the window every now and then to see what results have been dredged up recently.

License Issues

The Remembrance Agent has always been freely available, but only with the most recent version has it been licensed under the GNU General Public License. The package, although developed at the MIT Media Lab, was in part supported by two corporations: British Telecom and Merrill Lynch. Earlier versions were not free in the GPL sense of the word, because you couldn't distribute modified versions. Now that RA is unencumbered, it will doubtless show up in the form of Linux distribution packages, which should make the setting-up process easier.

Conclusion

Remember that this chapter and the preceding one are only a sampling of the available packages. To learn about others, browse the Emacs newsgroups, because a useful package tends to be discussed often.

The next chapter introduces packages that make life easier for programmers. Emacs is particularly strong in this area, because programmers were the first users of the editor.

Chapter 16: Packages That Make Programming Easier

Emacs was originally a programmer's editor. The various language-specific modes have a long history of tuning and refinement. As new languages are developed, either an existing mode is adapted or an entirely new mode is written from scratch.

Aside from the language modes, many programmer's utilities are available. By choosing a set of these that fits your programming style, you can create a customized Emacs-based programming environment that can be as useful as one of the modern IDEs (*Integrated Development Environments*) common in the commercial software marketplace.

Source-code files are differentiated from one another as a convenience for the programmer. As far as the compiler is concerned, a directory of these files could be just one large file. In a project's source files, the units that matter more to the programmer are code blocks such as function and variable definitions, classes, and preprocessor conditionals. A statement in one file might refer to or invoke a definition in another file. Emacs provides several different methods of navigating through a directory of source files and locating a particular block of code. etags, function menus, and the Speedbar window are three of these discussed later in this chapter.

A Mode for Nearly Every Language

What makes a language mode useful to a programmer?

- Font locking helps visually separate different types of code and comments.
- Special keybindings allow rapid movement between statements or function definitions, analogous to text-mode's sentence and paragraph movement commands.
- Indentation can be automated and set to a particular style.
- Parentheses, brackets, and curly braces can be checked for balance.
- It has a built-in interface with compilers and debuggers.
- It can jump to the source files responsible for compiler-reported errors, one after another.

Not every language mode has all these features. In general, the more widely-used languages, such as C, C++, and Java, have the most powerful Emacs modes.

Python and Perl, the two major interpreted languages, each have a mode that provides these features when appropriate.

Dealing with Comments

Emacs provides several keyboard commands that ease the task of delimiting comments with comment characters and keeping your comments formatted nicely. These commands work for all major languages and many minor ones.

The M-q key command, used in text-mode to reformat paragraphs to a particular fill-column, has been modified in the programming modes so that it preserves indentation and discards excess comment characters that might not be needed after the operation. Pressing M-q while within this C comment block:

```
/* Here are some comments which could
 * be evened out and
 * formatted, just for appearance's sake
*/
```

results in this:

```
/* Here are some comments which could be evened out
 *  and formatted, just for appearance's sake */
```

The `indent-for-comment` and `comment-region` commands can help you when you type comments. M-; moves point past the code and inserts opening and closing comment characters, leaving the cursor between them. The column that this command moves to is called the `comment-column`. By default, this is set to column 32. If your code is wider than 32 columns, you can use the `set-comment-column` command to set it to another value for the current buffer. Ctrl-x ; sets the current point position as the new `comment-column`. If you want it set permanently, you can use a line like this in your ~/.emacs file:

```
(setq comment-column 55)
```

As you type a comment to the right of a block of code, you might want your text to continue on a new line at the `comment-column` position rather than running off the right edge of the screen. Rather than pressing Enter for a new line, use the command M-j to indent for a new comment line. This key command also moves already-typed text down to a new indented line beneath the current line. If your comment looked like this, with point moved back between the words much and undo:

```
Fixnum undo_threshold;          /* Two thresholds controlling how much undo
information to keep.  */
Fixnum undo_high_threshold;
```

pressing M-j would format the comment lines like this:

```
Fixnum undo_threshold;          /* Two thresholds controlling how */
Fixnum undo_high_threshold;     /* much undo information to keep. */
```

Sometimes it is easier to type in comment material while the ideas are fresh in your mind and not bother with comment characters until after you have finished. The comment-region key command, Ctrl-c Ctrl-c, surrounds a marked region with comment characters.

This can also be used on code you want to make "invisible" to the compiler, perhaps while diagnosing a malfunctioning source file. If you use the Ctrl-u Ctrl-c Ctrl-c command, the Emacs "universal argument," it removes all comment characters from a selected region.

The next section introduces cc-mode, which evolved over the years from simpler C and C++ modes.

A Mode for C, C++, and Java

cc-mode is a highly-evolved and well-maintained mode. It was developed from an earlier C mode by several people, including Barry Warsaw, coauthor of the Emacs Python mode. Currently, this mode is a team effort, with Martin Stjernholm acting as maintainer.

Unlike some other language modes, it has no provision for font locking, leaving those duties for font-lock mode itself. Some programmers don't use syntax highlighting; cc-mode works equally well with or without it. The choice is up to the user.

If your source files have any of the conventional file name suffixes, such as .c, .h, .C, .cxx, .cpp, or .c++, cc-mode should start automatically when you view these files. You can see a complete list of recognized suffixes by using the Ctrl-h v [variable] help command. Requesting help on the auto-mode-alist variable causes a Help buffer to display a list of all suffixes that automatically call a particular mode.

If you use nonstandard file name suffixes, you can either start cc-mode manually (M-x cc-mode) or use a line such as this in your ~/.emacs file:

```
(add-to-list 'auto-mode-alist '("\\.CXT\\'" . cc-mode))
```

This makes cc-mode the default for any files ending in .cxt.

This mode's power lies in two areas: syntactic navigation and maintaining a defined indentation style.

Navigating through Source Files

Words, sentences, and paragraphs might be logical units to move by in a text file, but cc-mode ignores these (except within comment blocks), providing keybindings that enable quick movement between expressions, functions, and lists:

M-Ctrl-a	Moves point to the beginning of a function.
M-Ctrl-e	Moves to the end of a function.

These two commands are extensions of M-a and M-e, which move point to the beginning or end of a sentence in text-mode. In cc-mode, these two key commands are used for movement within a statement:

M-a	Moves point to the beginning of a statement.
M-e	Moves to the end of a statement.

The next key commands enable quick movement through preprocessor conditional statements:

Ctrl-c Ctrl-u	Places point at the beginning of a preprocessor conditional.
Ctrl-c Ctrl-p	Moves to the previous preprocessor conditional.
Ctrl-c Ctrl-n	Moves point to the next preprocessor conditional.

The preprocessor conditional movement commands are particularly useful when you attempt to scan a source file in order to determine just which code is active under your platform. Conditional statements are heavily used in software that can be compiled for numerous operating systems, such as most GNU and open source software.

Indentation Styles

Several distinct styles of indentation have evolved over the years for C and C++ source files. Rather strongly-held views on which style is more logical and readable have inspired many disputes, but it's really just a matter of taste and custom. cc-mode's default is a basic style from which the others are derived. The K&R style used in Kernhigan and Ritchie's classic *The C Programming Language* is one of the choices offered, as is the GNU style, commonly used in many (but not all)

GPL-licensed software projects. The Linux source code is another variant style. Figure 16.1 shows C code indented in the default style, and Figure 16.2 is the same code in the Linux style.

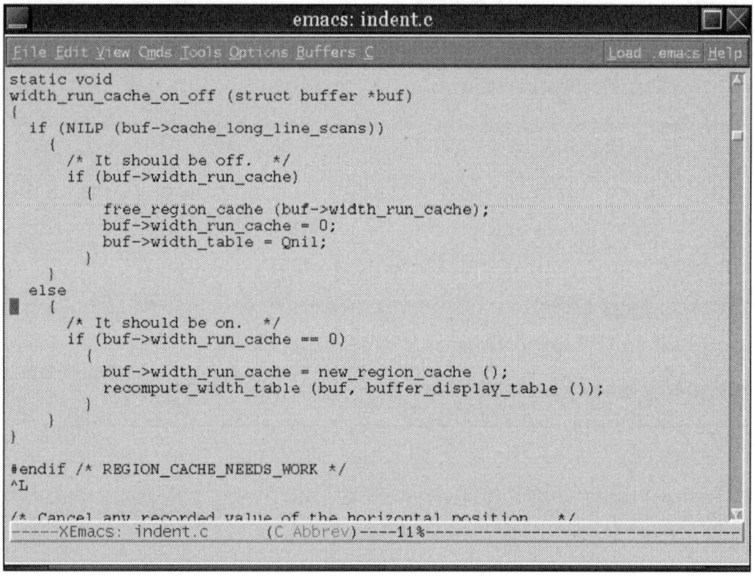

Figure 16.1 *Default cc-mode–Style Indentation*

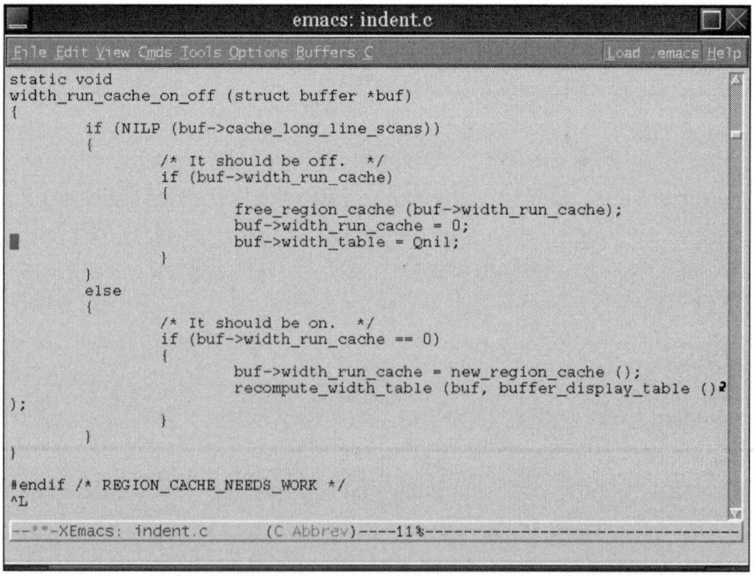

Figure 16.2 *Linux-Style Indentation*

As you can see, the styles aren't radically different; the brace alignment and amount of indentation vary between the styles. You can easily try any of the 11 available styles. Either press Ctrl-c . or press M-x and type

```
c-set-style
```

You are prompted for a style in the minibuffer. Delete the default value and press the Tab key. A Completion window opens with a list of all indentation styles supported by cc-mode. Choose one and type its name in the minibuffer. You won't see any change until you do one of two things: type in more code or select a region of existing code and reindent it with the M-Ctrl-\ command.

This keystroke calls the command `indent-region`, which uses whichever indentation style is in effect.

After trying these various styles, you might find one you prefer over the default. You can set this variable from within a Customize Group buffer (go to the "c" group), where you will find a Default Style setting. You need to remember the exact name of the style (as it was shown in the Completion window) so that you can type it in the entry field.

Otherwise, you can use a `c-mode-hook` setting in your ~/.emacs file, as in this example:

```
(add-hook 'c-mode-hook
    (lambda ()
    (c-set-style "name")))
```

Don't forget the double quotes around the name of the style.

Indenting Automatically

The Tab key has a special role in cc-mode. In a normal text-mode buffer, the Tab key inserts a configurable number of spaces (by default, eight); this simulates the behavior most people are accustomed to. In a cc-mode buffer, Tab inserts a variable number of spaces, depending on the syntactic role of the statement you are typing. This can be disconcerting if you aren't used to it, but what the mode is trying to do is keep your code indented according to your chosen style. This lets you concentrate on the code while the indentation is adjusted for you as you type. You can see a demonstration of this by pressing the Tab key, typing something (try a function definition), and then moving the cursor back to the beginning of the line and repeatedly pressing the Tab key. You would expect the definition you typed to be pushed to the right by these tabs, but you will find that once the Tab key has indented a line to the proper column, it refuses to let you insert more. If you need to insert real tab characters, you can always use the "insert quoted literal" key command, Ctrl-q Tab.

Another useful indentation command which is not restricted to cc-mode is the "indent-for-tab" command, Ctrl-i.

This command will indent a line in the proper way for the current major mode.

Automatic indenting will save you more time than any other single feature of cc-mode. It just takes a little practice to let it do its work while you do yours.

Electric Characters and Hungry Delete

These two features are turned off by default (probably to avoid scaring away skittish new users!), but they both are well worth trying out. You might find one or both of these features to your liking, in which case you can turn them on permanently.

The auto-newline feature changes the results of typing the comma, colon, semicolon, and curly brace keys. These characters all have a certain syntactical meaning in the C and C++ languages, so cc-mode can make general assumptions about what you need after you type one of them.

A semicolon is used to terminate a statement in C, and the convention is to start the next statement on a new line. The "electric" semicolon provided by auto-newline in effect presses Enter for you, and point ends up at the beginning of a new line. Let's say that your next character is a curly brace that is intended to enclose a function definition:

```
statement;
{
     |
```

As soon as you type the brace, a newline plus the proper amount of indentation is inserted. (The pipe character on the last line shows where your cursor would end up.)

To turn this feature on temporarily, press Ctrl-c Ctrl-a.

The same key command turns it off again.

The other optional feature is complementary to the auto-newline "electric" characters; it is called hungry delete. It increases the appetite of your Backspace and Delete keys so that they consume all spaces in their paths until either the beginning or end of a line is contacted or a nonspace character is encountered. What this does for you is speed up removal of indentation spaces when you've made a mistake and need to back up. It's easy when you're zippily backspacing through a row of spaces to hold down the key a little too long, inadvertently wiping out a character or two you wanted to keep. Hungry delete helps prevent this.

You can turn on this feature by pressing (while in cc-mode) Ctrl-c Ctrl-d.

Turn on both of these features simultaneously by pressing Ctrl-c Ctrl-t.

If you try these two features and you want them turned on permanently, you can insert one of the following statements into your ~/.emacs file.

For auto-newline only, use this one:

```
(add-hook 'c-mode-hook
    (lambda ()
    (c-toggle-auto-state 1)))
```

This one activates hungry delete:

```
(add-hook 'c-mode-hook
    (lambda ()
    (c-toggle-hungry-state 1)))
```

If you want both, this statement fills the bill:

```
(add-hook 'c-mode-hook
    (lambda ()
    (c-toggle-auto-hungry-state 1)))
```

These `lambda` functions can be typed into one of the `c-mode-hook` entry fields in the Customize buffer (discussed in the next section) as an alternative to plugging one of the preceding statements into your ~/.emacs file.

You can always tell whether either of these two submodes is active by glancing at your modeline. If the mode indicator is C, both are toggled off. If the indicator is C/a, auto-indent is toggled on. If it's C/h, hungry delete is toggled on. C/ah in the modeline means that they both are active.

Other cc-mode Variables

There was a time when developing a complete set of customized variables for cc-mode was a significant undertaking. It was done by constructing Lisp statements that redefined any of cc-mode's numerous tweakable settings. Luckily for the user, many of these variables now have a Customize interface. If you use cc-mode frequently, it is worthwhile to scan the mode's Customize Group buffer and see if you might want to change anything. You might guess that the group to look for would be cc-mode, but the name is just "c". Press M-x and type

```
customize-group
```

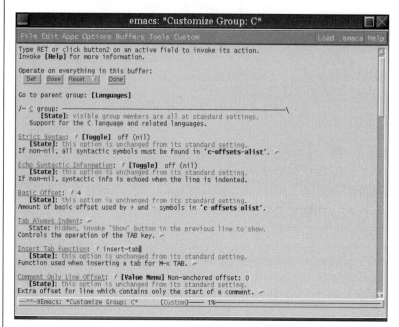

Figure 16.3   *cc-mode Customization Buffer*

When prompted, respond tersely with

c

The resultant Customize buffer will look something like Figure 16.3.

Possible Performance Problems

When you use the navigation key commands to jump from the body of a statement back to the beginning, or from a preprocessor conditional to the previous one, quite a bit of scanning and parsing are going on behind the scenes. With some coding styles, cc-mode can get lost and stalled, possibly even hanging the Emacs session. cc-mode prefers to scan forward in a file, because C and C++ can be difficult for the mode to interpret when moving backward, against the logical flow. The mode makes a leap backward, hoping to overshoot, say, the beginning of a function, and then scans forward until it is found.

There is an easy way to avoid these potential problems: Try to place the opening curly brace that begins a function definition (in C) or class definition (in C++ or Java) in the first column. Emacs and cc-mode try to encourage this by the way indentation and electric characters are set up.

The K&R style of indentation can cause problems with function argument declarations, because this style has them beginning in the first column. Indenting argument lists one space greatly speeds up cc-mode parsing.

See the cc-mode Info files for more on this topic.

cc-mode and Java

cc-mode can be used to edit Java code. It knows about Java syntax, commenting, and indentation, but an extension built on top of cc-mode is preferable. It's called the JDE, which stands for Java Development Environment. Read all about it in the next section.

JDE

The Java Development Environment is one of the "big modes"; it's large and complex, but it comes with well-illustrated HTML documentation. I can only scratch the surface in this chapter's coverage of the mode, but hopefully this section will be enough to pique your interest and get you off to a good start with JDE.

JDE, like many free software projects, began with a single developer. Paul Kinnucan started the project and is still the maintainer, but in recent years a sizable user community has arisen, complete with an active mailing list and many user contributions.

Requirements and Installation

You can use any Java Development Kit with JDE, but it will need some customization to be used with kits other than one of the official JDKs from Sun Microsystems. See the later section "Customizing JDE" for details.

GNU Emacs Installation

A GNU Emacs JDE installation requires several external Emacs packages:

- semantic
- beanshell
- elib
- eieio
- Speedbar

The Speedbar package is included with GNU Emacs, but it is a good idea to install a newer version in order to make it work with the other required packages.

You also need Netscape or another graphical Web browser for viewing the documentation.

All the Emacs extensions necessary for running JDE can be found, along with the JDE source itself, on this book's CD-ROM in the directory /cdrom/packages/JDE.

Install these extra packages by unpacking them into temporary directories and following the installation instructions. It is an involved installation process, but if you carefully work your way through the required packages, you should end up with a powerful Emacs extension.

In the directory on the CD-ROM where you found JDE and the other packages is a small text file called jde_init.el. This file contains initialization lines for all the packages. They can be copied and pasted into your ~/.emacs file. The file needs some editing beforehand, because you need to adapt the paths in the lines like this one:

```
(add-to-list 'load-path "opt/emacs/jde-2.2.6/lisp")
```

Using `add-to-list` statements like this one lets you install Emacs extensions anywhere you like, and they supersede the possibly older or incompatible versions that might be a part of your Emacs installation. This also helps keep your site-lisp directory from becoming cluttered.

Two of the statements in jde_init.el are optional:

```
(global-set-key [(f12)] 'speedbar-get-focus)
```

This statement lets you start Speedbar with a keypress and moves the cursor and focus to the new frame.

The next statement works only with GNU Emacs. It puts a Speedbar item on the Tools menu right after the Calendar item:

```
(define-key-after (lookup-key global-map [menu-bar tools])
   [speedbar] '("Speedbar" . speedbar-frame-mode) [calendar])
```

XEmacs Installation

The installation of XEmacs requires the following packages:

- JDE
- cc-mode
- semantic
- debug

- Speedbar
- edit-utils
- eterm
- mail-lib
- xemacs-base

All of these are preconfigured XEmacs packages that can be installed with the XEmacs package tools (see Chapter 12 for instructions). You probably have several of them already installed.

Maintaining XEmacs packages is a volunteer effort, so there is a possibility at any given time that the original source packages available on the Web might be more up-to-date. You can follow the same procedure described in the preceding section to install JDE and friends from the source archives, but it does take longer. You just have to balance the natural desire to have the latest and greatest software with time and inclination restraints.

Using JDE

Once you have JDE installed, try it out by loading a Java file. If the file has the widely-used .java suffix, you should notice two new menus, and "JDE" should appear in the modeline. Otherwise, you can manually start it up by pressing M-x and typing

```
java-mode
```

The Java menu, shown in Figure 16.4, is adapted from the underlying cc-mode C menu, with its motion and comment-filling utility commands. See the preceding section for details.

The JDE menu, shown in Figure 16.5, is where you find IDE-like commands, used for compiling Java source and then running and debugging compiled applications and applets.

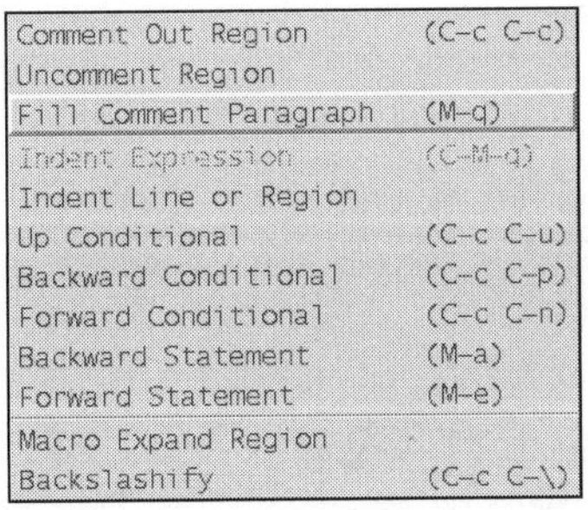

```
Comment Out Region        (C-c C-c)
Uncomment Region
Fill Comment Paragraph    (M-q)
Indent Expression         (C-M-q)
Indent Line or Region
Up Conditional            (C-c C-u)
Backward Conditional      (C-c C-p)
Forward Conditional       (C-c C-n)
Backward Statement        (M-a)
Forward Statement         (M-e)
Macro Expand Region
Backslashify              (C-c C-\)
```

Figure 16.4 *The Java Menu*

```
Compile          (C-c C-v C-c)
Run App          (C-c C-v C-r)
Debug App        (C-c C-v C-d)
Run Applet       (C-c C-v C-a)
Debug Applet     (C-c C-v C-t)
Build            (C-c C-v C-b)
Interpret        (C-c C-v C-k)
Documentation                ˅
Templates                    ˅
Wizards                      ˅
Speedbar         (C-c C-v C-s)
Project                      ˅
Help                         ˅
```

Figure 16.5   *The JDE Menu*

The Wizards and Templates submenus allow you to insert prewritten blocks of code into your files.

Directory Browsing

Eric Ludlam's Speedbar add-on works well with JDE. Select Speedbar from the JDE menu. A narrow frame appears, with the files in the current directory displayed in a tree arrangement, as shown in Figure 16.6.

Click on the plus symbol to the left of any file name in the Speedbar frame, and the hierarchy of classes in the file unfolds. Click on a class, and point is moved to

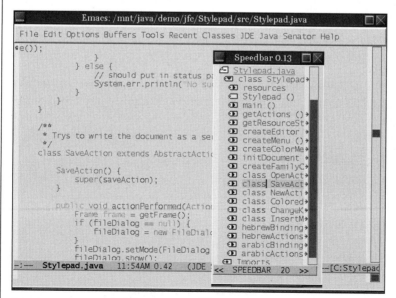

Figure 16.6   *JDE and the Speedbar*

that class; if the file isn't loaded, it will be. In effect, Speedbar is a graphical version of etags, but you don't need to generate a Tags file before you can browse the elements of your source files. Eric Ludlam's Semantic Bovinator is responsible for generating the tags. (Both Speedbar and etags are discussed in more detail later in this chapter.)

Using Speedbar, you can navigate through a source directory quickly and efficiently. Think of it as a programmer's version of a file manager. In source code, programming constructs such as classes and functions are the relevant units rather than files, which are somewhat arbitrarily separated from each other.

Speedbar has its own set of keybindings for managing the files in its frame:

Enter	Loads the file that is under the cursor.
g	Refreshes the display (rereads the directory from disk).
=	Expands the tree of tags (just like clicking the + button does).
-	Contracts the tree, hiding the tags.
C	Copies a file.
R	Renames a file.
D	Deletes a file.
I	File information (such as permissions).

The last four commands use the minibuffer for prompts and user input.

If you are comfortable with etags and its Tags files, you can use it instead of or in conjunction with Speedbar.

Debugging

There are two ways to debug Java programs with JDE. If you have the Sun JDK version 1.2 or higher, you can use a debugger that comes with JDE, JDEbug. JDE also has support for jdb, the native Java debugger. Both of these debugging interfaces are comparable to the debuggers you find in commercial IDEs, including features such as stepping through a source file, conditional breakpoints, menu-driven operation, and a prompt for giving commands directly.

If you have the proper JDK version, the JDEbug package might be preferable to the native jdb debugger. Here are some of the advanced features:

- Automatic local variable display. As you step your way through the code, local variables are shown, as well as at each breakpoint.

- Multiprocess debugging, which allows you to monitor execution of simultaneous processes.

- Stack navigation. At each program step and breakpoint, you can move up or down the stack with one command.

A certain amount of configuration is required before you can use either debugger. Consult the JDE HTML documentation for step-by-step instructions.

Customizing JDE

JDE is extensively (infinitely? There are lots of options!) integrated with the Customize utility. You could easily spend a day or more using Customize to tweak a JDE installation, but luckily the defaults are well-chosen. The Options submenu gives you a choice of five different JDE Customize group buffers to load. Space doesn't permit me to delve into all of them, but I have to call your attention to one especially impressive and useful group. The JDE Autocode group buffer lets you enter your own templates (or alter the existing ones). These will be subsequently available from the JDE menu.

In Figure 16.7, the first Customize option in the group is the text to use for the boilerplate at the top of every new Java file.

Imagine that you are working on a large Java project in which a certain block of code is repeatedly used in several different files. Naturally, Emacs provides several ways to avoid retyping the same or similar text; you could use abbreviations, macros, or the Clipper utility. The method that works well with JDE and Customize is using the tempo template-creation system. tempo.el is included with all current flavors of Emacs. html-helper-mode is another package that uses it heavily.

Tempo provides a way of writing simple Lisp code that defines a template that can be invoked by name or called by another Lisp mode or utility. The function used is called `tempo-define-template`. In the following example, a template called "hello" is created:

```
(tempo-define-template
       "hello"                                ;; template name
       '("System.out.println(\"hello\");")    ;; definition
       "h"                                     ;; abbreviation
       "Inserts a print hello message")        ;; documentation
```

This Lisp statement could be included in your ~/.emacs file, or several such statements could be included in one Lisp file that you could load before working on the Java project.

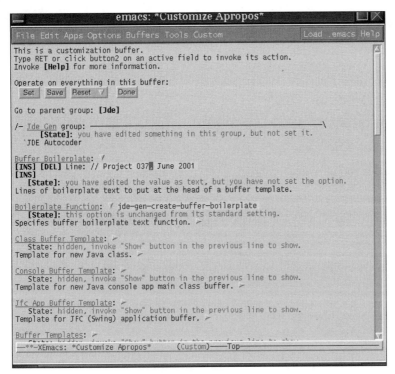

Figure 16.7   *JDE's Autocode Group*

After it's evaluated, pressing M-x and typing

```
tempo-template-hello
```

causes this string to be inserted in the current buffer at point:

```
System.out.println("hello");
```

Notice the backslash escape characters in the Lisp statement just shown. They are necessary, because the quoted string "hello" needs to be preserved from unwanted Lisp interpretation.

Now take a look at Figure 16.8. Notice the INS and DEL buttons to the left of each item. To add the "hello" template to the buffer, you click on the INS button at the bottom of the Code Templates category and fill in the name of the template and the command used to invoke it.

Make sure you save your changes by clicking on the State button. The next time you use JDE, you should be able to insert your new template with a menu selection.

JDE is one of the largest and most complex packages available for Emacs. Several chapters would be required to really do it justice. More background and installa-

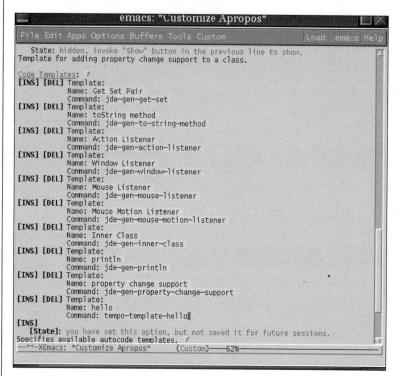

Figure 16.8   *Registering a New Template*

tion information (as well as links to the Web sites of the required packages) can be found at the official JDE Web site: http://jde.sunsite.dk.

CPerl-mode

Perl, Larry Wall's interpreted text-processing language, has been called the Swiss army knife of the World Wide Web. It is used extensively in the CGI scripts used by many Web sites, but it is also used behind the scenes in the maintenance of Linux systems. Perl scripts are responsible for many mundane tasks such as rotating log files, initiating certain actions at bootup and shutdown, and executing periodic cron jobs. The appeal of this language to system administrators is that functional, time-saving scripts can be written quickly.

There are two Perl major modes, perl-mode and CPerl-mode. This section describes CPerl-mode, because it has more features and is very actively maintained.

Some versions of Emacs default to perl-mode and others to CPerl-mode when a Perl file is loaded. In general, XEmacs is usually set up for CPerl-mode and GNU Emacs for perl-mode. In order for this section to make much sense while you try things out, I recommend that you find a Perl file, load it in an Emacs session, and press Ctrl-h m.

The mode help window appears. If it looks like Figure 16.9, you are running CPerl-mode. Notice also the "CPerl" mode identifier in the modeline. If the window identifies the mode as perl-mode, you might consider adding this line to your ~/.emacs file:

```
(autoload 'perl-mode "cperl-mode" "alternate mode for editing Perl programs" t)
```

When you evaluate this line or restart Emacs, CPerl-mode becomes your new default. (You can always delete this line later if you prefer standard Perl-mode.)

This mode was adapted from an early C mode years ago, so you will find some similarities to cc-mode, such as the motion keybindings (see Figure 16.10).

CPerl-mode has an intelligent interface to Perl Info files available on the Perl docs submenu. The mode looks up functions and symbols in a source file and then opens an Info window to the corresponding documentation. Unfortunately, most Linux distributions don't include an Info version of the Perl documentation in their Perl packages. You would have to snag a copy of the Perl source distribution (making sure that the release version of the source matches the version of your Perl binary installation), build the Info files, and install them in your Info directory. This would be worth the time and hassle if you do much Perl programming, especially for novices, because in effect context-sensitive help would be available at all times.

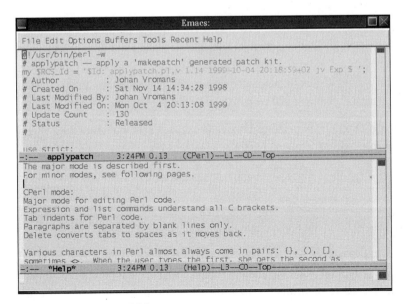

Figure 16.9 *CPerl-mode Help*

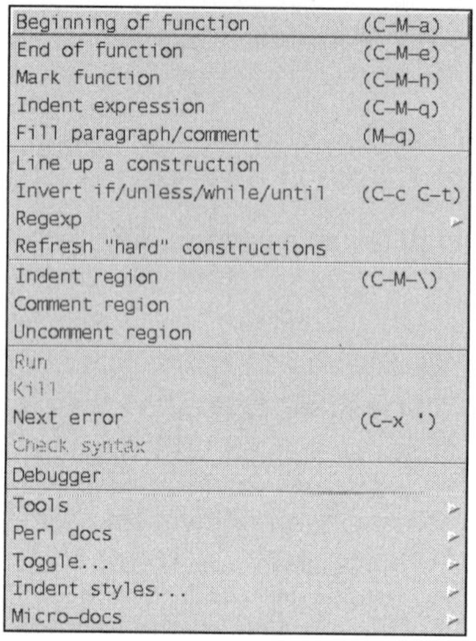

```
Beginning of function        (C–M–a)
End of function              (C–M–e)
Mark function                (C–M–h)
Indent expression            (C–M–q)
Fill paragraph/comment       (M–q)
Line up a construction
Invert if/unless/while/until (C–c C–t)
Regexp                                   ►
Refresh "hard" constructions
Indent region                (C–M–\)
Comment region
Uncomment region
Run
Kill
Next error                   (C–x ')
Check syntax
Debugger
Tools                                    ►
Perl docs                                ►
Toggle...                                ►
Indent styles...                         ►
Micro–docs                               ►
```

Figure 16.10   *The CPerl Menu*

Another unique form of documentation is available from the Micro-docs submenu. The items there summon any of several short essays concerning CPerl-mode usage and features, which are then displayed in a Help window. These docs are actually the documentation strings of unused variables buried in the cperl-mode.el Lisp file. The menu items call for help on a variable, just as you do when you press Ctrl-h v. This is a clever way to co-opt Emacs' help facility, and it's also a way to imbed help in a Lisp file but make it easily accessible.

After you finish editing a Perl script, two menu commands let you easily run or debug the file. If you select Debugger from the menu, a shell window opens with Perl running (with the -d debugging switch) and ready for your input. Pressing h at the prompt yields a list of commands with short descriptions, but to get much good out of the program, you should read the perldebug man page.

As befits an old and extensively-refined Emacs mode, CPerl's variables are for the most part changeable using Customize. Press M-x and type

```
customize-group
```

Respond with

```
cperl
```

You can access several pages of settings you can change. If you want CPerl to do as much as possible for you, look for settings that enable "hairy" options. These include electric characters such as in cc-mode, so that typing an opening brace automatically inserts the matching closing brace and leaves the cursor between them. CPerl uses more than the standard font-lock faces, which you might already have customized. These new faces are listed in a subgroup of the CPerl Customize group.

Customize is an indispensable part of Emacs, and I'd hate to do without it, but when experimenting with a new package, you might want to fool around with different combinations of settings without bringing up a Customize buffer. The developers of CPerl-mode realized this and built into the mode a way to let you quickly try out several settings via menu choices.

The various indentation styles, such as K&R and GNU, were introduced earlier. Similar styles are used in Perl programming as well. The Indent styles... submenu lets you toggle any of seven different styles. This is especially handy if you haven't yet settled on a style, because you can quickly change from one to another in order to compare them.

You can use the Toggle submenu to try out various "electric" features, such as electric parentheses and keywords. You can also turn on the auto-newline, similar to cc-mode's auto-newline, discussed earlier.

All in all, considering the built-in documentation and the abundance of menu commands, CPerl-mode is surely one of the more user-friendly Emacs programming modes.

Python Mode

Python is an up-and-coming interpreted scripting language with some similarity to Perl. It is an object-oriented language, like C++ and Java, but it uses an entirely different syntax than those two or Perl. Rather than use curly braces, brackets, or parentheses to separate statements or code blocks from one another, Python uses nothing but indentation levels to group statements under a header. Indentation control is a large part of cc-mode and CPerl-mode, but only for reasons of convention and readability. In Python, the Python interpreter uses white space in order to make sense of the source code. A Python mode for Emacs should make it easy to create and maintain consistent levels of indentation, as well as provide font locking and keyboard/menu commands.

Barry Warsaw's python-mode.el does all this and more. The standard Python mode for XEmacs, this mode has been under active development for years and is continually being improved as the relatively new Python language evolves. It works fine in GNU Emacs as well. For some reason, it has never been included in the official GNU Emacs distribution, but you can drop a copy of python.el in your site-lisp directory and byte-compile the file, and you will be almost ready to use Python-mode.

Activate the mode with these lines in your ~/.emacs file:

```
(add-to-list 'auto-mode-alist (cons "\\.jrn\\'" 'text-mode))(add-to-list 'auto-
mode-alist
      (cons "\\.py\\'"  'python-mode))
(add-to-list 'interpreter-mode-alist
      (cons "python"  'python-mode))


(autoload 'python-mode "python-mode" "Python editing mode." L)
```

These lines are necessary only for GNU Emacs users.

The Python Menu

In Figure 16.11, you can see that the familiar motion commands for navigating to the beginning or end of a statement are included, although in Python mode, the statements are definitions or classes. Because indentation levels are so important in Python, commands for marking the current definition or class as a region are included. After it is marked, the region can be shifted one tab width either direction or passed to the Python interpreter.

The tab width is a matter of preference. Too wide of a tab stop tends to push nested code blocks off the edge of the Emacs frame. Whenever a Python file is loaded, the

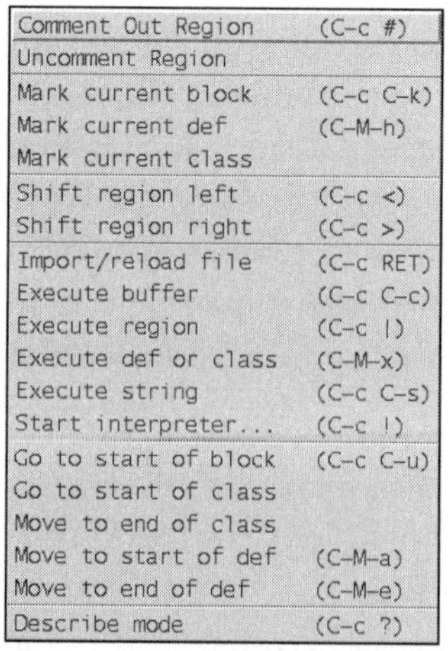

Comment Out Region	(C-c #)
Uncomment Region	
Mark current block	(C-c C-k)
Mark current def	(C-M-h)
Mark current class	
Shift region left	(C-c <)
Shift region right	(C-c >)
Import/reload file	(C-c RET)
Execute buffer	(C-c C-c)
Execute region	(C-c |)
Execute def or class	(C-M-x)
Execute string	(C-c C-s)
Start interpreter...	(C-c !)
Go to start of block	(C-c C-u)
Go to start of class	
Move to end of class	
Move to start of def	(C-M-a)
Move to end of def	(C-M-e)
Describe mode	(C-c ?)

Figure 16.11 *The Python-mode Menu*

tab width is set to whatever width was used by the file's author, ensuring that any additions you make to the file will fit in with the file's native indentation format. When you write a new Python file, the default four-space tab width is used, but this variable can be changed with Customize.

Execution Commands

There are several ways to execute Python code in this mode. You can hand over the entire buffer to the interpreter by pressing Ctrl-c !. A new window opens, showing you the output of the process (see Figure 16.12). A shell window running Python can be summoned, giving you an interactive Python session. The advantage of running this session in an Emacs window is that you can copy regions from another Python buffer and submit these chunks directly to the interpreter.

Customization

Among the many settings you can set in the Python Group Customize buffer is the name of the python executable you are using. In most cases, this is the default, "python," but a new version of Python written in Java has recently been gaining popularity. Python-mode makes a usually accurate guess as to which one you are using the first time you open a Python file. The Java-Python executable is nor-

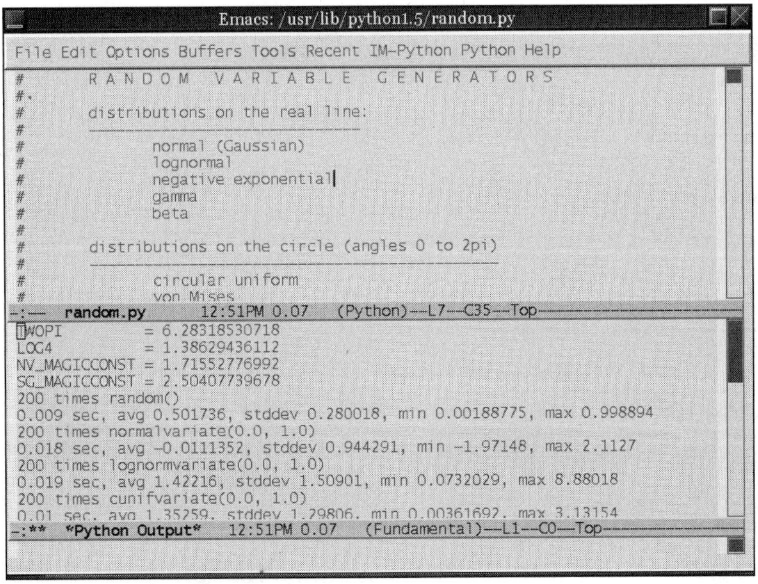

Figure 16.12   *The Python Output Buffer*

mally called "jpython", but if yours isn't, or if you call it using an alias, you can set the variable `py-default-interpreter` to the name of your executable. You could do this with a `setq` statement like many of the other variable-setting statements earlier in this book, but this might be a good time to investigate the Customize buffer for Python. Press M-x and type

```
customize-group
```

Respond to the prompt with

```
python
```

Figure 16.13 shows the initial Python Customize buffer.

The first items are the names of the default Python-mode executables, both Java and C, and the one that should be set as default. Among the other settings you might take a look at are the default indentation width, whether to use various "electric" features, and whether to beep a warning when the mode has changed the tab width (when a Python file with a different indentation setting has been loaded).

Python-mode uses the standard font-lock faces such as `function-name-face` and `string-face`. If you have already set the font-lock faces to your liking, you shouldn't have to do anything special for this mode.

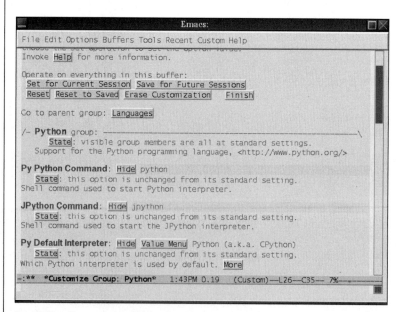

Figure 16.13   *Customizing Python-mode*

The Python Debugger

Python-mode doesn't have direct support for the Python debugger module, pdb.py. You can still use it in the Python Shell buffer, though. Import the module with these lines, typed at the python prompt:

```
>>> import pdb
>>> pdb.run('statement')
```

Don't type the three angle brackets. They are the default Python prompt characters that you see in any interactive Python session.

The standard Python documentation includes several help files explaining how to use the debugger module, but you can get a quick overview of the available commands by pressing h at the pdb prompt. You can substitute any Python statement copied from another Python buffer for the word statement in the second line.

Although the version of python-mode.el on this book's CD-ROM is the most recent as I write this, it's very possible that a new version will have been released by the time you read this book. The latest version can always be found at the official Python Web site (look for the "Emacs support" link): http://www.python.org.

Searching in Multiple Source Files

Earlier in this chapter, you saw how a combination of the Semantic Bovinator and Speedbar makes it possible to navigate through source files using tags, which are location markers used to find functions or classes by name. This is not a new idea. For years, programmers have used various utilities to generate tag files that index directories of source code. Other software, either stand-alone tag browsers or editor extensions and features, is used to navigate to tagged code blocks. Speedbar is a graphical tag browser that runs as an Emacs frame, but Emacs has nongraphical tag-browsing facilities as well.

Introducing etags

When you install Emacs, several auxiliary programs are installed as well. Most of them aren't used directly by the user. Instead, they are used by Emacs to perform certain jobs that are more efficiently done by a separate program rather than by Emacs itself. One program that is run by the user is called etags, a contraction of "Emacs tags".

etags has a long list of switches you can append to the command, most of which you will rarely need. The command's syntax is simple:

```
etags *.[ch]
```

When you run this command in a directory of C source files, etags scans each *.c and *.h file and compiles a list of every function declaration, global variable, external variable, and preprocessor constant definition in all the files, along with their locations. The tag file it creates is by default called TAGS unless you specify another name.

This program isn't just for C files; it also works with C++, Perl, Python, Emacs Lisp, and Java, as well as several other languages. Naturally, it doesn't look for the same code structures in all of these languages, but it modifies its behavior accordingly.

What You Can Do with a Tag File

Now that you have generated a shiny new TAGS file, you might take a look at it in an Emacs buffer. Here is a chunk of a TAGS file that indexes some of the XEmacs source:

```
^L
alloca.c,814
#define ADDRESS_FUNCTION( ADDRESS_FUNCTION^?,2287
#define ADDRESS_FUNCTION( ADDRESS_FUNCTION^?,2350
typedef void *pointer; pointer^?71,2431
typedef char *pointer; pointer^?73,2460
#   define xfree  ^?83,2743
#define     NULL     ^? 90,2830
#define malloc  ^?104,3301
#define     STACK_DIRECTION     ^? 121,3754
#define     STACK_DIR     ^?126,3840
```

Aren't you glad you don't have to read files like this? Tag files aren't meant to be read by humans, but you can see some meaning in this brief excerpt. alloca.c is the source file, followed by a list of definitions and so on, with their line-number location directly after the ^? character, which looks like two characters but is really an ASCII control character.

Emacs has several commands available for searching a TAGS file and opening a file that contains a particular tag.

Emacs reasonably assumes that a file named TAGS in the current directory applies to the files in that directory. If your tag file is elsewhere or has a different name, you need to tell Emacs about it. Press M-x and type

```
visit-tags-table
```

You are prompted for a file name, but if you want etags to use the default name, TAGS, just press Enter.

The command you will use the most is M-..

If the cursor is on the function name or whatever you are searching for, Emacs uses that as a search term. Otherwise, type in a term. It doesn't need to be a complete name, but if you type too small a fragment of the name you are looking for, there will be too many results.

This command finds the first match in alphabetical order. If it isn't the one you had in mind, press M-,. The next one will be found. You can execute this command repeatedly until you find the right one.

When Emacs finds a tag, it loads the source file and places the cursor on the code.

The tags facility can also be used to search for any other text in the source files and replace it with other text, similar to using the GNU grep file-searching utility but with replacement added to it. This search is similar to the standard query replacement command M-%, the difference being that the replacement is in every file listed in the TAGS file. To issue the command (which can be bound to a key), press M-x and type

```
tags-query-replace
```

Just as with the standard query-replacement command, pressing ! replaces the remainder of the matches automatically, but only in the current file. You have to keep pressing the M-, tags continuation key to advance to the next match, which might be in another file.

There are several more etags commands (see the etags section of the Emacs Info files), but a modern menu-and-mouse-based alternative to etags offers much of the same functionality and is easier to learn and use. There are two implementations of the same idea—one used by GNU Emacs and the other by XEmacs.

The GNU Emacs version is called imenu. If you would like to try it out, load a source-code file, such as a C or Emacs Lisp file. Most programming modes have built-in imenu support. You might or might not see a new menu on the menu bar. It might be called Index or, in the case of Python-mode, IM-Python. The menu lists programming constructs in the file, such as functions and variables. If you want this menu every time you load files in particular modes, you can add imenu to the mode-hooks with statements like these in your ~/.emacs file:

```
(add-hook 'c-mode-hook (lambda () (imenu-add-menubar-index)))
(add-hook 'emacs-lisp-mode-hook (lambda () (imenu-add-menubar-index)))
```

You might find the slight delay (longer for larger files) whenever a source file is loaded annoying. In this case, you can start up imenu only when you need it by pressing M-x and typing

```
imenu-add-menubar-index
```

You can also access a mouse menu by pressing Ctrl-mouse button 3.

The XEmacs equivalent is called `func-menu`, which adds a new Functions menu to the menu bar. To turn this on, insert these lines in your ~/.emacs file:

```
(require 'func-menu)
(define-key global-map 'f11 'function-menu)
(add-hook 'find-file-hooks 'fume-add-menubar-entry)
(add-hook 'c-mode-hook 'fume-add-menubar-entry)
(add-hook 'c++-mode-hook 'fume-add-menubar-entry)
(add-hook 'emacs-lisp-mode-hook 'fume-add-menubar-entry)
(add-hook 'python-mode-hook 'fume-add-menubar-entry)
(define-key global-map [(control c) (l)] 'fume-list-functions)
(define-key global-map [(control c) (q)] 'fume-prompt-function-goto)
(define-key global-map '(shift button3) 'mouse-function-menu)
(define-key global-map '(meta  button1) 'fume-mouse-function-goto)
```

Not all of these lines are necessary. For example, you might not need the keybinding in the second line or the mouse bindings in the last two lines.

The main advantage of the more primitive etags method discussed earlier is that once you have generated the TAGS file, every file in a directory is indexed, whereas the imenu and func-menu interfaces show only the functions and so on in the current buffer. Plus, you get a time lag when loading new files.

The Speedbar was introduced earlier in this chapter. It has the advantage of being a graphical index of an entire directory, but it does take up more screen real estate.

Speedbar is included with GNU Emacs and is available as a preconfigured XEmacs package. To use these versions, press M-x and type

```
speedbar
```

If you find yourself using Speedbar often, you might want to bind the command to a key that will toggle the frame on and off:

```
(global-set-key [(f12)] 'speedbar)
```

As is usual with Emacs, you are faced with a choice of several different ways to extract and make use of the language elements of your source code files. Part of learning to use Emacs effectively is trying out various extensions and coming up with a subset of them that suits your programming and editing style.

Emacs As an IDE

Earlier in this chapter, you saw how JDE can turn Emacs into a full-featured integrated environment for programming in Java. By combining and customizing various Emacs extensions, you can create a similar Emacs setup for other languages as well.

Settling on a comfortable method of navigating code blocks such as function declarations is a first step, as you saw in the preceding section. What you need now is a method of building and debugging projects from within an Emacs session.

Compile-mode

Emacs has a main entry point to the compilation of C and C++ code—the command M-x `compile`.

Naturally, you need a makefile for your project if it is made up of multiple source files. If you need to compile only a single source file, you might as well use a shell window and invoke your compiler from there. One advantage to using a Compile buffer for even the simplest projects is the "next-error" command which advances point in the compiler output to the next error. See the "Access To Errors" section below.

Compile-mode calls the make program with the `-k` switch. This causes the compilation process to ignore files that fail to compile correctly and go on to the next. You will have a chance to edit the make command line in the minibuffer. If `make -k` is what you want, just press Enter.

While your compiler is working, it doesn't prevent you from working on other buffers in the Emacs session. A Compilation window appears, as shown in Figure 16.14, displaying any error messages generated by the compiler. When the process is finished, an exit status numeral is shown. An exit status of `0` indicates that the process completed successfully.

If this were all that the compilation mode did for you, it wouldn't be much of an improvement over running a compiler from an xterm window. The error-handling features are what make this mode useful.

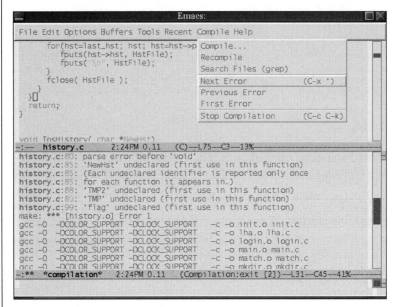

Figure 16.14 *The Compilation Window*

Access to Errors

When some error messages appear in the compilation buffer, you can use the next-error command by pressing Ctrl-x '.

Note that this command has a backquote rather than a single quote. When you type this command, the source file responsible for the error is loaded, and point is left at the trouble spot. After you have corrected the error, repeat this key command to visit the next error, which might be in the same file or in another one.

If you want to start over at the first error message, give this command the "universal prefix" by pressing Ctrl-u Ctrl-x `.

While you're in the Compilation buffer, several other key commands allow you to move around the buffer:

M-n	Moves to the next error (not the source).
M-p	Moves to the previous error.
Ctrl-c Ctrl-c	Loads the file containing the error at point.
Delete	Scrolls up.
Spacebar	Scrolls down.
Mouse-button-2 or Enter	Jumps to the line in a source file which caused an error.

Emacs As an IDE

makefile-mode

When you load a makefile into an Emacs session, a special mode designed for this type of file becomes active, as shown in Figure 16.15. This mode provides font locking, several motion and completion key commands, and a menu. You can open a simple Makefile Browser window, but using Speedbar in conjunction with makefile-mode is much more intuitive and useful, as shown in Figure 16.16.

The motion commands are similar to those in the programming modes. Several useful key commands aren't included on the menu, such as Ctrl-c Ctrl-\, which appends backslashes to the lines in a selected region. This forces the make program to see several consecutive lines as one long line. The mode help key Ctrl-h m shows you a complete list of makefile-mode keybindings.

EDE: The Emacs Development Environment

Eric Ludlam has been developing several interesting packages that significantly enhance Emacs. The Speedbar is one, and several others were mentioned earlier as required packages for a JDE installation.

One of his packages complements and extends compile-mode: The Emacs Development Environment (EDE) emulates commercial IDEs through its usage of the concept of a development project. A project can be more than just a directory

Figure 16.15   *makefile-mode*

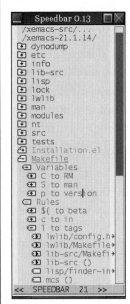

Figure 16.16   *The Speedbar*
View of a Makefile

of source files and a makefile; it can include several subdirectories, each with its
own makefile.

EDE ties together Speedbar, compile-mode, and the GUD (*Grand Unified
Debugger*) so that they can be accessed from a common menu and command set.

While I was evaluating this add-on package, I came to the conclusion that perhaps
it isn't quite ready for general use. The documentation is scanty, and some features
don't seem to be completed. Nonetheless, I think this project has promise, and
development is ongoing. If such an IDE-like project interests you, you might consider visiting Eric Ludlam's CEDET Web site (http://cedet.sourceforge.net), where
you will find EDE and his other projects, many of which depend on each other.

Debugging

A debugger is an application that runs another program in a controlled way. Execution can be stopped and resumed, and problems can be traced to the particular
source file culprits.

The default debugger for C and C++ programs on most Linux systems is gdb, a
GNU program. gdb is strictly a command-line program. It's very powerful and

well-maintained, but it has a steep learning curve. Emacs has been used as a front end to gdb for many years, and several modes have been written to serve as the interface glue between editor and debugger.

gdb commands are mostly English words such as "run" and "break". The Emacs debugging modes let you use shorter keystroke commands instead. A further advantage is that files that trigger errors in the binary being debugged can quickly be loaded into the Emacs session with point at the spot that needs fixing, similar to the behavior of compile-mode.

gdb can't do much with a binary that has been stripped of its debugging symbols. Programs compiled with the gcc compiler switch -g are suitable fodder for gdb.

The Grand Unified Debugger

The name of the most-used Emacs debugging mode requires a bit of explanation. gud.el began years ago as gdb.el, which provided a front end for the GNU debugger, gdb. In those pre-Linux days, a large proportion of Emacs users were running one of the proprietary UNIX variants, such as HPUX or System 5. Each of the commercial UNIX operating systems tended to have its own compiler and debugger. The GNU debugger mode was gradually expanded to include support for three of these proprietary debuggers: sdb, dbx, and xdb. From a present-day perspective, this might not seem quite as grand as it did at the time, but the user landscape has changed. The GNU programming tools have steadily improved in quality, to the point that even the dwindling numbers of users of commercial UNIX variants often use them in preference to the bundled compilers and debuggers.

The entry-point to the debugging mode is M-x gbd.

You are prompted in the minibuffer for the name of the executable you want gdb to run, which gdb assumes is in the current directory. Normally, you start the GUD when you have a source file loaded; its directory is therefore the current working directory.

A new debugging window opens, a Shell window with a gdb prompt. Nothing happens until you give gdb a command, either directly at the prompt or with one of the keybindings or menu commands.

If you type run at the prompt, the binary runs normally and, once initialized, slips from gdb's grip. Setting a breakpoint is how you make the process stop, perhaps at a function declaration or other construct that is giving you trouble. Once the running binary hits that particular function, gdb steps in and suspends the process. From there, you can step through the source file line by line. Figure 16.17 shows the menu and keyboard commands available. One key command I didn't see mentioned in the mode help is Ctrl-x spacebar. This is very useful, because it is a short, often-used command that is run from a source-file buffer. It sets a breakpoint at the cursor in the current buffer.

The Speedbar frame has GUD support built in. Using it gives you a graphical display of the functions and variables in your source files, making it easier to choose breakpoint locations.

What makes Emacs debugging useful is the simultaneous display of the source file as you step your way through. This makes it easy to make changes and try again. You don't even have to leave the source buffer to give the debugger commands. Rather than Ctrl-c, prefix a command with Ctrl-x Ctrl-a, and the command will be passed to the debugger window.

The gdb debugger is a complex program with many commands available. Only a small subset of these commands have keybindings in the debugger window. The developers of the mode bound keys to the most commonly used commands; any of the others can be entered directly at the gdb prompt.

The gdb debugger has extensive documentation available in a variety of formats. Most distribution-packaged versions of gdb come with the docs in Info format, making them easily accessible from within Emacs. You will get much more benefit from the gdb-Emacs combo if you first familiarize yourself with gdb by doing some reading.

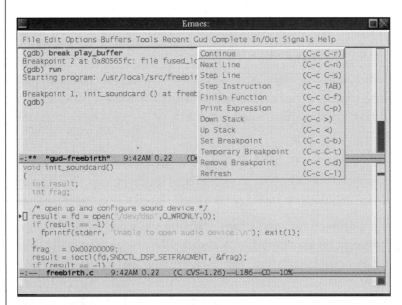

Figure 16.17   *GUD in Action*

The XEmacs Debugging Mode

The XEmacs Debug package includes gud.el, but it currently doesn't work well and isn't enabled by default. Another older mode called gdb.el is the default XEmacs debugger; you start it with the command just described for gud.el. This mode is more for those who are already accustomed to using gdb. There is no menu, but many of the keystrokes are the same as in gud debugger mode. This mode also has the useful Ctrl-x spacebar command that was just mentioned.

Conclusion

In this chapter, space was given to modes for the more popular programming languages and utilities. If yours wasn't included, chances are good that a mode has been written for it. Try loading a source file. An appropriate mode just might be summoned from one of the Lisp directories. The supported languages include Awk, Assembly, Fortran, Scheme, Modula, Prolog, Simula, and Tcl, among others.

Modes not covered in this chapter resemble the modes that were covered, because certain keybindings and menu conventions are followed by most authors of programming modes.

The next chapter introduces the various ways you can use Emacs to deal with your e-mail.

Chapter 17: Different Approaches to E-Mail

First, a Warning

Writing E-Mail in Emacs

Rmail for Basic E-Mail

The VM Mailer

Emacs As an Editor for Other Mail Programs

Gnus As a Mail Client

I f you have never used Emacs for e-mail, you might be wondering why you would even want to, considering that dozens of serviceable Linux e-mail clients are available. One reason so many Emacs users use it for e-mail is for the convenience it provides. Once you get used to features such as abbreviations, dynamic completion, and transposing letters and words, writing a message with the stripped-down basic editors often built into e-mail programs can be a trial.

Emacs by nature is acquisitive, accumulating modes and options as the years go by but rarely discarding them. You might rightly suspect that Emacs has several different ways of sending and receiving e-mail rather than just one unified approach. That would be too easy! This burdens the user with yet another evaluation process and decision, but the upside is that one of those e-mail methods is more likely to suit you to a tee than a one-size-fits-all Emacs mail client.

Naturally, there is another obvious option you can choose: Skip this chapter and go on to the next. Your current mail client might be perfectly satisfactory; you might have learned its ins and outs so thoroughly that it would be painful to change. Many experienced Emacs users use other e-mail programs. Even if you don't use one of the complete Emacs mail modes, the basic mail composition mode can still be used to send simple e-mail without attachments.

This chapter introduces three of the four available e-mail modes. VM and Gnus are large, intricate, and powerful modes, and Rmail is the original Emacs mail mode, lightweight and without features such as message attachments. The fourth mode is called mh-e; it is not as widely used as the others these days. If you are curious, you can read about it in the Emacs Info documentation. The bulk of this chapter is about VM. The last section is a quick introduction to Gnus, which is dealt with in detail in the next chapter.

Toward the end of this chapter, a hybrid approach is discussed that has become increasingly popular: using Emacs as an external editor for a mail program such as Mutt.

First, a Warning

Just about every e-mail program is afflicted with a certain amount of hubris, even the Emacs mail modes. They seem to think that just because you are trying out a program or mode, you will be so bowled over by the ease of use and feature set that you will barely notice or care that all your spooled e-mail messages have been moved willy-nilly to the new program's idea of the perfect mail-storage scheme.

What if you try a new e-mail program and don't like it? You want to go back to your familiar old program, but your messages have been moved, perhaps even converted to a different file format. This has happened to me a couple of times, and believe me, it's annoying! It is possible to convert mail from one format to another, but with a little foresight, you won't ever have to.

The best way to deal with this is to get into the habit of copying your mail-spool file to a temporary directory before you install any new mail client. You can move it back later if you decide to go back to your original e-mail setup.

Writing E-Mail in Emacs

There are certain interrelationships between the different e-mail modes. Rmail and VM both use mail-mode, the basic mail-composition mode. VM expands upon mail-mode, giving it more power and flexibility. Gnus uses its own composition mode, known as message-mode.

mail-mode can be used by itself; you can compose and send messages without making use of the full-blown mail modes at all. You can continue to use another non-Emacs mail program for both receiving and sending mail.

Enter mail-mode by pressing Ctrl-x m.

A Mail buffer appears, complete with a set of standard mail headers that can be edited, as shown in Figure 17.1.

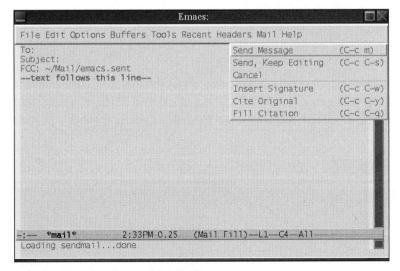

Figure 17.1   *The Mail Composition Buffer*

The Headers menu lets you insert optional headers that aren't needed for every message, such as CC and FCC. As you can see in Figure 17.2, the keybindings are long, so using the menu is quicker. You might wonder why keybindings are even included at all, because not many users will bother to memorize them. One reason is that the developers have gone to great lengths to ensure that every command is available to users on simpler displays, such as the Linux virtual console. Emacs in a nonwindowed, nongraphical environment has no menu bar, though the menu items can be accessed by pressing F10. The great majority of Linux Emacs users run the editor in an X Windows session, ignoring complicated keybindings when a menu is available.

Nearly every e-mail program has an address book, because nobody enjoys repeatedly typing often-used e-mail addresses. mail-mode doesn't have a graphical address book; instead, it uses the concept of mail aliases. Creating aliases is no more difficult than entering e-mail addresses in an address book window. All you need to do is create a file in your home directory and name it .mailrc. Enter one e-mail address per line, using a format modeled after either of these examples:

```
alias hank hdt@walden.net
alias jorge "Jorge Luis Borges <jborges@biblio.ar>"
```

Any address in an alias that includes spaces, such as the second one shown here, must be enclosed in double quotes.

When you enter mail-mode, Emacs checks to see if you have a ~/.mailrc file. If one is found, it is read into memory. If that file contained the first of the preceding two imaginary entries, typing `hank` in the To: field would automatically be expanded to `hdt@walden.net` as soon as the message was sent. XEmacs does this a little differently. As soon as the cursor moves out of the To field, the real e-mail address is inserted. This is a worthwhile safety feature, because it lets you make sure that the alias points to the correct e-mail address.

Sending mail successfully requires that you have one of the available mail-delivery agents installed and configured. Sendmail and Exim are two of the most popular. Your Linux distribution will have chosen one of these (or possibly another) as the

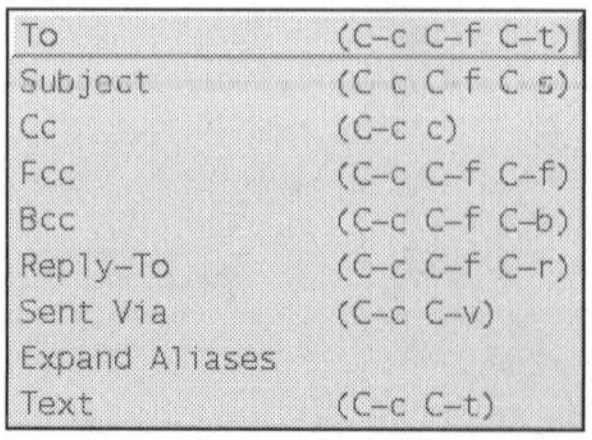

To	(C-c C-f C-t)
Subject	(C-c C-f C-s)
Cc	(C-c c)
Fcc	(C-c C-f C-f)
Bcc	(C-c C-f C-b)
Reply-To	(C-c C-f C-r)
Sent Via	(C-c C-v)
Expand Aliases	
Text	(C-c C-t)

Figure 17.2   *The Headers Menu*

default. Current distributions almost always provide a mail setup program, often as a part of the installation process.

You type the message body starting on the line just below `--text follows this line--`. That line is a delimiter that separates the body of the message from the headers, but it doesn't appear in the message itself, because Emacs deletes it first.

Signatures (or sigs) are the lines you want appended to your messages—often a professional identification or a quote. If you want your default sig tacked on to the end of your message, the key command Ctrl-c Ctrl-w or the menu command Insert Signature will do this for you. This was left as an option because you might not want a sig on every message. Emacs uses the file ~/.signature as the default signature file.

When you are ready to send the message, Ctrl-c m hands it over to your delivery agent. You don't have to be online, because the first destination of a message is a mail queue directory. Delivery agents typically "wake up" every few minutes and try to send the messages that have accumulated in this directory. If the mail server can't be found (meaning you aren't connected to the Internet), the agent will go back to sleep and try again later.

Teaching Emacs Your E-Mail Address

Depending on how your Linux installation is set up, Emacs might or might not be able to figure out your name and e-mail address. Just to make sure, it is wise to insert a few lines into your ~/.emacs file that set these variables permanently:

```
(setq user-full-name "Your Name")
(setq user-mail-address "your@email.address")
(setq mail-archive-file-name "~/Mail/emacs.sent")
```

The last line sets the location and file name of your archive of all messages that have been sent from Emacs. This file is the equivalent of the outbox file or directory used by other e-mail programs. The file can become gargantuan if you send many messages with attachments (only possible with VM and Gnus), so it is advisable to edit the file periodically and delete the portions you don't need to save.

Now that you can send mail with Emacs, receiving new messages involves using either Rmail, VM, or Gnus.

Rmail for Basic E-Mail

Rmail is the oldest of the Emacs mail packages. It was developed in the early days of e-mail, when attachments were unknown and just being able to send and receive

ASCII messages was an achievement. Today there are still many e-mail users who have little need for MIME attachments and who value a simple and uncluttered interface. Because of these users, Rmail survives. If your needs aren't complicated and you don't mind having your mail stored in an incompatible format, Rmail might be what you need.

The Babyl Mailbox Format: a Warning

Rmail stores mail in a unique format called Babyl, a format understood by no other mail software. You can try out Rmail, and if you decide it meets your needs, everything is fine. If you later decide to switch to an e-mail program or Emacs mode that uses the standard Linux mailbox format (in which all messages are concatenated into a single file), a command is provided to translate Babyl mail files into the more widely used format. Press M-x and type

```
unrmail [file-name]
```

This leaves the original Babyl file alone while creating a new mailbox-format file from the contents.

XEmacs doesn't have the `unrmail` command, and the documentation is vague about converting Babyl files. XEmacs users are therefore advised to stick with Gnus or VM. Rmail is fully documented in the GNU Emacs Info files but is given nothing but a brief mention in the XEmacs Info files.

Probably the main reason so many users have migrated to VM or Gnus from Rmail is Rmail's lack of support for e-mail attachments. Once seen as unnecessary frippery, MIME attachments are now being used by the majority of e-mail users. If you feel that you will need to attach image files, Microsoft Word documents, sound files, or any other non-ASCII file to your messages, you should skip ahead to the VM or Gnus sections.

There is at least one third-party Rmail extension which adds attachment capabilities. It is called etach; you can learn more at http://etach.sourceforge.net/.

Using Rmail

Start an Rmail session by pressing M-x and typing

```
rmail
```

or by selecting Read Mail from the Tools menu. The first thing Rmail does is move any messages from your inbox file (usually /var/spool/mail/your-user-name) to ~/RMAIL, Rmail's default mailbox file. All messages are converted to Babyl format before the file is saved.

Rmail doesn't by default fetch new mail from wherever your e-mail comes from, such as a POP or IMAP server. This is up to you to set up. Many Linux users use Fetchmail to retrieve new messages. Both VM and Gnus can connect to mail servers and pull down new messages.

> The Rmail Info manual (in the section "movemail and POP") describes the set-up necessary for connecting directly to a POP server for mail retrieval. Briefly, rather than using an inbox filename, an entry such as this is used:
>
> ```
> po:[username]:[mail hostname]
> ```
>
> You will be prompted for your POP password.

Rmail mode redefines many of the letter keys so that they run message-related commands. Most have mnemonic values:

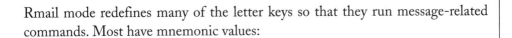

m	Writes a new message (the recipient needs to be entered in the To: field).
r	Replies to a message.
f	Forwards a message to another address.
d	Marks a message for deletion.
u	Undeletes.
x	Expunges (actually deletes marked messages).
s	Saves a message to a file and then deletes it from the folder.

The first three commands open a mail-mode window, as described earlier.

You create the Rmail Summary buffer by selecting one of the items on the Summary menu or using the keyboard equivalents. Pressing h makes visible a new window with all messages shown in chronological order. Rmail can sort and filter the messages in a variety of ways. Figure 17.3 shows a summary chosen with a regular expression, LISTSERV*. The menu in the figure shows the other message-filtering possibilities.

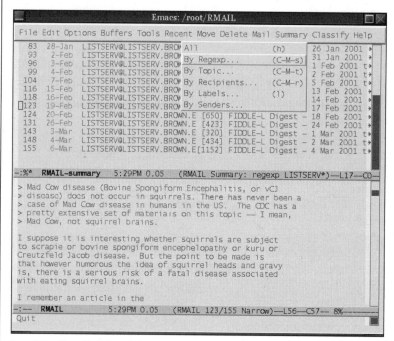

Figure 17.3 *Rmail–Filtered Summary*

When you click the middle mouse button on a message in a Summary buffer, the message appears in another window. When you read a message, the spacebar pages down and the Delete key pages up. (The Page Up and Page Down keys also work).

One advantage Rmail has over VM is that it has an extensive Customize interface. Press M-x and type

```
customize-group
```

Respond to the prompt with

```
rmail
```

You will find in these nested buffers many Rmail variables to examine or change.

Rmail Output and Labels

Rmail offers a nice variety of commands for dealing with messages. You can save messages to files in either standard UNIX mailbox format or in Rmail's Babyl format:

o [file-name]	Appends a copy of the current message to an Rmail-format file. This procedure can be used to create the equivalent of folders in other e-mail programs, collections of messages with a common subject origin.
Ctrl-o [file-name]	Does the same thing as o, except that the message files are saved in the standard mailbox format. Use this command if you want to be able to read these messages with another e-mail client, Emacs-based or independent.
w [file-name]	Copies the body of the current message to a new text file, stripping away all header lines in the process. The contents of the Subject: header will appear in the minibuffer as a default choice for a file name, giving you an opportunity to edit it or substitute another name.

Labeling messages lets you define your own categories that might be unrelated to subjects or sender. This gives you some of the advantages of separate mail files while still retaining your messages in a single file. When a message has been assigned a label, it is visible in the Summary buffer. These two commands assign and remove labels:

a [label]	Assigns a label to the current message. After you press a, the minibuffer becomes active. After you have typed a label, press Enter for it to take effect.
k [label]	This command is like a, but it removes a message's label instead.

Once you have given a group of messages the same label, you can use some new commands:

Ctrl-M-n [label1,label2]	Moves to the next message with the one of the listed labels. If no labels are specified the most recent label used with this command is re-used.
Ctrl-M-p [label1,label2]	The same as Ctrl-M-n [label1,label2], but moves backward.
Ctrl-M-l [label1,label2]	Creates a new Summary buffer displaying only those messages with the specified comma-separated labels.

Rmail might not have as many extra features as VM or Gnus, but many Emacs users find it sufficient for their needs.

The VM Mailer

Kyle Jones created and currently maintains the VM mailer for Emacs. It is available as a preconfigured XEmacs package. The XEmacs documentation recommends VM as a good choice for beginners, although the package is configurable and is powerful enough to be a favorite with many experienced users.

Here is a partial list of the features VM offers:

- Sending and receiving MIME attachments
- Creating and "bursting" message digests
- Many ways to organize messages
- Virtual folders
- Many menu commands
- Configurable toolbars (on XEmacs and GNU Emacs 21)

VM is very configurable, but unfortunately it has no Customize support. If you have become addicted to the ease Customize brings to Emacs package configuration, Rmail or Gnus might be a better choice. Changing VM's defaults involves inserting Lisp variable statements in a file named ~/.vm, which is read when VM starts up. The variables are well-documented in the VM Info files; they can be copied directly from the Info window and then pasted into the ~/.vm file.

That being said, VM's default settings are reasonable, so you might not need to change any of them.

Installation

GNU Emacs users need to install VM as an external package, because it is not included in the Emacs distribution. Before doing this, it wouldn't hurt to find out if your Linux distribution has a packaged version of VM available. If a package is available, it might save you some time compared to manually building and installing the source distribution.

You can find a copy of the VM sources on this book's CD-ROM, in the directory /cdrom/packages/vm. Unpack the archive and look for a file called README, which contains step-by-step installation instructions. You need to edit the makefile so that the files will be installed where you want them. A subdirectory of your site-lisp directory would be a suitable home for the VM Lisp files. You could put them in site-lisp itself, but it's generally a bad idea to install large multifile packages directly in the site-lisp directory. This makes it difficult to keep track of your Lisp files if you ever want to uninstall or upgrade a package.

The README file also contains a set of Lisp autoload statements that can be copied and pasted into your ~/.emacs file.

First Steps with VM

The first time you press M-x vm or select Read Mail (VM) from the menu (in XEmacs only), your primary inbox or mail-spool file is emptied. Remember to make a copy of your inbox in case you want to go back to your original mail program). The messages are transferred to ~/INBOX, and the VM window appears.

The screen is split into two windows, as shown in Figure 17.4. The top one is a Summary buffer in which each message is given a single identifying line, and the bottom window displays a preview of the first unread message, or optionally the complete message.

The preview is just a display of the message headers that is intended to allow you to decide if you really want to read that message. Pressing the spacebar reveals the

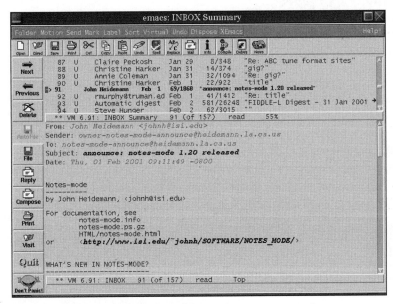

Figure 17.4   *VM Summary and Message Windows*

remainder of the message. Pressing the spacebar repeatedly pages through the message. Pressing b pages backwards. Note that these keys work while point is in the Summary window, so you don't have to move point and keyboard focus back and forth between the two windows.

Many VM users would rather not have this previewing action, preferring that a message be displayed in full. This leads to the subject of VM's configuration file, a Lisp file named ~/.vm, which you will need to create if you want to change any of the default settings. Actually, any VM-related Lisp statements could go right into your ~/.emacs file, but they are easier to deal with in a separate file. VM reads this file if it exists every time it is started up.

The variable that controls previewing is vm-preview-lines. The default value is 0, which means that only the headers are previewed. A number larger than 0 causes that many lines of the message body to be displayed. The following statement disables previewing and forces VM to display the entire message when one is selected:

```
(setq vm-preview-lines nil)
```

In Figure 17.4, you can see that VM substitutes its own menus for several of the standard menus. You can switch back to the normal menus by clicking the XEmacs or Emacs button on the right side of the menu bar. When you do this, you see a VM button that toggles the VM menus' visibility.

Sorting and Threading Messages

VM inherits many of its commands from Rmail, as you can see from the entries on the Sort menu, shown in Figure 17.5.

Figure 17.5 *VM's Message Sorting Menu*

These sorting commands are also available from the keyboard by pressing g. You are prompted in the minibuffer for one or more sorting criteria, such as subject or author. Press the Tab key twice, and a help window shows you all the valid choices.

A useful item on this menu is Toggle Threading, bound to Ctrl-t. It displays related messages in a hierarchical tree-like form, with later messages in a thread indented to the right.

Message Digests

A digest is a message made up of many separate messages condensed into one. Many mailing lists offer subscriptions to a digest form of the list; this protects your inbox from a daily flood of list messages. You receive a single digest in their place.

VM has commands for "bursting" a digest into separate messages so that you can select and read them just as you would the normal messages in your mail folder. This makes it easier to respond to a particular message in the digest, because you can quote just the relevant message rather than the digest message itself. Typing the asterisk character splits the current message (if it is a digest) and merges the messages into your mail folder. If you click the middle mouse button on a digest message in the Summary buffer, the header is displayed in the message window, along with an icon representing the digest messages, as shown in Figure 17.6. Clicking again on the

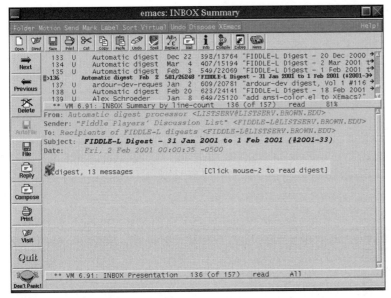

Figure 17.6 *Expanded Digest Summary*

prompt line that is displayed next to the icon opens a new VM frame with a new Summary buffer filled with the contents of the digest message.

You can create a digest of marked messages or of your entire folder and then mail it. A variety of marking commands found on the Mark menu, all of which are prefixed with M. MM, which marks the current message, can be used to mark messages intended for a digest. The @ character bundles the marked messages into a digest and mails it.

Virtual Folders

A virtual folder is a subset of your mail folder made up of messages that share a common subject line, author, label, or any of several other criteria. This isn't a real folder or file; it's just a method that VM uses to selectively display some of your messages. This is similar to Rmail's labels and selective labeled-message view.

You can create one of these using the commands on the Virtual menu, but it will last only as long as the VM session is active. Creating permanent virtual folders requires a Lisp statement in your ~/.vm file. The statement can be modeled after this one:

```
(setq vm-virtual-folder-alist
   '(

      ("First-virtual-folder"
       (("/path/file-name")
        (header "Durco")))
      ("Second-virtual-folder"
       (("/path/file-name2" "/path/filename3")
        (and (header "Bulletin") (author "Benson"))))
   )

)
```

This statement creates an associated list, a type of Emacs Lisp variable discussed earlier in this book. Remember auto-mode-alist, the list of correspondences between file name suffixes and major modes? Think of this as a way Emacs can group several related variables under one name.

The preceding associated list has just two members, each of which defines a virtual folder. To use this as a template, substitute virtual folder names for First-virtual-folder and Second-virtual-folder. The path sections should point to any VM mailbox file. The last sections of the definitions are the specifiers, which can include regular expressions. The first specifier (header Durco) tells VM to look in the mailbox file for any messages that have the word Durco anywhere in the header lines. The second uses a conditional keyword. and in this context means that all the following specifiers must be true in order for a message to qualify for inclusion in the folder.

The and specifier line (the last statement in the alist) could be translated like this: A message must have the word Bulletin included in one of the header lines, but it also must have the word Benson in the From: header.

This associated list can have any number of virtual folder definitions. It helps to turn on blinking or highlighted parenthesis mode while working on nested statements like this one.

Consult the VM mode help or the VM Info files for more details on the many different specifiers you can use in this alist variable definition.

Admittedly, this could be easier to do, but like other Emacs configuration tasks involving Lisp, you can do the work once and use the results for years.

VM and MIME Attachments

VM can decode and encode the BASE64 and Quoted-Printable MIME types by using either internal (although slower) Lisp routines or external programs. If you want VM to use an external decoder or encoder, you need to change a couple of variables. The VM source distribution includes the C source for four such programs—qp-encode, qp-decode, base64-encode, and base64-decode. If you install VM using the supplied makefile, the binaries are built and installed in /usr/bin. These four lines in your ~/.vm file tell VM to use them in preference to the built-in Lisp decoder and encoder:

```
(setq vm-mime-qp-encoder-program "qp-encode")
(setq vm-mime-qp-decoder-program "qp-decode")
(setq vm-mime-base64-encoder-program "base64-encode")
(setq vm-mime-base64-decoder-program "base64-decode")
```

The XEmacs VM package doesn't include these small C programs, but in any recent version of XEmacs you can find a base64 encoder/decoder in the /[usr]/[local]/lib/xemacs-[version-number]/i[4,5 or 6]86-pc-linux directory, which is where miscellaneous non-Lisp utilities are installed. The program is named mmencode, and these lines in ~/.vm will make it become VM's default base64 encoder/decoder:

```
(setq vm-mime-base64-decoder-program  "mmencode"
      vm-mime-base64-decoder-switches (list "-u")
      vm-mime-base64-encoder-program  "mmencode"
      vm-forwarding-digest-type "mime")
```

The mmencode program isn't in your executable search path, so to avoid the necessity of typing the complete path to mmencode in the preceding Lisp lines, you can make a soft link from the mmencode file in the XEmacs installation directory to /usr/local/bin:

```
cd /[directory where mmencode is installed] [Enter]
ln -s mmencode /usr/local/bin/mmencode [Enter]
```

Unless you frequently send and receive bulky MIME-encode messages, you probably don't need to bother changing these variables.

There are a slew of VM MIME-related variables—too many to do justice to in this chapter. The VM FAQ, which can be found on this book's CD-ROM in the same directory as the VM source, has an informative section on MIME variables.

VM's Toolbar

If you are running XEmacs or GNU Emacs 21 (or higher), VM displays a toolbar either along the side of your window or at the top, replacing the standard toolbar. When you have used VM for a while, you might want to regain the window real estate taken up by the toolbar, because all the icon commands are available from the menus and key commands. Here are some toolbar-related variables that can be plugged into the ~/.vm file:

```
(setq vm-use-toolbar nil)
```

This variable turns off the toolbar.

```
(setq vm-toolbar-orientation 'top)
```

If you would like the toolbar placed on a different window edge, substitute bottom, left, or right for top in this statement.

If you like the toolbar but you want to change the icons and the commands they run, you need to read the VM Info files, which include a section with details.

Configuring the Display: Frames and Windows

There's no denying that VM simply likes making new frames. A new folder opened, a digest burst, a new mail composition buffer—all of these open in a new frame. You can control this to some extent by setting these frame-related variables to nil:

```
(setq vm-frame-per-folder nil)
(setq vm-frame-per-composition nil)
```

If you want VM to never create a new frame, no matter what, set this variable to nil by inserting a line in ~/.vm:

```
(setq vm-mutable-frames nil)
```

Once this variable is set, VM will always use the current frame for new VM buffers.

You have a choice: Do you want a summary window along with a window displaying the first unread message? This behavior is controlled by the value of a variable that might be set one way or another by your particular VM installation. Changing the initial window layout involves changing this variable:

```
(setq vm-startup-with-summary t)
```

This statement causes VM to always generate a summary window when a new folder is opened. Set the value to nil if you want the first unread message displayed full-screen.

Retrieving Mail from Your Server

You can set up VM so that it can log in to your POP or IMAP mail server and download new messages. Many users would rather use an external program such as Fetchmail so as to avoid being tied to Emacs and VM for mail retrieval, but if this approach sounds like it would suit you, here are the details.

You need to insert your server information as an entry in VM's list of spool files. VM doesn't need such a list when you are moving mail from your main inbox to VM's ~/INBOX, but if you want to tell VM to look for new mail in other locations, you need to use a statement that resembles this one:

```
(setq vm-spool-files '("/var/spool/mail/layers" "~/Mail"))
```

Substitute a server for one of these spool files, complete with port, username, and password, by altering the statement to resemble this:

```
(setq vm-spool-files '("mail.server.net:110:pass:username:password " "~/Mailbox"))
```

If you want your messages deleted from the server after VM has sucked them up (unless you access from more than one location, you probably want this), you need to add the server information to another associated list:

```
(setq vm-pop-auto-expunge-alist
    '("mail.server.net:110:pass:username:*" . nil)
)
```

The password doesn't need to be in this statement, because the asterisk indicates to VM that it should use the value set in the vm-spool-files variable.

Two more important variables limit the size and number of messages downloaded:

```
(setq vm-pop-messages-per-session 100)
(setq vm-pop-max-message-size 50000)  ;; this size is in bytes
```

The default value of each of these variables is `nil`, which means that VM downloads the remote mail no matter how long it takes.

The syntax for specifying an IMAP server is a little different:

```
(setq vm-spool-files '("imap:mail.server.net:143:pass:username:password " "~/
Mailbox"))
```

The port numbers 110 and 143 used in the POP and IMAP examples might differ on your system. You can look up these numbers in the file /etc/services on most Linux systems.

For information on other authentication schemes (`pass` in the preceding example is one of several), consult the VM Info files.

VM Resources

Although the VM Info files are comprehensive and useful, even more information about the many VM variables can be found in vm-vars.el, a very well-commented Lisp file that is included with any VM installation.

VM's home page on the WWW is http://www.wonderworks.com/vm.

The latest version, along with the VM FAQ and links to other VM resources, can be found there.

If you use VM, it is worthwhile to scan the postings in the two VM Usenet newsgroups from time to time. They aren't tremendously active groups, but you will find interesting ways to configure VM as well as solutions to problems. The groups are gnu.emacs.vm.bug and gnu.emacs.vm.info.

Emacs As an Editor for Other Mail Programs

Perhaps the preceding descriptions of Rmail and VM haven't convinced you that either is as convenient and full-featured as your favorite mail client. There is a way to have the best of both worlds by letting Emacs handle the message-composition chores for your mailer. This leaves the management of your archived and current mail to your current mail client, which might already be set up just as you prefer.

It would be a waste of system resources to start up an instance of Emacs every time you wanted to write a message. The solution to this is to use Emacs' client/server features. To set this up for GNU Emacs, insert this brief statement at the end of your ~/.emacs file:

```
(server-start)
```

After this has taken effect, you can load files into an Emacs session from an X terminal window, and other programs can do the same. The command to use is

```
emacsclient [file-name]
```

XEmacs uses a different initialization and a different client program. The line in your ~/.emacs file that starts the server is

```
(gnuserv-start)
```

and the corresponding remote client command is

```
gnuclient [filename]
```

Before you try setting up an e-mail program to use one of these commands, it's a good idea to try it out from an xterm window to make sure the system is set up correctly and functional.

E-mail programs differ in how they let you assign a default external editor. Often the setting is made in a configuration file, while other programs pick up the value of the environment variable $EDITOR and use that.

If you set $EDITOR to emacsclient or gnuserv, you won't have a default Linux editor if Emacs or XEmacs isn't running.

Variables such as $EDITOR are set in one of your login shell's initialization files, such as ~/.bash_profile or ~/.zshenv. After adding an environmental variable (or making any other change), type (in a terminal window or virtual console)

```
source [init-file]
```

so that the change will take effect immediately.

NOTE

What is needed is a fallback editor for the system to use when Emacs isn't available. A setting similar to this one tells applications to use vi when there is no available running Emacs process:

```
EDITOR="emacsclient --alternate-editor vi +%d %s"
```

Substitute `vim`, `vile`, or any other text-mode editor for `vi` in this statement if you prefer.

There doesn't seem to be an equivalent way to use XEmacs' gnuclient, so this environment variable setting is applicable only to GNU Emacs.

You need to consult your e-mail program's documentation in order to find out how to assign an external editor, although some of the newer graphical mail clients provide a dialog box for making such settings. Just remember not to specify Emacs or XEmacs as the external editor; use emacsclient or gnuclient instead.

Yet Another Method

An interesting Emacs mail possibility is a major-mode extension called post.el. This mode acts as a buffer between the popular Mutt mailer and Emacs and provides font locking, menus, and an emulation of Mutt's keybindings. This major mode has evolved from several ancestral Mutt modes, a good example of open source cross-fertilization at work. You can find a copy on this book's CD-ROM in the directory /cdrom/packages/mail. A more recent version might be available from http://astro.utoronto.ca/~reid/mutt/.

This mode is easy to install. Just drop the file into your site-lisp directory, byte-compile it, and add this line to your ~/.emacs file:

```
(require 'post)
```

The last step is to let Mutt know that you want to use Emacs as the default external editor. One of these lines should be inserted into your ~/.muttrc file; the first one is for GNU Emacs users:

```
set editor="/usr/local/bin/emacsclient"
```

XEmacs users should use this line:

```
set editor="/usr/local/bin/gnuclient"
```

These paths might need to be adjusted to match your Emacs installation. Don't forget to comment out any other `set editor` line in ~/.muttrc by prefixing it with a hash character (#).

Now when you want to reply to a message or compose a new one in Mutt, a new Emacs frame appears, complete with new menus, highlighting of headers and quoted text, and a full set of Mutt-like keybindings (see Figure 17.7).

Notice in Figure 17.7 the Done button on the menu bar. Click that button when you are ready to mail the message. You are asked whether you want to save the

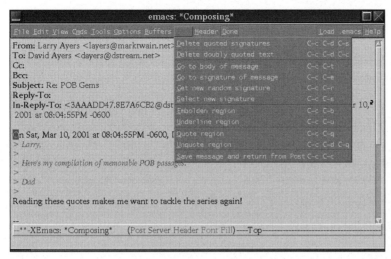

Figure 17.7 *A Post-Mode XEmacs Frame*

Mutt temporary file. You do want to save it; otherwise, Mutt won't be able to mail it. After you answer "yes" (or "no" if you want to abort the message), the Emacs frame disappears, and you are back in Mutt.

Many variables can be changed with Post-mode's Customize interface. Press M-x and type

```
customize-group
```

When prompted in the minibuffer, type

```
post
```

You will find all sorts of variables to set, either temporarily (just to try them out) or permanently.

The main objection to using Post-mode is that in order to use it at all, Emacs must be running. An easy way to get around this is to set up two shell aliases and two corresponding Mutt initialization files.

Here are the two aliases, which should be included in one of your Shell init files, such as ~/.bashrc, ~/.zshrc, or ~/.cshrc:

```
alias mutt-1 'mutt -F ~/.muttrc'
alias mutt-2 'mutt -F ~/.muttrc-2'
```

The file ~/.muttrc is your old Mutt init file, which either doesn't set an external editor for Mutt (which means that Mutt uses its built-in editor) or defines the external editor as a quickly-started editor, such as one of the vi clones—perhaps Vim or Vile.

The alternate Mutt init file (~/.muttrc-2) defines the external editor as one of the Emacs client programs, either emacsclient or gnuclient.

Once these aliases and Mutt init files have been created, you can start Mutt with either the Emacs/Post-mode command, `mutt-2`, or the alternate command to be used when Emacs isn't running, `mutt-1`. If you want to include these two ways of running Mutt in your window manager's menu-definition file, you can use the alias definitions just shown directly. Here is an example for the Blackbox window manager that could be included in the ~/.blackbox/rootmenu file:

```
[exec] (Mutt-Emacs)     {mutt -F ~/.muttrc-2}
[exec] (Mutt-Vim)       {mutt -F ~/.muttrc}
```

Every window manager has a different init file syntax, but there almost always is a method of defining the visible root menu entry (which is enclosed in parentheses in this Blackbox example) and the actual command to be executed (enclosed in curly braces).

The main limitation of Post-mode is that it works only with Mutt. Mutt is well worth using, though. It is well-maintained and almost rivals Emacs for configurability. You can read more about it at the Mutt Web site: http://www.mutt.org.

Gnus As a Mail Client

The next chapter is devoted to Gnus, one of the most complex and Byzantine of all Emacs packages. Many hard-core Emacs/XEmacs users use Gnus as their only mail and news client. Gnus has a very active user community. The maintainer, Lars Magne Ingebrigtsen, keeps up a rapid pace of development.

This section is a quick once-over evaluation of Gnus. Hopefully, reading this will help you decide whether to read the next chapter and try out Gnus.

First, allow me to state that Gnus isn't for everyone. If you don't take delight in a multitude of options, software that with a certain amount of work can be configured in manifold ways, and the markedly humorous attitude of the developer, you might be better served by a standard newsreader such as slrn.

Pros and Cons

Gnus pros:

- An enormous and detailed, if somewhat flippant, Info manual. (If you have been searching for a software manual that quotes poetry by Charles Reznikoff, your quest is over!) This manual is the place to go when you get confused, as you probably will at some point.

- An extensive Customize interface. However, to know how to set the many variables, you need the Info files at your beck and call.

- Handles MIME attachments well. Naturally, this can be configured.

- The ability to download batches of news postings while online, cache them, and then read them while offline at your leisure. Any postings you make are stored as drafts until you are online again. This is known as "Gnus unplugged".

- You have a choice of several different mail message storage schemes, each of which has advantages and disadvantages.

- Like VM, Gnus can connect directly to your mail server and fetch messages.

Gnus cons:

- Life is short. Who has time to figure out how to make Gnus do what they want? (The answer probably includes graduate students and the minimally self-employed.)

- Gnus is different. It has an unusual perspective on e-mail, treating it as a variant of newsgroup postings. If you are accustomed to "normal" e-mail applications, you will face an adjustment period.

- One disadvantage of all Emacs Internet-related modes is that Emacs sub-processes don't run asynchronously very well. If there is a long delay in server response for some reason, your entire Emacs session can stall and become unresponsive. Some Gnus addicts solve this problem by running a separate Emacs process just for Gnus. If there is a network slowdown, the editing Emacs will still be responsive, while the Gnus Emacs can be sent to a corner until it behaves.

- Gnus can be slow when reading large mailbox files, especially compared with text-mode mailers such as Mutt and Pine. Some users see this as an inducement to keep their archived mail in several folders rather than one.

- Gnus runs best on a machine with abundant memory and processor resources. However, this is almost a nonissue these days, because fast and powerful machines have become so inexpensive. I say "almost" because there are still Emacs users out there running 486 machines with 16 MB of memory. If you are one of them, I recommend Mutt and slrn rather than Gnus. The slrn newsreader was in part inspired by Gnus and shares many of the same keystrokes.

After reading this outline, you should have an inkling as to whether Gnus is worth fooling with for someone in your situation. If you are interested, by all means proceed to the next chapter; otherwise, skip to Chapter 19.

Conclusion

Using Emacs for e-mail may not fit your needs if you are just getting started using Emacs. As you become more proficient with the editor the options outlined in this chapter may become more appealing.

The next chapter delves into the intricacies of Gnus, one of the largest Emacs extensions.

Chapter 18: Gnus Configuration and Usage

Network news is one of the oldest sectors of the Internet. It has evolved over a period of nearly 20 years from a primitive bulletin-board system connecting two East Coast universities to the worldwide collection of tens of thousands of groups we use today.

What helps make this system possible is a standardized protocol for the transport and storage of messages—NNTP (*Network News Transport Protocol*). Messages have dating and identification headers; like e-mail messages, they are in ASCII format.

Gnus is one of the largest Emacs extensions. It evolved from an earlier news-reading package called GNUS. Lars Magne Ingebrigtsen is the main author and maintainer of the package. Since the original raison d'être of Gnus was reading network news, the first sections of this chapter are devoted to setting up and using Gnus as your newsreader. Gnus as an e-mail client is the subject of the closing sections.

Gnus requires a certain amount of time and effort to convince it to do what you think it should. Think of it as a complex machine with numerous knobs to twiddle and gauges to watch. This software machine comes with a huge Info manual that is cleverly written and chock-full of information. Unfortunately, its size makes navigation difficult for beginners trying to get their bearings. The Info documentation system has a built-in navigation system using links and cross-references between files, but even with these aids, finding your way around a multifile Info set can be frustrating. The Gnus Info manual, if printed, would be a book about the size of this one. No wonder it's easy to get lost! This chapter is an attempt at a more condensed and basic approach to Gnus, aiming to help you learn to use Gnus comfortably without getting into the more esoteric and lesser-used configuration variables.

After reading this chapter, you should be able to use Gnus effectively at a basic level, which offers you about the same functionality as does a "normal" newsreader. Only after getting the hang of using Gnus at that level should you venture into the esoterica of Gnus advanced commands. The plethora of commands overflowing from many of the Gnus menus can be intimidating and confusing to new users, so this tutorial focuses on the core keyboard and mouse commands.

Starting Gnus for the First Time

Some applications are fairly self-explanatory; you start one up and find that you can use it effectively without needing to read the docs first. Gnus isn't like that. A new user starting Gnus without preparation will likely give up in confusion before much time has passed. Read this entire chapter before trying to use Gnus; you will be glad you did.

Installation

Gnus is included as a part of the GNU Emacs distribution, and a prebuilt package is available for XEmacs (see Chapter 12 for installation instructions). Installation really isn't an issue with Gnus, unless you want to install a version more recent than the one that came with your version of Emacs. If you are using a version of GNU Emacs previous to 21.0, you might consider installing a newer Gnus (or a newer Emacs), because Gnus has evolved considerably since the release of GNU Emacs 20.7. Both the latest stable Gnus release (in source form) and the XEmacs package are available on this book's CD-ROM in the directory /cdrom/packages/gnus.

Installing from source isn't too difficult if you use the included configure script and makefile. After it's configured, Emacs users can type `make`. XEmacs users should instead type `make EMACS=xemacs` followed by `make install`.

Read the README file, which you will find in the Gnus source package. You will find lines for your ~/.emacs file that tell Emacs where to find the new Info files.

News from an External Server

In order to browse newsgroup postings, Gnus needs to know the address of your news server. A Linux convention is the file /etc/nntpserver, a small one-line text file containing nothing but the address of the news server you want to use. Another possibility is the environment variable `$NNTPSERVER`, which may be set in one of your login shell's initialization files.

Gnus looks for one of these server definitions when it starts up. If neither can be found, you need to either create the /etc/nntpserver file or define the environment variable with a line resembling this in your ~/.bash_profile file (or the equivalent if you use a different shell):

```
export NNTPSERVER=your.news.server
```

Save the file and then "source" it, a command that forces the shell to recognize any changes you have made:

```
source ~/.bash_profile
```

Another possibility is to set one of the Gnus variables, `gnus-select-method`. Although you can put Gnus-specific settings in your ~/.emacs file, it is recommended that you create a new file named ~/.gnus.el and use it to hold your Gnus settings. The name .gnus is acceptable as well, but using the .el suffix lets you easily edit the file in Emacs-Lisp mode. This file is ignored until you actually start Gnus so that when Emacs starts up it doesn't have to expend time and effort loading Gnus variable definitions.

Here is an example of how `gnus-select-method` can be defined in your ~/.gnus file:

```
(setq gnus-select-method '(nntp "news.server.net"))
```

A Spool Directory As a Source

If your machine is on a local network, you might have access to what is known as a "local spool". This is a directory on one of the networked machines that receives a periodic supply of news postings and makes them available to users' newsreaders on the network. It is also possible to have a local spool on a single computer that accesses the Internet via modem, using a program such as Leafnode to automatically fetch and store new postings.

Gnus is much faster when it can suck news from a filesystem rather than through a relatively slow modem connection, so by all means, use the locally archived news if you have it available. You can tell Gnus that you want to use a spool directory as a news source with a variation of the preceding `setq` statement placed in your ~/.gnus file:

```
(setq gnus-select-method '(nnspool "location"))
```

Substitute the network or local path to the spool directory for the word `location` in the statement, but don't remove the double quotes.

There are a dozen or so other `nnspool` variables, some of which might need to be changed to make this selection method work in your situation. You can inspect them by loading the Gnus Info manual and going directly to the "New Spools" section, which is listed in the top-level index.

If you have never used Gnus, read the next couple of sections before starting it up for the first time; you will be glad you waited!

~/.newsrc and ~/.newsrc-eld

On Linux and other UNIX-like systems, the traditional name for the local list of available newsgroups is ~/.newsrc. Not only does this file contain the names of the groups your ISP's news server can provide, it also has the groups marked so that your newsreader knows which groups you want to read and which messages you've already marked as read.

You might already have such a file if you have been using other Linux software to read news. Netscape and a few other programs are exceptions, in that they don't make use of the standard location and format of news-related files.

If you don't have a ~/.newsrc, Gnus downloads the information from the server the first time it connects to your news server. These files can be quite large (often more than a megabyte), and Emacs will be unresponsive during the download, so don't start Gnus when you are in the middle of some editing in another buffer.

If your news is coming through a modem, you probably won't want the active file updated each time you start Gnus. The active file contains the information about groups and their available messages; this is what Gnus uses to update your ~/.newsrc file. The variable that controls this is called `gnus-read-active-file`. This variable can be set with a `setq` statement in your ~/.gnus file, but instead I will use this as an opportunity to introduce the extensive Customize support for Gnus. Rather than dive right in to the main Gnus Customize buffer, which can be overwhelming with its multiple subgroups and hundreds of settings, instead take a look at the subgroup that contains startup server variables. Press M-x and type

```
customize-group
```

When prompted, type

```
gnus-start-server
```

In Figure 18.1, notice the Value Menu, which shows the three possible settings for this variable. Setting it to `t` is appropriate for only direct and fast connections to the server, such as a T-1 line or local spool. This setting causes Gnus to download the entire active file when starting up.

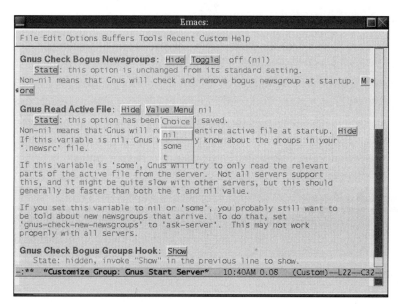

Figure 18.1 *A Gnus Customize Buffer*

A value of some would be an ideal compromise, but not all servers support it. With this value, only the information on subscribed groups is updated from the server, which is much faster. Try it out with your server to see if it works. The nil value prevents Gnus from reading the active file, forcing Gnus to use the information in your ~/.newsrc as its sole source of group information.

> Throughout this chapter, the term "back end" is used quite often. A Gnus back end is one of the modules used to gather a particular type of message. For example, network news articles or messages are pulled from the news server with the nntp back end. The mail back ends include nnml (*mail spool format*) and nnmbox (*UNIX mailbox format*).

If you are using a ~/.newsrc file created by another newsreader, it is possible that even if you set the read active file variable to some or nil, Gnus will persist in downloading the entire active file each time you start Gnus. This can be annoying: I've seen this behavior a couple of times, and it doesn't appear to be completely predictable. What you can do as a remedy is open the ~/.newsrc file in a normal Emacs session. Cut out the bulk of the file, leaving behind only groups to which you are subscribed or that interest you. Create a new file (you could call it something like ".newsrc-complete") and paste the cut groups into it. Save the file as a resource in case you develop an interest in one of the groups therein.

Default Group Subscriptions

If you have never used a news reader such as slrn or trn (both of which use the traditional ~/.newsrc file), you begin with a blank slate. Gnus automatically subscribes you to a pair of basic newsgroups such as news.announce.newusers, as well as the Gnus group gnu.emacs.gnus. You might know of some groups to which you want to subscribe. When the Group buffer appears, commands become available for subscribing and unsubscribing to the groups your server or spool offers. First, though, I'll explain the varieties of buffers Gnus uses at different times.

The Five Gnus Buffers

There are five main types of Gnus buffers, each one with its own commands and menus. The first one you will see after Gnus has connected with the server or spool is a listing of subscribed newsgroups, the Group buffer.

A List of Subscribed Groups

This is the entry point to the other Gnus buffers. It is always available as long as Gnus is running. The Group buffer appears after updated message information has been downloaded from the server as shown in Figure 18.2. You don't see this buffer unless a successful connection has been made.

> Most Gnus keyboard commands consist of a sequence of letters, some capitalized and others lowercase. To make the printed representations of these commands more legible, I've included a space between the letters. This space shouldn't be typed. These letter commands should be typed in sequence, not simultaneously. For example, you type the command S z by pressing S, releasing it, and then pressing z.
>
> Some of the commands begin with an uppercase M, which might be confusing, because M has been used in this book to represent the Alt key. There is a difference: An M that signifies the Alt key is always followed by a hyphen, as in the M-x minibuffer command. An M followed by a space is just what it looks like—a capital M.

NOTE

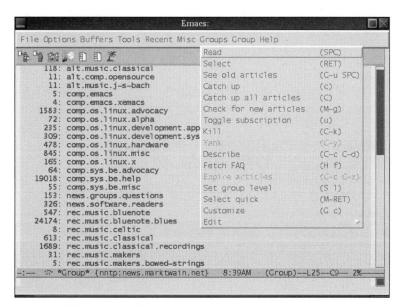

Figure 18.2   *The Group Buffer*

Here are the main commands in this buffer:

Spacebar	Brings up a Summary buffer (discussed in the next section), splits the screen into two windows, and displays the first unread message in an Article buffer. The middle mouse button can also be used to select a group.
Enter	Creates a Summary buffer for the selected group without opening an Article buffer.
A M	Adds to the listing of groups unsubscribed but available groups that match a regular expression. This command is in effect a regular expression search of the groups listed in your ~/.newsrc. For example, if you type A M `comp.lang.*`, groups such as comp.lang.c and comp.lang.lisp are added to the Group buffer and displayed. You can read the available messages, but a further command is necessary if you want to subscribe to one of these new groups.
u	Toggles a group's subscription on or off.
U	Prompts you for the name of a specific group you want subscribed.

Many more Group commands are available from the menus, but these few will get you started.

Another type of buffer available from the Group buffer is the Server buffer, shown in Figure 18.3. Type

^

to open it. This buffer is simply a listing of the various possible connections to servers (the word is to be interpreted loosely) that Gnus can access. These can

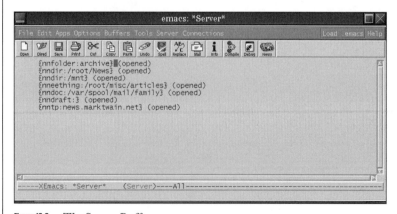

Figure 18.3   *The Server Buffer*

include your news server, mail back ends, WWW back ends, and directory groups you have created. Pressing Enter on any of the servers listed takes you to a Group buffer listing available newsgroups, mail folders, or whatever other types groups the server has available. You can subscribe and unsubscribe to any group by pressing u, the toggling key.

The last of the main groups you should be aware of is the zombie group. This is a group that Gnus knows about and can access but to which you haven't subscribed. Many zombie groups are newly available groups from your news server, and others are groups you have accessed in previous sessions but haven't subscribed to. Every now and then, it's a good idea to take a look at your zombies. There might be some to which you would like to subscribe with the u command; the others can be cast out with this command:

```
S z
```

The Summary Buffer

After you have selected a group, a new type of Gnus buffer is created—the Summary buffer, a list of unread articles or postings. The sender, subject line, and server's message number are shown, one article per line.

If you select your group by pressing the spacebar rather than Enter, the first unread article is shown in another window, as shown in Figure 18.4.

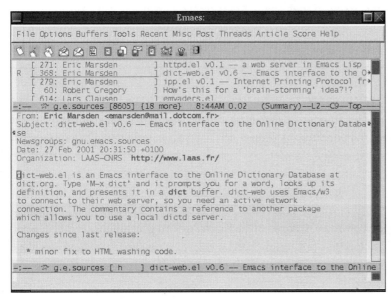

Figure 18.4   *Summary and Article Buffers*

There are several ways of moving focus from article to article. The up-arrow and down-arrow keys are intuitive, as is clicking the second mouse button, so use these for the time being since there are so many other keystrokes to remember.

Press Enter or the spacebar (or click with the mouse) to fetch an article from the server. It appears in a new Article window, and a capital R to the left of the message's line in the Summary buffer indicates that it has been marked as read.

Often, when reading news posts, you finish reading the messages that interest you and you never want to see the remainder again. Consign them to oblivion by pressing c, which stands for "catch up." What this really does is mark all messages in the Summary buffer as read. This is recorded in your ~/.newsrc file so that the next time you read news, only new messages in the group are seen. You can also press c on a group listing in the Group buffer, which marks all messages as read without opening the group.

The window focus never needs to leave the Summary buffer, because article-related commands in a sense "cross the modeline" between Summary and Article windows. Page up and down through an article with the spacebar and Delete keys.

There is a class of Summary commands that limit the groups displayed by using various filtering criteria. Here are the three most commonly used:

/s	After you type this command, only articles with the current message's subject are shown.
/a	Limits the display so that only articles by the current article's author are shown.
/u	Hides the messages already marked as read.

Gnus can display articles arranged in *threads*, which are hierarchical branching trees of articles. Sometimes this is useful, but in some groups, you might want to see all articles in a continuous sequence. You can toggle thread display with this command:

T T

Over the years, Gnus commands seem to have bred like rabbits. There are quite a few thread-related commands, some of them arcane but presumably used by some advanced Gnus aficionados (although it's amusing to speculate that there might be commands that no one has ever used!). Here are a few thread commands that make a good starting point:

T s	Fans out or exposes the threaded messages hiding beneath the current article.
T h	Collapses the current article's threaded replies, hiding them.
T S	Shows all threads.
T H	Conceals all threads.

The Gnus Info manual details the remaining thread commands, but using the mouse to navigate is nearly as fast, and you don't need to learn still more keyboard commands.

Articles

Once you have an article displayed in its own window, more commands come into play. As mentioned in the preceding section, the spacebar and Delete page back and forth through the message. Several categories of actions can be used on an article, including marking, saving, scoring, and caching (you will find more in the Gnus Info manual).

Marking or Tagging

Often there will be several articles in a Summary buffer that you would like to treat the same way. Gnus offers a variety of tags you can hang on an article. A marked article's particular tag shows up in the Summary buffer. Here are the most useful of these commands:

#	The basic processing tag. If you mark several articles with this, a subsequent command is applied to them all.
M-#	Untags the current article.
M P U	Untags all marked articles.
M P t	Tags all articles in the current thread.
M P T	Untags articles in the current thread.
?	Makes an article dormant. A dormant article isn't visible in the Summary buffer unless someone has replied to it. This, so to speak, "wakes it up". This command can be used when you have posted a message and you don't want to see it again until there is a response. The article is stored in the disk cache (see the section "The Local Cache").
M-u	Marks the article as unread, even if you have read it.
Ctrl-k	Marks all messages with the same subject as read.

k	Marks all messages with the same subject as the current one as read and then opens the next message.
M-s	Searches for regular expression matches in all articles in the current group.

As with all of these command categories, you can find many more marking commands on the menus and described in the Gnus Info files.

Saving Articles

If you follow certain favorite newsgroups, you are likely to happen across articles you would like to keep permanently. These might be wonderful examples of prose, software tips or code snippets, or possibly entire threads in which you participated. You also might be accumulating a collection of encoded image or sound files from one of the binary newsgroups.

Most news servers periodically discard articles when they reach a certain age due to disk space limitations, so you can't count on an article's being available from your server indefinitely. Gnus can save an article in a number of different formats, but if you save very many articles, keeping them organized and identifiable can become time-consuming. Consider using persistent caching (discussed later) if your collection becomes unmanageable. Here are the main article-saving commands:

o	Saves the current article to an Rmail (Babyl-format) file. This command appends the article to an Rmail folder. The default filename is the name of the newsgroup, but you can type in something else if you like. This is one way to accumulate an archive of valuable postings from a group. You might want to use this command if Rmail is your mail reader; otherwise, don't use it, because the Babyl format is understood by only Rmail and Gnus.
O m	Similar to o, but uses the standard UNIX mailbox format.
O f	Appends the entire article to a plain text file.
O F	The same as O f, but overwrites the file, destroying the file's contents.
O v	Appends the article to a VM-style mail folder. This is useful if you use VM, because you will be able to read the folder from your VM sessions.

Another way to save an article locally but still have it show up in future Summary buffers is to make it persistent. See the section "The Local Cache" for details.

Scoring

Scoring is a newsreader term for rating or assigning a relative value to an article. The idea is that similar articles in the future, perhaps those with the same subject or author, will inherit a score. Gnus will try to make the article more prominent if the score is high. Articles with a low or negative score won't even appear in the Summary buffer. The default score is a neutral 0.

You may be more familiar with kill files, used by some newsreader software for a similar purpose. A kill file is a list of patterns which match some combination of subject, author, or other header lines in a message. The newsreader ignores any message which matches one of these patterns. Gnus can use kill files but they are much slower to parse and less flexible than article scoring. Kill files require more user maintenance while scoring can be automated in various ways.

There are two varieties of scores—persistent and expirable. Persistent scores stay in effect forever unless you deliberately remove them, and expirable scores last for a limited time.

Roughly speaking, persistent scores tend to be used for scoring based on an author's name, because people tend to live on and keep their names. Expirable scores are well-suited for scoring based on a message's subject, because subjects come and go.

Scores are stored in Lisp files, one for each newsgroup. Armed with a basic knowledge of Lisp syntax (which you can glean from some of the earlier chapters), you can directly edit your score files. Sometimes this is faster than figuring out the exact command you need for scoring a message in a particular way, because score command syntax can become convoluted.

To edit the score file for the current group (assuming you are viewing a Summary buffer), press M-x and type

```
gnus-score-mode
```

or use a direct key command:

```
V e
```

The following command loads the current score file into a score-mode buffer for editing:

```
V f
```

You are prompted for the name of another score file, which will be loaded for editing. This file then becomes the current score file.

The subject of scoring takes up several chapters of the Gnus Info manual. You can really get tricky and elaborate with scoring if you are so inclined. What follows is enough of an overview to get you started using either interactive or adaptive scoring.

Interactive Scoring

The syntax of keyboard scoring commands is rather complex, but in actual usage, you will probably settle on a few favorite formulae. To score an article, you press four character keys. The first character of a command is either I, which increases the score, or L, which lowers it. Remember that articles start out with a neutral score of 0 unless a score file is already in effect.

The second character tells Gnus what part of the header you want scored:

a	Author
s	Subject
d	Date
f	Follow-up: this adds to the scores of follow-up messages
b	The body or content of the message
t	Scores on the thread

The third character is conditional; different choices are valid depending on which header was specified by the second character. If the header was of the `string` type, such as subject or author, use these characters:

e	An exact match
s	A substring match
f	A "fuzzy" or loose match
r	A regular-expression match

If the header specified by the second character was the date, these are your choices for the third:

b	Before the date of the message
a	After the date
n	The date of the article being scored

The fourth and final character determines whether the score will be permanent, temporary, or immediate (without adding to the score file):

p	Makes the score permanent
t	For an expirable score
i	For an immediate score

I'll bet you would just love to see some examples at this point!

Here's one: Say you wanted to permanently score up the current article on its subject line using fuzzy matching (so that the score will catch similar headings). This is the command:

```
I s f p
```

Here's another example. This time you want to score down a particularly annoying author who has been infesting one of your favorite newsgroups. This will push those offending messages into the background:

```
30 L a e p
```

You might be wondering what the number 30 is doing there, gratuitously stuck to the beginning of the command. I thought I'd throw that in to demonstrate how to give a numerical argument to a scoring command. Without that prefix, the command would have lowered the score by only 1 point. With it, the score is lowered 30 points, helping minimize the chances of your seeing postings from that author. You can use similar prefixes with any Gnus command where an amount is in question.

Here's one more example: Perhaps you want to temporarily lower the score based on a substring interpretation of the subject line:

```
L S
```

"Just a moment," you say. "I thought there were supposed to be four characters, with only the first one capitalized!" I just wanted to see if you were paying attention. Now that you mention it, this command doesn't look correct according to what you have read so far. The reason it is valid is because Gnus accepts a capitalized second or third character in this command. This signifies that the omitted character or characters should be assigned default values. These values are "substring" for the third character and "temporary" for the fourth.

This elaborate score-command syntax might seem unnecessarily complex, but from another point of view, it is empowering. You may never use most of the hundreds of possible permutations. Nevertheless, a little experimentation might provide you with the exact command you need. You might want to type up a cheat sheet containing your favorite score-command permutations or create simpler keybindings for them.

These commands can also be initiated from the menus, but you are prompted for the sequence of code letters. It is easier (for me, at least) to work up a few effective formulae and type them in directly as commands.

After your main groups have been affected by a score file, you can filter the Summary buffer with scores using these commands:

V m   You are prompted for a numerical score. All articles with a score less than the one you entered are marked as already read.

V x   This time, the score you enter at the minibuffer prompt is used to expunge or delete all articles with a lesser score by making an entry in the group score file.

Adaptive Scoring

If the explanation of score commands led you to reflect on our brief tenure upon this earth, you might be interested in letting Gnus do the scoring for you based on the articles you delete, read, and save. This is a transparent, behind-the-scenes technique of scoring with no direct user interaction. To enable adaptive scoring, you need to change the `nil` value of the variable `gnus-use-adaptive-scoring` to `t`. You can do this with a `setq` statement in your /.gnus file:

```
(setq gnus-use-adaptive-scoring t)
```

You can be more specific in this statement. In place of `t`, you can use either `word` or `line`. The former uses individual words in the subject header for scoring, and the latter uses several of the header lines in addition to the subject line. The `line` choice is probably more useful in most cases.

You can also use Customize to change the value. Press M-x and type

```
customize-group
```

When prompted, type

```
gnus-score-adapt
```

A Customize buffer appears, containing numerous changeable variables related to adaptive scoring, as shown in Figure 18.5. The first one is the toggle for adaptive

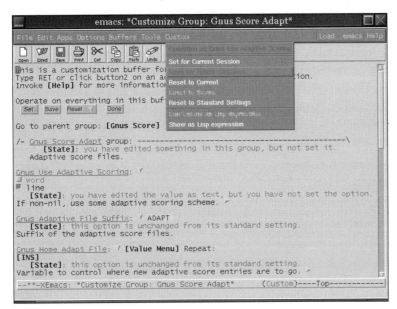

Figure 18.5 *Turning on Adaptive Scoring*

scoring itself. Just check one of the boxes next to "word" or "line" and save your change with the State menu.

When adaptive scoring is turned on, Gnus begins to notice which articles you delete unread, which you save, and the sort of threads that interest you. It accumulates this information throughout a news-reading session, and when you quit, it neatly deposits the information in one or more score files. It takes a while for Gnus to build up enough information in the score files to make a noticeable difference, but after a week of daily news reading, your Summary buffers will display interesting posts prominently, while the annoying stuff begins to recede into the background. Think of scoring as a form of self-defense.

The Local Cache

In Gnus terminology, a *cache* is a directory tree where articles can be stored, either temporarily (until you have time to read them) or permanently. You can use the cache (which is a subdirectory of your ~/News directory) as an alternative means of saving a local copy of an article. The cache can also speed up subsequent Gnus sessions, because Gnus will load an article from the cache instead of downloading it from the server if it has a choice. Here are a few of the commands that copy articles to the cache:

!	"Ticks" the article. Gnus downloads the message and copies it to the cache for later reading. After you have read it, it is deleted later. Ticked articles will be visible in the group's Summary buffer.
*	Makes the current article persistent. This causes Gnus to copy the article to your local news cache. A persistently cached article is never deleted. The article won't be visible in the Summary buffer unless you also tick the article with the ! command.
M-*	Removes the persistence tag from the article, causing it to be deleted after you read it.

Decaying Scores

This might sound rather morbid, but allowing your scores to decay into digital humus can be beneficial to your Gnus ecosystem. Turning on this subsystem of Gnus lets it evaluate your score files daily, gradually moving both positive and negative score values closer to the 0 baseline. This is especially valuable when you have enabled adaptive scoring, which over time can result in massive score files with conflicting entries that tend to average each other out.

You can turn this on by setting the variable `gnus-decay-scores` to a non-`nil` value such as `t`. This line in your ~/.gnus file does that:

```
(setq gnus-decay-scores t)
```

The default decay values should do what you want. Small positive and negative scores (between -3 and 3) are set back to 0. Larger scores (between 3 or -3 and 60 or -60) are shrunk by 3 every day. Scores larger than 60 (or smaller than -60) are reduced by 5% per day.

These are well-designed defaults. The smaller scores really don't mean that much and might as well be zeroed out. The larger the score, the greater the possibility that it really means something to you, so these gradually creep closer to 0. They get pushed back to their former values as either your scoring commands or adaptive scoring writes to the score files.

Message Composition

Being able to post follow-up messages and direct replies is the whole point of network news, so naturally Gnus provides a healthy variety of ways to do just that.

Rather than use the default Emacs mail-mode, Gnus provides a generic message-mode that is equally useful for both news articles and mail composition.

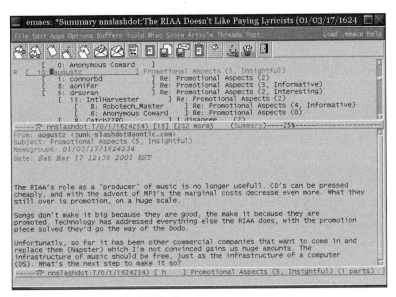

Figure 18.6   *A Message-Mode Window*

In Figure 18.6, notice how different levels of the quoting of previous messages are highlighted differently. This improves the readability of that part of your message, helping you see at a glance who has responded to whom.

Five basic commands open a message composition window so that you can write a response:

a   Use this command when you want to post an article that isn't a follow-up (the news-reading term for a public reply). In effect, you are starting a new thread when you do this.

f   The follow-up command. Your message will eventually appear as the next post in the thread.

F   The "quoted follow-up" command. The posting to which you are responding is inserted before your response in the composition buffer. Angle brackets precede each line in the quoted section in order to distinguish it from what you write.

r   Replies privately via e-mail to the author of the current article. You don't need to have Gnus enabled as your mail client to do this.

R   Similar to r, but quotes the current article in the reply.

Many variations of these commands are listed on the menus, but these are the workhorses.

After you have completed your posting, Ctrl-c Ctrl-c shoots it off to the news server.

Viewing Files and Directories with Gnus

Gnus is ambitious. The limited worlds of news and mail were not enough for it, so it expanded its territory to include just about anything on your filesystem and even the WWW. Not all of these Gnus extensions are compellingly useful. I wonder if Lars Magne Ingebrigtsen might have implemented some of them just to show that it can be done, perhaps as a demonstration of the extensibility of Gnus.

Directories and Document Groups

The directory group back end is an odd one with limited abilities. It lets you read a directory with numerical file names (even on a remote machine, using ange-ftp or efs file names). The directory looks like a newsgroup, but the access is read-only.

More useful is the nneething back end; it lets you read any directory as if it were a newsgroup. Files are marked as read when you open them, and this information is stored for future sessions. This is no substitute for Dired or a file manager, but it can be useful for browsing collections of documents and keeping track of which ones you have read.

The Document Group back end (nndoc) is quite versatile, allowing you to treat a variety of file types as newsgroups. Not all files are composed of discrete units that can be usefully broken up by nndoc, but this back end understands several message archive file types.

An example will help make this clear. Suppose that years ago, when using Netscape for e-mail seemed like a delightful novelty, you ended up with four months' worth of e-mail stored in a file that only Netscape can fruitfully read. You decide to turn Gnus loose on the file by typing

```
G f
```

You are prompted for a file name in the minibuffer, and you type

```
~/.netscape/nsmail
```

The nndoc back end is familiar with this type of mail file and separates the individual messages and displays a new Summary buffer.

You can feed nndoc Rmail files, standard mailbox files, saved newsgroup posting files (many news readers store saved messages in a single file per group), and several types. This is a great way to read old archived mail as mail messages rather than "in the raw."

If you have enabled one of the Gnus mail back ends, you can even "respool" these messages and make a native Gnus folder or directory from them (depending on which back end you use). Mark all the messages with the # process mark using this command:

```
M P b
```

Then respool with

```
B r
```

You are asked which back end to use (see the section "Selecting a Mail Back End" for a comparison of mail back ends). If you were to type nnml, the messages would be written to new files in a subdirectory of your ~/Mail directory.

The original mail file you started with remains unchanged.

You can also find all these back ends on the Foreign groups submenu of the Groups menu.

Gnus and the World Wide Web

It might not have occurred to you to try accessing Web sites with a news reader. For certain sites, this isn't such a bad idea. Web-based discussion forums and mailing-list archives have begun to eclipse traditional NNTP newsgroups in recent years. Gnus comes with several back ends for certain types of sites. There isn't room in this chapter to discuss them all, but one of the most interesting is described next. A chapter in the Gnus Info manual called "Browsing the Web" (in the "Select Methods" section) gives you more-detailed information about these back ends.

Slashdot

Slashdot is a news-and-message-board site popular with Linux users and open-source software users; you can find it at http://slashdot.org. You can enable this site's back end by inserting this statement in your ~/.gnus file:

```
(setq gnus-secondary-select-methods
    '((nnslashdot "")))
```

The Slashdot back end relies on W3, the Emacs Web browser (see Chapter 20). W3 is used to render the HTML in which Slashdot messages are written. If you haven't installed W3, skip ahead to Chapter 20 and install it so that this back end will work.

Once you have started Gnus and the Group buffer is visible, switch to the Server buffer by typing ^. You see nnslashdot listed as one of the available servers. Select it by pressing Enter. After a while, you see something like Figure 18.7.

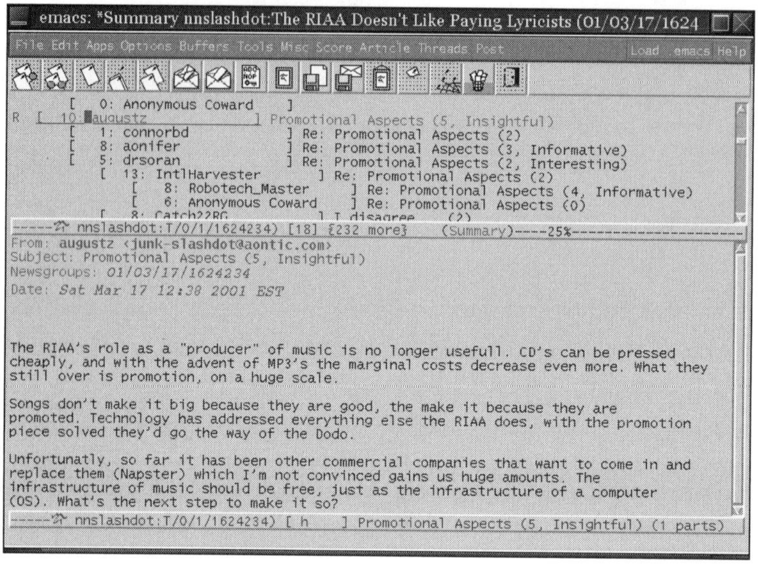

Figure 18.7 *Gnus and Slashdot*

Press F to subscribe to one of the "groups," which actually is a Slashdot news item along with reader comments.

If you press the spacebar on one of the articles shown, and Gnus retrieves the news item and the responses.

You can browse the Slashdot responses just as you would news postings.

I have to confess that recently I couldn't get the nnslashdot back end to work until I downloaded a snapshot of the most recent Gnus development version from http://www.gnus.org.

I didn't even install the entire snapshot distribution; I merely byte-compiled the nnslashdot.el file and substituted it for the old version of the file. The most recent Gnus snapshot is included on this book's CD-ROM in the directory /cdrom/packages/gnus, so if you are interested, you might want to extract the needed file.

Web sites change frequently, and their administrators don't really care about peripheral viewers (such as nnslashdot users!) who never see the banner ads that supposedly pay for a site. If the format of Slashdot is changed, it is unlikely that the Slashdot developers will bother to inform the Gnus developers. As a result, the Slashdot back end might not be functional at times.

A Caution

These Web back ends will probably never be as reliable as the core Gnus functions. When Web sites change, a part of the back end code might be disabled. Someone might eventually fix the Gnus code that was affected, but these peripheral back ends probably aren't a high priority to the developers.

Gnus for E-Mail

Don't expect Gnus to be a drop-in replacement for any other e-mail program you might have been using. Gnus treats your mail messages as it does news messages, and this can take some getting used to. You need to do more configuration than is necessary with other e-mail clients; the benefit of this is the potential for a highly personalized mail setup.

In particular, you need to understand the Gnus mode of mail expiration. Naturally, you don't want to lose messages you wanted to keep, but with the default settings, Gnus will never delete a mail message.

Several steps lead to a working Gnus mail setup. First, you need to select a mail back end. Next, you have to tell Gnus where to find new mail. Gnus can bring in mail from a local file or directory, a POP server, an IMAP server, or even a Web-based mail service such as Yahoo mail or Hotmail.

An optional next step could be to configure message expiration. You might consider doing this if you subscribe to high-volume mailing lists or if you receive quantities of junk mail.

The sky's the limit after you're past these first steps as far as Gnus configuration goes. Gnus has a massive series of Customize buffers available; most of the numerous Gnus variables can be changed from within one of these buffers. Press M-x and type

```
customize-group
```

Respond with

```
gnus
```

You see a top-level Gnus Customize buffer similar to the one shown in Figure 18.8.

The two mail-related subgroups to investigate are Mail Source and Nnmail.

Sometimes it's worthwhile to track down a setting in one of the Customize buffers, and other times it is easier to copy and paste a snippet of Lisp into your ~/.gnus file.

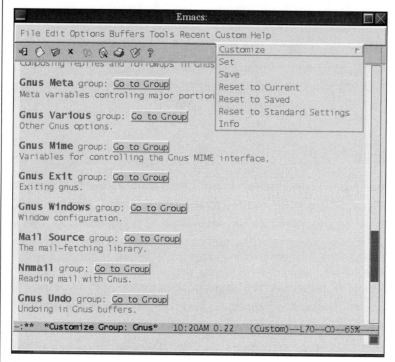

Figure 18.8   *Customizing Gnus*

Selecting a Mail Back End

Gnus doesn't have a single method of processing mail messages; it has several, each of which has advantages and drawbacks. Some are more appropriate for users who have much free disk space, and others are more efficient if you have large quantities of mail. Before you begin using Gnus for mail, you need to decide on one of these back ends.

These back ends differ mainly in the method used to store messages. The Summary and Article buffers introduced in the news-reading sections of this chapter are for the most part identical whether you're reading news or reading mail with any of the back ends. All the commands described earlier can be used with mail messages too.

Storing Mail on a Local Spool

The nnml back end is modeled on the way news servers store articles. The messages are split, one file per message, and are deposited in one or several directories. An active file and an overview file (similar to files that news servers use) provide an index that Gnus can use to quickly get at a particular message.

The drawback of nnml is that it uses many inodes, which are pointers used by the Linux ext2 filesystem to identify a file and its location on the hard disk. Each file uses one inode. Each filesystem has a limited number of inodes, which raises the dreaded specter of running out of them. This should be of concern to you only if you have vast quantities of mail or if you are on a shared filesystem administered by someone else.

This back end is a little slower when Gnus is absorbing a quantity of new mail, because the mail has to be split into its constituent messages and distributed to directories.

For many Gnus users, especially those unconcerned with maintaining compatibility with standard e-mail clients, nnml is the back end of choice.

Using an MH-Style Spool

The nnml back end was developed for users accustomed to the venerable MH mail-handling system developed years ago at RAND. It is a lot like nnml but without the rapid message access provided by index files. Use this if you are accustomed to such systems and want to maintain compatibility; otherwise, any of the other back ends is preferable.

The UNIX Mailbox Format

If you like the traditional mailbox format used by many other e-mail programs, the nnmbox back end should suit you. All messages are stored in one big file. Gnus can append new mail to such a file very quickly, but finding a message is slower than with nnml, because the whole file has to be searched for header identifiers. You might use this back end if it is important to you to be able to read the mailbox files with a traditional mailer such as Mutt or Pine.

Mail Folders

nnfolder is like a hybrid between the nnml mail spool approach and the single-file nnmbox back end. Mail is kept in several mailbox-style files, but each mail group you have set up gets its own file. Searching for a message is faster than with the nnmbox back end, partly because the files tend to be smaller. An active file is maintained; this provides some indexing for your mail.

The Rmail (Babyl) Format

Rmail users (but probably few others) might be interested in keeping their Gnus mail in Rmail's native format. This is another "one big file" back end like nnmbox, so performance is similar.

Informing Gnus

You can set up a mail back end either by writing Lisp in your ~/.gnus file or by opening a Customize buffer and entering your choice there.

The following is a sample Lisp statement that can be adapted to your situation. It sets up a new secondary select method; the primary one is your news server. Substitute nnmbox or any of the other mail back ends for nnml in this expression if you like:

```
(setq gnus-secondary-select-methods
      '((nnml "")))
```

Mail Sources

Now for some Lisp that tells Gnus where your mail folders are. The first could be used to fetch mail from a POP server that requires a username and password:

```
(setq nnmail-spool-file
    '(pop :server "pop3.mailserver.com" :user "myname"))
```

If you prefer to use a non-Emacs method of retrieving your mail (such as Fetchmail), all you need is a statement like this:

```
(setq nnmail-spool-file
      '(file :path "/var/spool/mail/user"))
```

Perhaps you use procmail to split your mail into files depending on the contents of the message header. In that case, point Gnus at the directory with a statement patterned after this one:

```
(setq nnmail-spool-file
    '(directory :path "/var/mail"))
```

You can list more than one mail source in an `nnmail-spool-file` variable definition. For example, the preceding statements could be combined. This would tell Gnus to gather mail from both the single mailbox file and the files in the directory:

```
(setq nnmail-spool-file
    '((directory :path "/var/mail")
    (file :path "var/spool/mail/user")))
```

Make sure you keep the parentheses balanced in a statement like this.

Splitting Mail

Many e-mail users appreciate the convenience of having mail separated into folders categorized by subject or origin. Procmail used in conjunction with Fetchmail is a popular means to this end on Linux systems. Gnus can do this as well, using a regular-expression-matching scheme similar to the one Procmail uses.

Here is an example that creates several new mail groups:

```
(setq nnmail-split-methods
      '(("kernel" "^Sender:.*linux-kernel*")
        ("family" "^From:.*Ayers*")
        ("xemacs" "^X-Mailing-List:.*xemacs-beta*")
        ("misc" "")))
```

The last group (misc) should always be present, because it is the catchall group where mail that didn't pass the first three tests ends up. If you leave it out, you might lose mail. Maybe Gnus would save the messages somehow, but I don't feel inclined to run a test!

Each item in this list of splits is a two-element list. The first part is the name you want the group to have, and the second part is a regular expression that is intended to match one of the header lines in a message.

Here is an English translation of the regular expression in the next-to-last item:

```
Any message that has at the beginning (^) of a header the characters "X-Mailing-
List:," followed by a single character (the period matches a space), followed by
zero or more characters (*), followed by "xemacs-beta," followed by zero or more
characters (*)
```

Sometimes it takes some experimentation to come up with a regular expression that matches every message you think it should. You can examine the header lines in an e-mail message by opening it directly in Emacs (not using a mail mode such as Gnus), or by simply pressing t in an Article buffer. Look at several messages from the source you are trying to filter, and try to find a header line that is common to all of them but distinctive enough that other messages won't match as well.

This is just the tip of the iceberg when it comes to Gnus splitting mail. See the "Fancy Mail Splitting" section of the Gnus Info manual for interesting but complex mail-splitting esoterica.

Expiring Mail

You can tell Gnus to expire messages in certain mail folders, in which case messages are deleted a week after you receive them. This time lag can be changed with a Lisp statement like this:

```
(setq nnmail-expiry-wait 9)
```

You can also change this variable in the `nnmail-expire` Customize group.

You can manually expire a message at any time by pressing E in the Summary buffer. If it's a big file and you want to dispose of it at once rather than wait until the expiration happens, just press

B Delete.

The following Lisp statement can be used as a template to fine-tune expiration periods for several mail folders. Check your parentheses well!

```
(setq nnmail-expiry-wait-function
      (lambda (group)
       (cond ((string= group "family")  60)
             ((string= group "junk") 1)
             ((string= group "main") 'never)
             (t 9)
)))
```

This chunk of Lisp creates a lambda (nameless) function, the main body of which is a conditional statement that says if the string "family" matches a mail folder's name, wait 60 days before expiring the messages. The expiry action to take with the main folder is `never`, which disables expiry completely for that folder. Don't forget the single quote before `never`, because it prevents the Lisp interpreter from trying to make sense of the word. It needs to be passed unaltered to Gnus. Another valid entry rather than an integer or the word `never` is `immediate`, which signals Gnus that you want all messages in a folder expired right now.

Attachments and MIME

All you need to do to attach a file to an outgoing message is press Ctrl-c Ctrl-a (or use the menu). You are asked for a file name (Tab completion comes in handy) and a MIME type. A default type is suggested.

When you receive a message with a MIME attachment, Gnus should know what to do with it. If you'd rather use external viewers for images, or if you need to have a certain type of MIME type passed to another application, you can use keyboard commands.

The MIME-related commands are numerous, but these few will handle most of your needs:

K o	Saves the attachment to a file.
K v	Views the attachment.
K l	Pipes the attachment to another program.
W M v	Views all the attachments in the current message.

These commands accept a numeric prefix. For example, you can type

```
2 K o
```

This saves the second attachment to a file.

Mail without News

You probably don't want to open a connection to your news server every time you get new mail with Gnus. There is another way to start Gnus so that only the mail back ends are activated. Press M-x and type

```
gnus-no-server
```

This command lets you read your mail offline. The next section demonstrates how you can effectively use Gnus as an offline news reader, an "unplugged" mode that is particularly useful for users connecting to the Internet intermittently with a slow modem.

Offline News Reading with the Gnus Agent

Recent versions of Gnus have included an entirely new mode of use called the Gnus Agent, also known as "Gnus Unplugged". The idea is for Gnus to download articles from selected subscribed newsgroups while you are online and then allow you to read them at your leisure and make follow-up replies while offline.

You can manually tag articles you want downloaded, or you can, with a little work, set up the Agent so that it downloads only messages that meet certain scoring criteria.

This sounds good, but be warned that configuring the Gnus Agent beyond the defaults requires some knowledge of Lisp if you want to be selective about which articles are downloaded. Space doesn't permit me to go into advanced Agent configuration. The Gnus Info manual details the code needed to set up Agent categories, which could be a next step after absorbing and using the material in this section, although the simplified approach given here might be all you need.

In the next section, you will learn to use the Agent manually, meaning that you will tell Gnus while online which groups or articles to download for later reading.

Setting It Up

One statement in your ~/.gnus file transforms Gnus into an offline reader:

```
(gnus-agentize)
```

This changes the whole personality of Gnus. Now you can start Gnus with a new minibuffer command. Press M-x and type

```
gnus-unplugged
```

This starts Gnus in such a way that it makes no attempt to contact a server. You can now read previously downloaded articles if you have any to read, but because this is the first time, you need to start your PPP connection (or however you get on the Internet). Once you are online, a new command lets Gnus know about it:

```
J j
```

Gnus is now "plugged" and will connect with your NNTP server. Now type

```
g
```

This tells Gnus to check the server for new articles in your subscribed groups. The command

```
J s
```

downloads all the unread articles and places them in newly-created subdirectories of ~/News/agent. Each group gets its own directory. But before you type this command, think of the possible consequences. Have you been neglecting to keep up with postings in your subscribed newsgroups? Perhaps some of them contain thousands of unread messages. Do you want this massive influx of messages flooding onto your hard disk?

Until you either set up some good scoring rules for your groups or catch up with the groups by marking old messages as having been read, you might be better off using the following approach to downloading.

In the Group buffer, notice that there is a new Agent menu (see Figure 18.9).

Notice the Group submenu on the Fetch menu. This command fetches all the new messages in the group under the cursor and stores them on your hard disk. The keybinding for this command is

```
J u
```

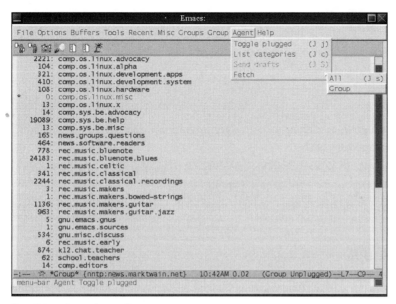

Figure 18.9   *Gnus Agent Groups*

Using this command, you can be selective about which group's messages are downloaded.

When your downloads are complete, select Toggle plugged from the Agent menu or type

```
J j
```

Now Gnus is in its "unplugged" state and doesn't care whether you are connected to the Internet.

You can read the new messages just as you do in a normal Gnus session but without tying up a phone line. Messages marked as read are subject to the normal expiration process, and you can use any of the usual Gnus commands for saving, making persistent, and so on.

You might have noticed that nearly all Agent key commands begin with a capital J. As an aid to remembering them, the letters that follow the J are often the same as the analogous Gnus commands.

When the Gnus Agent is enabled, you can still use the original startup command M-x gnus if you are already connected to the Internet. You will still be able to "unplug" at any time, whether you are connected or not.

The Agent and Mail

The Gnus Agent is intended for use with news servers. If you are using one of the mail back ends, you should type ^ while in the Group buffer; this opens the Server buffer, which was discussed earlier. Two commands are available here:

J r   Removes a server (such as a secondary mail server) from the Agent's list of servers to work with.

J a   Adds a server to the list. You shouldn't have to add your primary news server, but if you use others, you can add them.

Posting Follow-Ups

You can write as many follow-up or reply messages as you like while Gnus is un-plugged. Send them with Ctrl-c Ctrl-c, just as you normally would. Instead of being sent, they are copied to a Drafts folder.

Later, when Gnus is in its plugged state, you can select Send drafts from the Agent menu or type

J S

All your messages will be sent to the server.

Further Exploration

The Gnus Agent can be configured to be quite specific in what it is allowed to download. Unfortunately, the Customize support for this aspect of Gnus is incomplete, meaning that you have to delve into the Agent section of the Gnus Info manual for information on writing scoring categories. For example, you can limit the Agent to downloading only short messages, or messages that are less than three days old.

If you use a modem to connect to your news server, you owe it to yourself to at least try the Gnus Agent for a day or two. If you don't like it after all, just comment out the gnus agentize line in your ~/.gnus file, and Gnus will go back to the way it was. I switch over to the Agent if I get involved in a thread that requires some reasoned responses—the sort of writing that is easier while you're offline.

Some Gnus users, especially those with a dial-up Internet connection, prefer to install a local news-server such as leafnode rather than Agentizing Gnus. If you are on a multi-user network it would make sense to install such a news-server. A single news-spool could be accessed by all users no matter what newsreader is being used.

Miscellaneous Gnus Settings

Gnus is very (some would say pathologically) customizable. The easy way is to venture into the maze of Gnus Customize buffers and see what the default settings are. Not everything is included there, but the Gnus Info manual has enough material to get you started using Lisp statements in your ~/.gnus file to change the uncustomized variables and create new functions.

Highlighting

Nothing makes an Emacs mode more frustrating to use than a set of default font-lock highlighting colors that make text difficult to read. Gnus has its own font-lock types, so even if you have carefully set up the standard font-lock colors, the Gnus colors might need some work. You can find these settings easily by choosing the GNU Emacs menu item Options, Customize Emacs, Faces Matching Regexp. When prompted in the minibuffer, type

```
gnus*
```

A Customize buffer containing all the Gnus-specific faces appears.

XEmacs users can choose Options, Edit Faces. Scroll down until you find faces that begin with "gnus".

I have noticed that if a light background is used, the default Gnus font-lock colors are acceptable, but with dark screen backgrounds, some customization is needed.

Asynchronous Fetching

Although network operations in Emacs can never be completely independent processes (Emacs would need to be multithreaded, which it isn't), Gnus can prefetch articles while you are reading news. You need to set up this feature carefully, because you don't want Gnus to blithely prefetch too many or too large articles. A single line of Lisp in your ~/.gnus file turns on asynchronous fetching:

```
(setq gnus-asynchronous t)
```

You might want to tweak some variables associated with this feature. The easiest way to get an overview is to use Customize. Open the buffer by pressing M-x and typing

`customize-group`

Respond to the prompt with

`gnus-asynchronous`

Figure 18.10 shows the buffer that appears.

In this buffer, you can turn on asynchronous fetching, either temporarily so that you can try it out (recommended) or permanently. You might consider changing the number of articles that Gnus prefetches from 30 to a smaller number. It all depends on how fast your Internet connection is and how much of a user load is borne by your server.

Another option you might try is Gnus Use Header Prefetch. If this is toggled on, Gnus downloads the headers for the next group in the Group buffer while you are reading the current group. This makes sense only if you are in the habit of reading groups in strict sequence.

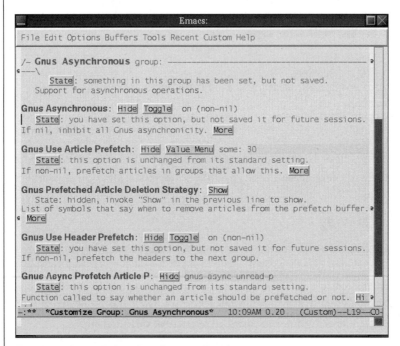

Figure 18.10   *Customizing Asynchronous Fetching*

Gnus opens two connections to your news server when asynchronous fetching is turned on. This might slow down Gnus if your server is busy. This is another reason to evaluate this feature carefully instead of just turning it on and forgetting about it.

Skill Level

Because Gnus is so complex, it makes sense to have two different skill levels. The default level is Novice, but as you gain proficiency with Gnus, you might want to bump up the level a notch to Expert. The difference between the levels is mostly in how solicitously verbose Gnus will be. If you tire of continually being asked questions like "Are you sure? y or n", you can change the level. Insert these lines in your ~/.gnus file:

```
(setq gnus-novice-user nil)
(setq gnus-expert-user t)
```

Once these lines take effect, Gnus cheerfully allows you to shoot yourself in the foot.

However, even with the expert-user option turned on, Gnus will query you when you try to do something extraordinarily destructive.

Another pair of options prevent Gnus from requiring confirmation when you try to "catch up" or mark as read all messages in a group and when you quit Gnus. Here are the ~/.gnus lines:

```
(setq gnus-interactive-catchup nil)
(setq gnus-interactive-exit nil)
```

Unless you are recklessly confident, it is advisable to leave these variables alone.

Gnus, XEmacs, and GNU Emacs 21

The Gnus developers have gone to great lengths to ensure that Gnus works well on both GNU Emacs and XEmacs. In actual usage, the differences are slim. If you are using a GNU Emacs version earlier than 21.0, you won't see the toolbars, which in my opinion aren't worth all that much. They give a beginner the option of clicking an icon rather than searching the menus for the four or five most common commands.

In XEmacs, you get to see graphical "smilies". These are little yellow icons that are cartoonish representations of the classic e-mail and news-posting abbreviations such as :-) and :-(. They are trivial, to be sure, but rather amusing.

Another graphical feature is the display of picons in a message's header. A picon (short for "personal icon") is a small bitmap that displays a low-resolution image of the sender's face. I get the impression that the usage of picons has decreased in recent years, so this feature might fall by the wayside as time passes.

The main difference between Gnus in XEmacs and GNU Emacs is that it is easier to keep up to date with newer versions of Gnus for XEmacs users. The XEmacs Gnus package is maintained independently of the various XEmacs beta and stable releases, so it is more likely to be up-to-date than the version that is bundled with GNU Emacs, which is updated only when a new GNU Emacs version is released. Naturally, Gnus users using GNU Emacs can obtain a new version and install it in a subdirectory of their site-lisp directory, as described in Chapter 12.

Conclusion

So now you have been introduced to Gnus. You might run screaming back to your familiar news and mail readers after reading this chapter, but there's also a possibility that you might be intrigued. Even if you eventually reject Gnus, it is interesting to explore, even if for only a short time, such a complex and powerful package constructed of nothing but a group of Lisp files.

The next chapter considers the various methods for accessing remote files. This won't be useful for every Emacs user, but if you ever need to edit a file on a remote machine, Emacs provides some very useful tools.

Chapter 19: Editing Files on a Remote Machine

T he normal technique for working with files on remote machines is to use the ftp file-transfer program (or something similar) to download a copy of the file you need, edit it, and then upload it back to its home, overwriting the original file. Of course, this assumes that you have read-write privileges on the remote machine.

> In this chapter, the term "remote machine" is used to refer to another computer accessible over a network. This could be either a local network or the Internet.

This technique works well but can become tedious if you have many files to edit or need to repeatedly edit the same file. Repetitious tasks like this cry out for automation. Enough people have felt this need that an Emacs package has been written and refined that makes this sort of file access transparent. The package can be found in two variant forms—ange-ftp for GNU Emacs and EFS for XEmacs. ange-ftp was originally written by Andy Norman. He no longer actively maintains it, so the GNU Emacs and XEmacs development teams each adopted the package, and the code began to fork. The XEmacs developers used as a starting point a re-written version by Andy Norman called EFS, while the GNU Emacs team continued development of the original ange-ftp.

Both offer roughly the same features and use the same file name syntax; in the course of this chapter, any usage differences will be pointed out along the way. In order to prevent constant repetition, I'll refer to both versions as ange-ftp, using the name EFS only when it differs in some way from ange-ftp.

ftp

The standard ftp program is the "man behind the curtain" here, the engine that ange-ftp uses to copy files across a network. ftp is a command-line console program that can display directory listings on remote machines and transfer files. It accepts commands such as get and put, used to request file downloads and uploads. When you use ange-ftp, this all happens automatically. You request that Emacs load a remote file, and before long, a buffer appears with that file in it. You edit, and then save the changes, and the file travels out over the network and silently replaces the original file. You could think of ange-ftp as a front end for ftp; it does all the tedious logging in and transfer for you so that you are free to do what you need to do: edit the file.

Requesting a Remote File

You might be wondering how Emacs is supposed to know that the file you want is on the network somewhere and not on your machine. A special path syntax is used. When Emacs sees a path entered in the minibuffer with that syntax, it makes no attempt to find the file in the normal way. Responsibility for fetching the file is handed off to ange-ftp. After the file has been downloaded, Emacs displays it in a buffer just as if it were a local file. ange-ftp doesn't sink back into complete dormancy. It waits until you save the file, and then it makes every effort to upload the modified copy of the file to its original location.

The syntax that alerts Emacs to your intentions is the mere presence of a colon, separating the remote machine's system name and the path and file name of the file you want. Optionally, a username followed by an @ character can come first. The whole sequence must start with a forward slash. The following are two examples—the first without a specified user ("anonymous" is the default), and the second with a username. Both of these would be typed after the find-file key command, Ctrl-x Ctrl-f:

```
/ftp.gnu.org:/pub
/juneau@ftp.esd.edu:/pub/user/juneau/great_bustard.tex
```

The first command wouldn't retrieve a file, because the path is that of a directory. A Dired directory listing would be displayed, from which you could select a file (see Figure 19.1). You could edit files, but you wouldn't be able to save them under the same name (which includes the path on the remote machine). Nothing would stop you from saving to a path and file name on your machine. You can also use the Dired copy command by pressing the key command C or by selecting Operate, Copy. An anonymous login, as in the first example, is almost always a read-only access to the remote file system.

The second example shows how an imaginary user with juneau as a login name can gain read-write access to his private directory on the ftp.esd.edu machine. This user would be prompted for a password in the minibuffer to gain access to the directory. This can be avoided; see the following section.

ftp sites usually don't let you stay connected for long periods of time without activity. Suppose you spend a couple of hours working on a file, and you want to save it to the remote machine. By this time, the ftp session has timed out and disconnected you. If you try to save the file, ange-ftp is smart enough to know that the connection should be reestablished first, and it does so.

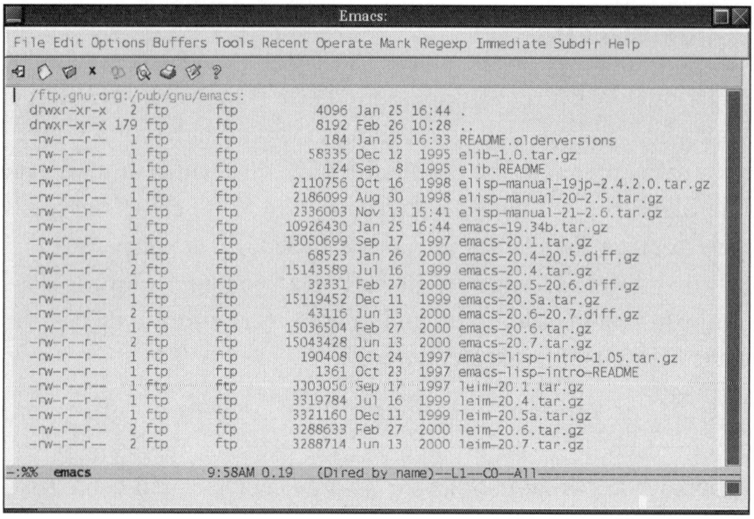

Figure 19.1 *An ange-ftp Dired Listing*

There is another optional element to an ange-ftp path-and-file name instruction—the port number. Most machines use the standard ftp port 21, but if you need to use another port for some reason, you can include #[digit] in the path:

`/linnaeus@ftp.silphium.org` **Error! Bookmark not defined.**`23:/pub/compositae/laciniatum.txt`

The space between "org" and the port number 23 has to be inserted using the "insert-literal" keystroke: press Ctrl-q Space.

The syntax is a little different in GNU EMacs 21; rather than entering the literal space a hash-mark can be used:

`/linnaeus@ftp.silphium.org#23:/pub/compositae/laciniatum.txt`

netrc and Passwords

Machines connected to a network may allow anonymous access, such as the public fileservers hosting various free software projects. ange-ftp, unless told otherwise, tries to log on to a server with the username "anonymous" and a password consisting of your e-mail address. This works fine if you plan on saving only local copies of the files you obtain. You won't be allowed to overwrite the original file with your version unless you have an account on the remote machine that has write permission.

There is a straightforward and simple method of informing ange-ftp of your usernames and passwords. A file named ~/.netrc has long been used on UNIX and

UNIX-derived systems as a personal file containing hostname, username, and password information. Networking programs such as telnet and ftp often have support for this file included. This is a simple text file with entries such as the following, which use the same imaginary users and so on as the earlier examples:

```
machine ftp.esd.edu login juneau password X387gtrk
machine ftp.silphium.org login linnaeus password chelone@turtle.net
machine ftp.gnu.org login anonymous password ogg@vorbis.net
```

The third example doesn't seem useful at first glance, because ange-ftp fills in the information for anonymous logins automatically. What make entries such as this worthwhile is that ange-ftp does Tab completion for you on any host machines listed in the ~/.netrc file.

There is a certain security risk in having unencrypted passwords in a plain-text file. Make sure that the permissions are set so that only you can read the file. If the permissions on .netrc are insufficiently secure ange-ftp will give you a warning message.

Binary and ASCII Transfers

Two methods are used by the underlying ftp program to transfer files—binary and ASCII. ange-ftp by default transfers files as ASCII text, although it does attempt to switch to binary transfer if the file's suffix is of a recognized binary type. If a binary file such as a tar archive or an executable is transferred with the ASCII method, the file will be corrupted, so if you have any doubt at all, there are several methods of making certain that a transfer is binary rather than ASCII.

Whenever ange-ftp has an ftp connection established, a Shell buffer is available with the ftp program's prompt displayed (see Figure 19.2). You can select this buffer from the Buffers menu. Doing so gives you an opportunity to override ange-ftp and give a direct command at the ftp prompt. Type `binary` and press Enter. ftp switches to binary mode (also known as image mode). All subsequent transfers will be in that mode. You can switch back to ASCII mode by typing `ascii` at the ftp prompt.

Another ftp command you can give is `bye`. This shuts down the FTP connection. Doing so might occasionally be necessary, because ange-ftp doesn't close the connection on its own. Killing the ftp Shell buffer also closes a connection.

ange-ftp recognizes the most common binary file name suffixes, such as .tgz and .zip. If you find yourself transferring binary files that have a new or nonstandard

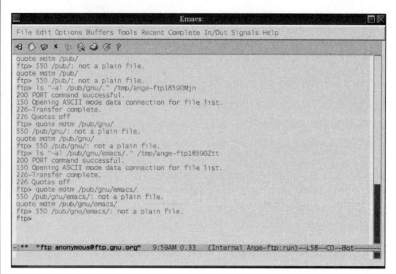

Figure 19.2 *ftp Shell Buffer*

suffix, you can change an associated list variable. Bring up an ange-ftp or EFS Customize buffer by pressing M-x and typing

```
customize-group
```

At the minibuffer prompt, type

```
ange-ftp
```

Or, for XEmacs, type

```
efs
```

You will see a Customize buffer similar to the one shown in Figure 19.3.

In Figure 19.3, notice the long regular expression just beneath "Ange Ftp Binary File Name Regexp". This regular expression is a list of acceptable binary file name suffixes. This list is in a text entry field, meaning that you can move the cursor there and type in new items. Here is what the very end of that regular expression would look like if you added the suffix .pck:

```
|\.taz$|\.tgz$|\.pck$
```

Don't forget the backslashes, because they are necessary to "escape" the periods so that they aren't interpreted as part of the regular expression. The dollar sign is also necessary, because it is a regular expression symbol that matches the end of a line. In this case, it stands for the end of the file name. If you make changes, remember to select Save for Future Sessions from the State button's drop-down menu.

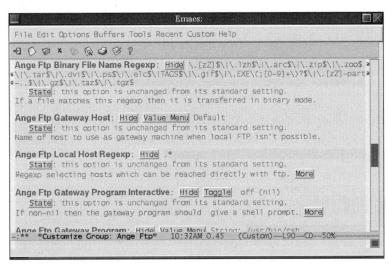

Figure 19.3   *Customizing ange-ftp*

While you have the Customize buffer open, you might look at some of the other settings that can be changed. You can change the default username, password, time to wait before a retry, and many other variables.

Host Types

ange-ftp tries to auto-detect the type of operating system the remote host machine is running. The mode was created in the days when non-UNIX servers such as DEC VMS and MTS were more common. In general, if the `ls` command fails to return a file listing, `dir` is substituted. Note that if you run across a host running VMS, you need to type your file names in uppercase letters.

Hosts running one of the Microsoft Windows operating systems are usually no problem, but when transferring text files, you should be aware of the differing line-end conventions between Microsoft operating systems and Linux. As an example, if you download a text file compressed with the zip or PKZIP program on a Microsoft Windows platform you should unzip the file with this switch:

```
unzip -a [file]
```

This switch automatically adjusts the end-of-line treatment so that it matches your platform.

Linux ASCII files use a single invisible line-feed character, and Windows uses a carriage return plus a line feed. If you want to make sure that the native text-file conventions are preserved at each end, you should transfer text files in text mode (see the preceding section). XEmacs users can set a variable that will enable this behavior:

```
(setq efs-treat-crlf-as-nl t)
```

This could be given a keybinding if you use it much.

If you use a version of Emacs which has MULE enabled (the Emacs international character set extensions; see Appendix D), the end-of-line conversions will be handled automatically.

Hash in the Modeline

Not corned beef, but ASCII hash marks (#), are displayed at the ftp prompt as a file is transferred if the `hash` command is sent to the remote. These characters are a primitive precursor of the progress bar that many windowed programs display. ange-ftp doesn't show the actual hash characters. Instead, it translates them into a running percentage of the total download and displays that number in the modeline. This works only with hosts that understand the `hash` command (most do). You can turn this off using Customize or by changing the value of one of these variables from `t` to `nil`:

```
(setq efs-send-hash nil)        [for XEmacs]
(setq ange-ftp-send-hash nil)   [for GNU Emacs]
```

ange-ftp doesn't monitor the flow of bytes constantly, because that would be a resource drain. It updates the percentage of each kilobyte sent or received.

Sources of Further Information

The GNU Emacs Info documentation for ange-ftp is rather scanty; about one page can be found in the Remote Files section of the Emacs Info manual. A better source of usage details is in the Commentary section of the primary ange-ftp Lisp file, ange-ftp.el. You can find this file in the /net subdirectory of the main Emacs Lisp directory, which is usually /usr/local/share/emacs/[Emacs-version-number]/ lisp. The "local" path element might or might not correspond to your installation. At the beginning of the Lisp file, you will find many pages explaining how ange-ftp works and the variables that can influence its operation.

The XEmacs EFS package contains its own Info manual, which is a useful asset. Much of it is a reworking of the Commentary material in the Lisp files.

Conclusion

This chapter, short as it is, should give you a head start on editing remote files. After you get it set up with your own passwords, ange-ftp is a straightforward package, transparent enough in use that you can easily take it for granted.

The next chapter introduces W3, the sole Web browser of the text-editor world.

Chapter 20: Web-Browsing with W3

S ome years ago, an Emacs hacker named Bill Perry had a quixotic idea. What if Emacs could be used as a Web browser? After all, Web pages are ASCII text documents; even the HTML tagging is composed of ASCII characters. What about the images? At the time (the early '90s), XEmacs was just beginning to be able to display images, so that was one possibility. The proposed Emacs browser could also be run strictly in text mode like the Lynx browser, which would let GNU Emacs users use this fantasized Emacs extension. A challenging project, to be sure, that would end up pushing the limits of what can be demanded of an interpreted language like Emacs-Lisp.

Perry plugged away at the project for several years. He was kept busy with W3, because this Emacs extension occupied an unstable area: the shifting ground between the two slowly-evolving versions of Emacs on the one side and the frantically mutating nature of HTML in the mid-to-late '90s on the other.

How did it turn out? Considering the difficulties inherent in the project, remarkably well. It's far from perfect; W3 can be slow to render Web pages, and due to the single-threaded nature of Emacs, it can cause Emacs to "zone out" if there are network slowdowns.

On the plus side, here are some of W3's hard-won features:

- It renders inline images well (on XEmacs and presumably Emacs 21).
- Stylesheets are well-supported.
- It has SSL encryption (with helper applications).
- It supports bookmarks and caching.

It won't replace Netscape or Mozilla, but W3 can be useful at times. Gnus makes good use of W3 when displaying HTML mail or newsgroup messages. It also can be handy for reading HTML files on your hard disk.

Installing and Setting up W3

XEmacs users can install a preconfigured package that should be ready to go. GNU Emacs doesn't include W3, so you have to install it from source, which isn't that difficult. The W3 source archive is much like those of Gnus and VM, because it includes a configure script that generates a custom makefile. A copy of the W3 archive can be found on this book's CD-ROM in the directory /cdrom/packages/w3.

If you would like to specify a particular directory for W3's byte-compiled Lisp files, run the configure script with this command:

```
configure --with-lispdir=/[path]/W3 --with-emacs
```

Substitute the path to your site-lisp directory (the recommended location) for [path] in this command. If your Emacs (for whatever reason) isn't called `emacs` or isn't in your executable path, substitute the name and the path (if needed) for `emacs`.

Running `make` and then `make install` should be all you need to do.

W3 makes use of several configuration files, some of which are automatically generated and then saved in the directory ~/.w3. You can change the way W3 works either by editing the files there or by accessing the W3 Customize Group buffer and changing the settings.

Images, XEmacs, and GNU Emacs

W3, shown in Figure 20.1, was one of the first Emacs extensions to take advantage of the built-in XEmacs image-rendering support. Users of GNU Emacs were denied this W3 feature until the release of Emacs 21, a significant event in Emacs history. W3 in its current released version doesn't work with Emacs 21, but the fixes are in the W3 CVS tree, which will eventually become a new version. This chapter focuses on W3 usage with XEmacs, but the usage and configuration details should be applicable to GNU Emacs when the code situation stabilizes.

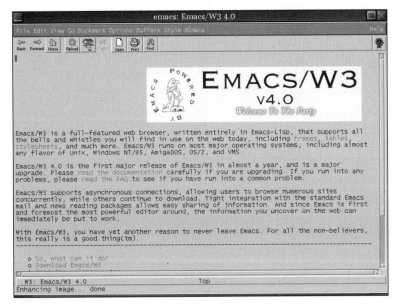

Figure 20.1   *W3 Displaying the W3 Home Page*

> Emacs 21 hadn't yet been released while this book was being written, but the release seemed so imminent that it will probably be available by the time you read this.

Turning off Image Display

Even if you are running an image-enabled Emacs, there might be good reasons to disable W3's image loading. W3 is slower than browsers such as Netscape and Opera and shouldn't be considered as a replacement graphical browser. With image loading turned off, W3 does a respectable job, similar to Lynx but with more-advanced page formatting. The W3 Options menu, shown in Figure 20.2, lets you turn off automatic image loading. Selecting the final item on the menu saves the current state of the listed options to an initialization file named ~/.w3/profile.

MIME Support

W3 is aware of the standard locations where it can expect to find a system's mailcap and mime-types files. Many Web browsers refer to these files to find a way to present a file to the user. The mime-types file (often /etc/mime-types) lists various file suffixes and which MIME-type the suffix indicates. Here are a couple of lines from a typical mime-types file:

```
audio/x-pn-realaudio           ra rm ram
application/x-httpd-php3        php3
```

The mailcap file (~/.mailcap or /etc/mailcap) maps files that have been identified as having a certain MIME type to corresponding programs that know how to handle such files. Here is a mailcap line that corresponds to the first mime-type line just shown:

```
audio/x-pn-realaudio;/usr/local/RealPlayer7/realplay "%u"
```

Figure 20.2   *W3's Options Menu*

This line associates the RealPlayer program with files that have been identified in the mime-types files as being of the `audio/x-pn-realaudio` type.

Basic Commands

There are two ways to start W3. The first is to press M-x and type

`w3`

W3 starts up and attempts to load the default home page, the W3 home site at Indiana University. If you aren't connected to the Net, W3 naturally won't be able to find the page. Pressing Ctrl-g aborts the search. If you want to be able to start W3 without being Net-connected, you can change the default page to a local HTML file on your hard disk. You can change the setting by pressing M-x and typing

`customize-group`

Respond to the minibuffer prompt by typing

`w3-files`

One of the items in the resulting Customize buffer will be `w3-default-homepage`. You can type any valid URL in the item's text entry field. Don't forget to select "Save for Future Sessions" from the State menu when you are finished.

You can also start W3 by pointing it directly at a local HTML file by pressing M-x and typing

`w3-open-local`

You are queried for a file name in the minibuffer.

W3 provides a great number of key commands, but you need to learn only a few to be able to quickly navigate Web sites:

Spacebar and Backspace	Scroll forward and backward through a page (Page Up and Page Down work too).
Enter	Follows the link at point (the middle mouse button also does this).
B	Returns to the previous page. A cached copy is used if you have turned on the disk cache.
F	Goes forward to the next page.
r	Reloads the page (g also does this).
Tab	Moves point to the next text entry field (such as a form).

Shift-Tab	Moves to the previous text entry field.
Ctrl-o	Prompts you for a Web site's URL.
o	Prompts you for a local HTML file.
s	Displays the HTML source for the current buffer.

There are many other key commands, but these are the ones you will need the most. Press Ctrl-h b to see a complete list.

To help Netscape and Lynx users adapt easily to W3, Bill Perry included emulation keybindings. These two commands replace the default keybinding with bindings similar to either of the two browsers:

> M-x `turn-on-netscape-emulation`
>
> M-x `turn-on-lynx-emulation`

These commands allow you to try out the new keybindings, but if you decide you want to use one of these emulations in every W3 session, you probably don't want to type the command each time W3 starts up. One solution to this is to insert this line in your ~/.w3/profile file:

`(setq-default w3-netscape-emulation-minor-mode t)`

Substitute `lynx` for `netscape` in this line if you prefer.

Bookmarks

By default, W3 recognizes the file ~/.mosaic-hotlist-default as its bookmarks file. You probably don't use Mosaic, the early precursor of Netscape, so you probably don't have such a file. If you select Add bookmark from the Bookmark menu while visiting a Web site, that site's URL is added to that bookmark file. If it doesn't exist, it is created.

If you would rather use a different bookmark file, you can specify it in the ~/.w3/ profile file with a line like this:

`(setq-default w3-hotlist-file "file:////[path]/file.html")`

There are several keybindings (as well as menu items) for working with bookmarks:

h i	Adds the current page to the default bookmark file. This command uses the buffer name as an identifier (this is what you see on the bookmark menu). If you want to give the bookmark another name, press Ctrl-u and type `new-name` before typing i i.

h l   Adds the link's URL at point to the bookmark file.

h v   Converts the bookmark file to HTML and displays it with W3.

h a   You are prompted for a regular expression. Type one in the minibuffer, and the bookmarks that match the expression are displayed. This is a handy way to find particular bookmarks in a large bookmark file.

h u   Lets you use Tab completion to jump to a bookmarked location. Type in a few letters of a bookmark's name (not the URL) and press Tab to insert the remainder of the name.

h r   Renames a bookmark. You might end up with bookmark names that are too long or that aren't good identifiers, such as index.html. This command also uses Tab completion. Type in a portion of the bookmark you want to rename, complete it by pressing the Tab key, and type the new name in the minibuffer when prompted.

These are the default bookmark key commands. If you have turned on Netscape or Lynx emulation, you can view the new keybindings by pressing Ctrl-h b.

Using Netscape's Bookmark File

W3 can load an external bookmark file and make it available on the bookmark menu, but you need to use a certain amount of caution when doing this. A typical Netscape bookmark file has hundreds of entries. The Emacs menu system has a difficult time displaying a large number of items in a readable and navigable fashion. W3 has trouble rendering many table-heavy Web sites, so it makes sense to keep a separate bookmark file consisting of sites that W3 can handle.

Netscape uses HTML as the file format for its bookmark file. Not all of the bookmark commands just mentioned work with this type of file—another reason to maintain W3's bookmarks separately.

Stylesheets

W3's display of HTML documents can be controlled through the use of Cascading Stylesheets (CSS). These are text files written with a particular syntax that CSS-enabled browsers interpret in order to control different attributes of an HTML file, such as fonts, colors, and text alignment. Stylesheets can exist both on the server that hosts an HTML file and on the machine running the browser. The point of using stylesheets is to separate the presentation attributes from the HTML file itself and to give both the viewer and the author a measure of control over how a page is displayed. The ratio between the influences of the viewer's and the author's stylesheets can be varied. The "cascading" of stylesheets is a metaphor for how multiple stylesheets can affect the ultimate presentation of the HTML file.

> W3 has the distinction of being the first web browser to include stylesheet support. Cascading Stylesheets were proposed as a standard long before the big-name browsers began to support the protocol.

The W3 distribution includes a sample stylesheet in the /etc directory called default.css. In the XEmacs package, it is named /etc/w3/stylesheet in the main package directory.

Here are a few sample entries from that file that give you a taste of CSS syntax:

```
/*
** Hypertext link coloring
*/


a:link     { color: #FF0000 }
a:visited  { color: #B22222 }
a:active   { color: #FF0000 }


/* W3-specific section for Emacs versions which
** can only display one size of font at a time
*/


@media unifont {
h1,h2,h3,
h4,h5,h6   { text-decoration: underline; }
        h1 { color: rgb(0,255,255); }    // cyan
        h2 { color: rgb(70,130,180); }   // steelblue
        h3 { color: rgb(106,90,205); }   // slateblue
        h4 { color: rgb(135,206,235); }  // skyblue
        h5 { color: rgb(0,0,128); }      // navy
        h6 { color: rgb(173,216,230); }  // lightblue

strong,em { color: red        }
      dfn { font-style: italic }
  s,strike { color: green       }
```

Several chapters of the W3 Info manual are devoted to the nuts and bolts of stylesheets. You will find ample detail that is outside the scope of this book. You can get a feel for how stylesheets work by copying the W3 sample stylesheet to ~/.w3/default.css and letting W3 know that this file is the one to use. Do this by pressing M-x and typing

```
customize-group
```

At the minibuffer prompt, type

```
w3-files
```

A buffer similar to Figure 20.3 appears. The setting to change is Default Stylesheet. Type in the entry field the path and file name of the sample file.

Save the changes by selecting Save For Future Sessions from the State button's menu.

Before starting W3, load your new stylesheet into an Emacs session and read through it. The color specifications can be in any of three formats: RGB number triplets, colors named in the X11 rgb.txt file, or 8-bit truncated RGB. All three formats are used in the example just shown.

As a first CSS experiment, try changing some of the colors in the file so that they show up well against your Emacs background color. The X11 application xcolorsel is a handy tool for browsing the available colors and finding their names in various formats.

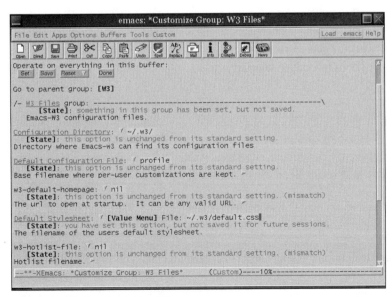

Figure 20.3 *W3 Configuration Files*

The relative sizes of the different headers can be changed if you are using XEmacs (and possibly Emacs 21). Don't make too many changes at once so that you will be able to track down any mistakes.

Sections of the file that seem obscure are explained in the Stylesheet Info chapters.

After you have saved your changes, load a local HTML file by pressing M-x and typing

```
w3-open-local
```

The changes you made should be visible in the W3 buffer. If they aren't, check over the file for errors.

One thing to keep in mind is that W3 reads its configuration files the first time it is started in an Emacs session. You can shut down W3 by pressing q, edit a configuration file or stylesheet, and then restart W3, and the changes won't take effect. W3 seems to hold its configuration variables in memory for the duration of an Emacs session. This means that you need to shut down and restart Emacs when you want W3 to notice any changes you have made to its configuration.

Security

W3 was designed with security in mind. You can install an external SSL (Secure Sockets Layer) program, and W3 will encrypt HTTP connections through an SSL channel. Cookies are files that many servers would like to leave on your hard drive that might contain password or identification information. You can disable all cookies or limit them to certain trusted servers.

Using SSL

In order to use W3's SSL capabilities, you must install an external program. The only one that is currently supported is SSLeay version 0.6.6 or later. The current status of SSLeay is that it has been orphaned by its original developers. The code was adopted by a new project known as OpenSSL, which is under active development as an open source replacement for SSLeay. W3 doesn't have direct support for OpenSSL, but with a little scripting, this disadvantage can be circumvented.

A warning: What follows are some suggestions for an SSL W3 approach that has worked for some people, but it likely will require some tinkering to get it to work on your system. Some background reading will help. You can find references and links on the OpenSSL Web site at http://www.openssl.org.

The W3 Info manual can also provide further help.

Start out by creating a shell script named emacs-ssl:

```
#!/bin/sh
exec 2>/dev/null
exec openssl "$@"
```

This script starts openssl with all error messages directed to /dev/null so that W3 won't become confused by them. Make sure you make the script executable, and then move it to /usr/local/bin or another binary directory on your path.

The next step is to change the values of several W3-SSL variables. The easiest way to do this is with Customize.

SSL Variables

Bring up a Customize buffer for SSL by pressing M-x and typing

```
customize-group
```

Respond to the prompt with

```
ssl
```

The resulting buffer, shown in Figure 20.4, lets you set such variables as the SSL certificate directory and the command-line options for the SSL program.

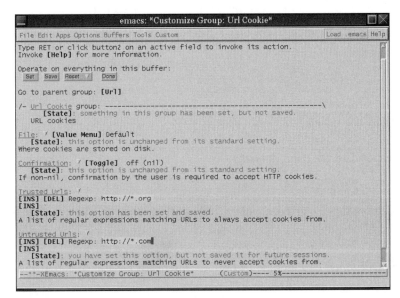

Figure 20.4 *Customizing W3–SSL*

The default openssl command-line arguments should be fine, but the Program Name variable should be set to `emacs-ssl` rather than `openssl`, ensuring that your new shell script is called rather than openssl directly. Save the new setting, and kill the Customize buffer.

The subject of SSL is quite involved; legalities vary by country, and several commercial interests demand fees for certificates. The WWW is your best source of up-to-date information on this rapidly changing area. The OpenSSL site, mentioned in the preceding section, and the W3 Consortium's site (no relation to the Emacs W3) are good starting points: http://www.w3.org.

Cookies

Cookies are controversial. Some people consider them evil violations of privacy, and others feel that they are nothing to worry about. These are files that have no meaning to any program on your system but serve to identify you to a previously visited WWW host the next time you visit. Registration and password information is stored in cookies. The result is that the next time you visit a site you won't need to manually log in.

Cookies are enabled in W3 by default. You can prevent W3 from accepting any cookies with this line in ~/.w3/profile:

```
(setq-default url-privacy-level 'paranoid)
```

You can use Customize to tailor W3's cookie behavior in more subtle ways. Figure 20.5 shows the Url Customize Group buffer. The Privacy Level checkboxes give you a range of levels from which to choose. Summon this buffer by pressing M-x and typing

```
customize-group
```

At the minibuffer prompt, type

```
url
```

Alternatively, respond to the prompt with

```
url-cookie
```

You will see in this new Customize buffer INS buttons next to the two items Trusted Urls and Untrusted Urls. Click on one of these buttons with the middle mouse button, and a new text entry field will open. You can then type in either regular expressions (which can include or exclude ranges of URLs) or actual specific URLs, as shown in Figure 20.6.

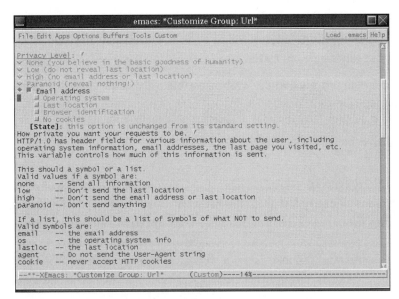

Figure 20.5   *Url Customize Group Buffer*

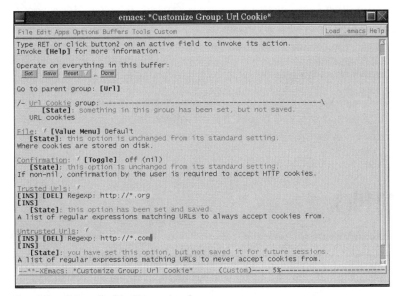

Figure 20.6   *More Cookie Customization*

As an example, many Linux users would rather not have cookies from doubleclick.com on their machines. You could enter this regular expression in the "Untrusted Urls" entry field:

```
http://.*\.doubleclick\..*
```

Notice how the second and third periods in the expression are escaped with backslashes so that they will be interpreted as periods rather than the regular expression symbol for any single character.

Judicious tweaking should give you a level of cookie usage that is just right for your situation.

Masquerading

Many Web sites query every browser that visits them. Behind the scenes, the browser is asked to divulge its identity—that is, the browser's name and version number. Why do these sites even care? They might be using advanced or variant features of HTML that are supported by only certain browsers. If an antiquated browser version shows up, the site might block access or display a warning such as, "This site requires Netscape 4.0 or later for optimal viewing." The option to view a text-only version of the site might be offered at a thoughtfully-designed site.

W3 can pretend to be either Lynx, Netscape, Internet Explorer, or arena. This is known as *masquerading* as another browser. This makes no difference in W3 usage, but it might let you visit more sites. You can set this variable in ~/.w3/profile by inserting this line:

```
(setq-default w3-netscape-masquerade-mode t)
```

Substitute another browser for `netscape` if you like. If you habitually browse the Web with graphics turned off, you might try masquerading as Lynx. Some sites automatically redirect Lynx browsers to an alternative text-mode site that might be well-suited to W3.

Downloading Files

There are several commands for saving pages and downloading remote files:

D	Downloads the file referred to by the hyperlink at point. A click of the middle mouse button is also effective. The destination on your hard disk will be editable in the minibuffer.
d	Downloads the current displayed page.
M-s	Saves the current HTML source of a visited page to either formatted text, HTML source, or LaTeX source, or in binary format. A related command is p, described next.
p	Sends the document to the printer in one of the four formats described in the preceding item.

Asynchronous Operation

W3 in its default state can cause Emacs to become unresponsive during a download. You can help prevent this antisocial behavior by turning on asynchronous download-ing. This feature allows you to continue editing files in other buffers while W3 is fetching a file. You can set this variable in your ~/.w3 file by including this line:

```
(setq-default url-be-asynchronous t)
```

This can also be toggled from W3's Options menu, or it can be set using Custom-ize. To bring up the proper Customize buffer, press M-x and type

```
customize-group
```

When prompted, type

```
url
```

Look for the Be Asynchronous item, toggle it to on with the middle mouse button, and save your changes by selecting "Save for future sessions" from the State drop-down menu.

W3's asynchronous downloading works well for the most part, but not as well as it would if Emacs could run in concurrent threads.

Caching Web Sites

Caching means saving to a directory on your hard disk a copy of every Web page W3 visits. If image loading is turned on, every graphics file is saved as well.

When you feed W3 a URL to visit, a quick check is made in the cache directory. If the file is found there and it is identical to the remote file, the cached copy is used rather than the original. This speeds up W3 substantially. The downside is that a cache can grow very large.

You have a choice of two different types of file names for your cached files. The file names can retain their original human-readable names, or they can be renamed using the MD5 message-digest algorithm. The second option is slower but en-sures that cache collisions are unlikely.

A cache collision happens when a Web browser is checking the cache for files that match a retrieved file. If it finds two or more with the same name, an arbitrary choice is made, and it might be the wrong file. Depending on the browser, any multiple file name matches might be rejected, causing the browser to consider the remote file uncached even though a copy is in the cache.

When W3 copies a file to the cache, it is given a new name by computing a 16-bit checksum or digest using the file's contents as input. The new file name looks something like this:

```
e6a26ab2a6b1b69337458536f348bff6
```

There are enough characters in such a name that the chances of two files ending up with the same name are negligible. What you give up is the ability to look at the file name and have any idea of what it is.

By default, W3 uses the MD5 method, but if you would rather have comprehensible cache file names, you can insert this line in ~/.w3/profile:

```
(setq-default url-cache-creation-function
  'url-cache-create-filename-human-readable)
```

Cleaning out the Cache

After a time, cached pages and images get "stale"; they may no longer correspond to an active page. It's useful to periodically "prune" the cache by removing all the files and letting W3 start over its incessant accumulation of files (assuming you have caching turned on). This keeps the cache from ballooning to a monstrous size. Too many cache files cause W3 to slow down as it is forced to compare so many files to the current page.

You can do this manually every so often, or you can use a shell script called clean-cache, which can be found in the /contrib subdirectory of the W3 source distribution. This script will probably need to be edited so that it can find your W3 cache directory. Alternatively, you can set the environment variable CACHE_ROOT in one of your login shell's initialization files with a line similar to this:

```
export CACHE_ROOT=/home/user/.w3/cache
```

A further refinement would be to make clean-cache a cron job, perhaps executed once a month. In the comments at the beginning of clean-cache, Bill Perry suggests this as a small shell script to be called by cron:

```
#!/bin/sh
CACHE_ROOT=/home/user/.w3/cache
CACHEMAXSIZE=5000
SIZE='du -s $CACHE_ROOT | awk '{print $1}'
if [ $SIZE -gt $CACHEMAXSIZE ] ; then
  /usr/local/bin/clean-cache
fi
```

The values of CACHE_ROOT and CACHEMAXSIZE as well as the location of the clean-cache script should be altered to fit. Consult your Linux distribution documentation for instructions on adding new cron jobs (man cron or man crontab, perhaps).

The XEmacs W3 package doesn't include a copy of clean-cache, so XEmacs users should snag a copy from the W3 source archive on this book's CD-ROM.

Caching Only

Once you've accumulated a quantity of documents in your cache, W3 offers you the option of reading them without attempting to access the Web at all. W3 is much faster in this mode, because all network operations are disabled. This is especially useful if your Net connection is intermittent and through a modem. You can visit content-heavy sites and read them more closely later while offline.

This option probably isn't appropriate for your ~/.w3/profile file, because you need to be able to toggle it on and off at will. Select Use Cache Only from the Options menu to turn on this feature.

Conclusion

W3 is an interesting and complex Emacs extension, but as the HTML used in writing today's Web pages evolves, more and more pages are becoming unreadable by this Emacs browser. Bill Perry has slowed down further development for the time being. Appeals on the Net for assistance with certain aspects have yielded little response so far. This might indicate that the demand for such a browser is not widespread.

The recent development of loadable module support in XEmacs might in time lead to a portion of W3 being rewritten in the form of compiled C modules. This would be a major boost in performance for W3, and rumor has it that such module support might be in the offing for GNU Emacs as well.

If W3 were a commercial closed-source product, we would have no choice but to abandon it if development lagged. W3 is GPL licensed, just as Emacs is, so the future may yet hold hope for its further extension and refinement.

Although W3 doesn't render well sites such as Amazon or Linux Today, there are still many simpler sites that don't rely so heavily on complex table layouts. W3 also serves Gnus and VM users well as a built-in interpreter for HTML mail.

On a lighter note, the next chapter introduces various games and amusements written for Emacs.

Chapter 21: Emacs Games

Text-Based Games and Hacks

Xmine

The Gamegrid Games

Emacs-Lisp programmers have been writing games for Emacs ever since the early days of the editor. The language, although optimized for text editing, is versatile enough to be effectively used for writing games similar to the familiar examples written in compiled languages such as C.

Emacs games, especially the graphical ones introduced toward the end of this chapter, will never run as quickly as their compiled C or C++ equivalents. Fortunately, the speed of modern computers makes the difference much less noticeable than in the past.

Text-Based Games and Hacks

Harken back to the days of yore, when text-based terminals reigned supreme and the idea of computer recreation was new. As a break from writing and running useful programs, many early users wrote games, hacks, and amusements. Emacs-Lisp programmers were not immune to the lure.

> The word *hack* has several meanings in computer jargon. The word was eventually expanded into the modern term *hacker,* which carries some negative connotations. In the context of this chapter, this definition from *The Online Dictionary of Computing* is apropos: "To interact with a computer in a playful and exploratory rather than goal-directed way. 'Whatcha up to?' 'Oh, just hacking.'"

Restricted to the ASCII character set and with no graphics or audio resources, it was a challenge to come up with an amusement or game that could hold a user's attention. A few of the following are playable games, and others can be seen as demonstrations of the flexibility of Emacs-Lisp. Some (such as the Tower of Hanoi) make use of the language's mathematical functions.

With the exception of readable-text modes such as Dissociated Press and Conx, most of these games and hacks need to be run in an Emacs that displays a fixed rather than proportional or scaled font.

Zippy

During the early days of Emacs, Bill Griffith's "Zippy the Pinhead" was a popular underground comic strip. Zippy, who had a skull shaped like an inverted cone, was prone to making surreal exclamations that often incorporated odd references to aspects of American mass-market low culture.

If you feel you are in a mental rut, press M-x and type

```
yow
```

A Zippy quote appears in the modeline. If the quote is too long for the modeline, GNU Emacs enlarges the area, whereas XEmacs shows the quote in a new window.

The quotes are randomly drawn from a file named yow.lines, included with GNU Emacs and a part of the XEmacs Cookie package.

Here is a typical utterance from Zippy:

```
I pretend I'm living in a Styrofoam packing crate, high in th' SWISS ALPS, still
unable to accept th' idea of TOUCH-TONE DIALING!!
```

Many of the lines betray their 1970s origin; think of them as period-piece humor from the era. Others are timelessly bizarre.

Similar to the Zippy quotes are the Spook lines. These are lines of deliberately subversive-sounding words or phrases that are intended to waste the time and effort of automated keyword search engines used by agencies such as the NSA.

The idea is to insert a random assortment of such phrases at the end of an e-mail message by pressing M-x and typing

```
spook
```

Here's an example of typical Spook output:

```
Janet Reno FSF arrangements Kennedy CIA explosion Nazi encryption Semtex terrorist
Honduras Paula Corbin Jones Roswell counter-intelligence Kibo
```

Already several of these items, such as Janet Reno, are not as current as they once were. Like the Zippy quotes, static entries tend to become outdated. The sources of the quotes or phrases are in text files, so nothing is stopping you from inserting new items or replacing old ones. The only requirement for these files is that entries must be separated by an ASCII null character. This character looks like ^@ but is really only one character. Insert one of these in a buffer by pressing Ctrl-q Ctrl-@.

You can even hijack the Spook or Zippy modes by substituting a completely new file for spook.lines or yow.lines. For example, say that you decide you want the sig for your e-mail messages to be chosen at random from a file of your favorites. All you have to do is first rename spook.lines spook.lines.orig and then give the name spook.lines to your sig collection. Make sure that the entries are separated by the null character. Now all you have to do to append a random signature to your message is press M-x and type

```
spook
```

If you try this with the Spook mode, you will probably need to change the value of the variable `spook-phrase-default-count` with a statement like this one in your ~/.emacs file:

```
(setq spook-phrase-default-count 1)
```

The default value is 15, but a value of 1 is more appropriate for inserting signatures.

Doctor

Eliza was one of the first and most popular pseudo-artificial-intelligence programs. It has been implemented in many programming languages, so naturally an Emacs version was developed. It is called Doctor, a remarkable simulation of a Rogerian analyst having a dialog with you.

Start the session by pressing M-x and typing

```
doctor
```

The "doctor" introduces himself and invites you to describe your problems. The Lisp file behind this doctor simulacrum scans your responses for keywords and attempts to formulate vaguely appropriate answers. Sometimes they sound like what a real person would say, but other answers are obviously a little skewed by the mode's limitations. Here is an example of a short exchange with the doctor:

```
I am the psychotherapist.  Please, describe your problems.  Each time you are
finished talking, type RET twice.

I'm plagued by baseless anxieties.

Why do you say you are plagued by baseless anxieties?

You asked me to describe my problems.

Is it because of your plans that you say I asked you to describe your
problems?

What do you mean?

Maybe your life have something to do with this.

Don't you mean "has"?
```

As you can see, the Doctor's grammar is a bit skewed at times.

Two factors help make this work as well as it does. The first is psychological: Even a partly-coherent response to something said or typed is assumed to be coming from another sentient person, even when you know better. Just as in ordinary conversation you try to interpret other people's speech as meaningful, filling in logical and factual gaps automatically, you tend to overlook the Doctor's lapses and pick out whatever meaning you can find. The incorporation of phrases from your entries into the Doctor's responses reinforces the illusion that there is someone behind the screen actually reading what you have typed.

The second factor is the mimicking of therapy techniques that try to coax forth a patient's ideas by saying little and using questions as responses. These techniques are easily faked by a mindless computer program, because little factual knowledge or analysis is displayed.

One variation of the Doctor gives him Zippy as a patient. Try pressing M-x and typing

`psychoanalyze-pinhead`

The Doctor's dialog with Zippy scrolls by too quickly to read. Press Ctrl-g to halt the dialog so that you can page up and read some of the output.

Dissociated Press

This mode and the next one are text scramblers that can yield amusing output. The input can be either an entire buffer or a selected region.

Dissociated Press is the older of the two modes. Start it by pressing M-x and typing

`dissociated-press`

A new Dissociation buffer opens. New sentences begin to appear, made up of sentence fragments semi-randomly plucked from the original buffer. The mode selects the next fragment to copy by attempting to match similar word beginnings and endings. The result is a nonsensical buffer filled with both real words and odd portmanteau words, which are new words made up of two real words conjoined.

Figure 21.1 is a Dissociation buffer formed using the Jane Austen novel *Mansfield Park* as grist for the dissociative mill.

This mode can be given two varieties of arguments. Positive-number arguments cause the operation to be character-by-character, with the number determining how many characters to overlap. For example, this command:

Ctrl-u 2 M-x `dissociated-press`

is the default behavior, whereas this command:

Ctrl-u 3 M-x `dissociated-press`

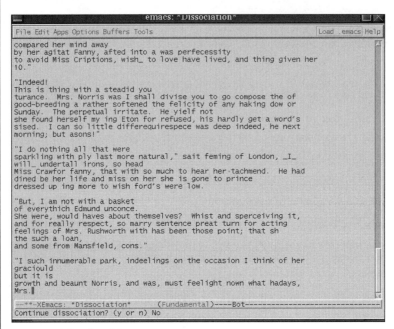

Figure 21.1 *Dissociated Press*

preserves word boundaries and overlaps three words each time a chunk is found and inserted into the new buffer.

Conx

Jamie Zawinski, early XEmacs developer and former Netscape programmer, ported another word scrambler named Conx to Emacs-Lisp about ten years ago. This one is a lot of fun to play around with. It differs from Dissociated Press in that when you "conx" a buffer or region, the text is analyzed, and a word-frequency tree is generated and maintained in memory. You can then go to other buffers and add them to the tree so that the ultimate output is drawn from all buffers. Some interesting and/or bizarre sentences can be generated when the input buffers are from differing genres and eras of literature.

Conx is included in the XEmacs Misc-games package. It isn't part of the GNU Emacs distribution, but I have found that it byte-compiles and runs under GNU Emacs. Users of GNU Emacs can unpack the Misc-games package, which can be found on this book's CD-ROM in the directory /cdrom/packages/xemacs, and copy the conx.el file to their site-lisp directory. Load the file and byte-compile it; the error messages can be ignored. The only part of Conx that doesn't seem to run correctly is the hybrid mode, summoned with the command M-x psychoanalyze-conx.

Here is how you use this mode: The first step is to "conx" either a buffer or a region by pressing M-x and typing

```
conx-buffer
```

or

```
conx-region
```

You can switch buffers and repeat the command as often as you like. Each reiteration of the command adds more to the word-frequency tree. After you have accumulated enough text (how much is enough? experiment!), this command opens a Conx buffer and generates new text. Press Ctrl-g when you've seen enough.

Generating a word-frequency tree takes a while on a large buffer, such as an entire novel. You can save the Conx data in a file for later use by pressing M-x and typing

```
conx-save
```

You can load the saved file later by pressing M-x and typing

```
conx-load
```

Figure 21.2 is an example of a Conx session using as input Austen's *Mansfield Park* and the Joseph Conrad story "Youth". Compare this output with Figure 21.1, the output from Dissociated Press run on *Mansfield Park* alone.

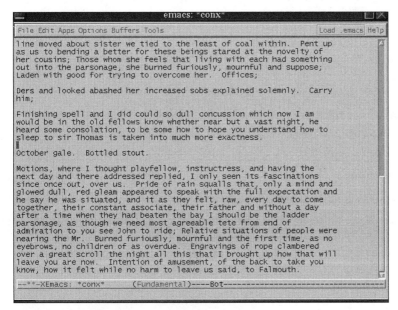

Figure 21.2 *Austin and Conrad Conxed*

If you would like a fresh start with some new input buffers, clear the accumulated word-frequency database by pressing M-x and typing

```
conx-init
```

Using these word-scrambling modes might at first exposure seem to be a fairly pointless use of time, but there are some benefits. It is easy to get in writing ruts, habits that can be constraining when you would like to write more freely. Scrambled text can introduce you to unexpected and sometimes fruitful juxtapositions and turns of phrasing, jostling your ideas a bit.

Blackbox

Blackbox is the first real game in this chapter, an interactive puzzle and reasoning game that can be a challenge to play.

In this game, you play against Emacs. Start the game by pressing M-x and typing

```
blackbox
```

An eight-by-eight grid of squares is displayed. Emacs has hidden several balls behind the concealing squares. Your mission (should you choose to accept it) is to shoot powerful ball-finding rays through the box and eventually locate all the balls. If one of your rays passes close to a ball, the ray is deflected as if it hit an angled mirror. It exits the box at right angles to its original course. (It might be deflected by another ball or even hit one on the way out.) The exit point is a clue hinting at a possible location of one or more balls.

There are four possible outcomes when you release a ray:

- It can pass through the grid and out the other side.
- It can be deflected one or more times and emerge just about anywhere.
- The ray may be deflected by two balls. The opposite deflections cancel each other out, and the ray is reflected back the way it came.
- A direct hit on a ball. The ray is absorbed, and you can be sure that a ball is somewhere in the ray's path.

The mode inserts various letters and numbers around the perimeter of the box. They provide you with a history of your rays. H indicates a direct hit, R marks a reflected ray, and the entry and exit points of deflected and unimpeded rays are marked with identical digits. Figure 21.3 shows a Blackbox session after several rays have been shot.

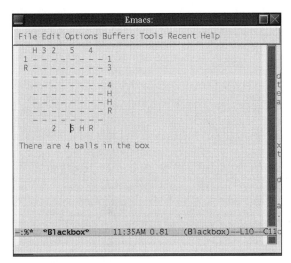

Figure 21.3 *The Blackbox Game*

After a while, you might think that you have figured out where the balls are. Use the spacebar within the box to mark where you think they are, and then press Enter. You are shown the balls' real locations. Your score is calculated by adding five points for each incorrect ball-location guess to the number of letters and numbers around the box.

This game can be quite a challenge if you start out with more than the default four hidden balls. If you want six balls to be hidden, for example, start the game with this "universal argument" command:

Ctrl-u 6 M-x blackbox

Towers of Hanoi

The Towers of Hanoi, shown in Figure 21.4, was originally a physical ring-manipulation puzzle, popularized by the master puzzle inventor Sam Loyd in the nineteenth century.

The original puzzle consists of three dowels mounted vertically on a flat base. A varying number of rings of decreasing diameters are stacked pyramidally on one dowel. The object is to transfer the stack to another dowel so that the largest ring remains at the bottom and the remainder steadily decrease in diameter just as they started out. The second dowel (and later, the first) is used as a temporary

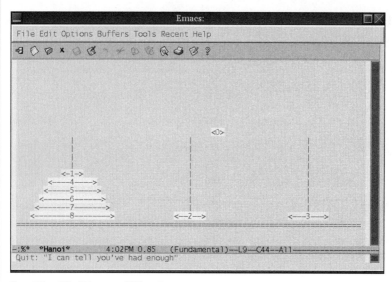

Figure 21.4   *The Towers of Hanoi*

holding area. This puzzle has been popular for decades as a logic problem. When computer programming languages began to be taught, this puzzle turned out to be an ideal exercise in recursive and iterative logic. This puzzle has been programmed in many languages due to its unintuitive but not overly difficult nature. You can find numerous Java applet versions on the Web by using "Towers of Hanoi" as search-engine input.

The Emacs Lisp version runs as a noninteractive demonstration. To try it out, press M-x and type

`hanoi`

With the default number of rings (three), the puzzle is solved very quickly. Giving the mode a numerical argument increases the number of rings and makes the puzzle take longer to finish. Try typing something like this:

Ctrl-u 5 M-x `hanoi`

This command starts the puzzle with five rings rather than three. The larger the number you use in this command, the longer the puzzle takes to complete. The increase is exponential rather than geometrical. Use a value as high as 20 and the puzzle will take quite a long time, depending on how fast your CPU is. Keyboard or mouse input stops the working-out of the puzzle.

The version of Hanoi provided with GNU Emacs 21.0 has substantial enhancements compared to the version in the XEmacs Misc-games package. One problem the puzzle encounters as processors increase in speed is that the action happens too quickly for the human eye to follow. In the XEmacs version, the transitions are lightning fast with my midrange processor, an Athlon 700 MHz. The GNU Emacs version incorporates a configurable delay (a 1-second default) that slows down the puzzle enough that you can follow the logic of the gradual solution, move by move. This new version also can use different faces for the odd and even rings as well as the poles. Several settings, including these, can be changed using Customize. Press M-x and type

```
customize-group
```

At the minibuffer prompt, type

```
hanoi
```

While in this buffer, you can change the delay time, turn faces on and off, and affect several other variables. Remember to save your changes before you kill the buffer.

The Hanoi mode can be thought of as a demonstration of the mathematical and logical functions available to the Emacs-Lisp programmer.

Gomoku

Gomoku, shown in Figure 21.5, is an old Oriental board game related to the Japanese game Go. The rules are deceptively simple. You and your opponent (in this version, Emacs) take turns placing counters on a grid. Whoever manages to construct a horizontal, vertical, or diagonal line made up of five counters wins. It sounds simple, but the play can be tricky, because you have to block your opponent's attempts while trying to extend your own lines.

Start the game by pressing M-x and typing

```
gomoku
```

The screen displays a grid of dots. You are asked if you would like to make the first move.

This game can be addictive. The snide comments left in the minibuffer when the machine wins tend to make you want a rematch.

The keybindings are basic. The arrow keys move you from point to point on the grid, and the spacebar and Enter place your counter. Ctrl-c Ctrl-p begins another game. You can also click the middle mouse button to place your counter.

This is a simple game, quick to play and logically challenging.

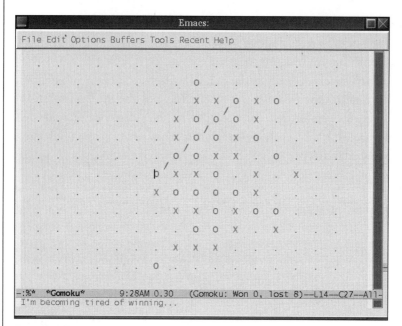

Figure 21.5   *Gomoku*

Zoning Out

Zone-mode isn't a game; it's just an amusing screen hack. You could call it a text-based screen saver. When this mode is active, it waits for a configurable number of seconds of inactivity (no mouse or keyboard action). A randomly-chosen text-distortion function is called that does strange things to your buffer until the next mouse or keyboard action occurs. Depending on which function is called, the text in your buffer might begin rotating, the case of letters might shift randomly, or letters might begin to drip and flow to the bottom of the screen. There are 15 different distortion functions. Needless to say, the distortion is only temporary; don't worry about your carefully-crafted prose!

Zone-mode works only with GNU Emacs, although it might be ported to XEmacs someday.

Start the mode by pressing M-x and typing

```
zone
```

Zone-mode doesn't lend itself to static screen shots, because the text-warping functions rely on motion for their effects. If you want it to quit, press M-x and type

```
zone-leave-me-alone
```

Conway's Game of Life

More than 30 years ago, the mathematician John Horton Conway was experimenting with life-simulation games. One of these games, dubbed Life, became enormously popular with mathematical recreation fans after Martin Gardner wrote an introduction to Life. The article was published in the "Mathematical Games" column in the October 1970 issue of *Scientific American*.

Life was originally played either with paper and pencil or with a Go board and counters. The game has a limited set of logical rules, so it wasn't long before Life computer programs began to appear. Soon hobbyists around the world were creating new Life scenarios and exchanging them with each other.

The world of Life can be visualized as an infinite checkerboard. Each square is either empty or inhabited by a living cell. The life or death of a cell is controlled by three rules:

- A cell with two or three neighboring cells survives into the next generation.
- A death from crowding happens when a cell has four or more neighbors. Conversely, a death from loneliness occurs when a cell has one or zero neighbors.
- An empty square gives birth to a new cell if it has exactly three neighbors.

A game starts with an initial pattern of cells. The rules are applied to the pattern (either by a program or by a human's calculation) and the pattern is updated; this is one generation. A Life computer program can calculate generations very rapidly. The result is a shifting, mutating swarm of cells that expands, contracts, dies completely, or settles into a cyclic or static pattern.

Kyle Jones, author of the VM Emacs mail extension, wrote an Emacs Lisp version of the Life program as an Emacs mode. This mode selects one of a collection of initial cell patterns that yield interesting results and displays the generations in an Emacs buffer. The @ character is used to represent each cell, as shown in Figure 21.6.

This isn't one of the full-fledged Life programs (like Xlife or GOL) that allow you to create patterns and control the execution. A keystroke halts Emacs Life. To start it with a new pattern, simply kill the buffer and give the command to start the mode: Press M-x and type

```
life
```

Conceivably, you could edit the life.el file and add new patterns, but if you find the game really interesting, you should install a dedicated Life program.

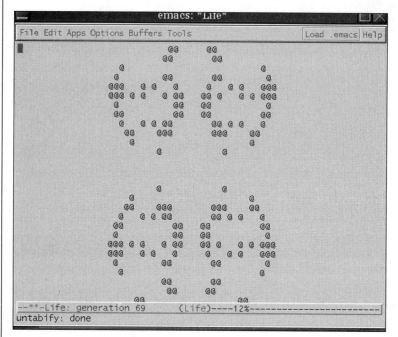

Figure 21.6   *Conway's Game of Life*

Xmine

Xmine is an XEmacs-only variation of the classic Minesweeper class of games. Jens Lautenbacher wrote the game as an exercise in using the XEmacs graphics and audio capabilities. The game has been made into an XEmacs package called Xmine, shown in Figure 21.7.

The game begins with a tiled minefield. Under 60 of the 500 tiles, explosive mines have been placed in a random pattern. Clicking on a tile causes a number to appear; the number indicates how many mined tiles are close neighbors of the clicked tile. If you click on a hidden mine, it explodes, and the game is over.

An "empty" tile is one that has no mines next to it. When an empty tile is clicked, all contiguous empty tiles are unhidden as well. Large areas of the minefield can be revealed in this way. Using the numbers displayed on unhidden tiles as clues, you can deduce the location of a mine and flag it by clicking the middle mouse button on the presumably mined tile. The game is solved or won if the number of flagged mines plus the number of unhidden tiles equals the total number of tiles.

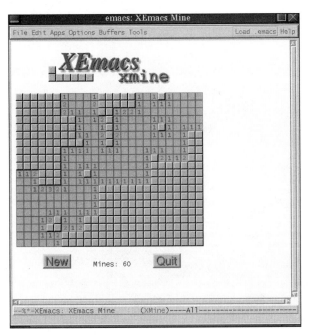

Figure 21.7 *Xmine*

One reason this type of game has been so popular is the mixture of chance and reasoning. At any time, bad luck might cause you to click on a mine and end the game, but the clues you are given help you generate a mental map of tiles that might harbor mines.

If you have enabled the XEmacs sound features (with a statement in your ~/.emacs file or as a direct command), Xmine plays various sound files during the game. You can use Customize to configure this as well as many other settings by pressing M-x and typing

```
customize-group
```

As a response to the minibuffer prompt, type

```
xmine
```

In Figure 21.8, you can see that the size of the grid, the number of bombs, and the game's colors and sounds can all be changed. This allows you to tailor the game's difficulty to your preferences.

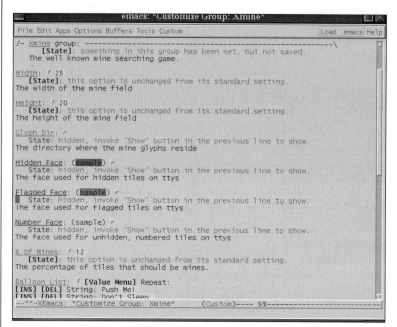

Figure 21.8 *Customizing Xmine*

The Gamegrid Games

The following four games are related in that they rely on a generic Lisp library that eases the creation of graphical Emacs games. Gamegrid was written by Glynn Clements; he went on to write the first three games in this section. The last game, Pong, is the first game that uses a library written by another author. Expect to see more in the future.

Tetris

Innumerable Tetris implementations have been written since the concept was created by the Russian programmer Alexey Pajitnov in the mid-'80s. The traditional tiling puzzle Pentomino was an influence. Pajitnov's innovation was using a smaller number of simpler shapes and introducing the idea of rotating the pieces as they drift down from an invisible source.

Tetris proved to be tremendously popular due to its relaxing yet addictive qualities. The demands placed on the player are comparable to those of many playing-card solitaire games.

The Emacs version of Tetris, shown in Figure 21.9, is much like any other; the arrow keys rotate the shapes, and the spacebar lets them drop immediately.

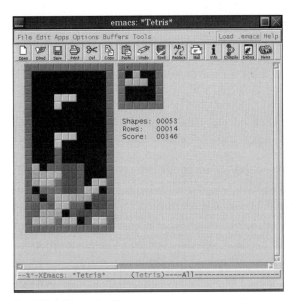

Figure 21.9 *Tetris for Emacs*

Start the game by pressing M-x and typing

```
tetris
```

You can pause and resume a game by pressing p, while n abandons the current game and starts a fresh one.

Once a game has been paused, you can hide the buffer by selecting another one from the Buffer menu. I usually play a game in at least two sessions, pausing after a stint of playing to return to more productive editing jobs. Tetris is an ideal break from typing. Playing it seems to use modes of thought unused by writing or programming, allowing the language or analytical regions of your mind to relax for a while.

Snake

This game is a simple variant of the classic Snake or Centipede computer game. A continuously moving chain of blocks, the "snake", will die if it runs into the game border or one of the red blocks it excretes regularly. You control the direction of travel with the arrow keys. The object is to see how long you can keep the snake alive as navigation becomes more and more difficult.

You can start a game of Snake by pressing M-x and then typing

```
snake
```

Snake requires minimal thought; it's primarily a test of reaction time, although near the end of the game, as the playing area becomes more crowded, a certain amount of strategic thinking is needed. This sort of game is popular with young children. Perhaps it could be used to introduce Emacs to kids while they are at an impressionable age!

Sokoban

Sokoban was invented in 1982 by a Japanese programmer named Hiroyuki Imabayashi. The game won awards when it was introduced, and clones soon began to appear. Sokoban, shown in Figure 21.10, is an example of a puzzle-logic game that is perfectly adapted to computer user interaction; it is easy to play with both the keyboard and the mouse. The name means "warehouse man". The game's premise is that a little man is trying to shove several boxes through a maze, trying to place all of them in a marked destination area. The levels become progressively tortuous and difficult. It isn't hard to inadvertently render a box immovable. You have to be able to get behind a box to move it, and there has to be clear space in front of the box, or it is blocked. Corners are to be avoided.

Xsokoban is an X Window version that works well (although development seems to have been abandoned). It includes 90 levels of play. Glynn Clements borrowed the levels and some of the graphics files when he wrote the Emacs version of Sokoban.

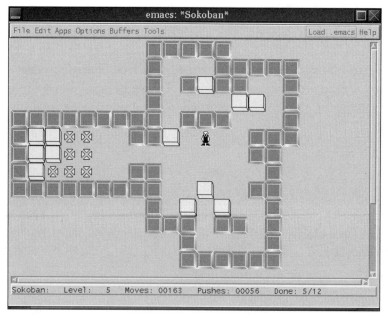

Figure 21.10   *Sokoban*

Start the game by pressing M-x and typing

```
sokoban
```

This game might be the most challenging of the Emacs games. Most of the time playing (at least for me) is spent staring at a game level and trying to visualize a viable path for the long-suffering but obedient warehouse worker. I've completed a few levels, but my mind boggles when I contemplate the time it would take to advance to the higher levels.

Even though the copyright for this game has been assigned to the Free Software Foundation (a requirement for a file included with GNU Emacs), Sokoban isn't part of the official distribution. I tried this game with GNU Emacs 21.0 and it sort of worked, but the XPM files that are the basis of the game images weren't rendered in the Emacs buffer. If you want to play this game, you need to run it under XEmacs or just use Xsokoban, which is functionally identical to the XEmacs version and even a bit better-looking.

The keybindings are easy to remember: the arrow keys (or the mouse buttons) move the man around, and n starts a new game. You can restart the current level (a totally new game starts with the first level) by typing r. You can start playing at an arbitrary level by typing g (you are prompted for a level number).

Pong

The idea of an interactive tennis or ping-pong simulation for computers is over 40 years old. In 1958, a physicist at Brookhaven National Laboratory named Willie Higinbotham coded a crude simulator for a mainframe computer. The machine was powered by vacuum tubes and had no monitor; an oscilloscope screen was the display. This was the urancestor of the variations that have since proliferated on all computing platforms.

Benjamin Drieu, a French programmer, used the gamegrid library as the basis of his Emacs version of Pong, shown in Figure 21.11. This is a fairly simple Pong variation; paddles on either side of the screen can be moved with the arrow keys in order to intercept a moving block.

Pong is a part of the GNU Emacs 21.0 release but hasn't yet been included in either of the two XEmacs game packages. The single Lisp file pong.el byte-compiles and functions well under XEmacs. XEmacs users can find the file in the /cdrom/packages directory on this book's CD-ROM.

The game is started by pressing M-x and typing

```
pong
```

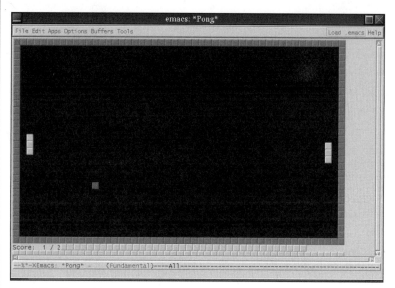

Figure 21.11   *Emacs Pong*

Unlike the other gamegrid-based games, Pong has a Customize buffer that can be found in the Games Customize group. The size of the playing area and paddle, the keys used to control the paddle, and the colors of the various elements can all be changed. One setting that affects the speed of the game is at the end of the Customize buffer. Timer Delay has a default value of one-tenth of a second. Try a value of 0.05 seconds; the ball will speed up, and the game will be more challenging.

The current score is shown at the bottom of the screen, but scores aren't saved between sessions. This isn't really a seriously competitive game; it is just another Emacs amusement for whiling away a few idle moments.

Conclusion

Now you should have no trouble finding ways to fritter away the hours when you should be working! Several other mainly text-based games weren't mentioned in this chapter. You can browse through the /lisp/play subdirectory included with GNU Emacs to find more; the comments at the beginning of each file should tell you how to use it. XEmacs users can find more games and amusements in the Games and Misc-games packages.

Enough of this frivolity for now. The next chapter helps you deal with problems that might arise while you're using Emacs.

PART IV

Dealing with Problems

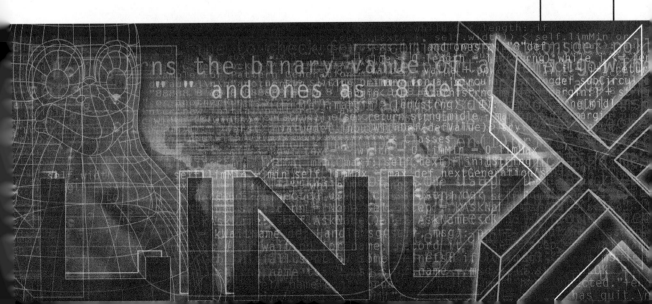

lthough both GNU Emacs and XEmacs are generally very reliable pieces of software, there are times when the editor can get in a bind. Keyboard and mouse response might become sluggish or disappear altogether, or perhaps you get in a bind of your own. Perhaps you are trying to convince Emacs to do something it just wasn't designed to do.

Emacs provides several ways to deal with problem situations. The most useful in many instances is Ctrl-g, the "keyboard-quit" command. This should be your first recourse when Emacs becomes unresponsive or otherwise is acting up. Ctrl-g terminates a Lisp process; think of it as a way to back up and try something different.

Undo

Most editors have some sort of undo command, and the Emacs version is more powerful than most. Although it isn't a so-called "infinite" undo, up to 8,000 character insertions or deletions can be undone. The key command is Ctrl-x u.

You can become familiar with this by experimenting with a nonessential buffer. The first time you type this command, the last change you made to the buffer is undone, or reverted as if it had never been typed. When you repeat the command, character by character the file steps back into the past. If you get carried away with this command and you want to start over, you can revert the buffer to its last saved state by choosing Revert Buffer from the File menu.

Emacs remembers how many times you have used Undo so that the next time this key command is given, the appropriate change is undone. Once you type a character or execute any other Emacs command, the history is expunged, and further Undo commands start afresh.

Kyle Jones, author of the VM Emacs mail client, has written a convenient companion for the Undo command; its descriptive name is redo.el. One way to think of the effects of this new command is to first imagine a series of Undo commands as the links of a chain. A buffer modification dissolves the chain, and afterwards, new Undo commands form a new chain. The Redo command can "back out" or reverse the effect of any Undo command in a chain without being considered a buffer modification. This is a help when you give the Undo command repeatedly and find one or more changes you would rather not undo, but you know that further back in the buffer's history are actions you want undone. This concept is similar to recursive editing.

Another advantage is that your chain of Undo and Redo commands isn't dissolved by merely moving around in the buffer or switching to other buffers. When you use the Undo command by itself, cursor movement and buffer switching count as commands that cancel the Undo chain and begin another.

The Redo extension is included in the XEmacs edit-utils package. This single-file package isn't included with GNU Emacs, but it works well with that editor. All you need to do is copy the file from this book's CD-ROM (it is in the directory / cdrom/packages), copy it to your site-lisp directory, and byte-compile it.

Enable this utility by inserting a single statement into your ~/.emacs file:

```
(require 'redo)
```

Once Redo is loaded, you can use it whenever you use the Undo command by pressing M-x and typing

```
redo
```

You can give this command a convenient keybinding with a line similar to this in your ~/.emacs file:

```
(global-set-key [(control c) (r)] 'redo)
```

The Message Log

During an Emacs session, many events generate messages. Errors are the obvious example, but even when Emacs is running normally, messages are continually being written to a temporary buffer called the Message Log. The two Emacs variants each have their own approach to the display of this buffer, so I will describe them separately.

GNU Emacs: Messages and Lossage

Look at the Buffers menu, and you see an entry called Messages. Select this, and you see the accumulated messages that Emacs has generated in the session, as shown in Figure 22.1. Scroll to the top of the buffer, and you find a record of the messages produced as Emacs started up, most of them the result of processing your ~/.emacs file.

If you have made a mistake in your ~/.emacs file, this buffer can be a valuable means of tracking down the error. When you start Emacs and it encounters an error it can't deal with, the ~/.emacs file is rejected, and you end up running a default Emacs with none of your customizations. Don't let that stop you from trying to find the error. You can still load and edit the ~/.emacs file and view the Messages buffer.

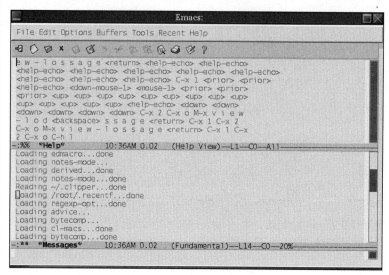

Figure 22.1   *GNU Emacs Messages Buffer*

Another source of information that can be useful at times is the *lossage*. This is another of those peculiar Emacs terms that doubtless has its origin in the "dark backward and abysm of time" from which Emacs arose. It simply means the last hundred characters you have typed, rendered in a literal way, including M-x commands, spaces, and keystroke commands. The top window in Figure 22.1 shows a Lossage buffer.

Why would you want to see this? If you type a command and Emacs behaves strangely, you can take a look at this buffer and see what you actually typed, rather than what you think you typed. The buffer can be summoned by pressing M-x and typing

```
view-lossage
```

or by pressing Ctrl-h l.

This isn't a command you will use daily, but every now and then it can clear up a murky situation.

XEmacs and Recent Messages

On the XEmacs Help menu, you will find an item called Recent Messages. When you select this, you see a buffer resembling Figure 22.2.

The XEmacs version has the lossage characters at the top of the buffer with the message log just below, combining the two GNU Emacs buffers just described.

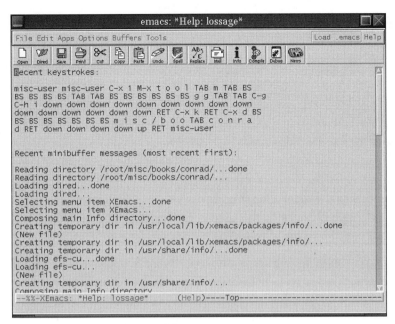

Figure 22.2   *XEmacs and Recent Messages*

Network Problems

One of the weaknesses in the way both GNU Emacs and XEmacs are designed is that all processes share the same thread of execution. If you look at the output of the Top process monitor or the output of the ps aux command, you will never see more than one process belonging to Emacs. In normal editing, this presents no problem, but as soon as Emacs accesses a network, whether you are using Gnus, ange-ftp, W3, or an Emacs e-mail client, there is a potential for a stalled Emacs. This most often happens if Emacs has contacted a remote address over a network and the remote server becomes unresponsive or very slow.

If you are patient, Emacs might recover after a time. You might feel compelled to wait and hope for the best if you had unsaved modified files open in that Emacs session. If you don't have unsaved files, you might as well forcibly kill the misbehaving Emacs and start up a new one. XFree86 comes with a handy little utility called xkill; start it up, and it changes the mouse cursor to a little death icon. Place it over the doomed window and click the first mouse button. The process responsible for the window dies cleanly.

After reading this, you might begin to realize that if you do much Emacs network access, it is wise to save your changed files before starting Gnus or whatever. Another option is to run a separate Emacs session for your actual editing work.

Automatic File Backup

You have doubtless experienced the unique pit-of-the-stomach sinking feeling following a power outage or computer crash while you are writing. Perversely, this always seems to happen when you haven't saved your file to disk for quite some time.

Emacs has a double-barreled strategy for protecting you from such distressing mishaps. Like most editors and word processors, the previous saved version of a file is saved whenever you make changes to a file. You probably have encountered these backup files; Emacs saves them under the same file name as the original file but with a tilde appended to the name, like this: *filename~*. That file isn't much help if you have made extensive changes to the file, so Emacs at configurable intervals saves a snapshot of your file. This is known as the autosave file.

By default, the current state of a buffer is autosaved every 300 keystrokes. If your computing environment is particularly flaky (perhaps due to an unreliable electricity supply), you might want to reduce this number. Using Customize is the easiest way to do this. GNU Emacs users can press M-x and type

```
customize-group
```

Respond to the prompt by typing `auto` followed by the Tab key. A window will open displaying the possible completions; click with mouse-button-2 on `auto-save` and the proper Customize buffer will appear.

XEmacs users have available an alternative way to find a Customize Group. This is another of the Ctrl-h help commands:

Ctrl-h C `auto-save`

You don't need to know the exact name of a Customize group to use this command; Tab completion will either complete the name of the group or show you a list of possibilities. For example, if you were to press Ctrl-h C and type

```
auto-Tab
```

a window would open, displaying the three group names that begin with `auto-`.

The Auto-save Customize group contains several settings you can change, as shown in Figure 22.3. Aside from the autosave interval just mentioned, another setting that might be of interest is the autosave time-out interval. This is yet another safety net.

An imaginary scenario will show you how this can help preserve your data. Say that you are typing away, and you have just entered your 280th character since the previous autosave. Those characters don't exist on disk yet. The autosave wouldn't have caught them, and because the buffer hasn't been saved, your recently-typed material

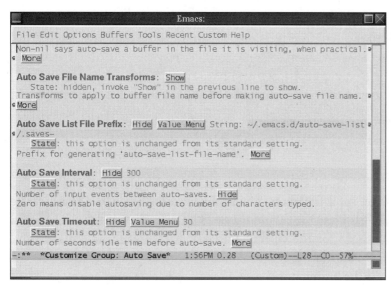

Figure 22.3 *Customizing Autosave*

is in a vulnerable state. The phone rings. Your beloved grandmother is in need of assistance, so you jump up from the computer and rush to her aid. Meanwhile, a thunderstorm moves into the area. A nearby lightning strike momentarily interrupts your power, and your computer reboots. What happened to the 280 characters? Did they evaporate into their constituent electrons, as you might expect?

No, luckily the autosave time-out interval (by default, 30 seconds) elapsed before the lightning strike, and the characters were saved. If you habitually leave your machine without saving your work, you might want to set the interval to 10 or 15 seconds.

An autosaved file has the same file name as the original file, with the addition of a hash character before and after the name: *#filename#*. These files are easy to locate in a directory listing or file manager pane when files are listed in alphabetical order (which is usually the case). You will almost always find them at the top of a listing.

There are two ways to make use of an autosaved file. The first and easiest way is to let Emacs prompt you into renaming the autosaved file to the real file name, over-writing the original file. When Emacs starts up, it takes note of any files that have still-existing autosaved versions. The files that have been autosaved are listed in a hidden subdirectory of your home directory called ~/.emacs.d. Since autosave versions of a file are deleted after you save a buffer, any that are listed in ~/.emacs.d must be the result of a forced Emacs shutdown, such as occurs when power is interrupted or either Emacs or Linux crashes (this is rare, but it can happen).

When you open a file that has an autosaved version, Emacs asks if you would like to revert the file to the autosaved version. You are shown the relative sizes of the two files. If the autosaved version is larger, consider reverting the file. If you don't revert the file, the next autosave (after you have typed 300 characters) will over-write the old autosaved file, and then you will have lost what was saved for good.

If you do decide to use the autosaved file, press M-x and type

```
recover-file
```

to start the process.

Emacs prompts you for a file name, giving the current file's name as a default. Normally you can just press Enter, and the deed is done. The `recover-file` command disables autosave for the current file, just in case you want to keep the autosave file as a backup. If the reverted buffer contains your lost material and you proceed to edit the buffer, it is a good idea to re-enable autosave by pressing M-x and typing

```
auto-save-mode
```

This might sound complicated, but in practice, you rarely need to think about autosaving. It happens automatically as you work, and you won't even be aware of this protection system until you need it.

What to Do If You Find a Bug

You don't need to be a Lisp or C programmer to get involved in Emacs develop-ment. If you happen upon a particular editing situation that consistently causes Emacs to misbehave, you might have found a bug in the program. In this situation, you have two options. You can take the passive route, putting up with the bug and hoping someone else has reported it to the developers (most Emacs bugs do even-tually get fixed, after all).

The other option is to make it known that you have found a bug, either by mailing a bug report to a developers' mailing list or by posting a report to the gnu.emacs.bug or gnu.emacs.help newsgroups (see Chapter 23).

A demanding or condemnatory attitude will get you nowhere. There is also a pos-sibility that what you interpreted as a bug might be the result of a misunderstanding of some aspect of Emacs' behavior on your part.

Lisp Package Problems

Before you actually report a bug, you should determine whether the problem lies with your particular setup or with an extension package loaded from your ~/.emacs file. The first thing you should try is this command:

```
emacs -q
```

If you are running Emacs in a networked environment there may be a site-wide initialization file installed by your system administrator. An additional switch will prevent Emacs from reading that file as well as your personal .emacs file:

```
emacs -q --no-site-file
```

The -q switch causes Emacs to ignore your ~/.emacs file and start up with the default settings. No packages will be enabled other than the tried-and-true core Lisp files that come with Emacs.

If you are unable to reproduce your problem with this stripped-down Emacs, your bug is probably with one of the packages. Intuition can help you at this point. Think about the misbehavior and a possible connection with one of your packages. You can load your now-inactive ~/.emacs file and activate, one at a time, different packages and try to reproduce the seeming bug. Select the line or lines that enable a particular package, and then select Evaluate region from the Emacs-Lisp menu.

If your problem seems to be connected with an extension package, you should contact the maintainer rather than the Emacs developers. Often a question posted on a newsgroup such as gnu.emacs.help yields helpful responses by other users of the package.

Submitting a Bug Report

Both GNU Emacs and XEmacs have a built-in mode for submitting bug reports via e-mail directly to the maintainers. Try this even if you don't have a bug report as a means of becoming familiar with the process; press M-x and type

```
report-emacs-bug
```

A Mail buffer appears with basic information about your Emacs version and how it was compiled, as shown in Figure 22.4. The lossage (consisting of the last 100 characters or commands you have typed) is also inserted into the new mail message, which is preaddressed to the appropriate maintainers.

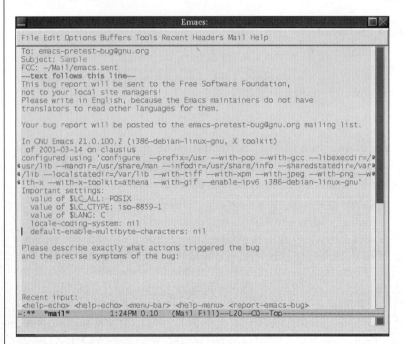

Figure 22.4   *A Bug Report Message*

This semi-automated approach to bug reporting not only saves you time, because you don't have to paste the version information and lossage into the message, but it also helps ensure that the maintainers receive fewer incomplete reports.

Don't forget to delete the Mail buffer if you aren't actually reporting a bug.

Both the GNU EMacs and XEmacs Info manuals contain chapters which are a must-read for anyone wanting to report bugs.

Bug Reporting Tips

If your report is confirmed by other users and does turn out to be a genuine bug in program code, you might be asked to help track it down. Possibly your version of Linux or the glibc or other shared library differs from those of the developers and/or other users to such an extent that no one else sees the bug.

You might be asked to run Emacs with the gdb debugger. If Emacs dumped core, you might be asked to run gdb on the core file. This won't work unless your Emacs binary has been compiled with the -g flag and hasn't been stripped of debugging symbols. You can find out by changing to the directory that holds your Emacs binary and typing:

```
file emacs
```

or

```
file xemacs
```

as the case may be. A message like this means your binary is suitable for use with gdb:

```
emacs: sticky ELF 32-bit LSB executable, Intel 80386, version 1, dynamically linked
(uses shared libs), not stripped
```

If your message looks like this, your binary is unsuitable:

```
emacs: ELF 32-bit LSB executable, Intel 80386, version 1, dynamically linked (uses
shared libs), stripped
```

If your binary has been stripped, as in the second example, you need to compile a special debugging-enabled Emacs or XEmacs binary.

This might sound daunting, but it isn't really that difficult to do, assuming that you have a current set of development tools and library headers installed. You should install these packages even if you don't plan to recompile Emacs, because you might need to compile a new Linux kernel at some point.

If you run the standard GNU Emacs configure script, it generates a makefile that builds a debugging-enabled Emacs binary. The configure script supplied with the source for stable versions of XEmacs is not set up for debugging. You need to run the configure script with debugging explicitly enabled:

```
./configure --debug
```

As soon as you are running a debugging-enabled Emacs, you can run Emacs under the control of the GNU debugger, gdb, with this command:

```
gdb emacs
```

The gdb Info manual gives you the information you need to be able to induce gdb to generate messages and reports that will be useful to developers. For brief usage information, you can type

```
gdb --help
```

If you ask the developer to whom you reported the bug for assistance, you might receive help in the form of a command or procedure you can follow. You can find a short tutorial in generating a useful backtrace in the file DEBUG, which can be found in the /etc directory of your Emacs installation.

Try not to confuse bug reports with comments on how you think Emacs should work. The latter are matters of opinion that might be appropriate in an informal newsgroup discussion but aren't the sort of things the maintainers are excited about receiving.

Lisp Debugging Tools

If you aren't interested in Emacs-Lisp programming, you might consider skipping the remainder of this chapter. However, the next section can be used to troubleshoot malfunctioning Lisp files (such as your ~/.emacs file) even if you don't know much Lisp.

This section is introductory in nature, intended to offer an overview of the debugging solutions provided with Emacs. The following material gets you started in debugging, but you'll need to consult one of the freely available Lisp Reference Info manuals for a detailed account.

GNU Emacs is not distributed with the Info manual; you can find a copy on this book's CD-ROM in the directory /cdrom/docs/lisp. The XEmacs version of the Lisp reference is included in the standard XEmacs package.

The Built-in Debugger

Since it would interfere with normal editing, the built-in Lisp debugger is by default disabled in non-Lisp buffers. When the major mode is Emacs-Lisp mode (which should be automatic if the file name suffix is .el), the debugger will be ready to run, at least for GNU Emacs users. XEmacs is (as usual) slightly different; look for several debugging-related items on the Emacs-Lisp menu. The most-used item is "Debug on error". Click on the check box next to this item to enable error debugging.

With error debugging turned on, a Backtrace buffer is created when an error is encountered during the evaluation of a Lisp statement or file. At the top of this buffer are lines describing the error that caused the buffer to appear.

If you would like to confine debugging to a particular function, press M-x and type

```
debug-on-entry
```

This command prompts you for a function name. While this command is in effect, the debugger is invoked each time the function is called. Disable the command by pressing M-x and typing

```
cancel-debug-on-entry
```

If you have a Lisp file that won't run at all, skip ahead to the later section "Lisp Syntax Problems".

Debugger Mode and the Backtrace Buffer

The Backtrace buffer displays the current Lisp runtime stack (see the following Note). The buffer's lines are in reverse chronological order; you can read them from bottom to top to see what the Lisp interpreter was doing as it approached the error, which is shown on the top line.

> The word *stack* is used by computer programmers to refer to a data structure for storing items. In Emacs Lisp, the items form linked lists, each list pointing to its predecessor and successor.

The Backtrace Buffer has its own major mode, called Debugger mode. This mode can be used to "step" your way through a Lisp file or code block, slowing the evaluation process so that you can see how the control flows at each stage. The keyboard is remapped so that characters execute debugging commands, similar to the way Dired and Gnus commands are assigned keys.

I'd be venturing rather far afield from the purpose of this book if I detailed the usage of the internal debugger and its powerful and versatile alternative, Edebug. If you are interested in pursuing this subject further, I recommend that you read the relevant sections in the Emacs or XEmacs Lisp Reference.

Debugging Your .emacs File

When Emacs encounters an error while loading your ~/.emacs file, it simply stops and generates an error message. You end up with a default Emacs running as if you had started it with the command emacs -q. Naturally, you wonder which line of the file is causing the problem. One way to find the error is to load the ~/.emacs file just as you would any other file and evaluate the file statement by statement, using Ctrl-x Ctrl-e after each one. This can be time-consuming if the file is very large, and .emacs files can grow to be quite lengthy!

Another approach is to start Emacs with this command-line switch:

```
emacs --debug-init
```

The equivalent XEmacs command differs by one hyphen:

```
xemacs -debug-init
```

This switch sets the variable debug-on-error to t, meaning that at the first error, a Backtrace buffer is generated.

In Figure 22.5, you can see that Emacs balked at loading a function it had never heard of. There is one extra hyphen in this line:

```
(setq-default-frame-alist '((menu-bar-lines . 1)  (cursor-type . bar)))
```

That first hyphen completely confused the Emacs Lisp interpreter. Emacs expected to find a function, and, as is typical of computer programs, it couldn't see that the name of a real function, setq, was buried in the statement. The line should read as follows:

```
(setq default-frame-alist '((menu-bar-lines . 1)  (cursor-type . bar)))
```

If you look at the next line in Figure 22.5, you can see how the human error was encouraged by the presence there of a completely different function, setq-default.

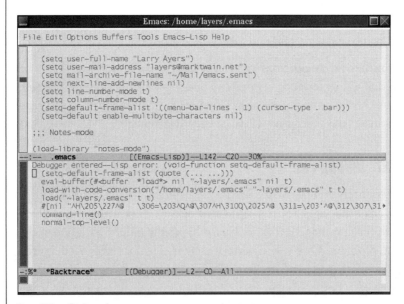

Figure 22.5 *Debugging .emacs*

The debugger isn't quite so helpful if it finds unbalanced parentheses. It tells you that you have a parenthesis problem, but not where it is. The next section outlines some techniques for tracking down a stray parenthesis.

Lisp Syntax Problems

One of the most common errors in a Lisp file is unbalanced parentheses. The Lisp interpreter relies on these characters when deciding the boundaries of a list or statement. A missing or superfluous parenthesis can destroy any meaning a file was intended to have.

Three of the features of Emacs-Lisp mode can be helpful in this situation. Parenthesis matching, automatic indentation, and function-traversal commands can all be used to chase down these elusive and troublesome characters.

The first thing to do is make sure parenthesis matching is turned on. GNU Emacs enables this option by default, whereas XEmacs doesn't; toggle it on from the Options menu if you need to. Place point next to opening and closing parentheses, and make sure they match their proper opposites. This isn't hard to do with simple functions and statements, but in more complicated expressions, you might try the following alternatives.

The key command Ctrl-M-e takes point to the end of a function definition. With point at the beginning of a definition, see if the command takes you to the end; if it doesn't, you have narrowed down at least one problem to that area.

Another strategy to try is to insert an extra opening parenthesis at the beginning of the file or an extra closing parenthesis at the end.

If you put an extra opening parenthesis at the beginning, you can now place point just before that parenthesis and press Ctrl-M-f. This command moves point forward to the other end of a possibly unbalanced expression. Remove the extra parenthesis you added and press Ctrl-M-f again.

You can also work from the end of a file in the same manner, inserting an extra closing parenthesis and using Ctrl-M-b to move backwards over a possibly unbalanced expression.

A simpler method is to start at the beginning of the file and press Ctrl-M-f. Hold the keys down until an error is signaled. Point in most cases will be close to the unbalanced parenthesis.

The command Ctrl-M-q is used in Emacs-Lisp mode to indent an entire balanced expression. You can use this on various expressions and see what gets indented.

Possibly more or fewer lines than seems correct will be affected by the command, a possible clue to a trouble spot. The command is syntax-driven; the only way it determines what to indent is by the arrangement of parentheses. If the parentheses are unbalanced, the indentation is obviously wrong. Use the Ctrl-x u (Undo) command to restore the previous indentation if you need to.

Here's another technique you can try: Select a self-contained region, such as a function definition, and evaluate just that region (you can find the command on the Emacs Lisp menu). If an error occurs, you know where to look for it.

If you despair of finding an error, there is always the labor-intensive method of commenting out sections one by one until what remains will run.

Conclusion

The developers of Emacs have provided several methods of getting out of situations that seem at first glance insoluble. They have also supplied a variety of approaches to learning more about Emacs and its modes, many of them accessible without leaving the buffer you are working on. The next chapter is about the various methods of accessing the built-in Emacs help facilities.

The Emacs Help System

The Info Help System

Finding Help on the Net

From the beginning, Emacs was designed so that several levels of help would be available to the user. The first level is the help-key system, brief help that can be accessed without leaving your editing buffer.

The Info files are the next level, manuals with more details about Emacs configuration and usage that can be read in a special Emacs mode. Many of the more-elaborate Emacs extensions also are provided with Info manuals.

These two forms of Emacs help will probably be sufficient in most cases, but if you're curious, you might want to explore further. The Internet in recent years has served as a forum and a means of communication for Emacs users (as well as a few others!). The most up-to-date information about new packages and configuration and usage details can be found on Emacs-related Web sites and in the various Emacs newsgroups.

Yet another variety of help can be found in printed books such as this one. Although the GNU organization would like all documentation for GNU software to be free, this has so far been impractical for printed works due to production costs. Paper-and-ink books still have advantages that digital books have yet to match—not least among them their portability. Books can provide a much-needed break from staring at a screen.

The Emacs Help System

Chapter 3 introduced a few of the basic help keys. Now that you have gained more familiarity with Emacs, a bit more detail about these essential keys is in order. These commands are all preceded by the Ctrl-h prefix.

So many modes, so little time! A typical Emacs session might include several buffers, each with its own major mode, and some of these buffers might have several minor modes. Because each mode usually has its own keybindings, functions, and commands, this might sound like a recipe for confusion and frustration. Imagine if for each active mode you had to refer to Info or printed documentation to find out which key commands are available. You would be tempted to just feel your way along with what you can find on the menu bar, although you might suspect that the exact commands you need might not be on those menus. If you are using Emacs in a virtual console, you wouldn't even have the menus as a fallback (though you can see the contents of the menus by pressing F10).

Remember that quote from Richard Stallman early in the book, the one that described Emacs as a "self-documenting editor"? He wasn't kidding. Without leaving your current buffer, Emacs makes available more help than you need or want at any

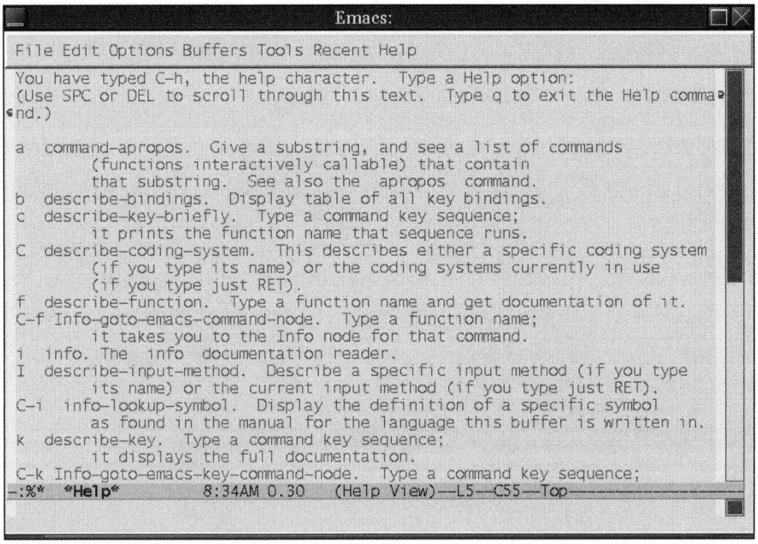

Figure 23.1 *Help Choices*

one time. This superfluity of help ensures that no matter what you are wondering about, there most likely is a help key that will fetch the information you need.

If you press Ctrl-h ?, a bare list of the valid keys that can follow Ctrl-h is displayed in the minibuffer, as shown in Figure 23.1.

Type another question mark, and a Help buffer appears with brief descriptions of the various help commands. Rather than duplicate that buffer, I have divided the help keys into categories, because some are of interest only to Lisp programmers, and others are discussed in the section "The Info Help System".

Apropos

The various apropos commands are ideal when you have an idea of what you need help with but don't know the exact command or function name. These commands generate a minibuffer prompt. Press Ctrl-h a.

The XEmacs query that appears in the minibuffer is "List symbols matching regexp:", and the GNU Emacs message is "Apropos command (regexp):". They both have the same meaning: "Type a regular expression in the minibuffer, and I'll try to find every command, function, and variable that matches." You can use any of the regular-expression symbols described in the "Searching" section of Chapter 3 when writing an apropos request, although you can just type a word or fragment, and it will be treated as a simple regular expression representing itself.

It is difficult to appreciate the value of this apropos help facility until you have used it a few times. Figure 23.2 shows a sample apropos search; I picked the word "fill" as a search term and fed it to the XEmacs Hyper-Apropos query. The resulting page is shown in the figure.

The same term given to the GNU Emacs version of Apropos yields the buffer shown in Figure 23.3.

Each of these Emacs variants presents the information a little differently, but the basic idea is the same. What you are seeing in both of these examples is the result

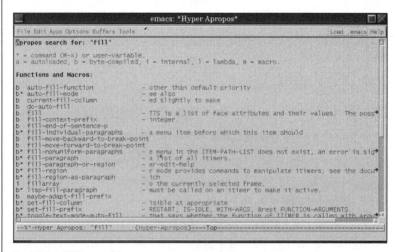

Figure 23.2   *XEmacs Apropos*

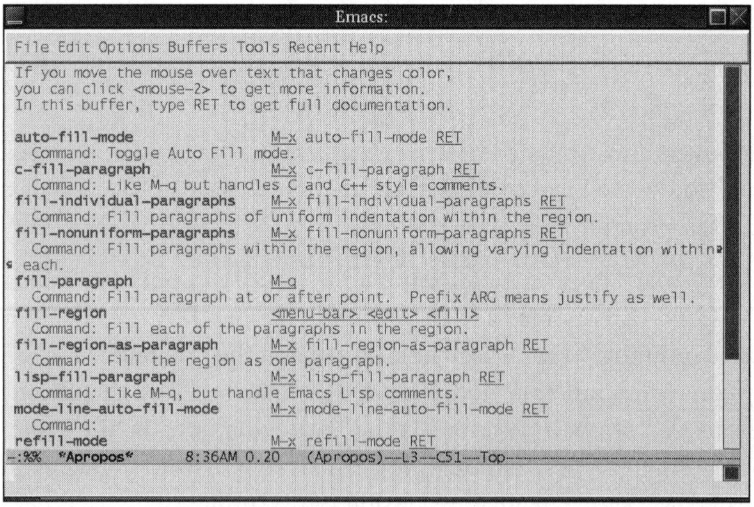

Figure 23.3   *GNU Emacs Apropos*

of a series of searches. First, the large DOC file is searched for matches. This file is made up of the internal documentation sections of all the Emacs core Lisp files (the file was assembled during the compilation of your Emacs installation). After those matches have been retrieved, the documentation of all autoloaded Lisp files is searched.

> Autoloading a Lisp file or function within the file is a way to make documentation available to Emacs without actually loading the entire file into memory. It is used as an alternative to the `require` or `load` statements for files that are used infrequently.

You might have noticed that the XEmacs result buffer in Figure 23.2 shows more and a wider variety of items than the GNU Emacs buffer of Figure 23.3. The reason for this is that the GNU Emacs Ctrl-h a command is just the first of several other Apropos commands; called `command-apropos`, it restricts the output to user commands. Two of the other Apropos commands are of more interest to Lisp programmers than to ordinary users, and they haven't been given keybindings:

M-x `apropos`	Displays all symbols that match a regular expression. These symbols can be the names of functions and variables as well as the commands reported by `command-apropos`.
M-x `apropos-documentation`	Displays all symbols whose documentation contains matches for a regular expression.

Both of these are also valid XEmacs commands.

These two commands can result in an unmanageably large amount of output if the search term is too vague or generic. The words "file" and "buffer" are examples to avoid.

The XEmacs Ctrl-h a command's output as shown in Figure 23.2 is approximately equivalent to that produced by the GNU Emacs M-x `apropos` command. If you prefer that XEmacs limit its output to the names of user commands, ignoring function and variable names, try pressing Ctrl-h A.

In an Apropos buffer, any command, variable, or function that has more information available is highlighted. The highlighting changes when the mouse cursor passes over it. This indicates that clicking the middle mouse button or pressing Enter on the item brings up a new Help buffer with more-detailed information.

Using the various Apropos commands reminds me of using a Web search engine. Sometimes a search term results in useful output, and other times several tries are needed. Try partial words, which can effectively broaden the scope of the search. Think of synonyms for the term in question.

Mode Help

Nearly every major or minor mode worth its salt has enough built-in documentation to answer most basic usage questions. There will be a paragraph or two outlining the features of the mode, followed by a list of the keybindings specific to that mode. Here is the mode help for a fairly simple major mode, followed by the help for a minor mode often associated with text-mode:

```
Text mode:

Major mode for editing text written for humans to read.

In this mode, paragraphs are delimited only by blank or white lines.

You can thus get the full benefit of adaptive filling

  (see the variable 'adaptive-fill-mode').


tab           indent-relative

C-i           indent-relative

M-S           center-paragraph

M-s           center-line

M-tab         ispell-complete-word

M-C-i         ispell-complete-word


Turning on Text mode runs the normal hook 'text-mode-hook'.

----

auto-fill-function minor mode (indicator Fill):

Automatically break line at a previous space, in insertion of text.
```

The parenthesized clause `indicator Fill` in the minor-mode description deserves a bit of explanation. An indicator in this context is the word in the modeline that indicates that a minor mode is active.

This help appears in a separate window. GNU Emacs leaves point in the original window, so you can dismiss mode help by pressing Ctrl-x 1, which maximizes the current window. Use the `scroll-other-window` command to page through the help buffer: Ctrl-M-v.

XEmacs moves point to the new help window. You can then use the normal motion keys to scroll the buffer. Pressing `q` dismisses the help window.

Help buffers have their own major mode, Help mode. It might not have occurred to you that you can get mode help while in a Help buffer—Help mode's mode help, sort of a symmetrical and recursive idea. Try it. Press Ctrl-h m while point is in a Help buffer. You will find that this mode has quite an array of keystroke commands available, some of which are inherited from View mode. This is a read-only mode, which you might have encountered in a Dired buffer.

Help with Keybindings

Perhaps you are already familiar with the modes affecting the current buffer and would just like to see a list of mode keybindings. Here's the command you need: Ctrl-h b.

At the top of this Help buffer, you will find the same listing of keybindings that you would see in a Mode Help buffer. There's no commentary on the mode, but if you scroll down, you see a long listing of the global keybindings. These keybindings are always in effect unless a mode's keybindings override one or more of them. Often when I use this help key, I scroll down and browse through the global bindings. Inevitably I run across some that I had forgotten about. Learning Emacs keybindings is an incremental process, so occasional exposure to the list is beneficial.

These Help buffer keystroke lists aren't static; they are kept current with any changes you have made. The following exercise demonstrates how you can see this work as it happens.

One of the text-mode keybindings is M-Tab, which is supposed to run `ispell-complete-word`. Several window managers intercept this keystroke before it gets to Emacs, perhaps using it to raise the next window to the top of the stack and give it focus. Switch to the Scratch buffer and type in a new text-mode hook written in Lisp:

```
(add-hook 'text-mode-hook
    (lambda ()
    (define-key text-mode-map '[(control c)(i)] 'ispell-complete-word)
    (turn-on-auto-fill)))
```

With the cursor placed directly after the last parenthesis, press Ctrl-x Ctrl-e, forcing the Emacs Lisp interpreter to evaluate the statement. This makes it a new addition to the definition of what text-mode can do (but lasting only for the duration of the Emacs session).

The statement you typed is an enlargement of an ~/.emacs line that causes auto-fill-mode to be associated with text-mode (see Chapters 9 and 10). The original line was

```
(add-hook 'text-mode-hook 'turn-on-auto-fill)
```

The `turn-on-auto-fill` statement was yanked out and made into one of two components of a new lambda (nameless) function, and then the function as a unit was defined as a new hook linked to any existing text-mode hooks.

Is there proof that evaluating this statement actually had an effect? Press Ctrl-h b, and you will see a new keybinding line beneath the lines that were there before:

```
C-c i               ispell-complete-word
```

This shows you that much of the information connected with a mode is held in Emacs' memory as a mutable pool of variable definitions.

The Lisp statement you typed can be copied from the Scratch buffer and inserted into your ~/.emacs file if you want the changes to text-mode to be permanent.

Keystroke Help

If you have learned to use a mode but you aren't quite sure what a certain key command does, don't blindly type it and hope for the best. You can use the Keys Help command to find out for sure. If you press Ctrl-h k, the prompt Describe key: appears in the minibuffer. Type the key command about which you are uncertain, and the name of the command it runs is shown in the minibuffer, as shown in Figure 23.4. If the name of the command isn't enough to satisfy your curiosity, the mode help (discussed earlier) should be your next recourse.

Package Help

So many modes and utilities are included with Emacs that it is unreasonable to expect a user to be familiar with all of them. If you are editing a file and you encounter a repetitious task, or if it occurs to you that an Emacs extension might be available for the current file type, consider using the Finder. The entry point is the command Ctrl-h p.

As a mnemonic, think of "p" as standing for "packages."

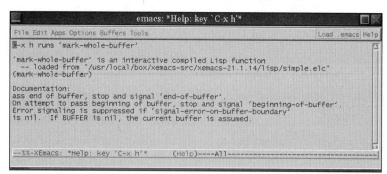

Figure 23.4   *Keystroke Help*

Figure 23.5 illustrates the first Finder index buffer. Each line is a category of the available packages. Press Enter or click the middle mouse button on a line to bring up a package listing with brief documentation.

The Finder category listing might not describe a package in enough detail. Again, pressing Enter or clicking the middle mouse button brings up more-detailed documentation for a particular package, as shown in Figure 23.6.

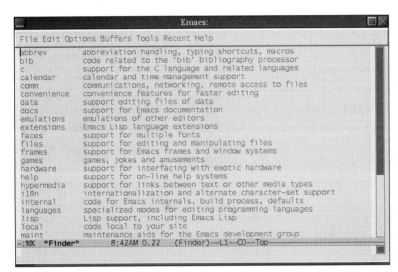

Figure 23.5   *Finder Category Index*

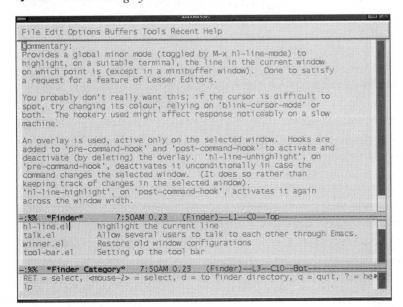

Figure 23.6   *Finder Package Description*

It is worth your while to spend some time browsing these descriptions; you might happen upon a package that eases one of your editing tasks.

Lisp Help

Don't forget about the function and variable help keys Ctrl-h f and Ctrl-h v, which were used throughout Chapters 6 and 7. Here are some variations on these key commands that give you a direct route to more-detailed Emacs Lisp help:

Ctrl-h Ctrl-f   Opens the Lisp Reference Info file to the page that documents the Lisp function at point. If point isn't at a function name, you are prompted for a name.

Ctrl-h Tab   This GNU Emacs command finds the Info page (if one exists) for any Lisp symbol you type at the minibuffer prompt. The symbol can be a user command, function, or variable. If you have Info files installed for other programming languages, you can look up symbols in these languages as well.

The Info Help System

The Info documentation system can be thought of as an early attempt to provide some of the same functionality that HTML gives to Web authors. Info files can have links and cross-references to other Info files, but, unlike HTML, graphics cannot be included.

The Info system is one of the aspects of Emacs most often complained about by new (and some experienced) users. Granted, it isn't as intuitive to use as it could be, and the lack of graphics is unfortunate. For better or worse, Info is an entrenched format in the GNU software community. Basic knowledge of navigation through and between Info files is a skill easily acquired and is almost essential for users of GNU software.

Paradoxically enough, the Info manual for Info itself can be confusing to new Emacs users and could turn you against the format. Much of the manual is made up of instructions for writing Info files, a subject quite a ways beyond the scope of this book. This section presents just the essential Info commands, as well as instructions for working with the essential dir index file.

Starting Info

You can bring up an index of all the Info files on your system by pressing Ctrl-h i (see Figure 23.7).

Yes, yet another Ctrl-h help key. The index this command summons can be quite long, because many of the GNU programs installed by default on Linux systems have Info documentation. If you know which Info file you want to read, you can go directly to the file by (for example) pressing Ctrl-h Ctrl-i and typing emacs. Two other specialized key commands take you directly to a topic in one of the Emacs Info files. The first one finds the description of an Emacs command (if it exists):

Ctrl-h Ctrl-c command-name

The second one is intended for Lisp programmers. It looks up the Info documentation for a function in the Emacs-Lisp reference Info manual:

Ctrl-h Ctrl-f function-name

The Lisp reference manual doesn't come with GNU Emacs, so you need to install it if you want to use this command. You can find a copy on this book's CD-ROM in the directory /cdrom/docs. The XEmacs Lisp reference manual is a standard part of the XEmacs distribution.

Info files have their own major mode that provides keybindings and mouse control.

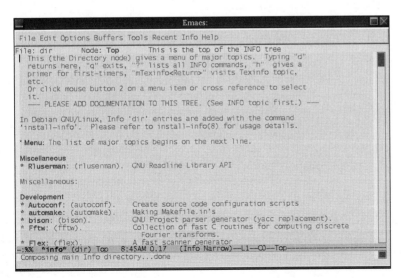

Figure 23.7   *The Info Index*

Info Navigation

Info manuals can be quite large. Some have several hundred pages. It isn't hard to get lost, because when you view a particular page, there isn't a visual cue to your location in the manual as a whole. Clickable links at the top of each page take you to the next page, the previous page, or up. It is important to understand the difference between going up and going to the previous page, because the distinction isn't immediately apparent and can result in aimless floundering through the pages. The previous page is the previous page at the same level, such as the previous subtopic. The Up page has links to the current, previous, and next pages.

Info manual pages are arranged in a tree-like hierarchy. Another way to think of Up is to realize that this link takes you up one level to the branch closer to the Top page, which can be thought of as the trunk of the manual tree.

The Top page of each manual is composed of some introductory material and a list of subtopic links (roughly equivalent to chapters in a book), as shown in Figure 23.8.

Notice in Figure 23.8 that the Up reference link points to dir, the main index of all Info manuals and pages. That page is as far up as you can go.

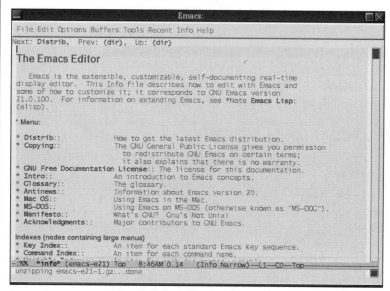

Figure 23.8   *Top Emacs Info Page*

The key commands are intuitive:

d	Stands for dir. This takes you to the main Info index page, usually /usr/info/dir. Select one of the highlighted entries by clicking the middle mouse button on it or pressing Enter. The Top page of the selected manual is loaded.
t	Returns to the Top page of the current manual.
n	The Next page in the current section of the manual. Sometimes the last page of a section or subsection links to the first page of the next one. Others are dead ends, and your only way out is Up, Top, or dir. Many manuals are set up so that continually pressing n takes you all the way to the end.
p	Takes you to the previous page in the current section.
b	Takes you back to the top of the current page.
s	Info's search command. You are prompted for a string to search for. Pressing Enter then takes you to the first occurrence of the string in the current Info manual. Press s again, and the prompt offers the same string as a default. Press Enter again, and the next occurrence is found.
Spacebar	Pressing the spacebar pages down, and pressing Delete pages back up. The Page Up and Page Down keys also work, but there is an advantage to using the spacebar and Delete keys. When you reach the end of a page, pressing the spacebar takes you to the next page, just as if you had pressed n. As you would expect, pressing Delete when you are at the beginning of a page moves to the previous page. XEmacs requires pressing these keys twice to get to the next or previous page.
m	Often a section (also known as a node) contains several subsections, each one indicated by a highlighted link preceded by an asterisk. If you type m (for "menu"), you are prompted for a link's name. Type in enough characters to distinguish the name from the others, and let Tab completion finish the name. Use this command if you prefer to use the keyboard. Otherwise, a middle mouse button click on the link takes you there as well.
x	The XEmacs version of Info mode allows you to set bookmarks in an Info file with this key command. You are prompted for a bookmark name. Choose a short and mnemonic name so that you will remember it. The bookmarks are saved in a file named ~/.xemacs/info.notes, a text file you can view if you need a reminder of the names of your bookmarks.

j	This "jumps" you to a previously-assigned Info bookmark. Tab completion can be used on a partially typed name. If you can't remember the name of a bookmark, press Tab twice. A window opens with a completion list of all your bookmarks. Click the middle mouse button on one of the bookmarks in the new window. The page is loaded with point left at the bookmarked line.
i	Look up a string in the Index of the manual.
q	The "Quit Info" command takes you back to the buffer you were editing before you started the Info session.

Problems with Info

Disorientation can be a drawback when browsing a large Info manual. There is no indication of the manual's size or of the relative size and importance of the constituent sections. It helps to conduct a quick survey of the entire manual before settling down to read sections of interest to you. Make brief exploratory excursions down a manual's various byways so that you can develop a mental map, returning to the Top page often so as to keep your bearings.

Watch out for cross-references. These are clearly marked as such, but be aware that following one can take you out of the manual into an entirely different one. In Figure 23.9, notice the link to CC Mode. This link and the other two in the same

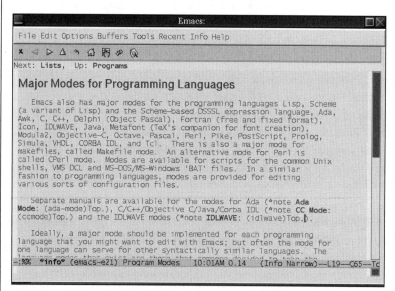

Figure 23.9   *Info Cross-Reference Links*

paragraph indicate that these links will take you to the Top page of another manual. Look for *note in front of a link rather than a single asterisk alone, because this is a sure sign of a cross-reference.

If you find that you have inadvertently ended up in another Info manual use the l key-command; this takes you back to the last node you were reading, even if it in another manual. If you have passed through several nodes before realizing that you are reading a different manual you will probably find it to be quicker to type d to return to the main Info index and find the link to the manual you unexpectedly exited. You end up at the Top page again, and you have to retrace the path that took you to the page with the cross-reference. This is an annoyance. A rule of thumb is to ignore cross-references when you are reading an Info file for the first time; save them for future readings.

Adding New Info Directories

The larger Emacs extension packages such as Gnus and AUCTeX come with large multiple-file Info manuals that you might be reluctant to add to your main Info directory (often either /usr/info or /usr/share/info). Perhaps you are installing a beta or newly-released version of a package and you want to keep the Info files separate so as to ease future upgrading.

Emacs looks for Info files in an associated list of directories called the Info-directory-list (although some versions of Emacs might use Info-default-directory-list instead). Use the variable help key (Ctrl-h v) to determine which of the two your Emacs uses.

Let's say you have a new directory of Info files called /home/user/info that you would like Emacs to know about. These statements in your ~/.emacs file use the Lisp functions cons and add-to-list to add your new directory to the front of the list:

```
(require 'info)
(add-to-list 'Info-directory-list (cons "/home/user/info" 'Info-directory-list))
```

The dir File

The Emacs Info reader has only one way to know the contents of your various Info directories. A specially-formatted file named dir in each directory contains the names and brief descriptions of each Info manual. Emacs reads the dir files from all known Info directories, concatenates them, and displays them to you in the Info:dir buffer. This is the main index that the Info d key brings up.

Normally you shouldn't need to manually add entries to any of these dir files. Packages such as Gnus, VM, and AUCTex come with their own dir files, which should work with any version of Emacs after you've added the new Info directory as just described. A utility called install-info is a part of most Linux distributions. This program can be a Perl script or a compiled C program, depending on the distribution. All the versions make it easy for software authors to install associated Info files and add the appropriate index entry to the dir file. You can also use the utility yourself if you need to install an Info file manually, but it might be easier to just add the entry yourself rather than figure out the proper switches for an `install-info` command.

This isn't that hard to do as long as you follow a few formatting rules needed for a valid entry. Here is an example:

```
* Ispell: (ispell).        ISPELL, an interactive spelling corrector.
```

The field on the right is a brief description that isn't absolutely necessary. The field on the left must follow this sequence:

- An asterisk followed by one space
- The English name of the program, followed by a colon and a space
- The actual name of the Info file (stripped of the .info suffix)
- Parentheses must surround the actual name
- A period follows the right parenthesis
- At least one space or tab separates the left and right fields

After adding an entry, you can check it by starting up Info in an Emacs session. If the new link entry is valid, it is highlighted like the other entries. Clicking the new entry should load the new manual.

Emacs constructs its composite dir file the first time you start up the Info reader. If you make changes to one of the dir files (such as adding a new entry), you need to exit Emacs and restart it so that your change will be recognized.

Finding Help on the Net

Few events have benefited the free software community more than the advent of common and inexpensive Internet access. The constant flow of patches, ideas, and requests for help is an asset to both users and developers. The Internet has grown to such an extent in recent years that it can be difficult to find the particular online community that has the information you need. This section offers pointers to the areas of the Net that offer the most help and information to the Emacs user.

The Emacs Newsgroups

Reading news postings with an NNTP newsreader such as Gnus or slrn can be a rewarding activity, but you can benefit even more by participating in discussions. There is a certain etiquette to be observed that can help you be accepted by long-time denizens of a group and that makes newsreading more fruitful both for you and others.

It is always a good idea when subscribing to a new group to hang around for a while before venturing a post. You can get a feel for the tone of a group: who are the most knowledgeable people, who is more likely to answer questions from beginners, and whose postings to avoid. You soon will notice the questions that are asked perennially and often ignored because they have been answered so many times. In many newsgroups, you see a periodically reposted FAQ (Frequently Asked Questions) among the other messages. Reading these helps you avoid posting questions that have been answered repeatedly.

An organization called The Internet FAQ Consortium maintains a Web site at which you can find official FAQs for nearly any newsgroup: http://www.faqs.org.

gnu.emacs.help

This group was created to provide help for Emacs users, but the boundaries between the various Emacs groups have blurred somewhat, partly because of people cross-posting messages to several groups. Nonetheless, I would guess that three-quarters of the postings in this group consist of questions and answers concerning the fine points of Emacs usage and configuration (see Figure 23.10). Several GNU Emacs developers frequently post to this list, so you can be sure that a valid question will be seen by some very knowledgeable Emacs experts. In newsgroups such as this one, a question that can be easily answered by reading the Info documentation might be ignored.

gnu.emacs.announce

This is a very low-volume group. New versions of GNU Emacs are released at varying intervals, averaging about 18 months between releases. Release announcements are posted here, but announcements are also made on the other Emacs groups.

gnu.emacs.sources

This, too, is a fairly low-volume group, but it has a high signal-to-noise ratio, meaning that a most of the postings are to the point and worth reading.

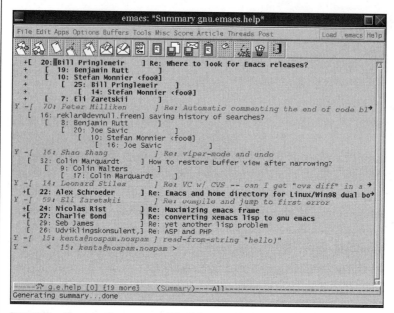

Figure 23.10 *Gnus and gnu.emacs.help Message Headers*

Emacs package authors post entire extensions to this group, although large multiple-file packages are announced here with a link to a Web or FTP site where the package can be obtained. This is the group to subscribe to if you want to keep up with the activities of Emacs Lisp programmers.

comp.emacs

This is more of a general Emacs discussion group, with some threads wandering from the subject. There might be 50 to 100 postings per day—not so many that it is a burden to scan the headers for interesting posts. A certain amount of cross-posting takes place between this group and comp.emacs.xemacs, meaning that XEmacs users will find much of interest here.

comp.emacs.xemacs

XEmacs users will want to at least occasionally monitor this group, because announcements of new stable and beta XEmacs releases are posted here. The maintainers of the XEmacs packages also post release information in this group. Many of the discussion postings are cross-posted to comp.emacs, so this group has a blend of XEmacs-specific messages and more-general messages that can apply to either flavor.

gnu.emacs.bugs

If you have found a repeatable bug in GNU Emacs, consider reporting it here. For your message to be of any use to the Emacs developers, you need to be specific about the actions that brought on the misbehavior. The `view-lossage` command can be useful as a record of the keystrokes you used prior to the bug's appearance. If you are experiencing crashes, the developers might want you to examine the resultant core file with the gdb debugger. Reporting bugs and helping developers track down the cause is one way a nonprogrammer can assist with free software projects such as Emacs.

gnu.emacs.gnus

This newsgroup averages about 50 messages per day, almost as many as the main Emacs groups. Abstruse discussions of Gnus configuration and usage can be found, along with a fair number of beginners' postings. Lars Magne Ingebrigtsen, main author and maintainer of Gnus, often posts here. This is also where announcements of new versions of Gnus can be found. The volume of postings to this group might seem surprising until you consider how complex and difficult-to-learn Gnus is.

If you want to try to learn to use Gnus, this group is a must.

gnu.emacs.vm.info

Users of the VM mail extension should monitor this list. It is a fairly low-volume list, but Kyle Jones (author of VM) answers user questions and announces new versions.

Useful Web Sites

The home sites for GNU Emacs and XEmacs are well worth visiting from time to time. They each provide philosophical rationales for the respective editors and links to other Emacs sites, as well as mailing-list and newsgroup information. The latest release news is generally kept up to date, although the newsgroups are more likely to have news as it breaks. The canonical sites are http://www.gnu.org/software/emacs and http://www.xemacs.org.

Nearly all of the Emacs extensions have Web sites these days. They serve as central news sites concerning the extension. They also have links to distribution sites, information on mailing lists, and general explanatory material. I won't list them all here (which would force you to type them in order to use them); you can get to any of them from the sites listed in this section. Instead, I'll direct you to two other general sites. The first is the Emacs Web Ring, a central site with circularly-linked Emacs-related sites: http://www.gnusoftware.com/WebRing.

The second is the Emacs-Lisp Archive site at Ohio State University: http://www.cis.ohio-state.edu/archive.

This site makes available many extensions that have been posted to the gnu.emacs.sources newsgroup.

The following URLs can be consulted if you would like to learn more about the history of Emacs, XEmacs, and the code-fork, as outlined in the Introduction to this book: http://www.gnu.org/gnu/thegnuproject.html, http://www.multicians.org/mepap.html, http://www.jwz.org/doc/emacs-timeline.html.

Conclusion

There certainly is no shortage of Emacs-related help; the problem is finding the time to make use of it! Part of adapting yourself to using open-source software is realizing that even though so much information is available, it might not always be in the form you prefer. A little extra work is necessary to learn how to use such documentation as Info files, manual pages, and the information contained in the Emacs Lisp files. Luckily, many skilled users are willing to part with some of their precious spare time in order to help new users. There are a variety of motives, but one of the most powerful is the realization that the free software community needs to welcome new users; otherwise, it will stagnate.

PART V

Appendixes

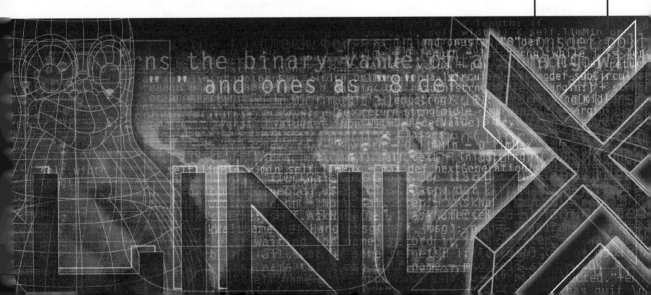

Appendix A: Key Command Reference

This is a task-sorted list of the most commonly needed commands that have default keybindings. Naturally, if you have created your own keybindings, you won't find them here.

See Appendix B for minibuffer commands that have no default keybindings.

Essential Commands

These are the commands you should learn first.

Ctrl-x Ctrl-f	Loads a file. You are prompted in the minibuffer for a file name.
Ctrl-x Ctrl-s	Saves the current buffer to disk, overwriting the original file.
Ctrl-x Ctrl-w	Saves a buffer to a different file name.
Ctrl-x s	Saves multiple changed buffers. You are prompted for confirmation.
Ctrl-x k	Kills a buffer. If you have unsaved changes, you are asked if you are sure you want to kill the buffer.
Ctrl-x i	Inserts the contents of a file into the current buffer.
Ctrl-g	Aborts or cancels an Emacs operation. Sometimes needs to be repeated.
Ctrl-x u	Undoes the last change. Repeat this to undo previous edits.

Movement Commands

These key commands allow you to move throughout a buffer by varying increments.

Ctrl-x b	Moves to another buffer—by default, the most recently visited.
Ctrl-x Ctrl-b	Brings up a list of buffers, allowing you to either visit or kill.
M-<	Moves to the beginning of the buffer.
M->	Moves to the end of the buffer.
Ctrl-a	Moves to the beginning of the current line.
Ctrl-e	Moves to the end of the current line.
Ctrl-p	Moves to the previous line.

Ctrl-n	Moves to the next line.
Ctrl-f	Moves forward one character.
Ctrl-b	Moves backward one character.
Ctrl-right arrow	Moves forward one word.
Ctrl-left arrow	Moves backward one word.
M-e	Moves forward one sentence.
M-a	Moves backward one sentence.
M-}	Moves forward one paragraph.
M-{	Moves backward one paragraph.
Ctrl-l	Redisplays the buffer with the current line centered.
Ctrl-v	Moves one screen forward. Equivalent to Page Down.
M-v	Moves one screen backward. Equivalent to Page Up.

Windows, Frames, and Buffers

These commands give you control over the number and size of windows and frames.

Ctrl-x 2	Adds another window to the frame, split horizontally.
Ctrl-x 3	Splits the frame so that two windows are side-by-side.
Ctrl-x o	Moves the cursor to the other window.
Ctrl-x 1	Makes the current window the only one.
Ctrl-x 0	Removes the current window (but not the buffer).
M-Ctrl-v	Scrolls the other window, leaving point in the current window.
Ctrl-x ^	Enlarges the current window; the other window shrinks.
Ctrl-x 5 2	Creates a new frame.
Ctrl-x 5 o	Moves the cursor to the other frame.
Ctrl-x 5 0	Destroys the current frame.
Ctrl-x 5 f	You are prompted for a file name to load in the other frame.
Ctrl-x 5 b	Switches to another buffer in the other frame.

Selecting a Region

These are the default Emacs commands for selecting text. If you would rather use the more conventional Shift-combined-with-movement-keys approach, you might try the Emacs extension pc-select. The latest XEmacs versions provide shifted motion keys as an alternative keybinding "out of the box".

Ctrl-Spacebar	Sets the mark. Any subsequent cursor motion defines a region or selected area.
Ctrl-x h	Selects the entire buffer as a region.
M-h	Selects the current paragraph.
Ctrl-x Ctrl-x	Exchanges point and the mark.

Cut, Copy, and Paste

M-w	Copies the selected region into the kill ring.
Ctrl-w	Deletes the region and saves it in the kill ring.
Ctrl-y	Pastes the last cut or copied region from the kill ring.
M-y	Pastes the next-most-recent cut or copied region from the kill ring. Can be used only after Ctrl-y.
Ctrl-d	Deletes the next character. The deletion isn't saved.
Delete	Deletes the previous character, like Backspace. See Chapter 10.
M-d	Deletes the next word.
M-Delete	Deletes the previous word.

Transposition and Case

Ctrl-t	Transposes the two characters on either side of point.
M-t	Transposes the two words on either side of point.
Ctrl-x Ctrl-t	Transposes two sentences.

M-c	Capitalizes the first letter of a word, or the next letter of a word if point is within the word.
M-l	Makes the portion of a word to the right of point all lowercase.
M-u	Makes the entire word uppercase.

Searching and Replacing

See Chapter 3 for more usage information.

Ctrl-s	Searches incrementally forward.
Ctrl-r	Searches incrementally backward.
M-Ctrl-s	Regular expression forward search.
M-Ctrl-r	Regular expression backward search.
M-%	Searches and replaces with prompting for actions.
M-Ctrl-%	Like M-%, but with regular expressions.

The following response keys are used during a search-and-replace operation.

Spacebar or y	Replaces the current search match and goes on to the next one.
.	Replaces the current match and quits the search entirely.
,	Replaces the match and pauses. Spacebar or y resumes the search.
Delete or n	Doesn't replace the current match and moves on to the next one.
^	Goes back to the previous match.
!	Replaces all search matches without asking for confirmation.
Ctrl-r	Begins recursive editing during a search.
M-Ctrl-c	Quits recursive editing and returns to the search.
Return	Exits and returns to normal editing.

Spelling Correction

See also the minibuffer spell-check commands in Appendix B.

M-$	Checks the spelling of the word at point.
M-Tab	In GNU Emacs, tells ispell to try to complete a partially-typed word.

The Dired File Manager

Ctrl-x d	You are prompted for a directory for Dired to list.

The following key commands are valid within a Dired buffer. Consult the Dired chapter of the Emacs Info manual for an exhaustive listing.

d	Tags a file for later deletion.
~	Tags all backup files for later deletion.
u	Untags a file.
x	Deletes all files tagged with d.
m	Tags a file for other operations, such as copying.
M-Delete	Untags all tagged files.
C	Copies a file.
R	Renames a file.
z	Compresses or uncompresses a file (by default using gzip).
Enter	Loads a file. (The middle mouse button also does this.)
v	Loads a file in read-only mode for viewing.
g	Updates the directory listing from disk.
s	Toggles the sorting of files by file name to sorting by date.
+	Makes a new directory.

Word Wrapping

M-q   Wraps the words in the current paragraph. No line will extend beyond
         the seventieth column.

Keyboard Macros

See also the macro-related minibuffer commands in Appendix B.

Ctrl-x (	Begins recording a macro.
Ctrl-x)	Ends macro recording.
Ctrl-u Ctrl-x (	Replays the most recent macro and allows more keystrokes to be added.
Ctrl-x e	Replays the most recent macro.
Ctrl-x q	Inserts a prompt or query within a macro as it is being recorded.
Ctrl-u Ctrl-x q	Inserts a recursive edit within a macro.
M-Ctrl-c	Quits the recursive edit and continues with the macro.

Shell Commands

See also the shell buffer commands in Appendix B.

M-!	Executes an external Linux shell command.
Ctrl-u M-!	Like M-!, but any output from the command is inserted into the current buffer.
M-|	Uses the contents of a selected region as input for a shell command.
Ctrl-u M-|	Takes the output of a shell command and uses it to replace a selection.

Rectangles and Registers

Ctrl-x r k	Kills the rectangle formed by positioning point and the mark diagonally from each other.
Ctrl-x r r	Copies a rectangular region to a named register.
Ctrl-x r y	Pastes the most recently killed rectangular region.
Ctrl-x r t	Inserts a text string to the left of each line in a rectangle.
Ctrl-x r c	Removes all characters from a rectangle and leaves spaces in their place.
Ctrl-x r Spacebar x	Saves the current point position in a register named x. You can have many of these saved positions at once, each with its own name. The name can be a word or a single character.
Ctrl-x r j x	Jumps to the point position saved in register x.
Ctrl-x r s x	Copies the selected region into a register named x.
Ctrl-x i r x	Inserts the contents of register x into the current buffer. This can be a normal or rectangular register.

Bookmarks

See also the bookmarking minibuffer commands in Appendix B.

Ctrl-x r m	Sets a bookmark in the current buffer at point.
Ctrl-x r m xxx	Sets a bookmark named xxx at point.
Ctrl-x r b xxx	Jumps to a bookmark named xxx and loads the file if necessary.
Ctrl-x r l	Opens a buffer containing a list of all bookmarks.

Abbreviations

See also the abbreviation commands in Appendix B.

Ctrl-x a g	Defines an abbreviation.
Ctrl-x a l	Defines an abbreviation for the current major mode only.
Ctrl-x a i g	Defines the word at point as an abbreviation.

Ctrl-x a i l	Like Ctrl-x a i g, but for the current major mode only.
M—	Ignores a prefix when expanding an abbreviation.
Ctrl-x a e	Expands the abbreviation at point.
M-/	Completes partially typed words using matches found in the current buffer or other buffers.

Sending Mail

See also the commands in Appendix C for entering Rmail, VM, and Gnus modes.

| Ctrl-x m | Opens a new message composition buffer and inserts the required headers. |
| Ctrl-c Ctrl-c | Sends the message and moves to the previous buffer. |

Mouse Commands

GNU Emacs and XEmacs mouse commands differ slightly.

Mouse Bindings Shared by GNU Emacs and XEmacs

| Button 1 | A click moves point. If the button is held down and dragged, a selection is made. |
| Button 2 | Pastes the most recently cut or copied selection. If the mouse pointer is over highlighted text or a button widget, the link is followed. |

GNU Emacs-Specific Mouse Usage

Button 3	Selects a region between point and the mouse pointer. Click again to cut the text.
Ctrl-Button 3	Major mode mouse menu.
Shift-Button 1	Font mouse menu.
Ctrl-Button 1	Buffer mouse menu.

XEmacs-Specific Mouse Usage

Button 3	Major mode mouse menu.
M-Ctrl-Button 3	Buffer mouse menu.
Ctrl-Button 1	Makes a selection and inserts it at point.
Shift-Button 1	Extends a selection.
Ctrl-Button 2	Sets point where the button is clicked and moves a selected region there.
Ctrl-Shift-Button 1	Cuts a selection with the mouse and inserts it without moving point.

The Help Keys

These are the most useful of the help keys. The Help chapter of the Emacs Info manual describes many more.

Ctrl-h m	Brief description of the currently active major and minor modes.
Ctrl-h b	Lists the active keybindings.
Ctrl-h i	Starts the Info help system.
Ctrl-h a	The Apropos command; regular expression help (see Chapter 23).
Ctrl-h c	Brief description of a key command.
Ctrl-h k	Longer description of a key command.
Ctrl-h t	Starts the interactive Emacs tutorial.
Ctrl-h v	Description of a Lisp variable—by default, the variable at point.
Ctrl-h f	Description of a Lisp function—by default, the function at point.
Ctrl-h p	Helps you find Emacs packages by keyword.
Ctrl-h W command-name	Displays keybinding information on a command.
Ctrl-h n	Shows you the changes made in your version of Emacs or XEmacs, with the most recent change shown first.

Quitting Emacs

Ctrl-x Ctrl-c	Ends the Emacs session.

Appendix B: Minibuffer Commands

E macs has so many commands available that it would be impossible to assign usable keystrokes for them all, given the limitations of the standard 101-key keyboard. The more obscure and lesser-used commands are therefore executed by prefixing the command's name with M-x, which signals Emacs that a user's command can be expected in the minibuffer. After you press the M-x prefix, further keystrokes appear in the minibuffer rather than in the main editing window. You execute a command by pressing Enter. After that, your keystrokes are directed to the editing window as before.

The following is a list of the most useful minibuffer commands.

M-x bookmark-save	Saves all the current bookmarks to the default bookmark file.
M-x bookmark-load	You are prompted for the name of a bookmark file to load. Pressing Enter causes the default bookmark file to be loaded.
M-x bookmark-write	You can specify a file name in which all current bookmarks will be saved.
M-x bookmark-delete	Deletes a bookmark by name. You are prompted in the minibuffer.
M-x bookmark-insert	Inserts at point the entire contents of a file that a bookmark refers to.
M-x bookmark-insert-location	Inserts at point the name of a file that a bookmark refers to.
M-x customize	Opens the top-level Customize buffer, which has links to all the Customize groups. If you already know what group or variable you want to customize, use one of the following customize commands.
M-x customize-group	You are asked to enter in the minibuffer the name of a group. Tab completion is a big help if you aren't sure of the entire name.
M-x customize-variable	Similar to the preceding command, you are prompted for a specific variable. Tab completion is available, as in all minibuffer commands.
M-x customize-face	You are prompted for the name of a face (a combination of font and other display characteristics, such as foreground and background color). A good one to start with is the default face.

M-x `fill-region`	Wraps long lines within a selected region so that they don't extend beyond the fill column, which by default is set to column 70.
M-x `goto-line`	Allows you to type a line number in the minibuffer, press Enter, and have point be moved to that line.
M-x `ispell-region`	Runs the ispell spelling checker on a selected region.
M-x `ispell-buffer`	Checks spelling for the entire buffer.
M-x `load-library`	After you type in the name of a Lisp file (without the .el or .ec suffix), the file is loaded. The file must be in a directory in your load-path such as the site-lisp directory. This is one way to try out an extension temporarily.
M-x `name-last-kbd-macro`	Gives a name to the last-created keyboard macro. This name is valid only for the duration of the Emacs session.
M-x `insert-kbd-macro`	You are prompted for the name of a macro you have created and named. A Lisp definition of the macro is inserted in the current buffer. Often used to insert a macro definition in an .emacs file so that it will be available for use in future sessions.
M-x `recover-file`	The command to use when Emacs has died unexpectedly due to a system or Emacs crash. You are prompted for a file name. If an autosave file corresponding to that file can be found, it is renamed, replacing the last saved version.
M-x `recover-session`	An extension of the preceding command that is useful when several changed buffers were unsaved at the time of a crash. You can use this command to pick and choose which autosave files to recover.
M-x `revert-buffer`	Discards all changes to a buffer and reloads from disk the original unmodified file, which is the last saved version.
M-x `server-start`	Starts the Emacs editing server, a background utility that allows you to load files from the command line or another application into an already-running Emacs session. The user program is called emacsclient.

M-x `gnuserv-start`	The XEmacs equivalent of M-x `server-start`. Used with the user program gnuclient.
M-x `shell`	Opens a shell buffer, similar to an xterm but running in an Emacs window.
M-x `write-abbrev-file`	Prompts you for a file name and then saves all current abbreviations to the file.
M-x `read-abbrev-file`	Loads an abbreviation file and makes the contents usable.
M-x `list-abbrevs`	Shows you the currently available abbreviations and their expansions.
M-x `edit-abbrevs`	Opens a buffer containing your current abbreviations. You can add, edit, and delete entries.

Appendix C: Miscellaneous Mode Commands

Although major modes are usually initialized when the appropriate type of file is loaded, there are times when manual loading is necessary. The following are minibuffer commands for the most commonly used modes.

M-x `auto-fill-mode`	Turns on automatic word wrapping.
M-x `font-lock-mode`	Enables syntax highlighting in the current buffer.
M-x `line-number-mode`	A minor mode that causes the line number to be displayed in the modeline.
M-x `column-number-mode`	A mode similar to M-x `line-number-mode`. Displays the column number in the modeline.
M-x `abbrev-mode`	Toggles word abbreviation mode.
M-x `auto-compression-mode`	Toggles automatic file compression and decompression.
M-x `transient-mark-mode`	Toggles the highlighting of selected regions (GNU Emacs only).
M-x `tool-bar-mode`	Toggles the GNU Emacs 21 toolbar.
M-x `rmail`	Starts the Rmail mail reader.
M-x `vm`	Starts the VM mail reader.
M-x `gnus`	Starts Gnus, the mail and news reader.
M-x `cc-mode`	Major mode for C and C++ files.
M-x `cperl-mode`	Major mode for the Perl programming language.
M-x `python-mode`	Major mode for the Python programming language.
M-x `lisp-mode`	A major mode for writing Lisp programs.
M-x `tex-mode`	A major mode for writing TeX files.
M-x `latex-mode`	A variant of tex mode for writing LaTeX files.

Appendix D: Emacs and Internationalization

Emacs in the beginning was designed and used by speakers of English, but it wasn't long before users throughout the world began to adopt the editor. The ASCII character set with unibyte encoding is well-suited for English letters and other characters. Other Roman-alphabet languages need ASCII variant character sets so that characters with breves and umlauts can be displayed.

> Every character set needs to be encoded before it can be used by a computer program or transferred over a network. Various coding systems have evolved to handle the varying needs of the character sets used to represent scripts throughout the world. A particular character encoding is classified as "unibyte" when every character can be represented in computer memory with no more than 8 bits (binary digits), which is equivalent to 1 byte. The standard ASCII character set uses only 7 of the 8 bits. The multibyte character encodings are used to represent scripts used for languages such as Chinese and Japanese, which have so many characters that a single byte is insufficient. These scripts use 2 bytes per character.

Syllabic and graphical-character scripts, such as those used to represent Oriental languages, needed a more involved solution. Multibyte or 16-bit character set encodings were developed for these languages, but a way was needed for Emacs to be able to make use of them. The Mule project, originally a separate project, was eventually merged with Emacs and now forms the core of Emacs' ability to both display and accept input in most of the scripts used by the world's major languages.

Setting Up

Your installed version of Emacs might or might not be able to display alternative character sets. Emacs and XEmacs each have their own method of dealing with this option. This is complicated by the differences in how Linux distributions package the editors. Typically, Mule and non-Mule packages are available. The default installation is non-Mule.

You can easily find out whether Mule support is available in your Emacs. Is there a Mule menu on your menu bar? In GNU Emacs 21, Mule is a submenu under Options. If this menu is missing, check your ~/.emacs file for a line disabling multibyte character support, as in this example:

```
(setq-default enable-multibyte-characters nil)
```

Comment out this line and restart Emacs. The Mule menu should now be visible. This variable is valid only for GNU Emacs.

If it turns out that Mule is not a part of your Emacs installation and you need the capabilities it offers, you have two options. You have to either install a distribution package of the Mule version of Emacs or compile it from source.

In order to use Mule-enabled GNU Emacs built from source, you need to install the Leim distribution, which is available on this book's CD-ROM in the same directory as the Emacs source: /cdrom/emacs/source. The GNU Emacs configure script needs no additional switches for Mule support, which is the default.

The XEmacs configure script does need a command-line switch to enable Mule:

```
./configure --with-mule
```

Consult the INSTALL file in the XEmacs source directory for further Mule-related configuration options.

The XEmacs Mule-based package is necessary. Depending on which language environments you need, you might also need the Egg-its (Japanese) and Leim (non-English and non-Japanese languages) packages.

Fonts

Now that you have a Mule-enabled Emacs, you probably need to install additional X Window fonts. Emacs provides a handy sample file called HELLO, shown in Figure D.1, which includes a line of text for every language currently supported.

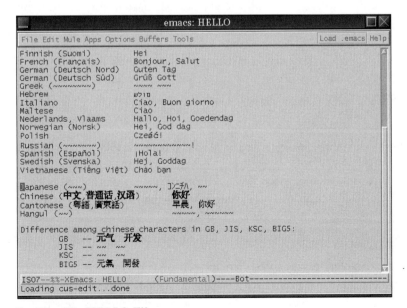

Figure D.1   *The HELLO File*

Loading this file gives you quick evidence of missing fonts. Press Ctrl-h and type H to load the file. Any missing fonts appear as empty boxes. In XEmacs, tildes are used.

Unless you are impressively multilingual, there is no reason to install the available X fonts for each of these languages. Your Linux distribution CD-ROMs contain installable international font packages. The package file-names should give you an idea of which language's fonts are in which file.

Input Methods and Language Environments

An input method is a set of instructions that tells Emacs how to interpret your keystrokes. The simplest input method is to simply interpret each character key as it appears on the keyboard. Typing an a causes a lowercase a to appear in the buffer, and so on. Variations of the basic English input method are used for European languages and some other languages that use characters such as umlauts and accented letters. In these methods, two keystrokes are necessary for the needed characters.

An additional layer of interpretation is needed for languages with different alphabets, such as Greek and Russian. When you use these input methods, the keyboard letters are mapped one-to-one to characters in the other alphabets.

Input methods become complicated for nonalphabetic languages such as Chinese and Thai. The number of characters tends to be in the thousands rather than the dozens. This means that several keystrokes are needed to type a character. You can view a descriptive list of all the available Emacs input methods by pressing M-x and typing

```
list-input-methods
```

A language environment is a collection of settings that includes a default input method and coding system.

A coding system is a system for encoding written characters into a form usable by digital computers. ASCII, for example, is a coding system that uses a unique sequence of 7 bits for each character. Emacs automatically translates text written in any coding system into an internal system when reading data and translates it back into the original system when writing a file.

When multibyte characters are enabled, Emacs can display text written in any supported language if the correct fonts are available. Setting the language environment changes the default coding system and the input method to appropriate settings for the selected language.

If you would like to read a short description of a particular language environment, press Ctrl-h, type L, and press Tab.

The Tab key summons a Completions window with a list of all the supported language environments. Choose one, type the name into the minibuffer, and press Enter.

You can change the language environment for the current Emacs session by pressing M-x and typing

```
set-language-environment
```

You are prompted for a name. If you aren't sure of the name or spelling, press Tab, and a Completions window appears.

You can also change this setting by selecting one of the items on the "Set language environment" submenu of the Mule menu.

GNU Emacs lets you permanently change your language environment with Customize. Press M-x and type

```
customize-option
```

When prompted in the minibuffer, type

```
current-language-environment
```

When the Customize buffer appears, type the environment you want as the default into the text entry field, and then select Save for Future Sessions from the State pop-up menu.

The Mule Project

In 1987, a group of Japanese Emacs users developed a Japanese version of Emacs called Nemacs. Once they had the new version working well with their language, these developers contacted the Free Software Foundation and offered the code as a possible addition to Emacs. The FSF demurred. Although the prospect of making Emacs available to a new community of users was tempting, the FSF thought that a more general approach that could support any language would be preferable.

This situation provided the impetus for a new project, the Multilingual Enhancement, or Mule. The Japanese developers began with the Japanese-language code used in the Nemacs editor and generalized it so that new languages could be supported. The result was an Emacs extension rather than a separate editor. Over the next few years, new languages were added as contributors from various language backgrounds joined the project. During this period, Mule was an external Emacs extension. In 1997, Mule was accepted as an integral part of GNU Emacs. The XEmacs team opted for making Mule an optional, although official, package.

Glossary

associated list (alist). An Emacs Lisp term for a special type of list in which each element is a keyword-value pair. See Chapter 7 for examples of how this type of list is used in an Emacs Lisp file.

atom. A basic unit of a Lisp expression. An atom can be a numeral, a symbol (which may identify a function or variable), or a quoted string. See **symbol**.

auto-save. Emacs periodically saves a copy of a buffer as you edit it to a file that is deleted after the buffer is successfully saved to disk. This temporary file is updated if either Emacs or the system crashes. The auto-save file can be recovered later, minimizing your chances of losing work. See Chapter 22 for more details.

bookmark. A location within a buffer saved to a bookmark file, allowing you to return easily. Normally, opening a file results in the cursor's being placed at the beginning of the new buffer. Selecting a bookmark is a way to load a file with the cursor placed at a saved spot.

buffer. A copy of a file that is visible in an Emacs window. When changes are made and the buffer is saved, the contents of the buffer overwrite the original file. Emacs also creates temporary buffers that don't correspond to an actual file, such as the Scratch buffer.

byte-compile. An Emacs Lisp file can be subjected to a process called byte compilation, which makes the file quicker and easier to load. The file becomes unreadable by humans, because some of the Lisp code is turned into byte-code, a compact form of code that is easily processed by the Emacs Lisp interpreter. A byte-compiled file can be identified by the letter "c" appended to the file's name. For example, code.el becomes code.elc.

car. An Emacs Lisp term meaning the first element in a list. See also cdr.

cdr. All the elements of an Emacs Lisp list except the first. What remains of a list when the list's car is removed. See also car.

comment. A human-readable section of a source code file that is tagged with special characters that force the interpreter or compiler to ignore the section. Text-formatting languages also have special commenting characters. When marked up, text is processed and the commented sections are skipped.

completion. Emacs can finish typing incomplete file names, commands, or names of variables. You just type a partial name and press Tab, and the remainder of the name is completed.

cons. In Emacs Lisp, to cons an element to a list is to add it to the front of the list. Cons is a built-in function.

evaluate. The Emacs Lisp interpreter built in to Emacs can read Lisp code and execute any instructions it finds. This is known as evaluating the code.

fill, fill-column. The Emacs term for word wrapping is filling a paragraph, meaning to break lines at a certain column number (the fill-column). The result is a paragraph that fits within a defined width.

frame. An Emacs X window that contains one or more Emacs windows. Many frames can be active at once. A virtual-console Emacs session is technically in a frame, but often a gnuclient or emacsclient frame in another virtual console serves the same purpose as multiple X frames.

function. A command or series of instructions written in Emacs Lisp.

GNU. A recursive acronym that stands for "GNU's Not UNIX." GNU is the name of a project under the aegis of the Free Software Foundation. The goal of the GNU project is to facilitate the creation of all the software a user might need. The software is licensed in such a way that anyone is permitted to modify it as long as the changes are made available. Emacs was one of the first pieces of GNU software. GNU software is a subset of free software, a broader category. Other varieties of free software typically restrict the rights of users in various ways. As an example, the BSD licenses allow closed-source derivative works to be created from BSD-licensed software.

This prevents other users from benefiting from or contributing toward the private enhancements.

GPL. An abbreviation of "General Public License," the licensing used by all GNU software. You can read about the GPL by pressing Ctrl-h Ctrl-c in an Emacs session or Ctrl-h Ctrl-l in an XEmacs session.

incremental search. A method of searching a buffer for a string as you type it. The search moves point to the first match for what was typed. As you type more, the search becomes narrowed down to more-specific matches.

kill. Killing selected or marked text means deleting it from the buffer but storing it in a circular internal list called the kill ring. Think of the kill ring as a clipboard of deleted chunks of text.

list. The basic unit of an Emacs Lisp expression. A list is composed of zero or more elements separated by white space and enclosed in parentheses.

macro. A sequence of keystrokes (which can include key commands) that is recorded for subsequent playback. Mouse events can also be included in a macro. See Chapter 4 for further information.

mark. A second invisible cursor that is moved in order to set a region's size. Imagine that the cursor or point can be split in two, with one half remaining in the original position and the other moved to enclose an area of text between the halves. See also **point**.

markup. Special characters that are understood by text-formatting systems and languages such as LaTeX and HTML. These characters are a code that tells external software how to display different sections of a file.

minibuffer. A horizontal strip in an Emacs frame just beneath the modeline. This is an area where the user communicates with Emacs. Messages from Emacs are displayed here. This is where you type in information Emacs needs to do its work, such as commands or file names.

mode. A bundle of Emacs settings optimized for a certain type of editing. A mode can be invoked manually or automatically, as when a file with a particular suffix is loaded. A major mode is a mode that alters many settings, such as the keybindings and screen appearance. Only one major mode can be active at a time. A minor mode affects just a few settings. More than one minor mode can be active at the same time along with a major mode.

modeline. Just beneath the editing area of an Emacs window is a multipurpose horizontal area, usually of a contrasting color, that is full of information about the current state of affairs. You can see the current file's name, whether it has been modified, where point is in the buffer, and the currently active modes. Several options control what you see in the modeline.

point. Synonymous with cursor location. Every buffer has a point position

that Emacs remembers even when you are editing another buffer. The cursor is present only in the current buffer. See also **mark**.

query-replace. A form of search-and-replace during which the user is asked whether each match should be replaced with the new string or left alone.

region. An area of text that has been selected or marked with either the keyboard or the mouse. The marked region may be highlighted, but this is optional and isn't the default in some versions of Emacs. A region can be copied or deleted (killed). In Emacs terminology, a region is an area of text between point (the cursor location) and mark. See **point** and **mark**.

regular expression (regexp). A technique used by software to find matches for strings of text. Special "wildcard" characters are reserved for matching characters and sequences of characters that fulfill certain requirements. A regular expression is a pattern of characters that match themselves, interspersed with the special characters. See Chapter 3 for a description of how regular expressions can be used in the various Emacs searching commands.

setq. A commonly used Emacs Lisp function that assigns a value to a variable.

shell buffer. A special type of Emacs buffer that contains a shell prompt. You can run text-mode Linux commands and use any of the Emacs commands on the output.

string. A sequence of text characters. A general term that includes but is not limited to words and sentences.

symbol. A type of atom. Symbols have names which consist of a sequence of characters uninterrupted by whitespace. They are used to uniquely identify Emacs Lisp functions. A symbol can also have a value associated with it, in which case the symbol identifies a variable. A single symbol can identify both a variable and a function. See **atom**, **function**, and **variable**.

variable. An Emacs Lisp symbol that has a value that can be changed, roughly equivalent to a setting. A variable can have more than one symbol associated with it. You can customize many aspects of Emacs behavior by changing the values of variables.

window. An editing area in an Emacs frame that has its own modeline. The frame can display one window that fills the available area. Two or more windows can share the same frame, with the division between them either horizontal or vertical. An Emacs window is not the same as an X window; an Emacs X window is called a frame so as to distinguish the two.

yank. The Emacs term for inserting previously cut or copied text into a buffer. Most applications use the term "paste" instead.

M